T0335846

Information Communication Technologies and Emerging Business Strategies

Shenja van der Graaf, LSE, UK

Yuichi Washida, Hakuhodo Inc. & The University of Tokyo, Japan

IDEA GROUP PUBLISHING
Hershey • London • Melbourne • Singapore

Acquisitions Editor: Michelle Potter
Development Editor: Kristin Roth
Senior Managing Editor: Jennifer Neidig
Managing Editor: Sara Reed
Copy Editor: Holly Powell
Typesetter: Jessie Weik
Cover Design: Lisa Tosheff
Printed at: Yurchak Printing Inc.

Published in the United States of America by
        Idea Group Publishing (an imprint of Idea Group Inc.)
        701 E. Chocolate Avenue, Suite 200
        Hershey PA 17033
        Tel: 717-533-8845
        Fax: 717-533-8661
        E-mail: cust@idea-group.com
        Web site: http://www.idea-group.com

and in the United Kingdom by
        Idea Group Publishing (an imprint of Idea Group Inc.)
        3 Henrietta Street
        Covent Garden
        London WC2E 8LU
        Tel: 44 20 7240 0856
        Fax: 44 20 7379 0609
        Web site: http://www.eurospanonline.com

    Library of Congress Cataloging-in-Publication Data

Graaf, Shenja Van Der, 1976-
   Information communication technologies and emerging business strategies / Shenja Van Der
Graaf and Yuichi Washida.
      p. cm.
   Summary: "This book explores new media such as online music stores, iPods, games, and
digital TV and the way corporations are seeking innovative ways to (re)engage with their
consumers in the digital era"--Provided by publisher.
   ISBN 1-59904-234-7 -- ISBN 1-59904-235-5 (softcover) -- ISBN 1-59904-236-3 (ebook)
   1. Electronic commerce. 2. Digital communications. I. Washida, Yuichi, 1968- II. Title.
   HF5548.32.G72 2006
   658.8'72--dc22
                                    2006010100

British Cataloguing in Publication Data
A Cataloguing in Publication record for this book is available from the British Library.

All work contributed to this book is new, previously-unpublished material. The views
expressed in this book are those of the authors, but not necessarily of the publisher.

Information Communication Technologies and Emerging Business Strategies

Table of Contents

Preface

Introduction Towards ICTs and Innovative Market Creation Strategies

At MTV we try to reinvent what we know as media—perspectives on innovative, upcoming media formats and where to effectively place products to make them 'buzz-worthy' in a time of online and offline convergence.[1]

MTV Networks (MTVN) kicked 2005 off by signing a strategic agreement with Microsoft to "create new ways for consumers to access MTVN entertainment programming and brands such as MTV, VH1, CMT and Comedy Central via a variety of digital entertainment products and platforms... [MTV is] committed to being on the platforms where our young consumers are today, and will be in the future, whether it is PC, mobile, portable device, Web or TV. Microsoft continues to innovate and change the game, and that is a great environment for our content and our consumers."[2] MTV and Microsoft also formed a *digital media strategy task force* that works to identify and collaborate on new strategic opportunities, that is, "the development of digital entertainment offerings, digital media co-marketing and new distribution initiatives."[3]

MTV is not an isolated example of a firm that is seeking ways to capture, engage, and retain consumers on multiple digital media platforms. Coca-Cola for instance, launched CokeMusic.com in June 2002, an online meeting place for teens with a real interest in music.[4] The site hosts, among others, the *Launching Pad*[5] which, each month, features music, videos, and bios of eight upcoming artists, and *Coke Studios* which is a virtual hang out place where registered users can create "their own music mixes and customized avatars, called V-egos. Each visitor's V-ego allows the person to extend his or her personality into the Web sphere"[6]—making it a vivid Coke brand community (Van der Graaf, 2004). The U.S. Army has also been very successful at generating buzz through their online game *America's Army: Operations*.[7] The game is part of the ad campaign "Together We Stand: An Army of One" which aimed at counteracting missed recruiting goals[8] and results have shown that they have succeeded very well (Van der Graaf & Nieborg, 2003).

Were digital technologies such as the Web previously seen as a direct threat or even competitor to various sectors—especially media? These examples show that the Internet is presently being incorporated into the calculus of major firms—consolidating multiple platforms and digital divisions. Two intertwined trends have emerged—particularly since the mid-1990s—that reflect the social, political, and economic impact of information and communication technologies (ICTs) on changes in the architecture of interaction. On the one hand, digital technologies have opened up ways for decentralization and diversification by enabling consumers to become participants in the production and distribution of media content rather than being endpoints for the delivery of a product or service. This shift can be marked by a transition from a message- and transmission-based architecture, where the sender controlled the rate and frequency of the information, to a network model with greater reliance on the user's self-regulation, bypassing traditional media controls. On the other hand, firms have aimed to use and leverage some of the unique qualities of ICTs by linking consumers directly into the production and distribution of media content for reasons of reputation and loyalty building and increasing returns on investment.

These two trends have attracted much attention across many academic disciplines and industrial sectors, especially regarding copyright issues, that is, the control over the distribution of copyrighted material and the collection of revenues for intellectual creations. More recently however, new ways of doing business are being sought by capitalizing on the features of the digital environment—ranging from slight variations of off-line models to more radical reconceptualizations of the roles of, and relationships among, content producers, intermediaries, and consumers (Slater et al., 2005). The relationship between a top down corporate-driven and a bottom up consumer-driven process involving digital platforms can be viewed as an emerging site for revenue opportunities, expanding markets, and reenforcing consumer commitments, laying bare the underlying structures by which both firms and consumers gain, process, and exchange information. In other words, digital technologies are said to have facilitated information and knowledge sharing to a far greater extent than previous media forms, while offering a structure of interdependence characterized by relations of minimal hierarchy and organizational heterogeneity (Jenkins, in press; Powell, 1990). This is achieved by permitting or even fostering a diversity of organizational logics that minimize conformity rather than maximize it by enforcing a hierarchical system through standardized lines of authority (Benkler, 2002; Stark, 2000).

In the current crowded state of the digital marketplace, firms increasingly are said to look for ways to specifically acquire, engage, and retain their consumers. In doing so, they hope to be enabled to enhance their ability to monitor and predict consumer *expression* and affiliation, while they rely on consumers to spread the word about a product. Looking then at various communication technologies and relevant practices seems to be an increasingly important aspect of emerging commercial strategies. The changing base underlying a firm's innovative activities can then be expected to have profound implications for the way firms create innovative market strategies.

ICTs and Emerging Business Strategies

This book provides a collection of theoretical and empirical strands that, with the growing usage of communication technologies such as the Internet and mobile phones, what used to be understood as the domain of consumption seems to have become a player in, on the one hand, production, distribution, and integration processes and, on the other hand, seems to potentially impact on a firm's competitive (dis)advantage. It is indirectly the result of a collaboration of Hakuhodo Inc., Ericsson Consumer & Enterprise Lab, and the Utrecht University that came up with an international comparative survey program, named Media Landscape Survey 2003-2004 to examine and compare communication technology environments in the U.S., The Netherlands, Sweden, South Korea, Japan, and China.

This very broad initiative brought us in contact with other researchers and practitioners interested in similar issues that center on the relationships among emerging and existing firms, markets, and consumers. Specifically, this book focuses on the wide and rapid diffusion of the use of various new media, such as e-mail, mobile phones, Internet, interactive TV, games, and Web logs, and the way they have impacted the paradigm of human and business communications.

These new communication means that are major products of ICTs, are gradually complementing or even replacing some more conventional communication means, such as physical mailing or using fixed phones rather than wireless ones. As some of the chapters will show, new technologies have contributed to changes in the way we communicate and seem to have given way to new or alternative social norms and cultures within and across cultures, for example, striking differences between Japan, Europe, and the U.S. regarding the way various media are used, seemingly based in each region's political, economical, cultural, and social contexts.

The most important viewpoint in the examination of communication means and new technologies are, we believe, innovation processes that occur while these technologies diffuse among users. Investigating the changes of interpretation in our society for each communication means and its technology is significant from various disciplines as we have sought to represent in this volume. By investigating such innovation processes, we can examine emerging business strategies—especially in the creative industries—processes of innovation, community-thinking, the evolution of social norms, and emergence of new (sub)cultures, emerging markets, and organizational cultures rather than merely tracing superficial trends of ICTs.

All chapters combined, provide an in-depth overview and at times a challenging framework, in which a variety of new media technologies are mapped, based on empirical and theoretical studies and not on mere subjective impressions or fashions in the forefront of ICT industries in the East and West.

Contributions Towards
Innovative Market Creation Strategies

This book is divided into four sections. *Innovation, Communication Technologies, and Consumer Clusters* is kicked off by Imar de Vries. He explores visions of mobile communication by focusing on idealized ideas surrounding wireless technology. By examining sources on the development, marketing, and use of wireless technology, he contextualizes these visions within earlier accounts of ideal communication found in media history and isolates the regularities that are part of these accounts. On close examination, a paradox reveals itself in these regularities, one that can be described as resulting from an uneasiness in the human communication psyche: an unfulfilled desire for divine togetherness clashes with individual communication needs. While the exact nature of this paradox—innate and hard-wired into our brains, or culturally fostered—remains unknown, the author claims that the paradox will continue to fuel idealized ideas about future communication technology. He concludes with the observation that not all use of mobile technology can immediately be interpreted as transcendental, and that built-in locational awareness balances the mobile communication act.

Gaby Anne Wildenbos and Yuichi Washida focus on the Japanese usage of digital products. Both the consumer and production side are addressed, whereby emphasizing the mobile phone industry on the basis of two consumer groups *otakus* and *kogals*. First, key characteristics of each consumer group are described. Second, social and cultural aspects related to consumption behavior of the otakus and kogals are examined, that is, collectivism, individualism and *kawaiiness*. This is followed by the production side of digital products in Japan, highlighting two major companies involved in mobile telephony: NTT DoCoMo and Label Mobile, which in their turn, are linked to the consumption cultures of otaku and kogals.

Michael Björn offers an empirical research report that describes the diffusion of mobile camera phones and picture mail services in Japan between the years 1997 and 2005, based on annual consumer surveys conducted by Ericsson Consumer & Enterprise Lab. A general framework based on sociocultural values and attitudes to telecom for describing the telecom market from a consumer perspective is presented. This framework is then used to put different consumer-life-stage segments in relation to each other in respect to product diffusion. The change over time of attitudes and behavior is described, and the conclusion is drawn that the product terminology spontaneously created by consumers themselves in order to relate to the product is an important step for mass market diffusion. Furthermore, the group of people who develop this terminology becomes a crucial catalyst for diffusion—the Japanese case presented here consists of female students.

Masataka Yoshikawa's chapter aims to explore the future trajectory of enjoying digital music entertainment among consumers comparing the characteristics of the usage patterns of digital music appliances in the U.S. and those in Japan. As the first step of this research, the author conducted two empirical surveys in the U.S. and Japan, and found some basic differences in the usage patterns of a variety of digital music appliances. Next, a series of ethnographical research based on focus-group interviews with Japanese young women was done and some interesting reasons of the differences were discovered. In Japan, sharing the experiences of listening to the latest hit songs with friends by playing them with mobile phones that have the high quality, ring tone functions can be a new way of enjoying music contents, while iPod has become a de facto standard of the digital music appliances in the world.

Section II is titled *Commerce, Community, and Consumer-Generated Content*. The next chapter, authored by Sal Humphreys, discusses ownership in massively multi-player online games (MMOGs). She considers how the interactive and social nature of MMOGs presents challenges to systems of organization, control, and regulation used for more conventional media products. She examines how the interactive structures of games cast players as producers of content, not merely consumers. This productive role creates a distributed production network that challenges the ideas of authorship which underpin copyright and intellectual property. The role of the publishers is shown to encompass community, as well as intellectual property management. The communities generated within these games are a key source of economic benefit to the publishers. The contract that determines the conditions of access and the forms of governance inside proprietary worlds is considered in light of this newly intensified relationship between commerce and community. Questions are raised about the accountability of publishers, the role of the market, and the state in determining conditions of access.

David B. Nieborg's overview on advertising practices surrounding the games industries views the use of digital games for the promotion of goods and services as becoming more popular with the maturing and penetration of the medium. He analyses the use of advertisements in games and seeks to answer in which way brands are integrated in interactive play. The branding of virtual worlds offers a completely new range of opportunities for advertisers to create a web of brands and it is the usage of marketing through games that differs considerably. This chapter offers a categorization of *advergames* and will address the use of advergames from a developmental perspective, differing between commercial games with in-game advertisement and dedicated advergames. Where TV commercials, print ads, and the World Wide Web rely on representation for the conveying of their message; advergames are able to add the extra dimension of simulation as a mode of representation, resulting in various interesting game designs.

This section ends with Alek Tarkowski's study on Live Journal user icons. He provides insight into Internet applications such as Web-based *blogging* and instant messaging tools or social networking sites that often provide their users with the possibility of displaying small graphic elements. Such *pictures* or *icons* allow users to represent and mutually identify themselves. He offers an analysis of user icons displayed on the Live Journal blogging site. Tarkowski treats such a user icon as a medium with particular characteristics and patterns of usage. Live Journal users use such icons to participate in what John Fiske calls popular culture. A case study of user icons discloses the life cycle of the media form, during which a medium with initial characteristics coded by its creators begins over time to support a wide variety of uses, innovation in usage, and active participation in culture. In this chapter, he considers user pictures and practices that are tied to them as an example of the manner in which popular culture functions in the digital age.

The third section centers upon the impact of digitization on *Creative Industries*. David Lee considers the emergence of the discourse of creativity in contemporary economic, political, and social life, and the characteristics of emerging labor markets in the cultural industries. In particular he is concerned with analyzing the working experiences of a number of individuals working in the cultural industries in London. Using a critical theoretical framework of understanding, he examines the importance of cultural capital, subjectivization, governmentality, network sociality, and individualization as key concepts for understanding the experience of labor in the creative economy. Lee considers how creative individuals negotiate the precarious, largely freelance, deregulated and de-unionised terrain of contemporary work. As the economic becomes increasingly inflected by the cultural in contemporary social life, the terrain of experience of individuals working in these expanding sectors has been neglected in cultural studies. This chapter seeks to critically intervene in this area, arguing that the "creative" turn in contemporary discourse can be seen to mask emergent inequalities and exploitative practices in the post-industrial employment landscape.

In their chapter, Nigel Culkin, Keith Randle, and Norbert Morawetz explore new business models of digital cinema. They see the distribution and exhibition of motion pictures at a crossroads. Ever since the medium was invented in the

1890s the "picture" has been brought to the spectator in the form of photochemical images stored on strips of celluloid film passed in intermittent motion through a projector. Now, at the beginning of the 21st century, an entirely new method has emerged, using digitally stored data in place of film and barely needing any physical support other than a computerized file. This opens an intriguing portfolio of revenue generating opportunities for the movie exhibitor. They provide an overview of current developments in digital cinema and examine potential new business models in an industry wedded to the analogue process. The authors consider the strategies of companies at the forefront of the technology; implications associated with the change; and how different territories might adapt in order to accommodate this transition.

Then, Eggo Müller writes an insightful piece on the Dutch treatment of interactive TV. Whereas, the advent of interactive TV has been discussed as one of the key added values of digitization and convergence of old and new media for years, current marketing strategies of the big players on the Dutch telecommunications market determinately avoid using the term *interactivity*. Promising the user "more fun" and more easiness of media consumption when digitally connected to the media world though a provider that offers broadband Internet, cable television, and telephony in one package, the competitors themselves aim at another added value of interactive media consumption: getting access to the living room means getting access to consumption patterns that can be traced back to the individual consumer. Müller's chapter discusses media convergence and the current development of interactive television in the context of the reconfiguration of the relation between producers and consumers in the new online economy.

Bas Agterberg offers a fresh perspective on high definition and the innovation of television by looking at the development of High Definition Television (HDTV). He argues that the way technological, industrial, and political actors have been interacting, has been crucial to the several stages of the development of this innovation. The central question is how industry, broadcasters, and consumers have debated and defined a medium and consequently redefined a medium through innovations. The complexity and the way actors have played a part within the changing media environment is analyzed by looking at the necessity for technological change of the television standard, by relating the media film and television in transition from analogue to digital and by examining case studies of political debates and policy in Europe and the U.S.

In the final section of this book *Emerging Markets and Organizational Cultures*, Karen Coppock classifies the types of partnerships employed to increase Internet demand in emerging markets. This classification system or taxonomy, is based on more than 60 in-depth interviews of about 32 partnerships designed to create Internet demand in Mexico. The taxonomy first classifies the partnerships into three broad categories based on the number of barriers to Internet usage the partnership was designed to overcome: one, two, or three. The partnerships are then classified into six subcategories based on the specific barrier or combination of barriers to Internet usage the partnership sought to overcome. The six subcategories of the taxonomy are: lack of funds; lack of awareness; lack of uses; lack of funds and lack of uses; lack of funds and lack of infrastructure; and lack of funds, lack of uses, and lack of infrastructure. This taxonomy gives empirical meaning and enables further analysis of this unique and increasingly popular type of partnership.

Kris Markman's study carefully examines the use of computer chat technologies for virtual team meetings. The use of geographically dispersed (i.e., virtual) teams is a growing phenomenon in modern organizations. Although a variety of ICTs have been used to conduct virtual team meetings, one technology, synchronous computer chat, has not been exploited to its fullest potential. This chapter discusses some of research findings related to effective virtual teams and examines some structural features of chat as they relate to virtual meetings. Based on these characteristics, she offers tips for using chat as an effective tool for distant collaboration.

Tracy Kennedy explores in great detail, the work-family interface by investigating home as a potential work space that must still accommodate the social and leisure needs of household members. By examining spatial patterns of household Internet location, she investigates the prevalence of paid work in Canadian homes, illustrates how household spaces are reorganized to accommodate the computer/Internet, and examines how the location of Internet access is situated within sociocultural contexts of the household and how this might affect potential work-from-home scenarios. Data collected from a triangulation of methods—surveys, interviews, and in-home observation—also illustrate the relevance of household Internet location from an organizational perspective. The relationship between individuals and business organizations is interactive and integrative, and the home workplace is complex and blurred with other daily social realities. This influences effective work-at-home strategies and potentially shapes productivity and efficiency.

In the last chapter, Yuichi Washida, Shenja van der Graaf, and Eva Keeris give way to the presentation of parts of the international comparative study that, as earlier explained, lies at the base of the come about of this book. This chapter examines the innovation in communication media, based on empirical survey results from five countries. First, the authors created a general framework of *the media life cycle* by exploring the replacement of communication media used in everyday life. The shift from voice communications to mobile e-mailing is at the forefront of the media life cycle in the personal communication area. This framework also implies future media replacements in other countries. Second, by comparing two empirical surveys, conducted in 2002 and 2003, of communication means used among Japanese family relations, the authors discover that certain consumer clusters lead in the innovation of communication media. This framework and discovery can be useful to deal with the vacuum between conventional media studies and the latest trends in information technology.

As a summarizing remark goes, the contents or frameworks offered throughout this book are by no means complete nor do they pretend to be inclusive of providing full accounts of occurring practices in new media technologies. Rather the primary objective is to yield insight into the dynamic relationships between the creation, diffusion, integration, usage, and sharing of technologies, innovative practices, and the potential impact on the boundaries of the firm in the managerial choices it faces in its adaptation of digital strategies. While this book does not seek to measure performance or competitiveness rather it has sought to establish a link between what can be observed as practices and understandings of strategy. As such, contributions made to this book have sought to contribute to both laying bare and filling in some important gaps in the theoretical and empirical characterization of seemingly altered relationships between firms and the marketplace signaling a shift in the organization of production, distribution, and consumption.

References

Benkler, Y. (2002). Coase's pengiun, or, Linux and the nature of the firm. *Yale Law Journal, 112*(3), 369-446.

Jenkins, H. (in press). *Convergence culture*.

Powell, W. (1990). Neither market nor hierarchy: Network forms of organization. *Research in Organizational Behavior, 12,* 295-336.

Slater, D. (2005). *Content and control: Assessing the impact of policy choices on potential online business models in the music and film industries*. The Berkman Center for Internet & Society at Harvard Law School.

Stark, D. (1996). Recombinant property in east European capitalism. *American Journal of Sociology, 101,* 993-1027.

Van der Graaf, S. (2004). Viral experiences: Do you trust your friends? In S. Krishnamurthy (Ed.), *Contemporary research in e-marketing*. Hershey, PA: Idea Group Publishing.

Van der Graaf, S., & Nieborg, D. B. (2003). Together we brand: America's army. In M. Copier & J. Raessens (Eds.), *Level Up: Digital Games Research Conference*. Utrecht University.

Endnotes

[1]   Henrik Werdelin, VP Strategy and Product Development at MTV Networks International, June 21, 2005.

[2]   Retrieved May 9, 2005, from http://www.microsoft.com/presspass/press/2005/jan05/01-05MTVAgreementPR.asp

[3] Ibid. In addition, *MTV Overdrive* was launched which is a hybrid channel that provides consumers with a linear viewing experience and video-on-demand capabilities in a Web-based application covering music, news, movies, mini-sodes, and so on. Then in July MTV Networks UK & Ireland tried to fight declines in TV ratings with *MTV Load* and 2 months later they teamed up with IssueBits to work on a text-to-screen service *Mr Know It All* which allows viewers of MTV Hits to use SMS to ask questions which will—along with the answers—appear live as a way to boost viewers and put them in "'collective control' of content, look, and tone." Towards the end of the year MTV Networks International announced a global series of *mobisodes* to be distributed via MTV's mobile channels and Motorola's Web site. They also announced a collaboration with mobile content provider Jamster!, to embark on a joint research project to see "how the role of mobile content is evolving around the world and how that can inform MTV to develop compelling, new entertainment that is even more relevant to consumers." All these developments can only leave us wondering what MTV will announce in 2006, as the latest addition to their multi-platform strategy delivering content to consumers everywhere they demand it: on-air, online, wireless, video-on-demand, and so forth.

[4] It has over a million views a day, the number of new visitors increases monthly with 200,000 and people spend about 25 minutes on the site.

[5] It is based on a partnership with AOL Music.

[6] This means that users can chat, post messages, and listen to each other's music mixes with other V-egos. It pays off to be a good music mixer, which is contextualized within the community by a contest where a user can win *decibels* that are a virtual currency and can be used to buy furniture and the like to decorate one's private room. All kinds of games can be played and new games (e.g., *Uncover the Music*), skins, and music among others are frequently added to attract and retain users. See http://www.turboads.comcase_studies/2003features/c20030514.shtml

[7] See http://www.americasarmy.com

[8] The answer to this recruiting problem was to change the way the U.S. Army communicates with young people in the USA. A short-sided approach to rely simply on its name, the U.S. Army learned that they needed ongoing insights in research-based advertising in order to understand the attitudes and needs of young people.

Section I: Innovation, Communication Technologies, and Consumer Clusters

Chapter I

Propagating the Ideal: The Mobile Communication Paradox

Imar de Vries, Utrecht University, The Netherlands

Abstract

In this chapter, visions of mobile communication are explored by focussing on idealised concepts surrounding wireless technology. By examining sources on the development, marketing, and use of wireless technology, I contextualise these visions within earlier accounts of ideal communication found in media history and isolate the regularities that are part of these accounts. On close examination, a paradox reveals itself in these regularities, one that can be described as resulting from an uneasiness in the human communication psyche: an unfulfilled desire for divine togetherness that clashes with individual communication needs. While the exact nature of this paradox—innate and hardwired into our brains, or culturally fostered— remains unknown, however, I assert that the paradox will continue to fuel idealised ideas about future communication technology. I conclude with the observation that not all use of mobile technology can immediately be interpreted as transcendental, and that built-in locational awareness balances the mobile communication act.

Introduction

In October 2003, two British climbers were caught in a blizzard on a Swiss mountain. Rachel Kelsey and her partner Jeremy Colenso, both experienced climbers, were forced to stop behind a large rock at 3000 meters up and wait for the weather to clear. They soon realised that their chances of finding the abseil points in heavy snow were very slim, which meant they were stuck. They texted five friends, one of whom received the message in London at 5 a.m. and immediately notified the rescue services in Geneva. After having to wait another 36 hours because the conditions were too severe for the rescue team to pick them up, the two climbers were finally rescued (Allison, 2003).

The idea that Earth is becoming entirely networked is not new,[1] but the characteristics of mobile communication media have—just as with the first wireless revolution in the beginning of the 20th century[2]—fiercely fuelled the Western notion that through better communication technology all problems of communication will—finally—be solved (Peters, 1999). The "anywhere, any-time, anyhow, anyone" slogan, subliminally attached to every mobile apparatus, opens up a vision of a universally accessible communication space, in which the exchange of information comes to stand for the single most important condition of human progress. More than at any other time in history, this human progress is thought to depend on technological progress.

Rescue stories as those described in the opening paragraph play their part in keeping the idea alive that improvement through technological progress can be measured. The conventional wisdom is that human lives are the single most valuable things we can think of, and if new technology can help save them, it must be treasured. Moreover, if new technology such as mobile telephony makes possible a way of life that is never forsaken of human contact—which therefore is taken as *safe* because there will always be someone who can help—this technology is surely poised to be seamlessly adapted to and integrated in our being (Katz, 2003). Through the remediation of older dominant forms of communication and entertainment technology, the mobile device (or personal digital assistant (PDA) or smart phone, as it is increasingly being called by mobile phone operators and providers) does seem to try to provide an ultimate extension of the natural balance of our sense organs (Levinson, 1997, 2004). Future visions of mobile communication strive for setting up globally accessible meeting points that cater bodiless but perfect interaction, and ultimately for opening up a communication space in which everyone is represented.

This is the inherently human dream of reaching an ideal state, which is cunningly exploited by advertisements, telecom operators, service providers, and the like. We know it is a dream, and we know that we are confronted by it day after day. It will probably haunt us for centuries to come. However, just as "our desire for each other [is] a poor substitute for the primary Eros—and therefore doomed to fail" (Campe, 2000), so are our telecommunication media substitutes for the primary *closeness*—and bound to fail (Vries, 2005). The end result of this is a tragic search for ideal communication through a continuous so-called improvement of communication technologies, a search that will never end.

This chapter will investigate the paradox of this eternal futile quest that we seem to keep embarking on, and will do so by looking at how mobile discourse is framed within quest-ending narratives. By analysing texts from influential scholars such as Pierre Lévy, Howard Rheingold, and Paul Levinson, we will get a grasp of how idealised ideas of the power of new communication technology have pervaded the mobile realm. From there, an attempt is made to single out the recurrent elements in those ideas, whose pervasiveness in our culture will then be examined. Finally, we will look at a few current trends in mobile cooperation techniques that potentially realise certain ideals of communication, albeit in a more pragmatic sense than a sublime one.

Unwiring the Knowledge Space

So far, it has mainly been cyberspace and its accompanying access points in the form of personal computers and laptops that are associated with potentially establishing the universally accessible communication realm. However, with the amount of mobile phones growing at an enormous pace,[3] the mobile device has with stunning speed become an essential tool to establish and maintain social networks, as well as managing all kinds of data flows. In this capacity, the device seems perfectly poised to morph itself into the logical choice of medium when accessing the ever-expanding Über network, the Internet.[4] Wherever, whenever, whatever: downloading or uploading information on the move, sharing news events as they happen with your carefully filtered online friends, checking in on your favourite weblog while lying on the beach; it is already possible and will be even more so when the devices grow into always-on mode. It is at this point where Pierre Lévy's (1997) imaginative *collective intelligence*, located in what he calls the knowledge space, starts to come into its own on an immense scale.

Lévy describes the evolution of earthbound living as being immersed in a succession of four types of space, in which man's identity is determined by the tools and symbols predominantly available in that space (see Table 1). The knowledge space is the fourth—and final—space in which we have come to live, and can best be seen as an informational cloud, a "space of living-in-knowledge and collective thought" (Lévy, 1997, p. 140). An important premise for its existence, growth, and preservation is that people interact with the informational

Table 1. Succession of spaces according to Lévy (1997)

Space	Identity
Nomadic Space of Earth	totems, lineage
Territorial Space	territorial inscription
Commodity Space	position within the domains of production and consumption
Knowledge Space	skill, nomadic cooperation, continuous hybridization

cloud by adding, changing, and retrieving data in whatever way possible.[5] It is to "unfold and grow to cover an increasingly vast and diverse world" (Lévy, 1997, pp. 111-112), ultimately creating a universally accessible information realm. Already, we can recognise this vision in descriptions of the multiple thrusts behind both the Internet and the mobile revolutions, such as those found in marketing publicity and open source movements' manifests alike.

Lévy's hierarchical description of the four levels of space invoke Borgmann's (1999) distinction between information *about* ("my shed can be found next to the willow tree"), *for* ("this is how you build a cathedral"), and *as* reality ("hi, I am Imar's avatar, shall we start exchanging data?"). Both Lévy and Borgmann show us historical shifts that expose a dematerialising transition of the dominant form of information. Although—as is conspicuously evident from the title of his book *Holding on to Reality*—Borgmann warns us for a Baudrillard-like potentially dangerous split between information about/for reality and information as reality, Lévy is not so much concerned about the danger of leaving reality behind, as he frames the knowledge space firmly within the other three spaces: "[It is n]ot exactly an earthly paradise, since the other spaces, with their limitations, will continue to exist. The intention of collective intellect is not to destroy the earth, or the territory, or the market economy" (Lévy, 1997, p. 141).

Paradise or not, Lévy cannot help but describe the knowledge space in terms of "a u-topia ... waiting to be born," "a cosmopolitan and borderless space," "an electronic storm," and "a sphere of artifice shot through with streaks of light and mutating signs" (Lévy, 1997, pp. 138-141), thereby mimicking the eccentric cyberpunk style of William Gibson's *Neuromancer*. There is undeniably a religious element visible in the way Lévy writes about the knowledge space, in which information is to be uncoupled from its static base. This dematerialising movement fits perfectly with the transcendental nature of going wireless: liberating things by releasing them from their carriers (be it wires, paper, or the brain) promises more opportunities to interconnect those liberated entities, as they form free-floating nodes in a dynamic network. In the end, in its most radical form, the idea is that every node can be connected to all others, providing instant and perfect transferral of whatever form of data.

As asserted previously, although the knowledge space is self-regulated and its transcendental nature gives rise to the supposition that it might leave the other spaces behind, Lévy holds that it can not be entirely separated from the three preceding spaces. Moreover, in a circular movement—"a return of the earth to itself," as Lévy (1997, p. 141) calls it—the knowledge space connects back to the first space through the recurrence of the nomadic identity. Again, this is a characteristic that is typically found in the mobile device, as has been shown by scholars in recent literature (Gergen, 2003; Kopomaa, 2000; Meyrowitz, 2003). The multiple social roles we possess are called upon in increasingly diverse geographical and social environments when a mobile device is carried along: we can perform parental tasks while at work, we can keep in touch with friends while on vacation, and we can consume entertainment while sitting in class-rooms. Slowly, urban design is responding to the diminishing need to build strict and fixed divisions between sites for work, leisure, and family, creating hetero-geneous zones in which the individual's social status is defined by the type of communication he or she engages with. The use of mobile technology therefore does not entail a full-circle return to the nomadic in the sense that it forces *us* to change location in order to find more fertile ground, as was the case in Lévy's first earthly space, but it forces our *locations* to adapt to our dynamic modes of being.

The transcendental and nomadic nature of the knowledge space calls for an intricate investigation of the points where it meets other spaces, and of the materiality of these meeting points. Considering the ease with which the mobile device has found its place as the essential data tool, such meeting points, which according to Rheingold (2002) seem to call for a "marriage of bits and atoms" (p. 100) or for us to be able to "click on reality," (p. 95) are set to be facilitated by the smart phones of the future. Or, as we will see in the next section, this is how it is envisioned in idealised ideas of communication.

The Lure of the Ideal

Although he admits to being utopian, and has subsequently tried to capture the dynamics of the collective intelligence in a formal language in order to make it more visible and tangible, Lévy has been criticised for painting an exaggeratedly pretty picture, ignoring the tough reality of political, economic, social, and other factors that influence the way communication technology is developed, pro-duced, distributed, and used. In the fourth chapter of their book *Times of the*

Technoculture: From the Information Society to the Virtual Life, Robins and Webster (1999) accuse Lévy of "promot[ing] and legitim[ising] the prevailing corporate ideology of globalization," and hold that "there is a desperate need for a richer debate of knowledges in contemporary societies — in place of the shallow, progressivist marketing that attaches itself to the cyberculture slogan (and reflects the hegemony of corporate interests)" (Robins & Webster, 1999, pp. 225, 227). In the same chapter, the aforementioned Rheingold receives similar flak for his—supposedly uncritical—belief in the Internet as a means of restoring communities.

However, Lévy and Rheingold are influential writers and are certainly not alone in taking an optimistic and idealised view on the possible contributions new communication technology can make to finally bring people together in an intelligent collective—nor will they be the last. If the years between the launch of the world's first graphic Internet browser in March 1993 and the crash of the dotcom boom in early 2000 marked the building up of the cyberspace hype, then the subsequent years can be characterised as having been labelled the new and improved mobile or wireless era: countless press releases, research papers, news articles, advertisements, books, radio shows, and television programmes have heralded mobile technology as the ideal solution to many communication problems. Two books I would like to bring to the fore in this respect are *Smart Mobs: The Next Social Revolution* by Howard Rheingold (2002) and *Cellphone* by Paul Levinson (2004), as their structures show interesting similarities with Lévy's (1997) approach—and with it, the same dangerous tendency to overestimate communication technology's power to fulfill longtime ideals of communication.

Comprised of a large series of anecdotal, interview, and travel journal material, *Smart Mobs* intends to uncover the characteristics of the "next social revolution," which is to be cranked up by the new mobile devices that "put the power of instant and ubiquitous communication — literally—within everyone's grasp" (Rheingold, 2002, back cover). Describing an impressive amount of trends, experiments, news reports, and commercial projects within the global realm of mobile telephony and computing, Rheingold shows how "technologies of cooperation" have an inherent tendency to group people together—and where there is a group, there are opportunities to learn, create, or topple over. The well-known (albeit somewhat overused) example of the protest demonstration in the Philippines in 2001, in which more than 1 million people were rallied by text messages to oppose Joseph Estrada's regime, is used by Rheingold as a key argument in describing a pivotal cultural and political moment: the power of mobile, ad hoc social networks is not to be underestimated; it can even influence politics on a momentous scale! To be fair, Rheingold's argument does not hinge upon this example alone; next to three other activist movements, he also mentions the squads of demonstrators that, thanks to mobile coordination, *won* the "Battle of Seattle" during a World Trade Organization meeting in 1999. These *movements*, however, have been minor in impact and longevity, and do not appeal to the imagination as much as the Philippine regime change does. It is therefore that *Smart Mobs* focuses mainly on events and projects that contain a clearly visible potential to change things; after all, what better way is there to show that the social impact of mobile technology is not only measurable, but can also be described in terms of setting in motion an unstoppable voyage towards a better future?

Other examples of what the consequences of ubiquitous mobile communication might be are equally carefully chosen for their provocative nature. Among the phenomena that await us, Rheingold (2002) names WiFi neighbourhoods; wearable computing that makes our environment aware of our presence and can react accordingly; RFID tags that provide contextual information on any object; and swarm intelligence that makes possible useful emergent behaviour. He does his best to convince us of the inherent potential of these things to fundamentally change the way we are living—and does so with an obligatory nod to the possibility that some of those changes might not be as pleasurable as we would like—but fails to go much further beyond stating the mantra *together is good*. The majority of Rheingold's examples, however tangible and useful they may be within their own context, are used to construct a vision of a futuristic world in which the possibility to connect things (people and machines) is most highly rated. To connect is to solve, to evolve, to come closer to the ideal of sublime togetherness.

Levinson's *Cellphone*[7] is another very good example of how opportunistic ideas found in much cyberculture literature have been transferred to the mobile realm. Not wasting any time, the book's subtitle, which is as subtle as it is provocative, already promises to tell us "[t]he story of the world's most mobile medium **and how it has transformed everything**" (bold in original). Working from within his Darwinian approach to media evolution—only the fittest media persist in the human environment—Levinson holds that "the cellphone has survived a human test," and that the human need it satisfies is "as old as the human species — the need to talk and walk, to communicate and move, at the same time" (Levinson, 2004, p. 13). This need, which "even defines the human species" (Levinson, 2004, p. 13), is satisfied by the mobile device to such an extent that Levinson foresees the end of the digital divide; the rise of new and more honest forms of news gathering and dispersal; and the birth of a smart world.

The most important (and obvious) characteristic Levinson stresses is that the mobile device blurs the boundary between inside and outside, rendering it unnecessary to confine ourselves to brick and mortar rooms when we want to call someone or find information. The consequence of this blurring is that it will enable us to "do more of what we want to do, be it business or pleasure, pursuit of knowledge, details, companionship, love," and that it will make "every place in the world in which a human may choose to thread ... well-read, or 'intelligent'" (Levinson, 2004, pp. 60-61). Dubbing this intelligent world a "telepathic society"—accompanied by the obligatory but hollow disclaimers that "our progress ... will be tough going at times" (Levinson, 2004, pp. 60-61) and that the mobile device not only solves things but generates new problems of privacy as well—Levinson sides with previous visions of emerging all-encompassing intelligence that have proved to be vulnerable to easy critique, including the Noosphere of Teilhard de Chardin (1959), the morphic fields of Sheldrake (1989) and the global brain of Bloom (2000). As we will see in the next section, the recurrence of these ideas is not coincidental.

Researching Regularities

Clearly, optimistic visions of new futures are often met with scepticism, but this does not stop them from reoccurring through time; especially when new information and communication media find the limelight. To understand why this "almost willful, historical amnesia," as Mosco (2004, p. 118) calls it, occurs, it is necessary to investigate the underlying regularities of such idealised claims, and to map the basic elements that make up those regular elements. By focussing not on a new medium itself—nor on what it is that makes it unique—but on the path that lies before that medium, we can get a detailed view of the moments in time that mark significant contributions to the medium's earlier discourse. This can best be achieved using the so-called media archaeology approach, which aims to prevent historical amnesia by "(re)placing [the histories of media technologies] into their cultural and discursive contexts" (Huhtamo, 1994). Doing so, the emphasis is shifted "[f]rom a predominantly chronological and positivistic ordering of things, centered on the artefact, ... into treating history as a multi-layered construct, a dynamic system of relationships" (Huhtamo, 1994). It is these relationships that can clarify the intricate ways in which idealised regularities in the dynamic communication media discourse may have changed face, but not their core.

Huhtamo proposes to call the regularities *topoi*, or topics, which he defines as "formulas, ranging from stylistic to allegorical, that make up the 'building blocks' of cultural traditions." He stresses that these topoi are dynamic themselves: "they are activated and de-activated in turn; new topoi are created along the way and old ones (at least seemingly) vanish" (Huhtamo, 1994). In other words, topoi are highly political and ideologically motivated. As an example of a topos found in media history, Huhtamo considers the recurrent "panicky reactions" of public being exposed to visual spectacles, and finds these in illustrations of the Fantasmagorie shows at the end of the 18th century, in reports of the showing of the arriving train in the Lumière brother's *L'Arrivee d'un train a La Ciotat* (1895) and in the stereoscopic movie spectacle *Captain EO* in Disneyland. There is, of course, a danger of over-interpreting historical sources that may well have served another function than to give an accurate account of what actually happened, but this is exactly Huhtamo's point: "unrealized 'dream machines,' or discursive inventions (inventions that exist only as discourses), can be just as revealing as realized artefacts" (Huhtamo, 1994). The Lumière showing may well not have created any panic at all, but it still remains a poignant reference, a media myth that is repeatedly used in numerous books, articles, and essays in which the reception and impact of new media is discussed. Media archaeology tries to expose these dubious but persistent stories, to collect and dust off forgotten elements of a medium's history by looking at discursive connections, however weak those connections may be. By looking at the many levels on which the discursive construction of a communication technology presents itself, media archaeology bridges the revolutionary gaps that are often found in teleological historiographies of that technology.

This archaeological approach has been put to practice by several scholars in recent years,[8] and has so far been successful in revealing and critically analysing media topoi such as the desires for immediacy, presence, liveness, and simultaneity. The most powerful (or overarching) topos, however, is the gnostic longing to transcend earthly life by improving technology, and to create a Universal Brotherhood of Universal Man. This ultimate topos unites every imaginable description of fulfillment, perfection, pureness, and harmony, and can be found in accounts of every communication medium, in every stage of its development, production, distribution, and use. The dream to finally fulfill the ultimate topos through improvement of communication technology can be comprehensively traced through media history, as many scholars (Mattelart, 2000; Mosco, 2004; Peters, 1999) have already shown. As I have written elsewhere, "[w]ireless telegraphy was seen as 'the means to instantaneous free communication'; telephony seemed to promise banishment of distance, isolation and prejudice; radio would pave the way for contact with the dead and television would transform its viewers into eyewitnesses of everything that went on in the world" (Vries, 2005, p. 11). With every development, be it technological, political, economical, or social, the regularities in discursive accounts of older media have been passed on to newer versions, thereby changing form but not essence.

The argument here is that mobile technology fits into a long line of media in which a limited set of regularly used *modes of reflection* determines the discursive domain of media reception. By analysing the discursive construction of mobile technology and comparing it to that of previous communication media, we can get a grasp of the topoi that have flourished or been revived—be it essentially unchanged or in disguised form—and of those that have floundered or been abandoned. Some of the most interesting indicators of these topoi are to be found in rationalisation techniques people use when explaining why they buy mobile phones, or what they are mainly going to use them for. On the surface, these explanations mostly point to very pragmatic reasons. Field study has shown that common justifications for acquiring a mobile phone are business, safety, and security (Palen, Salzman, & Youngs, 2000). On a deeper psychological level, however, these pragmatic reasons can be tied to fears of solipsism, a desire to increase the amount and strength of communication channels in the social network, and a wish for greater control over one's overall connectivity and availability. Just as we have seen in Rheingold's *Smart Mobs*, a need for the potential to increase *togetherness* is expressed in the mobile discourse, reflecting the ultimate topos of ideal communication.

The hints of religious elements present in these uncovered communication ideals is not surprising; just as Ludwig Andreas von Feuerbach stated in the middle of the 19th century that God is the projection of the human essence onto an ideal, so is an ultimate communicative Being One a projection of a human essence onto communication ideals. The religious motifs continue to exist today: authors such as Erik Davis (1998) and David Noble (1997) have written elaborate accounts of how contemporary technological discourses are still undeniably intertwined with religious beliefs, despite the widely held notion that since the Enlightenment these categories have slowly but surely separated. Such is the case with the topos of ultimate togetherness: the fears and desires disseminated by that topos are exponents of a mixture of the autonomous behaviour of the liberated Cartesian subject on the one hand, and a dream of a bodiless sharing of minds, described by Peters (1999) as angelic communication, on the other. This is a deeply paradoxical mixture, however. Angelic communication shows all the hallmarks of a divine togetherness: with no physical borders and direct one-on-one mappings of minds, every entity will ultimately know and be the same. This loss of individuality collides with the search for more control over ones individual connectivity found in the modern subject's autonomous behaviour. Both angelic communication and complete autonomy are idealised opposite poles on the same scale, and will therefore remain forever out of reach.

Thinking through Paradox

The crux of the communication paradox can be described as an uneasiness in the human communication psyche, born out of the tension between the desire for ideal communication and the knowledge of never being able to reach that goal.

This is not to say that every individual always wants to strive for perfection. Moreover, reaching perfection may not be what would actually be beneficial for human kind, as many dystopian answers to utopian projects, proposals, and literature have shown; there is no room for individuals or deviations in a society that can only function perfectly if every citizen is synchronised in the grand scheme.[9] Still, the paradox holds, as even in dystopian visions the utopian looms; in the end, Armageddon, the ultimate dystopian event, does nothing more than to destroy old structures in order to lay the foundation for a new, perfect one. A similar argument can be made for a dominant part of the communication media discourse: New media strive for the abolishment of old media in order to provide improved togetherness (Bolter & Grusin, 1999).

As we have seen in the previous section, the successive observations that the development phase and subsequent promotion of communication media are almost always framed within idealised expectations, that these are always accompanied by dystopian rebuttals, and that this process of touting and dismissing keeps reoccurring through time, give rise to the assumption that there is a steady undercurrent present, a topos that can be described as an idea of ideal communication that drives humankind to keep searching despite guaranteed failure. The objection to this assumption might be that this process is merely a marketing mechanism, but such a mechanism can only work if it addresses a human longing, one that is sensitive to promises of solving the communication tension.[10] The question, then, is whether the paradoxical attitude towards communication technology is innate, or if it is just a temporary, culturally sustained concept of progress left over from the Enlightenment, which, at some time in the future, is to be replaced by another concept. If it is innate, we will not be able to escape it; if it is not, we might be able to understand how to change or manipulate the structures in which the paradox resides.

To ask the question of innateness is to enter the realm of epistemology, the study of how we can know the world around us. Until the middle of the 18th century, this field had known two fairly opposed visions: the rationalist and the empiricist view. The rationalist Innate Concept thesis holds that there are some concepts that are already in our minds when we are born, as part of our rational nature. The notion that we can have a priori knowledge, that we have some innate awareness of things we know to be true that is not provided by experience, rests on the premise that the concepts used to construct that knowledge are also innate. Empiricists, however, argue that there are no innate concepts, and that experience alone accounts for the raw material we use to gain knowledge. The most well-known proponent of empiricism, John Locke, wrote that humans are born with a blank mind, a tabula rasa, which is *written onto* by experience. Knowledge, therefore, is not brought to consciousness by experience, but is provided by that experience itself.

This distinction largely disappeared toward the end of the 18th century when the two views were brought together by Emmanuel Kant, who divided reality into the phenomenal world (in which things are what they appear to us to be, and can empirically be known) and the noumenal world (in which things are what they are *in themselves*, and where rationalism rules). According to Kant's transcendental idealism, innate concepts do exist, but only in the noumenal world, where they remain empirically unknowable. Arguably, these innate concepts are philosophical in nature and therefore proof of their existence remains hard to formulate, but this does not mean *innateness* is always metaphysical. For instance, genetic theory, a late 20th century science, claims to provide empirical evidence for the existence of innate mechanisms in cognitive evolution: Human brains are not tabula rasa, but prestructured in specific ways so that they can learn things other organisms can not. While some elements of evolutionary psychology (EP) are highly controversial,[11] it is increasingly accepted that we all come wired with what Chomsky (1957) has called a Language Acquisition Device (LAD): Not only do we possess an innate capacity to learn, but also an innate set of universal language structures. This means that, independent of our social, cultural, or ethic environment, we already *know* how language works before we even speak it. It is on this level that we have to look for the communication paradox if we believe it to be innate: Are we in some way hard-wired to have a tendency to long for goals that are impossible to reach, to be fascinated by things that are and yet are not? Is there some sense of divine togetherness that we come programmed with, that is at some point in time to be fulfilled but keeps slipping away when we think we come close? The long history of trying to overcome distance and time through the use of media makes a strong argument for such a claim, especially when looking at the positivist discourse this search is usually framed in.

Seen this way, the topos of increased togetherness through idealised communication is but one manifestation of a central paradoxical tendency generated by our brains, albeit one of the most dominant. An imaginative account of how this paradoxical core pervades all aspects of life is found in Hofstadter's (1979/1999) *Gödel, Escher, Bach: An Eternal Golden Braid*. In the new preface in the 20th anniversary edition Hofstadter stresses the paradoxical motive for writing the book by stating that he had set out to "say how it is that animate beings can come out of inanimate matter" (Hofstadter, 1979/1999, p. xx). Introducing so-called strange loops, instances of self-reference that can often lead to paradoxical situations, Hofstadter shows that these loops can not only be found in math, perspective drawings, and music, but also—and this is his main argument—in the very essence of conscious existence itself. Without paradoxes, it seems, life as we know it could not exist. A similar argument is made by Seife (2000), who explores our uneasy relationship with zero and infinity in *Zero: The Biography of a Dangerous Idea*. Innocent as they might seem, in many situations in many times the notions of zero and infinity have been difficult to grasp, use, and explain;

to such an extent even that people have equated them with the work of God and ignored them as not allowed by God at the same time. It was through the use of zero and the infinite that Zeno could create his paradoxical race, in which Achilles never overtakes the tortoise, and it is zero and the infinite that plague contemporary physicists' current understanding of our universe. Opposite poles that invoke as well as fight the paradoxical will always be with us, because we are born out of a paradox, Seife concludes.

EP is a relatively young field, and as such has not yet found very stable ground. The argument that there is a universally active module in our brain that triggers— or is even responsible for—a life with paradoxes is therefore to be very cautiously approached. As asserted previously, it may well be that our paradoxical attitude towards communication is not the manifestation of an innate concept, but of a culturally constructed one. A helpful nongenetic argument for the paradoxical inclination is found in existentialist theories, especially in Heidegger's treatment of *Gelassenheit* (releasement) and Sartre's description of *mauvaise foi* (bad faith). Whereas the former concept deals with fully accepting one's Being-in-the-world as something that has no intrinsic goal or pregiven content, as something that can only receive its significance through the meaning one chooses to give to it, the latter is the result of *not* accepting the open-ended nature of our existence, of continuously asking "why"? and trying to find the answer outside of one's own will. Such a denial of things-as-they-are and things-as-they-happen actively feeds and sustains a two-pole system, in which paradoxes reside: There is no coincidence when everything happens for a reason, and there is no sense when everything is contingent. People with bad faith—and there are a lot, according to Sartre—often face and cannot accept the most fundamental paradox: Sometimes things are just what they are, even when they are not.

Now all these observations may seem a far cry from our day-to-day experience of using mobile phones, but whenever we transfer any information in any way we are positioned as a node in a communication network, one that exists foremost because we as humans seek contact. We hope and strive for this contact to be instantaneous, clear, under control, and ideal, even when we want to mislead or deceive the other person; if we manage to use the medium and channel in such a way that it serves our intent, the contact has been ideal for its purpose. The desire is for a technologically induced complete fulfillment, which is omnipresent in mobile discourse. There is never any certainty about having reached this ideal state, however, as we have seen. The communication paradox makes sure that something always gets in the way of pure experience.

The Return of Location

In light of this knowledge, the best way we can act, as Peters (1999) also argues, is to embrace the impossibility of ideal communication and make do with what forms of communication we *can* realise. The transcendental nature of wireless technology may at times lure us into thinking we have come close and need just a little push in the right direction, but this would be like chasing a mirage. What then are the elements of more appropriate pragmatic approaches to using new communication technology, ones that defy the urge to hand out idealised promises? Some interesting trends in recent innovative wireless concepts show that the independency of locality, the characteristic that seemingly constitutes the *essence* of mobile telephony, can be turned on its head. Where the most pure form of communication is equated with a bodiless presence and is therefore situated in a nondescriptive *anywhere,* part of the current crop of wireless projects inject exactly this sense of locality into the mobile communicative act. The resulting location based services (LBS) are put to use in a variety of ways: backseat games that merge road context with virtual content (Brunnberg & Juhlin, 2003), portable devices that support the tourist experience by supplying on the spot information (Brown & Chalmers, 2003), systems that provide virtual annotation of physical objects (Persson, Espinoza, Fagerberg, Sandin, & Cöster, 2002), and mobile phone applications that can *sense* the proximity of people on your buddy list (Smith, Consolvo, Lamarca, Hightower, Scott, Sohn, et al., 2005). Of course, all these projects in some way reflect a drive towards making things easier, quicker, better, or simply more enjoyable, and therefore do not completely escape paradoxical idealised thinking, but they do not ostentatiously try to transcend our present experience of communication by denying its inherent grounding in lived space and time.

Another area where mobile phones are undeniably making a difference without having to resort to metaphysical musings is in developing countries. By leapfrog-ging older communication technology—in most cases this concerns landlines that had been too expensive to be installed nationwide—mobile technology is used to quickly set up cheap networks, thereby facilitating measurable boosts to local economies and communities. The mobile networks do not instantly connect all parts of a country, but remain localised in existing urban or rural environments. This localisation is further strengthened by the fact that, less tempted to use the mobile device to mix different social locales into one heterogeneous zone, as is more the case in Western metropolitan areas, people in these developing countries tend to see the mobile more as a landline that happens to be wireless. If there would have been a landline the impact would have largely been the same, something communication theorist Jonathan Donner (2003) concurs with. He conducted several field studies in Rwanda, and found that the use of mobile phones by Rwandan entrepreneurs enhanced their ability to do business, but also to satisfy their emotional and intrinsic needs. This is mostly due to the mere presence of a communication channel, and not to the mobile's intrinsic essence. Again, the underlying idealised implication is that appointments, deals, and transactions can occur faster and more streamlined when people are increasingly brought together in whatever way, but in cases such as those in Rwanda the results of introducing wireless technology are clearly visible and do not remain mostly theoretical.

Conclusion

With the global proliferation of mobile communication devices, a reinvigorated sense of ubiquitous connection possibilities has emerged. Covering large parts of the Earth, a networked informational skin seems set to revolutionise our way of living. The key new paradigm that is stressed in this "mobilisation" of the world is the ability to tap into an all-encompassing knowledge space, thereby making information addition, retrieval, and communication virtually instantaneous. The fundamental driving force behind this endeavour can be ascribed to a desire for establishing connections to everyone or everything in whatever way possible, a bodiless omnipresence. The radical consequences of this—almost angelic—desire are affecting traditional modes of interaction such as dialogue and dissemination.

This dream of idealised communication is subconsciously stressed by the dominant image of wireless communication that is found in advertisements, press releases, books on social change, government policies, and the like. Promises that things will get better, fuel our impatience when contemporary technology fails to deliver. In other words, the desire for ideal communication itself is part of a paradoxical system found in all layers of our existence. The dream can never be realised, and will therefore continue to recur through time. Whether we will be able to change our attitude towards this strange loop depends on its nature: If it is hard-wired into our brains, we will have to live with the paradox forever. If it is not, who knows, we might come to see mobile communication for exactly what it is, a specific but not definitive "Being" of communication.

References

Allison, R. (2003, October 7). Climbers on Alpine ridge rescued by text message. *The Guardian*. Retrieved May 16, 2005, from http://www.guardian.co.uk/uk_news/story/0,3604,1057271,00.html

Analysys Press Office (2005, May 5). Mobile penetration in Western Europe is forecast to reach 100% by 2007, says Analysys. *Analysys*. Retrieved May 16, 2005, from http://www.analysys.com/Articles/StandardArticle.asp?iLeftArticle=1897

Bloom, H. K. (2000). *The global brain: The evolution of mass mind from the big bang to the 21st century*. New York: Wiley.

Bolter, J. D., & Grusin, R. A. (1999). *Remediation: Understanding new media*. Cambridge, MA: MIT Press.

Borgmann, A. (1999). *Holding on to reality: The nature of information at the turn of the millennium*. University of Chicago Press.

Brown, B., & Chalmers, M. (2003). Tourism and mobile technology. In K. Kuutti & E. H. Karsten (Eds.), *Proceedings of the 8ᵗʰ European Conference on Computer Supported Cooperative Work* (pp. 335-355). Dordrecht: Kluwer Academic Press.

Brunnberg, L., & Juhlin, O. (2003). *Movement and spatiality in a gaming situation: Boosting mobile computer games with the highway experience*. Interactive Institute. Retrieved May 16, 2005, from http://www.tii.se/mobility/Files/BSGFinal.pdf

Campe, C. (2000). *Spheres I: An introduction to Sloterdijk's book*. Goethe-Institut Boston. Retrieved May 16, 2005 from http://www.goethe.de/uk/bos/englisch/Programm/archiv/2000/enpcamp100.htm

Chomsky, N. (1957). *Syntactic structures*. The Hague, The Netherlands: Mouton.

Clark, T. (2004). *Mobile communications and the wireless Internet: The Japanese experience*. Receiver 11. Retrieved May 16, 2005 from http://www.receiver.vodafone.com/11/articles/pdf/11_02.pdf

Davis, E. (1998). *Techgnosis: Myth, magic, mysticism in the age of information*. New York: Harmony Books.

Day, R. E. (1999). The virtual game: Objects, groups, and games in the works of Pierre Lévy. *The Information Society, 15*(4).

Donner, J. (2003). What mobile phones mean to Rwandan entrepreneurs. In K. Nyíri (Ed.), *Mobile democracy: Essays on society, self and politics* (pp. 393-410). Vienna: Passagen.

Gergen, K. (2003). Self and community in the new floating worlds. In K. Nyíri (Ed.), *Mobile democracy: Essays on society, self and politics* (pp. 103-114). Vienna: Passagen.

Hofstadter, D. R. (1999). *Gödel, Escher, Bach: An eternal golden braid.* New York: Basic Books. (Original work published 1979)

Huhtamo, E. (1994). *From kaleidoscomaniac to cybernerd: Towards an archeology of the media.* De Balie Dossiers Media Archaeology. Retrieved May 16, 2005 from http://www.debalie.nl/dossierartikel.jsp ?dossierid=10123&articleid=10104

Katz, J. E. (2003). *Machines that become us: The social context of personal communication technology.* New Brunswick, NJ: Transaction Publishers.

Katz, J. E., & Aakhus, M. A. (2001). *Perpetual contact: Mobile communication, private talk, public performance.* Cambridge, UK; New York: Cambridge University Press.

Kopomaa, T. (2000). *The city in your pocket: Birth of the mobile information society.* Helsinki, The Netherlands: Gaudeamus.

Levinson, P. (1997). *The soft edge: A natural history and future of the information revolution.* London; New York: Routledge.

Levinson, P. (2004). *Cellphone.* New York: Palgrave Macmillan.

Lévy, P. (1997). *Collective intelligence: Mankind's emerging world in cyberspace.* New York: Plenum Publishing Corporation.

Malik, K. (1998, December) The Darwinian fallacy. *Prospect, 36,* 24-30.

Mattelart, A. (2000). *Networking the world, 1794-2000.* Minneapolis: University of Minnesota Press.

Medosch, A. (2004). Not just another wireless utopia. *RAM5.* Retrieved May 16, 2005, from http://www.rixc.lv/ram/en/public07.html

Mosco, V. (2004). *The digital sublime: Myth, power, and cyberspace.* Cambridge, MA: MIT Press.

Noble, D. F. (1997). *The religion of technology: The divinity of man and the spirit of invention.* New York: A.A. Knopf.

Palen, L., Salzman, M., & Youngs, E. (2000). Going wireless: Behavior and practice of new mobile phone users. In W. A. Kellogg & S. Whittaker (Eds.), *Proceedings of the 2000 ACM Conference on Computer Supported Cooperative Work* (pp. 201-210). New York: ACM Press.

Persson, P., Espinoza, F., Fagerberg, P., Sandin, A. & Cöster, R. (2002). GeoNotes: A location-based information system for public spaces. In K. Höök, D. Benyon, & A. Munro (Eds.), *Designing information spaces: The social navigation approach* (pp. 151-173). London; New York: Springer.

Peters, J. D. (1999). *Speaking into the air: A history of the idea of communication.* University of Chicago Press.

Rheingold, H. (2002). *Smart mobs: The next social revolution.* New York: Perseus Publishing.

Robins, K., & Webster, F. (1999). *Times of the technoculture. From the information society to the virtual life.* London; New York: Routledge.

Seife, C. (2000). *Zero: The biography of a dangerous idea.* New York: Viking.

Sheldrake, R. (1989). *The presence of the past: Morphic resonance and the habits of nature.* New York: Vintage Books.

Smith, I., Consolvo, S., Lamarca, A., Hightower, J., Scott, J. Sohn, T., et al. (2005). Social disclosure of place: From location technology to communication practices. In H. W. Gellersen, R. Want, & A. Schmidt (Eds.), *Proceedings of the 3rd International Conference on Pervasive Computing* (pp. 134-141). London; New York: Springer.

Standage, T. (1998). *The Victorian Internet: The remarkable story of the telegraph and the nineteenth century's on-line pioneers.* New York: Walker and Co.

Teilhard de Chardin, P. (1959). *The phenomenon of man.* New York: Harper.

Vries, I. de (2005). Mobile telephony: Realising the dream of ideal communication? In L. Hamill & A. Lasen (Eds.), *Mobiles: Past, present and future.* London; New York: Springer.

Endnotes

[1]   See Standage (1998) for a comparison of the telegraph age with the rise of the Internet.

[2]   See Medosch (2004) for an account of how both wireless eras are very similar in the way the technology was received.

[3]   Mobiles in Europe are predicted to exceed Europe's population in 2007 (Analysys Press Office, 2005).

[4]   See Clark (2004) for an account of how "educational policy, peer pressure, and most importantly, soaring use of internet-enabled mobile handsets" drive young people in Japan to use mobile phones instead of computers when sending and receiving e-mail.

[5]   A fitting current example of an implementation of such a cloud would be Wikipedia, which thrives on user input and moderation. Other methods of

knowledge storage and retrieval such as Google and archive.org rely on algorithms and filters, which makes them more archival than dynamic modes of knowledge preservation.

[6]   See http://www.aec.at/en/festival2003/wvx/FE_2003_PierreLevy_E.wvx for a Webcast of his lecture at the 2003 Ars Electronica conference, in which he presented the system of this formal language.

[7]   Levinson prefers to call the device a *cellphone* instead of a *mobile phone*, because "[it] is not only mobile, but generative, creative." On top of that, it "travels, like organic cells do," and it "can imprison us in a cell of omni-accessibility" (Levinson, 2004, p. 11). I tend to use *mobile device*, as this category includes not only the mobile (or cell) phone, but also smart phones and PDAs.

[8]   Huhtamo names Tom Gunning, Siegfried Zielinski, Carolyn Marvin, Avital Ronell, Susan J. Douglas, Lynn Spiegel, Cecelia Tichi, and William Boddy (Huhtamo, 1994).

[9]   Eager to show that a collective intelligence does not mean a loss of individuality, Lévy acknowledges that it is important to ask, in Day's words, "how we can pass from a group mentality characterised by a modern notion of the mass (and with that, mass broadcasting) to a collective intelligence wherein persons may remain individual and singular" (Day, 1999, p. 266).

[10]   Claims that support the idea of a universal disposition towards what mobile communication is supposed to be about can be found in Katz and Aakhus (2001).

[11]   Malik (1998) criticises EP because it can be used to explain sexual and racial discrimination as "biologically meaningful." Because our genes have not been able to keep up with cultural evolution, the EP argument goes, we are "stone age men in a space age world," and therefore cannot help but to exhibit hunter-gatherer behaviour. Malik claims that this would completely deny the fact that culture has evolved out of natural selection too, and that we consciously make choices.

Chapter II

Beauty and the Nerd:
Ethnographical Analyses in the Japanese Digitalization

Gaby Anne Wildenbos, Utrecht University, The Netherlands

Yuichi Washida, Hakuhodo Inc. & The University of Tokyo, Japan

Abstract

This chapter focuses on the Japanese usage of digital products. Both the consumer and production side are addressed, whereby emphasizing the mobile phone industry on the basis of two consumer groups otakus *and* kogals. *First, key characteristics of each consumer group are described. Second, social and cultural aspects related to consumption behavior of the otakus and kogals are examined—that is, collectivism, individualism and kawaiiness (cuteness or coolness). This is followed by the production side of digital products in Japan, highlighting two major companies involved in mobile telephony: NTT DoCoMo and Label Mobile, which in their turn, are linked to the consumption cultures of otaku and kogals.*

Japan in Relation to the West

Japan plays a key role throughout the world, especially regarding technological innovation. Barclay (2004) surveys the state of contemporary Japanese technology in his report *The Technology of Japan*. In this survey it is apparent that Japanese technological capabilities are on the same level as those of the U.S. Moreover, Japan and the U.S. have a long-lasting relationship regarding this matter, which dates from the postwar period. Together with Russia, the U.S. has been in charge of Japan after World War II until the beginning of the 1950s. With regard to technology it wanted to make sure that Japan would loose its military nature. Evidently, it can be said Japan owes its strong economic position to this occupation period: "They chose to forge a new path, a path that led to postwar Japan being a military-political dwarf but an economic giant." (Nakayama, 2001, p. 2). Japan cannot afford to withdraw from the technological relationship with the U.S., since its technological dependence on America is essential. Another way of saying it would be that the technological alliance between both countries is a matter of strategic interest for the U.S., whereas it is one of economic and technological necessity for Japan (Barclay, 2004).

Where does this place other Western countries, like Europe? Although some countries in Europe import technologies from Japan, their relationship on this matter is less strong than the Japanese-American alliance. Nevertheless, Europe's influence on Japan is noticeable in a more general sense, namely Japan's movement towards Westernization. Westernization was first offered to Japan in the 16th century through southern European countries. Not only did the Europeans transport an interesting cuisine, more importantly, they brought medical and scientific knowledge. However, at that time the European or Western influence was limited, since the practical needs for their science and technology was small. The second period when Japan came into contact with Westernization was at the beginning of the 20th century. Then they did experience an internal need to adapt to some of the Western modernization (Kasulis, 1995). The Japanese saw Westernization as an import item; they could use modern European and American ideas or products for practical needs related to political, military, and economic necessities. Nowadays, it is even said that "seeing the skyscrapers of Tokyo's downtown districts, hearing Western rock or classical music even in village coffee shops, or tasting the French cuisine of its fine restaurants, it is easy for one to think of Japan as part of the Western-based family of cultures" (Kasulis, 1995, p. 1).

Japan vs. the West

Yet, apart from Westernization, Japan seems to present totally different characteristics as well. Ian Condry (personal interview, March 24, 2005), Professor of Japanese Cultural Studies, says that Japanese see their country as: "Japan is that which is not the West." This can be related to the period that stands in between the first and second introduction of Westernization, in which the foreign influence was kept to a minimum. After this period of isolation the Japanese realized that in order to "relate and compete with the U.S. and Europe, it is they who would have to adapt." Within the process of modification it seems as if the Japanese value their modes of behavior insignificant compared to the ones of the West, which shows itself in their ability to copy almost any Western attribute. Idealized versions of the West are presented in Tokyo Disneyland, German Happiness Kingdom, Canadian World in Hokkaido, Garasunosato "the Venice of Japan," Huis ten Bosch "Dutch Village," and so on.

Paradoxically, every time Japan tries to catch up with the West, their national identity becomes stronger in this process:

They [Japanese] ended up ahead of the power they were catching up to and redefining their own uniqueness. The Japanese view their entire past in terms of foreign influence and native sentiment. They consciously distinguish what came from China and the West and what is natively Japanese. (Eckstein, 1999, p. 9)

In other words, by means of westernization, Japanese people are in search of what is "Japaneseness"—A pursuit that is accompanied by the West. Other than Japanese technology, Japanese popular culture and lifestyle also appear to be booming in Western countries, especially in the U.S. Since it is not exactly clear where this interest comes from, recent writings on the influence of Japan on Western countries seems to be focusing on which specific Japanese characteristics attract the West, which can be exemplified by this chapter.

Consumption:
Beauty and the Nerd

What is most striking about Japanese mobile communication or usage of mobile phones? First of all, mobile phones appear everywhere: on the streets, in the elevators, in the trains, during lunch, during meetings, in back pockets or Louis

Vuitton bags of girls (and boys), and so on. This would imply that everywhere mobile phones will be ringing; however the usage of the mobile phones is apparently silent. When people use their phones to communicate with each other they mostly speak quietly. Moreover, the ability to send a text message is frequently used; especially in young girls, they send more text messages than they use their phone to actually make a call. More then 70% of Japanese send e-mail through mobile phones at least once a day (Washida, 2005). Another characteristic of the silent usage differs from the original communication means of a (mobile) phone. The phones are often used as wireless devices to obtain information and entertainment. It is possible to use your phone to listen to original music, to get information about your favorite restaurants, and what is more, discount coupons of that restaurant can be stored in the same device. Recently, even systems are developed to use your mobile phone as a mobile wallet; for example, to pay for your train ticket. Besides a communication tool or content provider, mobile phones are used as a means for self-expression. Although the design of the mobile phones is rather similar, the added straps and decorations speak for themselves.

There are two important consumer cultures surrounding digital products, that is, the otaku and the kogal culture. These terms may sound familiar yet there exists no detailed analysis of these cultures in relation to digital products. Therefore, I attempt to provide an in-depth study of these cultures in order describe their relevance to the Japanese usage of digitalization whereby focusing on both the production side and the consumption side.

Otaku:
Technologies as Life Value

Otaku and kogal do not mean male and female, still their association with gender is evident (Washida, 2005). They are of importance to the Japanese high-tech manufacturers since they offer a double-feedback structure; the small group of otakus give detailed technological feedback, whereas the large cluster of kogals provide information that is useful for a wide-ranging market. In general this means that the manufacturers use otakus to do test marketing when they initially release their products. The information obtained during this test marketing is used to improve products successfully. On the other hand, manufacturers get hold of kogals' curious behaviors regarding digital products. Feedback provided by marketing research helps the manufactures to make their products more attractive and competitive for the general market. Manufacturers even imitate kogals' behavior: They transform the new uses invented by the kogals into their own new commercial services (Washida, 2005).

Originally the term otaku can be translated into "fanboy" or "geek." "It refers to a person who is so involved with a particular kind of fan subculture that he or she comes obsessed with it, or even insane" (Newitz, 1997, p. 1). This is probably the most known reference. Nevertheless, the term can be put into a broader perspective. Nowadays otaku is used in the U.S. to describe the affiliation and love of fans towards a specific category differing from anime to motorcycles. This goes for Japan as well, however here the term is still mostly associated with males.

The first generation of otakus in Japan are generally referred to as "banana generation" and they are now in the end of their 30s and early 40s. They are today's managers of small companies, which they run according to the traditional business hierarchy in Japan. The second generation of otakus is called *dankai* junior generation. They are in the end of their 20s or in the beginning of their 30s and the main difference with the former otakus is that they do not support the traditional (business) hierarchy in Japan, because they experienced the difficulties in getting jobs or promotions due to the poor economic situation after the Japanese economic bubble.

Key characteristic to otakus is that they find out about new information and products soon. Therefore, they are "usually the impulse buyers of electronic devices in the very early phase of the development of products, and also abandon them easily if they find the product unsatisfactory" (Washida, 2005, p. 27). This specific consumption behavior is rooted in deep and narrow personal desires. In general, otakus experience trouble in their social life; it is difficult for them to establish a good relationship with the elderly or girls. The label otaku did not come out of the blue, since the Japanese nuance of this word includes the meaning of "you isolated in your house" (Washida, 2005, p. 27). As a solution to dissatisfaction with their social life otakus constitute a technological dream. Successful technological stories, like *Star Wars* movies and the rise of Apple Macintosh or NASA, influence the otakus in such a way that they believe that technology can make everything in life pleasant, whereas reality cannot. Consequently, even some of the otakus detract from society.

One could say that otakus think technological innovations can help them to accomplish things in society; things like status, marriage, and moreover, a better future. Probably they can be best compared with *hackers*, since hackers are also influenced by technological innovations by which they think they can change society for the better (Levy, 1984).

Some of these ideas are confirmed by information from the contemporary otakus that is obtained at interviews that were conducted with two employees of Hakuhodo, Japan's second largest advertising agency. These young men are employed in the branding and marketing division of Hakuhodo and appear formally dressed with a willing attitude to cooperate; both seem content with working at a large advertising agency and are adjusted to the corporate style.

However, they do want to be noticed as an individual. This shows itself for instance in their clothing, which is formal as well as distinctive from most outfits in the company. In other words, although they may not agree with the traditional business hierarchy, still the otakus choose to change society by accomplishing success within an organization. On the contrary, the hackers attack an organization with the same purpose. Nevertheless, both hackers and otakus posses the aspect of fanaticism. The fandom of anime is typical for otakus and consequently it is at the core of our interview.

Both men knew that the interview would be focusing on otakus and therefore they brought two anime DVDs with them: *Gundam* and *Innocence*, which shows loving anime is characteristic for otakus in their opinion as well. As a result they use these movies as an example to explain more about this topic. Most apparent is their passion for anime along with their enthusiasm to talk about it; they categorize it into different types, explain which people are attracted to what type, and why this is the case. Their interest shines through in the detailed knowledge they have. In a fragmented manner they tell about many different anime examples and almost without pausing they anticipate each other's information. During this explanation the relation between anime and technology is at the center. *Gundam* and *Innocence*, both masterpieces of anime according to the interviewed otakus, deal with technological subjects since it involves humans next to robots and the interaction between them. The otakus state they go beyond Hollywood movies like *I-Robot*, because the main question in the anime movies is how to identify yourself rather than a battle between humans and robots. Moreover, anime seems to be an inspiration for Hollywood—though it can be questioned how the main theme of these specific Hollywood movies differs from anime movies as robots in anime movies seem less threatening to human beings. They often function as a protection shield or weapons that support humans fighting evil creatures.

This observation may be helpful when contemplating the approach of otakus to technology. As one man said during the interview: "These [anime movies] make you think more about life, and that is why those anime movies can be recognized as masterpieces." In other words, the anime does not make him question the (threatening) difference between technology and humans; instead technology and humans seem to be familiar with each other in the otaku's perspective. It must be said this line of thought is mere speculation, because the relationship between technology and otakus is a personal matter which makes it impossible to expect a straight answer while questioning them on this topic. Still, there is a noticeable observation which has less to do with the explanation of anime from the otakus themselves. That is to say, since the otakus alternate in talking during the interview, one otaku is drawing anime pictures in his notebook to kill time while being silent. All the more this indicates their unconscious familiarity and passion towards the animation style.

The passion for anime does not only express the fandom associated with otakus, it also concerns their values in life. When asking the otakus what is most important to them in daily life they fall silent. After some thinking they answer that, of course, working and friendships are essential. Nonetheless, of more importance is thinking about life, looking deeper, and being moved; the effects they experienced while watching anime movies. Consequently, they have ideas about how life and technology or digitalization is involved with each other. This might sound paradoxical regarding the previous statement that the otakus have no answer on the subject of the relationship between technology and themselves—A paradox that can be justified. In Japan it is not custom to share personal information with unfamiliar persons, which makes it difficult to obtain information about the otakus themselves in relation to technology and digitalization. On the other hand, it is less complicated to talk about this matter in general and therefore some interesting insights on this matter are provided during the interview.

When discussing the concept of digitalization with the otakus the technological or digital dream comes to mind. Especially in their childhood they used to have specific thoughts about how technology and digitalization would be at hand in the future. One of the men explained that at school there was a special name for the child who had many of these futuristic ideas: doctor. Children, like a doctor, used to have dreams about a technological world that were very physical, such as flying cars. These dreams turned out to be different in the perspective of the interviewee. He thinks digitalization is humanistic; it can make a package of life. For instance, when using digital systems and products a person can make a "blog" to let someone in on his own thoughts or share files adjusted to personal taste. These insights are interesting since they confirm the presence of a technological dream in the minds of otakus. Yet, the current otaku perspective on technology can be best seen in the final words during the interview. At the question why one of the men understood technology, his colleague took the privilege to answer: "Because he loves it! He just bought a new gadget, just because it is cool!"

Kogal:
Collectivism vs. Individualism?

Kogal literally means "girlish female." "They are very active young girls, who love shopping, chatting, and being fashionable" (Washida, 2005, p. 27). Whereas the kogals used to be associated with the Japanese girls dressed up in school uniforms on purpose, nowadays their fashion is quite different and varied.[1]

Another important characteristic is that "they are surprisingly good inventors of new ways of using electronic devices" (Washida, 2005, p. 27). These innovations are an expression of the heavy use of electronic devices. For instance, through the 24-hour use of mobile phones kogals thought of adding music data to phones to change the traditional tone into a music ring tone; a popular feature nowadays.

Kogals can also be divided into different generations. The first generation of kogals is now 30-34 years old. These women, however, used to be kogals in their teenage years and in their early 20s. At that time, they suffered from the economic depression and had to develop a new lifestyle. The second generation consists of today's teenagers and can generally be said to be in their early 20s. They are used to the shifting economy in Japan, which causes them to think they have to be unique in order to succeed in making a living. They use new media and technologies to experiment with different lifestyles and to promote their uniqueness.

Before discussing the importance of the kogals' use of mobile phones, it is necessary to explain some aspects of the Japanese culture to understand the kogals' consumption behavior, that is, collectivism and individualism in Japan. The concepts of collectivism and individualism have been widely researched in the fields of psychology as well as sociology in order to explain cultural differences. Initially, the difference between collectivism and individualism was viewed as a contrast. Psychologists Strunk and Chang (1999) write:

Collectivism *promotes a sense of the self as interdependent. Collectivistic people are motivated by the norms and duties of their collectives, give priority to the goals of the collectives and emphasize their connectedness to members of the collectives. In contrast,* individualism *promotes a sense of the self as independent. Individualistic people are motivated by their own desires, give priority to their personal goals and use reason to analyze the advantages and disadvantages of associating with others.* (p. 2)

Since the beginning of the 1990s, scholars have sought to revise the contrast between the terms. Niles (1998) explains this by describing the writings of Harry Triandis, a well-known professor in psychology. Triandis (1995) states that most cultures include a mixture of collectivism and individualism. Moreover, the dimensions became characterized by rather specific attributes of which the ones most important to the situation of the kogals are described. The difference in defining oneself as part of a group rather than focusing on a concept of the self that is independent of the group stays the same. More significant is the contrast in commitment to a group or relationships. The social behavior of collectivists tends to be driven by duty and obligations, whereas among individualists social behavior relates to attitudes and other internal processes. Furthermore, relationships are of great importance among collectivists, even when it requires personal sacrifice. Individualists tend to let go of relationships when they involve too many personal costs (Niles, 1998).

Perspectives on collectivism and individualism in Japan are changing, due to Western influences such as globalization. In particular the younger generation is less keen on the traditional values including collectivism. This does not mean that they do not hold on to these values, but they are open to other perspectives or lifestyles as well. In other words, nowadays the contradiction between collectivism and individualism is not as straightforward as was once thought. Relating to the statement of Triandis, a mixture of both dimensions can be found in Japan. Indeed so, this is a complicated mixture, since either collectivism or individualism takes lead depending on a particular context.

Considering now kogals, it seems difficult for these young girls to cope with what direction in life to choose. Or, how can you decide on a way of life if your options are not clear? As a result, the kogals wish not to choose at all, which can be associated with mobile phone usage. The mobile phones of the girls that are interviewed are mostly used for sending e-mails; this includes keeping in contact with close friends as well as making new friends, which is an important difference as will be shown later. The girls divide their friends in categories, based on which school they attended. In other words, they talk about friends from elementary school, junior high school, and high school. Moreover, they value high school friendships as less close than primary school and junior high school friends; the latter seems to be valued as being closest to the interviewed kogals, which can be related to their use of mobile phones.

When kogals are asked when they got their first mobile phone, they said that it was during the period they attended high school. Then they started to use their mobile phone to communicate with friends rather than talking to them face-to-face which is referred to by the terms *pre-mobile-phone-stage-of-life* and *mobile-phone-stage-of-life*. Although perhaps slightly exaggerated and simplified, owning a mobile phone is important in the process of making new friends. The first thing to do is the exchanging of e-mail addresses, preferably mobile addresses as it makes an instant reply possible. Getting an immediate response implicates you are going to become friends. On the other hand, not receiving a response at once means you most likely are not going to be friends. The use of mobile e-mail gives the young girls the opportunity to have more control over who they include as their friends. Therefore, they can use it as a tool to form groups as well.

Also, it allows them to manage the distance or closeness of communication within these groups, which gives the girls a chance to keep in touch with many friends and to belong to many groups, while simultaneously not becoming a true part as the communication device allows them to have little intimacy. Put aptly by Leopoldina Fortunati in *Towards a Sociological Theory of the Mobile Phone*:

Cell phones can even better be used to shield oneself from wider surroundings by escaping into the narrower realm of highly familiar, predictable and self-controlled social relationships with close kin or friends. (Geser, 2004, p. 10)

Although the Japanese girls do make new friends through their mobile phones, their families and close friends are those they are most intimate with. The information derived from the interviewees confirm this by stating that they value friendship most with friends with whom they communicate face-to-face more often than friendships with friends from the mobile-phone-stage-of-life.

Another example that may indicate that kogals face a hard time making decisions can be illustrated by the mobile phone devices themselves and their ability to provide entertainment and information. Although the design of mobile phones is rather similar, the decoration of the phones is not. For example, each phone has different straps that can be a means of self-expression or individualism. On the other hand, the decoration often includes many pictures of friends as well, which shows the girls belonging to a group. The phones of the girls interviewed are a good example as well: They are made fancy with straps and key cords, most likely to express the girls' own vision on *kawaii*.

Then, what does *kawaii* mean? Moreover, why is it important within the description of the kogals consumption behavior? It is difficult to translate what this word exactly means. "Cute" is one translation; "adorable" might also be used. Japanese people use the word kawaii to describe the value of wishing to own the described object. In other words, where Japanese people use kawaii, Western people would probably use the word "cool."[1] In the interviews it became apparent that the girls choose their products on kawaiiness. A mobile phone is kawaii for communication and e-mail. However, it is less kawaii to use it for listening to music. Instead, an iPod is most kawaii for listening to music nowadays.

Choosing products on kawaiiness is most likely related to the role models of the girls. In general, they do not have a straight answer to who their role model might be; they describe powerful women who are beautiful, successful, and independent. Moreover, they have a strong focus on study and career for their futures and are eager to put effort into achieving this image of the powerful woman. This causes them to appear very strong and well balanced; even the conductors of the interviews are impressed by the seriousness and confidence of the girls. Nevertheless, from in-depth conversations with researchers from Hakuhodo Institute of Life and Learning (HILL) it becomes clear that this seriousness can be easily mistaken. It is rather loneliness that causes the girls to appear that way.

The description of the kogals' usage of mobile phones tells us about the combination of silent communication and the longing for entertainment and information through mobile phones—a combination causing the girls feeling pressured. Contemplating this and the framework of collectivism and individualism, it seems plausible that this pressure can be said to derive from the inability to choose a lifestyle. On the one hand, there is the longing to become part of a group which brings along obligations and personal sacrifices. On the other hand, they see new opportunities to let go of certain relationships, which involves both courage and anxiety since this choice is rather unfamiliar to these Japanese girls. A feeling of loneliness is the result of these pressures.

Consequently, the mobile phone becomes more than just a device; it becomes an indispensable friend. All the girls say that they "freak" if they do not have their phone near or if the network is not working properly. In other words, the mobile phone becomes an item to fill the lonely gap since it is capable of fulfilling both desires of the kogals: belonging to a group as well as being an individual. Moreover, consumption of other (digital) products based on kawaiiness can conceal their loneliness as it contributes to the image of being a powerful woman.

Production: NTT DoCoMo And Label Mobile

Today the penetration rate of the mobile phone among Japanese consumers has reached approximately 70%. The usage frequency of mobile phones in daily life has surpassed that of fixed-line phones. The biggest market share is held by NTT DoCoMo, who has approximately 56% of the market share. The key factor for success of NTT DoCoMo is its aggressive strategy to expand data communication usage, for example, text messaging and Web browsing via mobile phone, based on the popular i-mode service that launched in 1998, while competitors focused on voice communication services and pricing strategies. For the ordinary Japanese, the mobile phone has become the primary everyday life communication tool (both voice and data) alike, for example, the situation of a cell phone in the U.S.

Another important aspect of the Japanese mobile phone industry is the emergence of other mobile-phone-related markets such as the ring tone business. In 2004, the total market size of the Japanese ring tone business—including the latest digital music distribution business via mobile phone—had reached approximately $1 billion per year, while that of traditional music products such as CDs, is approximately $4 billion indicating that, in Japan, the mobile phone industry has become a "hub" for various other digitalized industries.

The influence of production on the use of (digital) products can be divided into three key elements: organization structure among the producers, motivation, and the actual production itself. Information deriving from several interviews with Japanese manufacturers illustrates these three aspects. Two of these interviews are most relevant for this research. The first is a meeting with a marketing manager from NTT DoCoMo. The second is a conversation with a marketing manager at Label Mobile, a company that offers music ring tones, called *chaku-uta's*. Both will be discussed in relation to the three aspects of the production side.

It has been said that manufacturers imitate kogals' behavior regarding digital products. NTT DoCoMo is an example of such a manufacturer—kogals can be said to be responsible for using mobile devices for written communication. Initially, the girls used pagers to exchange information with each other silently. NTT DoCoMo noticed the kogals' use of pagers and applied it in their development of i-mode; they developed the idea of developing an e-mailing service together with their subscriptions targeted at young people. One of the founders of i-mode says:

At first, a lot of people didn't understand our decision. But I knew (...) young people had strong communication needs. (...) Plus, they were attracted to new things; they liked innovation. I felt that if we could capture this group of people, everyone else would follow their lead. (Moon, 2002, p. 3)

The reason why NTT DoCoMo is able to pick up on this information from kogals, and create services like i-mode, is related to their organizational structure.[2] During the interview the manager at NTT DoCoMo made clear that they invest a lot of money in research that can help to develop and improve their products along with their services. Sometimes this research is put out to contract to survey companies, for instance when mapping the future market. Nevertheless, most research is done by NTT DoCoMo's significant research and development division.

Label Mobile is another company that learned from kogals as well. They copied the invention of adding music ring tones to mobile phones. Label Mobile was founded by record companies; these included almost all major record companies in Japan. Its mission is to make a structure for distribution for music content. In other words, the record companies use Label Mobile to sell their music to consumers, in which Label Mobile adjusts the systems and the Web sites properly to provide and distribute the content.

During the development of Label Mobile, the record companies have put shared effort into making it a success and they still have numerous meetings to maintain its popularity. Moreover, the relationship of Label Mobile with the handset makers and providers of mobile phones is beneficial, since the latter have influence in the development of chaku-uta's. In other words, the organizational structure of this company is trustworthy and stable as well as unique, motivated by its employees that besides making money, have a love for music, which they want to share with their clients. As a result, the actual production of chaku-uta's is fast, adequately targeted at consumers, and has been profitable for a few years now.

The examples of NTT DoCoMo and Label Mobile can then be linked to the otaku and kogal cultures. This is best explained by the example of NTT DoCoMo. Here, the motivation to produce (digital) devices and services is highly related to a belief in the technological dream. To illustrate this, a recent press release article from NTT DoCoMo states: "Every employee of the NTT DoCoMo Group will create MAGIC by following our DREAM" (1999, http://www.nttdocomo.co.jp/). This is result of the influence of the otaku employees working at large companies such as NTT DoCoMo. Otakus are motivated to create technological innovations as they believe these innovations will benefit and enrich their lives. Nevertheless, (digital) technology can not survive without the social and cultural aspects of consumption surrounding it, shown by the influence of kogals' consumption behavior. The examples of NTT DoCoMo and Label Mobile explain how innovative behavior of kogals impact on the development of new products, which—indirectly—relates to the kogals' emotional consumption behavior; kogals invent new usages of digital products by using these products extensively which, in turn, helps them to experiment with different lifestyles.

Conclusion

This chapter has investigated Japanese consumption behavior of (digital) technological products by providing an overview of consumer groups: otaku and kogal, followed by the production side of technology in relation to these consumer groups. In so doing, it hoped to provide accurate information on the Japanese consumption and production of (digital) technologies in order to widen the Western perspective on Japanese digitalization. This study also meant to trigger questions about which aspects of what characteristics attract the West. How do consumer groups in the West correspond to Japanese consumers? How are economical issues related to "emotional" consumption behavior on a global scale? Where is the attraction of Japanese technology and popular culture heading for? Will Japan become of growing importance in these matters or is the interest of the West in Japan just a fad? What gives the West the idea that Japan is "awesome"? Having raised more questions than answers, further investigation is needed to build a theoretical and empirical framework on the relations between West and East and digitization issues.

Acknowledgment

We appreciate the great contributions and stimulating collaborations through personal interviews, focus group interviews, and discussions with Kasai, M. (on 6 April 2005 at NTT DoCoMo), Mizuno, S. (on 11 March 2005 at Hakuhodo Inc.), Oval Communications (on 12-13 April 2005), Takeuchi, K. (on 26 April 2005, Hakuhodo Inc.), Tamura, H. (on 11 April 2005, at Hakuhodo.Inc.), Uchihama, D. (on 26 April 2005, at Hakuhodo Inc.), Yanagi, M. (on 1 March 2005, at Hakuhodo Inc.), Yokoi, M., (on 10 March 2005, at Label Mobile Inc.), and Yoshikawa, M. (on 5 April 2005, at Hakuhodo Inc.). We also appreciate the great suggestion by the personal interview with Condry, I. (on 24 March 2005 at Hakuhodo Inc.).

References

Barclay, D. (2004). The technology of Japan. *Massachusetts Institute of Technology Undergraduate Research Journal - MURJ, 11,* 13-18.

Eckstein, A. J. (1999). *Japan's national identity: Nationalists or not?* Retrieved January 4, 2006, from http://www.lehigh.edu/~rfw1/courses/1999/spring/ir163/Papers/pdf/aje3.pdf

Geser, H. (2004). Towards a sociological theory of the mobile phone. Retrieved December 21, 3005, from http://socio.ch/mobile/t_geser1.pdf

Kasulis, T. (1995). Sushi, science, and spirituality: Modern Japanese philosophy and its views of Western science. *Philosophy East & West, 45*(2), 227-248.

Levy, S. (1984). *HACKERS: Heroes of the computer revolution.* Garden City, NY: Doubleday Books.

Moon, Y. (2002). NTT DoCoMo. *Marketing i-mode.* Boston: Harvard Business School.

Nakayama, S. (Ed.). (2001). *A social history of science and technology in contemporary Japan: Volume 1: The occupation period 1945-1952.* Melbourne, Australia: Trans Pacific Press.

Newitz, A. (1997). Anime otaku: Japanese animation fans outside Japan. In J. Lyon (Ed.), *Bad subjects: Political education for everyday life.* New York University Press.

Niles, S. (1998). Individualism-collectivism revisited. *Cross-Cultural Research, 32,* 315-335.

NTT DoCoMo (1999). *2010 NTT DoCoMo Future Vision.* Tokyo, Japan: NTT Publishing. Retrieved from http://www.nttdocomo.co.jp/

Strunk, D. R., & Chang, C. (1999). *Personality and individual differences, 27*(4), 665-671.

Triandis, H. (1995). *Individualism and collectivism: New direction in social psychology.* Bolder, CO: Westview Press.

Washida, Y. (2005). Collaborative structure between Japanese high-tech manufacturers and Consumers. *Journal of Consumer Marketing, 22*(1), 25-34.

Further Reading

Bolter, J. D., & Grusin, R. (2000). *Remediation: Understanding new media,* Cambridge, MA: MIT Press.

Dohi, T. (2004, June). A cut above. *The Japan Journal, 6,* 26-29.

Fisher, C. (1992). *America calling: A social history of the telephone in 1940.* Berkeley: University of California Press.

Hakuhodo Institute of Life and Living. (2004). *HILL bi-annual report 2004.* Hakuhodo Inc. Tokyo, Japan.

Hirsch, E. (1998). New technologies and domestic consumption. In C. Geraghty & D. Lusted (Eds.), *The television studies book.* London: Arnold.

Mul, J. de (Ed.). (2002). *Filosofie in cyberspace: Reflecties op de informatie-en.* Amsterdam.

Communictatietechnologie. Kampen, Rotterdam: The Netherlands.

Sudoh, O. (2004, August). Community stores in cyberspace. *The Japan Journal, 8,* 22-23.

Endnotes

[1]   Some scholars and students at Harvard University named these phenomena *cutism* and explored how influential it has been to current Japanese society at the *Cutism Conference in 2004* (Harvard Project for Asian and International Relations, and the Reischauer Institute of Japanese Studies at Harvard University, Cutism, Harvard Hall 201 in Harvard Yard, 2004). They discussed that kogal generation is significantly important not only when we think about Japanese youth culture such as girl's comics and female celebrities, but also Japanese marketing trends and transnational

culture diffusion among East Asian countries. The exact definition of cutism was not given at the conference. However, they shared the certain significance of the kogal phenomena, using this keyword, to identify current characteristics of Japanese society.

2   The organization structure is intertwined with the business goals of the company. The Web site of NTT DoCoMo explains it is NTT DoCoMo's intention to stimulate "further growth of the mobile communications market via mobile multimedia, and thus improving the quality of life and revitalizing industry." The opportunity for NTT DoCoMo to achieve this goal is provided by investments in research and development. These major investments are also used to show recent achievements of NTT DoCoMo regarding technological innovations. For instance, the Web site of NTT DoCoMo contains a short movie of a future vision, titled *Vision 2010*. In this movie the company presents their "insight into a world enriched by wireless communications services in the near future." Nowadays NTT DoCoMo presents their actual production as a step forward towards that future. Nevertheless, the recently released services which are related to videophones and e-commerce rather appear to be entertainment or convenient, instead of resembling the future as portrayed in *Vision 2010*. For example, according to NTT DoCoMo the main advantage of video phones is that people can see each other anytime and anywhere, regardless of the distance between them. In contrast, at this time the actual service of video phoning offers the ability to create an avatar in case you do not want to be seen.

Chapter III

The Right of Interpretation:
Who Decides the Success of Picture Mail?

Michael Björn, Ericsson Consumer & Enterprise Lab, Sweden

Abstract

This chapter is an empirical research report describing the diffusion of mobile camera phones and picture mail services in Japan between the years 1997 and 2005, based on annual consumer surveys conducted by Ericsson Consumer & Enterprise Lab. A general framework based on sociocultural values and attitudes to telecom for describing the telecom market from a consumer perspective is presented. This framework is then used to put different consumer life stage segments in relation to each other in respect to product diffusion. The change over time of attitudes and behavior is described, and the conclusion is drawn that the product terminology spontaneously created by consumers themselves in order to relate to the product is an important step for mass market diffusion. Furthermore, the group of people who develop this terminology becomes a crucial catalyst for diffusion—and in the Japanese case presented here consists of female students.

The iPOD's Like a Can of Coca-Cola...

Apple Computer has been very successful in the increasingly crowded MP3-player market. There are technical differences, the iPod can play AAC (also known as MPEG-2 Part 7; it was designed as an improved-performance codec relative to MP3) format songs and is tightly integrated with the iTunes store, but our studies at Ericsson's Consumer & Enterprise Lab (here referred to as ConsumerLab) indicate that very few people are even aware of technical differences, and that purchasing songs over iTunes is a minority activity. Instead softer issues come into play, such as design, image, and values connected to the product.

"At this point, the iPod's like a can of Coca-Cola—it's a given" says Beastie Boy Diamond in a *Wired* magazine interview (Steuer, 2004, p.187) and he is not alone in having made such statements. Instrumental in catapulting the iPod into the ranks of the ultimate of "cool" seems to be the fact that musicians and other users themselves were early in taking a liking to the product; and, most importantly, were quite vocal in advocating its superiority. The fact that Apple had no control over this spontaneous endorsement campaign made a big difference. There is even an example of a full-featured but totally unendorsed ad film that in a matter of days had been watched 37,000 times (Kahney, 2004).

One might venture to say that although Apple undoubtedly designed and marketed the iPod, it was actually the consumers themselves who decided what was important with it. This is exactly what "right of interpretation" in this chapter's heading is referring to.

In the current media landscape, it may well be that the meaning or significance of the product as perceived by the consumer is increasingly likely to have been imparted on it by other consumers. In other words, Apple still owns the iPod product—but the market (i.e., the sum total of potential buyers of the product) has decided what its benefits are.

To explore this point, this chapter presents a case study from Japan, based on research carried out by ConsumerLab in the years 1997-2005. The focus will be on mobile phones equipped with cameras and the picture mail service (sending pictures via mobile phones), and on how the meaning of this service was indeed decided by the market itself.

Methodology and the MarketReality™ Monitor

The basis of the research at ConsumerLab is annual quantitative studies (1000-2000 respondents per study, adding up to around 12,000 respondents globally per survey round) in a culturally heterogeneous sample of countries: Brazil, USA, France, Germany, Italy, UK, Sweden, Malaysia, China, and Japan. All studies are based on national representative samples in the age groups 15-69 years, except in China and Brazil, where we make urban samples because of large economic and social differences.

For Japan, specifically, the research is carried out as a mail-out questionnaire administered in late spring of each year by a well-known research institute with long-term operations in Japan.

The studies contain approximately 400 questions that are asked in the same way and same order across all countries. This questionnaire has been built up gradually since 1995 and tries to encompass a broad scope of technology-mediated information and communication, including radio, TV, computers, the Internet, and (fixed and mobile) phones (with more space given in the questionnaire to telephony). Approximately half of the questions are phrased as attitudes to telecom, from the general to the specific. The attitudes are measured using questions with seven-point Lichert scales (very important—not important; I agree completely—I do not agree at all; etc.)

The MarketReality™ Monitor

ConsumerLab has developed a conceptual MarketReality™ Monitor (hereafter referred to simply as the Monitor) based on consumers' sociocultural values and

Figure 1. The monitor (Copyright Ericsson Consumer & Enterprise Lab. Used with permission)

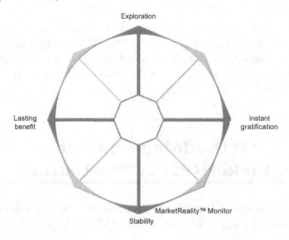

attitudes to telecom. The Monitor is built in three steps: Identification of two-dimensional regional value maps, identification of a global two-dimensional telecom attitude map, and finally, a merging of the value and attitude dimensions based on standardized axes values with a 50/50 impact. Respondents are distributed in the model based on individual factor scores. This way we have been able to create a space where each individual is plotted and where it is also possible to plot different segments, behaviours, attitudes, and so forth—while still always describing the telecom market from a consumer perspective.

The Monitor consists of two dimensions: "Exploration ↔ Stability" and "Lasting Benefits ↔ Instant Gratification," shown in Figure 1.

Dimensions in the MarketReality™ Monitor

The first dimension, "Exploration ↔ Stability," is the most important as it differentiates best between consumers on overall interest in telecom technology as well as on telecom product and service penetration. It also gives an indication as to the pace at which people need and require changes in their lives.

The higher a respondent is towards the *exploration* side, the higher her interest is in telecom technology and the more she is likely to have a large number of telecom products and services. On the *stability* side, we instead find a conservative attitude to telecom technology, and a low willingness to try telecom products or services that have not yet been tried and tested by others, and that have not received a social "seal of approval."

Whereas the first dimension is usually present in some form in many models with a sociocultural heritage, we believe that the second dimension, "Lasting Benefits « Instant gratification" is unique to our own research. This dimension has to do with the relationship between oneself and others, but also with the reasons for using technology.

By lasting benefits we mean a tendency to take a more long-term view of the need for and use of telecom technology. This indicates a more rational approach to the choice of telecom products and services, although it may well be that these explanations are made up "after the fact" and do not constitute truly rational behaviour.

By instant gratification, on the other hand, we mean a tendency to be more oriented towards satisfying one's feelings and needs of the moment when considering telecom technologies. This indicates a shorter attention span when evaluating new telecom products and services, and less patience when expecting benefits from them.

A more in-depth description of the Monitor is given in the book *Situation Analysis* (Sekizawa, Washida, & Bjorn, 2002).

Diffusion of Picture Mail in Japan 1997-2005: Who Decides the Success of Picture Mail?

Triggers for Diffusion of Services

If we apply our accumulated knowledge of triggers at ConsumerLab (i.e., something that makes people go from just showing an interest in a product or service to *act* on that interest) to diffusion (Rogers, 1995) of mobile services, we see a pattern of differences in the Monitor.

At the explorative top of the Monitor, we find the earliest adopters (often referred to as *innovators* in marketing literature), who are triggered to use new mobile services because they are new and exciting.

In the first stage of diffusion, the explorative people towards the lasting benefits side are triggered by efficiency and the time saving they would get by using the new mobile services, whereas the explorative people at the instant gratification side are more triggered by the fun, speed, and spontaneity they get by using new mobile services. We might call this first diffusion stage early diffusion.

The second stage of diffusion is where the differences between those products (or services) that remain consigned to a niche market and those that go on to reach a broader market tend to appear—Moore (1991) coined the term *chasm* for this stage and it is used here in this sense. In our experience, the set of triggers in the chasm depend on which segment (i.e., which location in the Monitor) it is that adopts the service.

The segments towards the lasting benefits side are triggered by the convenience of the service. This convenience trigger is rationally oriented in the sense that it gets a task done in a dependable way, that is, the service fulfills an already existing need in a better way.

On the instant gratification side, triggers relate to the social enrichment offered by the new mobile service, that is, the need fulfillment is put in a social context rather than in a task-oriented context. Since the social context can change without active participation from the specific individual, chances are greater here that the need also arises implicitly in conjunction with the diffusion of the service.

Less explorative segments towards the instant gratification side are looking more for visual or (sub)cultural statements as an important ingredient to the identity they are building in relation to their surroundings—the needs in this segment are more related to confirmation and status.

Provided that the new service does not flounder in the chasm stage, diffusion continues and reaches the mass-market diffusion stage. Here, the more stability-

Figure 2. Diffusion pattern in the monitor (Copyright Ericsson Consumer & Enterprise Lab. Used with permission)

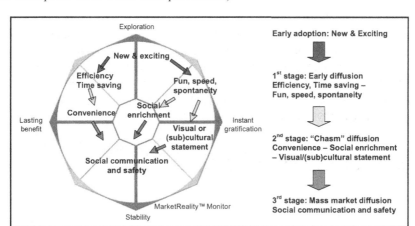

oriented people in the Monitor that are often the late adopters are mainly triggered by social communication and safety. It is however hard to trigger this group and many will only follow when the rest of the market is mature and everybody else is using the particular new service, which means that they have to use it in order not to be left out. Thus, we get the flow or diffusion pattern indicated in Figure 2.

We do not see this diffusion pattern in itself as anything controversial, and it could most likely be supported by evidence from adherents of linear schools of diffusion as well as by adherents of convergence diffusion models (although the naming of the various stages would certainly vary). Instead, the controversy lies in what process is needed to take place for any given product or service to move through the different stages. In order to explore this process, we will look at ConsumerLab survey data from Japan from the years 1997-2005 and follow the actual diffusion process of picture mail on the Japanese market. Interestingly, as you will see, the story is less of a diffusion story and rather more a story of how end users build a mass market!

At ConsumerLab we did our first quantitative survey in Japan in 1997 and the survey has continued on an annual basis since 1999, comprising in total over 10,000 respondents. For the sake of brevity, we only present data from the odd years (i.e., 1997, 1999, 2001, 2003, and 2005) here, but inclusion of the even years (i.e., 2000, 2002, and 2004) does not change the results in any way.

In order to look at the data, let us first establish what life stages (McDonald & Dunbar, 2004) are relevant for the different stages of diffusion, by plotting them in the Monitor.

Life Stages (Gravity Centres¹)

Figure 3 shows a plot in the Monitor of life stages in Japan 2001, the middle year in our series (the positions of the life stages vary very little over time). The major difference in comparison to life stages in our global (i.e., 10 countries) sample is that the group *men married no kids* is in the upper left side of the model (whereas it is in the upper right side of the model in the global sample).

Now let us look at the data year by year. Roll back your clock; imagine that you are back in year 1997 and visiting Japan.

Graphic Communication: Japan, 1997

Back in 1997, mobile phones were used for talking. Yes, it does seem like the Stone Age, but in fact it was not such a long time ago. New things were already happening that would change the way we view mobile phones for ever; SMS or text messaging was already popular and the idea that the phone would become a multimedia communications device no longer seemed like science fiction. Specifically at Ericsson, we believed that inclusion of other media types in the

Figure 3. Life stage in the Monitor (Copyright Ericsson Consumer & Enterprise Lab. Used with permission)

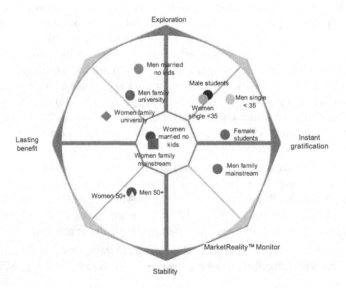

communication process would provide powerful means to enrich phone conversations. Although there were no camera phones in the market, 1997 was the year when we started doing market surveys to understand the interest for camera phones (and Ericsson later became a driving force in the global standardization of picture messaging, MMS).

Figure 4 describes the starting point for diffusion of graphic communication services in the mobile phone in Japan. All the data for the years 1997, 1999, 2001, 2003, and 2005 will be presented in this manner. Indexes presented in the graphics are calculated so that the average for all twelve life stage groups is 100 (where, for example an index of 160 means 60% above the average). The picture shows the upper half of the Monitor and is focusing on two extreme life stage segments; the *men family university* group (i.e., men who have a university degree and also have a family) and the *female students* group. The left half of the graphic contains information pertaining to the *men family university* group and, correspondingly, the right half of the graphic contains information pertaining to the *female students* group (unless otherwise stated). We have selected these two life stage segments for a number of reasons:

- They are present in the early stages of the diffusion flow and are thus key segments for initial product uptake.
- They are the most consistently different segments and turn out to play unique roles in the diffusion process.

Figure 4. Starting point (1997) for diffusion of graphic communication services in Japanese mobile phone (Copyright Ericsson Consumer & Enterprise Lab. Used with permission)

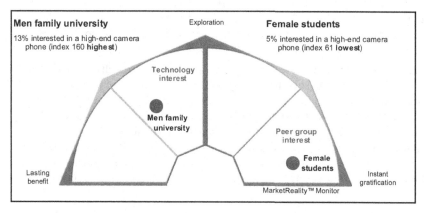

- They correspond reasonably well to the popular Japanese ideas of otaku[2] (for *men family university*) and kogal[3] (for female students); whereas the *men family university* group are driven by an interest for technology (at least for the type of product/service category we are investigating), the *female students* group are driven more by an interest in what their friends are doing (their peer group).
- They are of sufficient size for statistical analysis.
- They are stable in comparison to the same groups in other countries (as is opposed to the *men married no kids* group that moves to the upper right side of the Monitor in other countries).

In 1997 the *men family university* group showed the strongest interest of all 12 life stages for a high-end camera phone (at a price level of around 375 euro) with picture mail capacity (i.e., the possibility to include photos or pictures in a message). On the other hand, the *female students* group had the lowest interest of all 12 groups.

Our interpretation of this is that the *men family university* group saw a range of possibilities with this type of a product and were also excited by the new digital photo technology as such. The *female students* group on the other hand saw no relation between this product and their daily needs.

Graphic Communication: Japan, 1999

In 1999 we can see that it is not the camera phone that has been introduced on the market, but instead the digital camera. The *men family university* group have clearly followed up on their early interest in digital photo technology and are the early adopters as well as usage leaders of this product. However, they still see quality as an issue and are probably already upgrading to second-generation digital cameras. Having already been "burnt" by e-mail in the phone turning into nothing more than paging (or simple text messaging), they do not see the need anymore for having the digital camera integrated into the phone.

The female students, however, have a totally different approach to digital photos. Thanks to the interest shown by early adopters (i.e., the *men family university* group—possibly their fathers) already back in 1997, they have gotten used to the idea of digital photos, and they already find the quality good enough. They are in fact already using digital photos in the form of Print-Club pictures. Print-Club is a photo machine reminiscent of passport and identity card photo machines found in train stations and so forth in many countries—with the big difference that the photographs are in colour, can be decorated with frames, and are printed as

Figure 5. Diffusion in 1999 (Copyright Ericsson Consumer & Enterprise Lab. Used with permission)

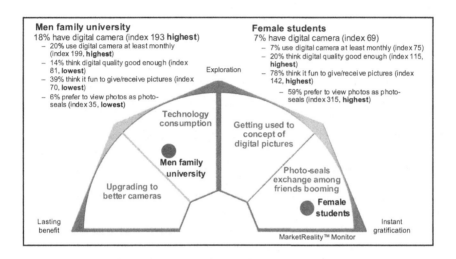

stickers. At this point in time, Print-Club pictures were shared among friends and many youngsters carried around albums with pictures of all their friends to show other friends when meeting them.

As you can see in Figure 5, the female students were the group most interested in viewing Print-Club pictures (*photo-seals*). Although female students are also most satisfied with digital picture quality, it is important to point out that Print-Club pictures paradoxically at this point in time were of downright awful quality (when understood as pixel density and colour range); instead their quality judgment was probably influenced by the usefulness of the pictures, namely in sharing with friends, where they also score higher than any of the other life stage segments. The indication is that for them, it would be almost as natural to move the Print-Club into the mobile phone, as it was to move the pager into the phone. This was also the gist of the message that ConsumerLab was giving our Japanese customers in this time frame.

The bottom line, however, is that digital photography in the form of a personal device, was not yet spreading from the early adopters, as the digital camera was not a device that the female students—or other groups with average or lower interest in technology—could fully relate to.

Graphic Communication: Japan, 2001

In 2001 we can see the gap widening between the two groups, indicated in Figure 6: The *men family university* group are more and more concentrating on the digital camera, and this product is becoming relatively harder to find a need for among the female students. The digital camera starts diffusing into the mass market, but as a direct replacement to the analogue camera with film (as we can see from analysis of other questions in the survey not presented here). The female students play no active role in this diffusion.

On the other hand, female students score highest on all counts relating to digital photography in the mobile phone. Their interest for Print-Club pictures is starting to migrate to an easier-to-use and more convenient platform, although the actual application is not changing and neither is their peer group interest: taking pictures of themselves together with friends in various situations and showing them to other friends in other situations. The platform they are moving to is Sha-Mail, a picture mail application that was introduced in the year 2000 by the Japanese mobile phone operator J-Phone (now Vodafone Japan K.K.). The other Japanese operators would eventually follow suit and introduce similar picture mail platforms, but since this is not a description of the development of the competitive market situation in Japan, we will simply refer to Sha-Mail and the other competing applications as picture mail in this presentation. (However, it might be interesting to point out that the Print-Club machine vendors also responded to the

Figure 6. Diffusion in 2001 (Copyright Ericsson Consumer & Enterprise Lab. Used with permission)

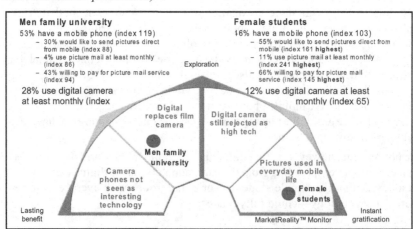

new threat by starting to put their machines online—however, ultimately without great success.)

Graphic Communication: Japan, 2003

In 2003, shown in Figure 7, the definition of picture mail as a form of social communication has become firmly established on the market by the female students, and although they remain the most avid proponents for this type of usage, the service is now in the mass market (i.e., roughly 50% of mobile phone owners have camera phone and/or picture mail). However, usage rates are extremely much higher in the *female students* group than in other segments, with almost half of the group sending picture mail at least once a week.

The *men family university* group is reacting negatively to the apparent success of picture mail among youngsters in the market, and turns in the lowest score of the 10 life stage segments below age 50 measured on the interest in sending pictures directly with their mobile phones. One might say that their reaction is one of outright rejection of picture mail as an interesting technology.

Graphic Communication: Japan, 2005

In 2005, shown in Figure 8, the hype around picture mail is gone, but usage in the *female students* group remains reasonably high—the levels we see this year

Figure 7. Diffusion in 2003 (Copyright Ericsson Consumer & Enterprise Lab. Used with permission)

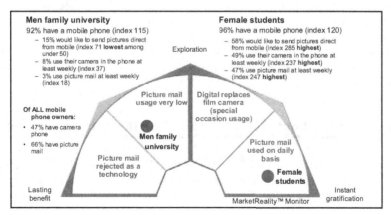

Figure 8. Diffusion in 2005 (Copyright Ericsson Consumer & Enterprise Lab. Used with permission)

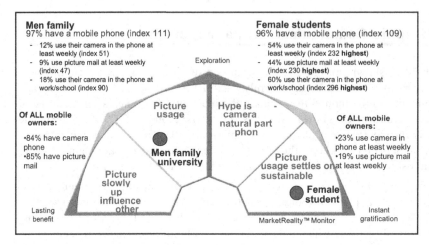

probably reflect lifestyle usage on a practical level and may be the type of usage we can expect in the long run from this group now that the camera has become a naturally integrated part of the mobile phone.

Totally on the market a critical mass of users (i.e., roughly 30% of mobile phone owners use camera phone and/or picture mail at least weekly) has evolved, leading us to believe that picture mail will remain a mass market service in the 2006-2010 time frame.

Interestingly, the *men family university* group is still lagging far behind the general market uptake, both when it comes to using the camera in the phone and for sending picture mail. While they have rejected camera phones on the basis that stand-alone digital cameras represent better technology, they are still influenced by usage uptake in society surrounding them—their gradually increasing usage likely represents a need to communicate in a manner suitable to the receiver of the message rather than a need to express themselves in a richer way.

Who Decides That Picture Mail Will Become Successful?

What we have seen here is a total reversal of initial interest and actual behaviour. Although the *men family university* group showed the strongest initial interest in a mobile phone with built-in camera—and would have been the obvious recommended target group by market researchers (with a high-end phone model)—they end up nearly at the bottom of the ladder with very low usage rates even eight years later. Conversely, the *female students* group go from showing the lowest interest to being the group that drives usage and thus general adoption.

While this may seem paradoxical, the answer lies in the triggers for behaviour that we discussed earlier. The difference in triggers between these two life stage groups in the Japanese context—and the inherent opposition between them—has been observed by others, such as Fujimoto (2005), who would most likely define the diffusion pattern described here as a third-stage (socializing) paradigm of adoption. And although we had labelled the different triggers with words, it turns out that the process behind that label is the crucial part.

Early adopters in the top of the Monitor in Figure 9 are triggered to use new mobile services because they are new and exciting. They see the possibilities with the specific technology behind the service (product) and try it out. However, this group is often too technical or "nerdy" to communicate their vision or the benefits they see with the product to others. Others may call upon them as experts when problems arise, but this happens at a later stage when they already have started using the service for other reasons.

In the first stage of diffusion, the explorative people towards the instant gratification side are more triggered by the fun, speed, and spontaneity they get by using new mobile services. This group of people can be seen as lifestyle

Figure 9. Diffusion process (Copyright Ericsson Consumer & Enterprise Lab. Used with permission)

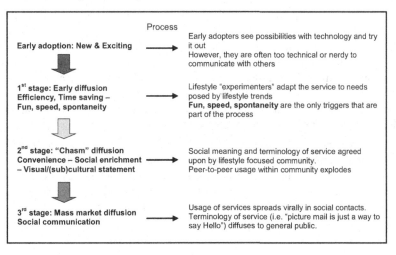

experimenters, in the sense that they are on the cutting edge of lifestyle-related trends such as fashion, food, music, and social behaviour. While not being interested in technology per se, this group takes high tech for granted and is thus willing to try out the service in order to see if it can be adapted to the lifestyles they are currently exploring.

In the second stage, the chasm diffusion stage, a process of redefinition of the need for and the social meaning of the specific service takes place. The social meaning of the service and terminology used to describe it is agreed upon inside of the lifestyle-focused community. By *social meaning* we here refer to the meaning of the service as it is actually interpreted by the users, it is social in the sense that the meaning is derived through interaction and exchange of opinions with others, and essentially a *conjuncture* as described by Hebdige (1979).

In other words, it does not have to be the same meaning as the provider of the service intends the service to have—but it still needs to have a meaning, lest it will slip off the radar and be forgotten. The importance of meaning for retention is well documented by cognitive psychologists (Anderson, 1990).

Similarly, the terminology used to describe the service may be different in the user group from that used by the service provider. For branded services both users and service providers will probably use the brand name, albeit with different connotations. In this case, Sha-Mail would be used by end users to denote something pragmatic and useful like a "graphic hello"[4] whereas, the service provider probably had a somewhat more technical association for the name.

Furthermore, usage within the community explodes. It seems that the explosion of usage is necessary in order to turn the service into a focus for behaviour in the peer-group community. There is a strong sense of a "we" in the peer group which stands in (implicit) opposition to a "them." So the service becomes almost like a secret link between the members of the group, where a cultural behaviour basically unknown to the rest of society is developed. The Japanese term for this type of sudden and drastic increase in usage would be *my boom*[5]—and explosions are indeed the cause of booms. This leads to the service becoming perceived both as some form of social enrichment and as a direct visual or otherwise (sub)cultural statement. The difference in perception depends on which market segment the observer belongs to.

Provided that the social meaning of the service and the terminology used to describe it as defined in the *chasm* diffusion stage is relevant and makes sense to a broader part of the market, diffusion continues and reaches the mass-market diffusion stage. In the case of picture mail, the terminology comes from ordinary greetings: "picture mail is just a better way to say Hello," the need of which is relevant to and easily understood by most people.

Figure 10. Diffusion process in the Monitor (Copyright Ericsson Consumer & Enterprise Lab. Used with permission)

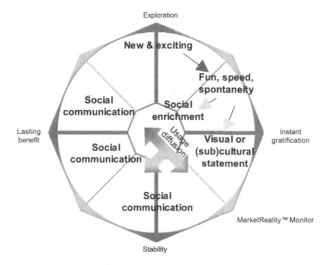

The later adopters of the service are mainly triggered by social communication. As diffusion progresses, it becomes increasingly harder to trigger users and they will only follow when the rest of the market is mature and everybody else is using the new service, which means that they have to use it in order not to be left out.

Putting back the triggers into the Monitor, we actually get a much simpler picture, shown in Figure 10, than what we started out with. The complexity lies not in the triggers but in the processes that actually make these triggers go off.

Implications for Other Markets and/or Other Services

A relatively common point of view is that Japan is a very different country (in various senses, depending on whom you ask)—and that, consequently, results from the Japanese market are not applicable to any other market. When combining the different perspectives of politics, technology, value chains, marketing, and so forth, this may or may not be true. However, from a strictly individual-oriented perspective, our experience is rather the opposite. There are large differences between many countries in the world, but Japanese people are not more "different" than people in many other countries. This view is also corroborated for example in the Inglehart Values Map,[6] which puts Japan very close to Protestant Europe, especially on the Secular-Rational dimension, but also on the Self-Expression dimension. At ConsumerLab, we have also done measurements on the cultural effect of globalization on consumers, and the indication is that Japanese people to a quite high degree are affected by globalization (more so than Americans, for example).

The important insight is that the results presented here just may be the norm rather than the exception. In order to open the table for discussion, we will look at diffusion data for two other services, SMS (or text messaging) over the mobile phone and music download over the Internet. The first example points to a mechanism very similar to the picture mail case, but on a global scale; the second example is inconclusive.

Diffusion of SMS Over the Mobile Phone

It is safe to say that SMS (or text messaging) was the first successful nonvoice application for the mobile phone. However, since the industry probably was not aware of the large impact that SMS ultimately would have, it is difficult to find good data from the early years of SMS usage. While not going back that far, we will here in Figure 11 look at SMS data for basically the same time period as we did for picture mail. In this case, then, the focus is consumers who send and/or receive SMS in the mobile phone at least once a week, but now covering all countries in the ConsumerLab survey sample.

First, however, some methodological points must be made: The countries in this sample are at various points of sociotechnological maturity and any interpretation of the results must bear this in mind. An age-gender division has been used instead of life stages for the reason of presentation brevity (8 groups instead of 12) and because of larger variation between countries in sizes of life stage groups. The usage levels have been indexed on a age-gender group per country and year basis, so that the usage level in a specific age-gender group in a certain country and year has been divided by the average usage level for that country in the same year—in effect giving us the relative importance of a specific age-gender group for SMS in that specific country and year. After that, all individual age-gender groups have been added for all countries in a specific year and finally normalized so that all countries have equal weight—in effect giving us the relative global importance of any age-gender group for SMS in that specific year. Furthermore, the years 1996-1997, 1998-1999, and 2000-2001 have been combined, since ConsumerLab's survey program was not fully annualized for all countries until the year 2002.

Figure 11. Diffusion of SMS usage (Copyright Ericsson Consumer & Enterprise Lab. Used with permission)

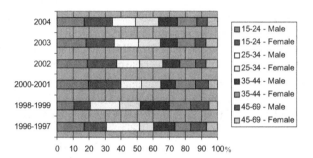

As shown in Figure 11, although the relative importance of the youth market is clearly seen, the result of the analysis also shows three distinct phases: The first phase is represented by 1996-1997, where there is a clear male dominance—with relatively higher incomes and a tech orientation similar to the *male family university group* mentioned elsewhere in this chapter. Usage levels of SMS are typically in the 15% range on a weekly basis. The second phase is represented by 1998-1999, where there is high growth but still some exclusivity in the user base. SMS usage levels are now typically in the 30% range on a weekly basis. In this phase we seem to be in the chasm and the overall equalling out of the age-gender groups; here it may be indicative of a reevaluation of the social meaning of SMS. Initially many possible meanings are present, including meanings related to efficiency and time saving, but by the beginning of the third phase one meaning has taken hold over the other—and that is the real-time oriented conversational (or chat-like) meaning that is also dominant today. It is interesting to see that the 15-24 female age group is the largest group for the first time in 2000-2001, indicating a new phase, and that it remains as large as the 15-24 male age group for the rest of the data series. The third phase is then the mass-market diffusion scenario with weekly usage levels of up to 90% in the most recent data. For this reason the relative market importance of the 15-24 female (and male) age groups diminish over time as the behaviour and use pattern initiated by this group spreads to other segments in the market.

Diffusion of Music Download Over the Internet

Our second multi-country diffusion pattern example deals with downloading of music from the Internet (legally or illegally). The data set presented in Figure 12 is taken from our syndicated survey partner NOP World, as ConsumerLab's own historical data are not as consistent in asking about specific services on the Internet, and for this reason the time period is slightly different. However the countries are the same as in ConsumerLab's own scope —except for the fact that Sweden has been omitted—and sample sizes are similar with around 1,000 respondents per country and year. Apart from this, the calculation methodology used is exactly the same as for the SMS over the previous mobile phone example.

In the data set in Figure 12, the male dominance throughout the whole series is the most striking feature—especially the 15-24 male age group. Moreover, there is no indication whatsoever that more than one diffusion phase is present in the series, even though there is a big downward movement in relative market importance for the 15-24 male age group from 1999-2000. Considering that music download music levels in 1999 were typically only in the 10% range of the population surveyed, the explanation rather seems to be a movement from the very earliest adopters to a larger but still early adopter-oriented type of user base. In the year 2000 typical usage levels are approaching the 20% range although there are still big variations between countries. From that point usage levels gradually move up to the 30% range without any major movements in the market composition. This example has been added to show that cases that do not fit the Japanese picture mail pattern are readily available, although this is not the place to go further in analysing music download over the Internet. However, it should be pointed out that this example may well show influence of anti-downloading activities from the music industry—portraying music downloaders as "leeches" (Ebare 2004) and possibly forcing a peer-group-generated social meaning of music downloading back into the underground again.

Support for this idea also comes from the comparison of downloading of music from the Internet to downloading of music over the mobile phone using only 2004 data from the same data set indicated in Figure 13.

Figure 12. Diffusion of music download over the Internet (Copyright Ericsson Consumer & Enterprise Lab. Used with permission)

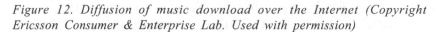
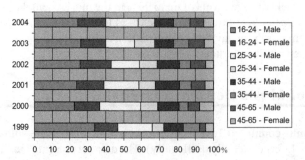

Figure 13. Music downloading in 2004: Comparing via mobile phone and over the Internet (Copyright Ericsson Consumer & Enterprise Lab. Used with permission)

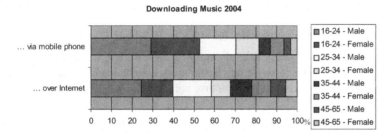

Although it is in the early days of downloading music over mobile phones, with typical usage levels in the 5% range and extreme youth orientation, it is interesting to see that the male domination is much weaker on the mobile phone than on the Internet. Because of earlier involvement from the music industry on mobile phone downloads, there is very little illegal downloading happening in this market, and it seems obvious that the music download market for mobile phones is poised to take a different route from music downloading on the Internet.

Another obvious interpretation is that the diffusion mechanism for services over the mobile phone follows one pattern and that services on the Internet follow one or several different patterns. In other words, the Japanese picture mail example may be highly relevant for other mobile-phone-based services (in other countries) such as SMS and music download—but provide less insight on diffusion patterns on the Internet.

Summary and Discussion

The point of this chapter is by now hopefully very clear to the reader: The Japanese female students were not the earliest adopters of the picture mail service, but they were the crucial group to capture in order to make the service successful on the mass market. This is true to the point where it actually becomes irrelevant who the early adopters were. For the picture mail service—or, we believe, for any service based on new technology—it is relatively easy to find a small group of explorative people who are willing to try the service out, but it is more difficult to find a group who can translate the ramifications of the inherently new technology that the service implies into something meaningful for the mass market.

As shown in Figure 14, the life stage group *men family university* is the group originally interested in picture mail—but since the cameras in the mobile phones as well as the technical limitations in the messaging service do not live up to their expectations, they totally lose interest.

Female students start using digital images because they are delivered faster (e.g., in Print-Club machines) and fit better in a spontaneous lifestyle. Gradually they then focus this behaviour on picture mail in the mobile phone, creating a mass market in the process.

The answer to the question posed in the title of this chapter then becomes: The female students are the decision makers. It was they who decided that picture mail was bound for success; not the product managers, not the marketing people, and not even the early adopters. Obviously, they did not make a joint conscious decision at any point in time—instead many relatively unimportant individual decisions proved to have synergetic effect.

Compared to the *men family university* group (i.e., the early adopters in this case) they have lower social status, less individual power, and certainly lower income. But at least in the case of the picture mail service, it seems that their peer group networking nevertheless is a powerful vehicle for influence over other groups in society.

Moreover, the influence of the female students on other groups in society is at least twofold, since their adoption of picture mail has the effect of deciding the social meaning of picture mail (e.g., the usage style and code of conduct) and the terminology used to refer to the usage of picture mail (e.g., "a graphic hello"). The diffusion of social meaning of the service as defined by the female students, as well as the diffusion of their terminology was in essence what paved the way for the diffusion of the actual service itself.

This chapter has dealt mainly with communication services (and primarily with the Japanese picture mail service)—services that to some extent are all exposed to a network effect, as formulated with respect to individuals in Metcalfe's Law[7] ("the value of a network equals approximately the square of the number of users of the system"). As an idea for possible further exploration, it is interesting to note that when the terminology for picture mail fuses with ordinary language, a network effect is created in the sense that the more people that use this terminology the more natural it seems to become (and the greater its social value). In the same way, we may even attempt to describe the failure of the *men family university* group to have any impact on this market as a network externality effect (Liebowitz & Margolis, 1995)—since their terminology may be too difficult for others to internalize (i.e., adopt as part of their natural vocabulary).

The relevance of this story for other services in other markets could be argued, but from the data for other countries presented here, we have reason to believe that it may be quite relevant for mobile phone services such as SMS and music download—although it may provide less insight on diffusion patterns on the Internet. But even if the details of the diffusion patterns as such differ, the evidence is that it will be increasingly difficult to ignore the effects of how individual users themselves interpret product and service offerings and pass the word on to others. "At this point, the iPod's like a can of Coca-Cola—it's a given." Indeed.

References

Anderson, J. R. (1990). *Cognitive psychology and its implications* (3rd ed.). New York: W. H. Freeman and Company.

Ebare, S. (2004). Digital music and subculture: Sharing files, sharing styles. *First Monday, 9-2.* Retrieved from http://www.firstmonday.org/issues/issue9_2/ebare/

Fujimoto, K. (2005). The third-stage paradigm: Territory machines from the girls' pager revolution to mobile aesthetics. In M. D. Okabe & M. Matsuda (Eds.), *Personal, portable, pedestrian: Mobile phones in Japanese life* (pp. 77-101). Cambridge, MA: MIT Press.

Hebdige, D. (1979). *Subculture: The meaning of style.* New York: Routledge.

Kahney, L. (2004, December 13). Home-brew iPod ad opens eyes. *Wired News.* Retrieved from http://www.wired.com/news/mac/0,2125,66001,00.html

Liebowitz, S., & Margolis, S. (1995). Are network externalities a new source of market failure? *Research In Law And Economics, 17,* 1-22.

McDonald, M., & Dunbar, I. (2004). *Market segmentation: How to do it, how to profit from it.* Oxford: Butterworth-Heinemann.

Moore, G. (1991). *Crossing the chasm.* New York: Harper Business Collins.

Rogers, E. (1995). *Diffusion of innovations* (4th ed.). New York: Free Press.

Sekizawa, H., Washida, Y., & Björn, M. (2002). *Situation marketing.* Tokyo: Kanki Publishing.

Steuer, E. (2004). The remix masters. *Wired Magazine, 12*(11), 184-187.

Endnotes

1   The meaning of *gravity centres* here is related to the fact that this analysis
     was originally based on Ericsson's Take 5 consumer segmentation model.
     More specifically, only Take 5 segments that are over represented (index
     over 120) in a life stage have been used to represent the place of that life
     stage in the Monitor. As an example, there are some respondents in the *men
     family university* group who are classified in the Take 5 segment Achiev-
     ers—but since the segment Achievers is underrepresented in that life
     stage, they have been excluded when plotting *men family university* in the
     Monitor.

2   The online encyclopedia Wikipedia describes otaku as "an enthusiastic fan
     of any one particular theme, topic, or hobby" (http://en.wikipedia.org/wiki/
     Otaku). If you speak Japanese you can also take a test and become a
     certified otaku. Retrieved from http://www.otaken.jp/image/OTAK01.pdf

3   The online encyclopedia Wikipedia describes kogal as "a subculture of girls
     and young women in urban Japan" and continues "They are characterized
     by conspicuously displaying their disposable incomes through unique tastes
     in fashion, music, and social activity." Retrieved from http://en.wikipedia.org/
     wiki/Kogal

4   See http://dailysoy.blogspot.com/2004_12_01_dailysoy_archive.html for a
     typical usage example, in this case of people watching Christmas displays
     on town: "Few linger to bask in the festive goodness; just take a quick pic,
     possibly sha-mail it to a friend, and move on."

5   Japanglish, Paperlantern Web site describes *my boom* as "something you
     are really into, absorbed in, a craze." http://www.paperlantern.net/culture/
     japanglish/

6   Inglehart Values Map, http://www.worldvaluessurvey.org/library/index.html

7   Metcalfe, R., http://en.wikipedia.org/wiki/Metcalfe's_law

Chapter IV

Foreseeing the Future Lifestyle with Digital Music:
A Comparative Study Between Mobile Phone Ring Tones and Hard-Disk Music Players Like iPod

Masataka Yoshikawa, Hakuhodo Inc., Japan

Abstract

This chapter aims to explore the future trajectory of enjoying digital music entertainment among consumers comparing the characteristics of the usage patterns of digital music appliances in the U.S. and those in Japan. As the first step of this research, the author conducted two empirical surveys in the U.S. and Japan, and found some basic differences in the usage patterns of a variety of digital music appliances. Next, a series of ethnographical research based on focus-group interviews with Japanese young women was done and some interesting reasons of the differences were discovered. In Japan, sharing the experiences of listening to the latest hit songs with friends by playing them with mobile phones that have the high quality, ring tone functions can be a new way of enjoying music contents, while hard-disk music players like iPod have become a de facto standard of the digital music appliances in the world.

Introduction: Central Questions

The November 2001 debut of iPod and the subsequent opening of iTunes Music Store have brought a rapid expansion of the digital music market around the world. Some estimate that the market will be worth $1.7 billion dollars by 2009 (Jupiter Research). Now, iTunes Music Store service is available in 30 countries around the world, with the total number of downloaded songs surpassing the 500 million mark in July 2005.

The store only opened in Japan in August 2005 and sold over 1 million songs in the first 4 days. This is an astonishing achievement, considering that Japan's largest online music store Mora has monthly sales of around 450,000 songs. In March and April 2005, SONY, which has long led the portable music player market, released a new digital music player under the Walkman brand, offering both the hard disk type and USB flash memory type to launch a marketing drive against iPod. The developments have finally begun to provide Japanese music lovers with an environment whereby digital music contents are broadly enjoyed in terms of both services and hardware devices.

One of the major characteristics of Japan's digital music market has been the presence of digital music contents for use on mobile phones. The use of digital music contents on mobile phones, which started as regular ring tones, has gradually evolved into Chaku-uta® (true-tone ring tones) by December 2002, and to Chaku-uta Full™ (mobile-phone-based music distribution service launched in December 2004 by the mobile carrier "au"). Chaku-uta® and Chaku-uta Full™ have sold over 100 million songs and 10 million songs respectively, making the digital music service the largest segment in mobile-phone content services.

The environment for enjoying digital music content is set to expand even further into the future. How would such a development affect the way Japanese music fans listen to music in general? This paper examines future ways of enjoying digital music content in Japan, and the competition between music players like iPod for use with personal computers and mobile phones that have adopted the usage as music players.

Japan's Digital Music Content Market and the Proliferation of Mobile Phones Before 2005

Firstly, let us examine past developments of the digital music content market in Japan. Japan's first digital music distribution service started in April 1997. A company called MUSIC.CO.JP began offering songs mainly from independent labels. Coinciding with the launch of numerous music download services in the U.S., a number of online music Web sites opened one after another, orchestrated by individual artists and record labels. In December 1999, SONY Music Entertainment became the first major record company to start an online music store bitmusic. Toshiba EMI, Avex Records, and other major companies followed suit. Yet, since early 2005, the system for online distribution of digital music contents has been underdeveloped, as can be seen in the fact that Mora's supposed largest online music catalog in Japan contained just 100,000 songs, as opposed to iTunes Music Store's lineup of 1 million songs upon its launch in August in Japan.

There is no denying that mobile-phone-related music services have been the driving force of the nation's digital music market. The launch of the i-mode service by NTT DoCoMo in February 1999 marked the start of digital content downloading services via mobile phones. The connection speed of 9600bps in those days made it, initially, difficult to distribute songs in high audio quality. Faced with the adversity, businesses began offering Chaku-melo music ring tones, instead of distributing actual music contents, achieving dramatic growth. The Chaku-melo market has rapidly expanded to 80-90 billion yen in 2002. What makes this development unique was the fact that this service was initiated not by record companies rather by major online Karaoke service providers like GIGA and XING, computer game companies like SEGA, and other companies operating in the peripheral areas of the music industry itself. The market size of 80-90 billion yen as of 2002 is among the highest of all mobile-related digital content services, proving the market-led proliferation of digital content services for mobile phones.

Amidst the flourishing success of the Chaku-melo market, supported by peripheral music businesses, record companies that lead the music industry initiated a move to provide the Chaku-uta® service, offering true-tone music as ring tones, instead of Chaku-melo MIDI-based ring tone melodies. The service was initially started solely by Japan's second largest mobile carrier au in December 2002. While the Chaku-melo service was employed by all mobile carriers rapidly, the Chaku-uta® service was not adopted by the industry leader NTT DoCoMo until February 2004 and by the number three mobile carrier Vodafone until March

2004. However, the service picked up substantial support from younger generations. As the preceding proliferation of the Chaku-melo service had already familiarized mobile phone users with the concept of *obtaining music over mobile phone*, Chaku-uta® sales reached 100 million songs by July 2004, and surpassed 200 million songs by April 2005 to establish a market of substantial scale. Record companies joined forces to establish Label Mobile, which currently provides around 300,000 songs, approximately three times the catalog size of computer-based online music stores.

After Chaku-uta® came the Chaku-uta Full™ service, which provides whole songs as ring tones to become a de facto digital music store over mobile phones. It reached its fifth million download in April, just 6 months after its launch in October 2004. The cumulative total of downloaded songs reached 10 million in June, causing a dramatic expansion in market size. Although the number of songs available remains smaller than Chaku-uta® at 37,000, the catalog is expected to keep on expanding.

As described thus far, the digital-music-content industry has rapidly mushroomed as one of mobile phone services, but it has been less than 1 year since a full-scale music distribution service (Chaku-uta Full™) was launched. Music has been merely distributed as an additional function to mobile phones, that is, the ring tone. Consumption has been initiated by mobile phone use, instead of music itself. In other words, an explosive proliferation of a new communications device called mobile phones, has triggered the consumption of digital music content as a natural course of evolution. Amidst this situation, a series of dedicated digital music players called iPod has emerged with major success, triggering the launch of the iTunes Music Store offering downloads of digital music content. With the development of a fully fledged environment for computer-based consumption of digital music contents, what has been the course of competition between different types of devices in today's digital music content market? Let us examine the overview based on the results of a quantitative survey.

Today's Digital Music Content Markets: Japan and U.S. Markets

In order to grasp the state of today's digital music content market in Japan, we have simultaneously conducted a survey consisting of identical questions for use in both Japan and the U.S. Results from the two countries were compared against each other in order to identify characteristics of the Japanese market. The survey was titled *Survey on Digital Contents*, and the survey period it ran online was between February and March 2005.[1] The following samples were included: Japan, N=677 aged 15-59 and in the U.S., N=700 aged 18-59.

First, let us take a look at the rate of music-terminal use in the two countries: 6.9% of Japanese respondents used hard-disk music players like iPod, whereas the ratio was almost double at 11.5% in the U.S. The ratio of people using USB flash-memory music players was 7.2% in Japan and 16.1% in the U.S., more than double the Japanese figure. However, the ratio of those using mobile phones as music players was 19.8% in Japan, nearly three times the U.S. result of 6.1%. These figures demonstrated a clear tendency of U.S. users opting for hard-disk or flash-memory devices with music transferred via computers, and Japanese users choosing mobile phones to listen to music.

Next, the survey examined how samples typically downloaded digital music contents: 28.9% of U.S. respondents have downloaded music via computer, over 10 percentage points higher than the Japanese ratio of 17.4%. On the other hand, 42.2% have downloaded music (music ring tones) over mobile phones in Japan, around three times the equivalent U.S. figure of 14.2%. The ratio of people who have downloaded true-tone ring tones was 20.4% in Japan, an astonishing lead of around seven fold compared to the U.S. result of 3.0%. The clear tendency of computer orientation in the U.S. and mobile phone orientation in Japan, observed in the choice of music-playing terminals, was also evident in terms of the practice of music downloading.

As explained in the previous section, these findings are a natural outcome reflecting how the digital-music-content market emerged and established itself around mobile phones from the early days in Japan in contrast to market development that evolved around computers and the Internet in the U.S. However, there is some interesting data—the survey asked those who do not own a portable digital music player which type of device they would like to possess. The results indicated almost identical tendencies between Japanese and U.S. respondents, unlike the stark differences they demonstrated in previous questions. Those who intend to purchase a hard-disk music player accounted for 26.7% in Japan and 26.1% in the U.S. The figures for flash-memory players were also very similar at 21.4% in Japan and 21.7% in the U.S. Finally, the ratio of those using a mobile phone as a music player is 5.3% in Japan and 3.0% in the U.S. Even though the Japanese figure is slightly higher than the U.S. figure, they can be viewed as almost at the same level, in comparison to the ratio gaps observed in other questions.

This data demonstrates a strong contrast to previous data, which showed a noticeable computer orientation for the U.S., and mobile phone orientation for Japan. In both countries, purchase intention appears higher for computer-based music players based on either hard disk or USB flash memory, and relatively low for mobile phones doubling as music players.

Until now, Japan's digital-music-content market has been characterized, in terms of hardware, with proliferated use of mobile phones, as opposed to the U.S. market where more users download music via computer. However, as the results of the aforementioned survey suggest, computer-based music players will be used increasingly for the consumption of digital music content, in addition to mobile phones, in the future Japanese market. Then, what changes will emerge in consumer's music playing styles when such hardware competition (spread of computer-based music players) evolves?

Future Style of Digital Music Listening in Japan: Overall Trend

We have projected future changes in the style of digital music listening in Japan, dividing the samples of the aforementioned survey into the following three groups and comparing the profiles, music listening styles, and mentalities of the current and future users.

1.   Current digital music content users—Those who own hard-disk/USB flash-memory music players N=42.

2.   Digital music content potential users—Those who intend to purchase hard-disk/USB flash-memory music players N=307.

3.   Nonusers of digital music contents—Those excluding the above two groups N=319.

We made a particular comparison between current digital music content users who have constituted the computer-oriented digital music market, and digital-music-content potential users who intend to join the market from now, so as to identify how the listening style of this market is likely to change, and what impact such changes will have on the market, which has evolved through downloading by means of mobile phones thus far. First, we compared samples' demographic profiles and basic indicators in music consumption.

Gender Comparison

Current digital-music-content users mainly consist of men, accounting for 66.7%, as opposed to women at 33.3%. Digital-music-content potential users have a more even gender distribution, consisting of men and women at respectively 54.4% and 45.6%. Nonusers of digital music contents have a greater proportion of women at 58.4%, compared to men at 43.6%.

Comparison by Gender and Generation

The generation factor was then incorporated to characterize the three groups more clearly. Among current digital-music-content users, men in their 20s claimed the largest proportion at 29.6%, followed by women in their 20s at 23.8%, and men in their 30s at 16.7%. These three groups alone represent over 70% (70.1%), indicating that digital music content is primarily enjoyed among younger people—both men and women. In comparison, among digital-music-content potential users, men in various age groups accounted for around 10% each, that is, men in their 20s at 11.1%, men in their 30s at 10.7%, men in their 40s at 15.3%, and men in their 50s at 11.7%. Women in their 20s and 30s also represented, around the same proportion, at 11.4% and 8.5% respectively. Compared to current digital-music-content users, there is a more even distribution of age and gender groups. As for nonusers of digital music contents, women in the middle to high age groups made up over 40%, including women in their 30s at 14.7%, women in their 40s at 12.3%, and women in their 50s at 16.3%. The data analysis incorporating generation factors highlighted distinctive characteristics among the three user categories.

Comparison of the Number of CDs Owned

When asked how many CDs they own, 18.7% of current digital-music-content users said 50 to 99, followed by 23.8% owning 100-199 CDs and 11.9% owning over 200 CDs. These three groups represent over 50% (54.4%). Among digital-music-content potential users, 18.2% own 0-9 CDs, whereas those owning 10-19 CDs, 20-29 CDs, and 30-49 CDs accounted for 14.0%, 13.7%, and 16.3% respectively. Combined, over 60% (62.2%) owned less than 50 CDs. Almost 70% (69.8%) of nonusers of digital music contents also own less than 50 CDs, broken down into those with 0-9 CDs, 10-19 CDs, 20-29 CDs, and 30-49 CDs at respectively 31.7%, 14.7%, 12.2%, and 11.6%. As the figures show, current users have a large proportion of people with a substantial CD collection, where as nonusers have a large proportion of people with limited CD ownership.

Comparison of Monthly Music Spending

Similarly to the former, the ratio of those spending over 3,000 yen (equivalent to the cost of one CD album) per month was 61.8% among current digital-music-content users but less than 40% (39.1%) among digital-music-content potential users. Over 70% (75.9%) of potential users spent at least 1,000 yen (equivalent to the cost of one CD single) per month. Nonusers of digital music contents demonstrated a similar tendency to potential users, with 28.8% spending over 3,000 yen, and 66.1% spending over 1,000 yen. As the figures indicate, current users have a large proportion of people who spend more on CDs, whereas nonusers have a large proportion of people who spend less on them.

Summarizing the results thus far, current digital-music-content users are mainly young men and women in their 20s, with substantial CD ownership and high music-related spending per month. They can be described as *music fans* with substantial music-related consumption. Potential users of digital music content, who are expected to enter this market, are distributed across both genders and broad generations, from youth to those in middle age. They are characterized as middle-level users in music consumption. Nonusers of digital music content are mainly women in higher age groups, with relative inactiveness in terms of music consumption. The results illustrate clear differences in demographic character-istics and music consumption behavior. There are major differences between consumers who have bolstered the computer-based, digital-music-content mar-ket until now, and those who will support the market from now on. These facts alone point to the possibility that the current market is set to undergo substantial changes in its nature. In order to examine details of anticipated changes, we have compared the three groups in their attitude and mentality in listening to music.

Formats of Music Ownership

Of current digital-music-content users 61.9% acknowledge the desire to store all of their CD collection on the computer, a significantly higher ratio than digital-music-content potential users at 26.7% and nonusers of digital music contents at 17.2%. Current users appear to have a strong desire to manage their music by computer and use computers as the main device for handling music content. In comparison, such desire is not as strong among the other two groups.

Intention Regarding Songs Available for Downloading

Next, in order to examine the number of songs that are available for downloading, we looked at whether people want a greater selection from download services via computer or those via mobile phone. When asked whether the number of songs downloadable via computer on the Internet should be increased, 45.2% of current digital-music-content users said "yes," much greater than 30.0% among digital-music-content potential users and 15.0% among nonusers of digital music content. As for whether they want to see the number of songs available via mobile phone increased, just 7.1% of current users agreed, whereas the ratio was more than double at 15.0% among potential users, and 9.7% among nonusers. Although with not as stark a difference as the last paragraph, these groups clearly demonstrated different preferences in catalog enhancement between downloading services via computers or those via mobile phones. In short, current users want to see enhancement of the computer-downloadable catalogs, while potential users want enhancement of mobile-phone-based catalogs just as much as of computer-based catalogs. The results, once again, indicate a strong preference among current users on computer-based services. In comparison, potential users are requesting catalog enhancement to both computer-based and mobile-phone-based services. In other words, potential users and nonusers wish to use both computers and mobile phones to listen to music rather than mere computers.

Style of Using Songs

We also asked several questions on how people wish to use songs they own. Of current digital-music-content users 35.7% said they want to store all CDs they own on a computer and edit them, for example, compiling a collection of favorite songs. The ratio was 22.5% among digital-music-content potential users and 11.0% among nonusers of digital music contents. These figures again confirmed the computer-oriented style of current users and highlighted another of their characteristics, that is, actively using downloaded songs for their personal enjoyment. This characteristic became even more evident in the next question.

People were asked whether they like to compile a collection of songs from CDs they own according to specific themes and use the original CD as a gift for friends on a suitable occasion of some sort. Of current users 11.9% said "yes," whereas the ratio was 15.3% among potential users and 6.0% among nonusers. A greater proportion of potential users expressed preference to this style than current users.

The third question was on whether they wanted to burn their favorite songs on CD-R or DVD more casually to give away to friends and acquaintances. The results showed a similar tendency to the results for the second question. Of current users 7.1% agreed, while the ratio among potential users was greater at 12.7%. Even nonusers had a greater proportion at 9.1%. Looking at the results to these three questions, current users have a self-contained approach in enjoying music with a preference to downloading via computers, whereas potential users are more inclined towards exchanging and distributing music with others.

Finally, we asked whether they wanted to give away or exchange songs, downloaded via mobile phone, to friends over the mobile phone. Again, only 7.1% of current users, who have the preference to computer-based song purchase, agreed to the concept, whereas the ratio was greater among potential users (9.1%), with even nonusers reaching the same level as potential users (8.8%). All the numbers point to the computer-oriented and self-contained nature of current users, and the potential users' tendency of combined computer and mobile phone use and a strong inclination towards distributing and exchanging songs.

When these analysis results are combined with the demographic characteristics and basic indicators in music consumption, current digital-music-content users can be defined as those with a strong computer preference, wishing to use digital music content for their personal enjoyment in a self-contained approach. In contrast, digital music content, potential users who are entering the market from now, are combining computers and mobile phones for this purpose and are inclined towards enjoying music with others in addition to appreciating it by themselves. This group has a particular tendency of using music as one of the tools for communicating with other people around them.

Let us take a closer look as the results to enable us to explore the direction of how Japan's digital music market may change, while reflecting upon the trends of both hardware and people's music listening styles.

The digital-music-content market in Japan originally evolved from the distribution of mobile phone ring tones. Then, music content was merely one of the functions or menus available in using mobile phones. They did not go beyond the ring tone boundary. Amidst this situation, the market embraced the emergence of a new type of music device that contains a hard disk or USB flash memory, designed to be used with a computer. Contemporary music fans were among the first to adhere to such devices, consisting of men and women in their 20s that are most active consumers of music. They stored and managed all music content they already had in a computer, thereby converting them into digital content, and began carrying songs in portable music players and in so doing they were enjoying music for themselves in a rather self-contained fashion.

Today, digital music content that takes the form of mobile phone ring tones exists alongside digital music content that can be carried on hard-disk or USB flash-memory music players. We have investigated the future course of the market in view of the profile and music mentality of potential users of digital music content, who are making a full-scale entry into this market in the future. Future users will be combining computers and mobile phones, and, unlike contemporary users, enjoying music as both a communication tool with others and for personal entertainment purposes. Digitizing music contents gives music a new function as a communication promotion factor, in addition to the current functions as ring tones and personal enjoyment.

In order to further clarify this new style of enjoying digital music content, we conducted an oral qualitative survey on two groups, that is, current iPod users who represent those enjoying digital music content via computers, and Chaku-uta® and Chaku-uta Full™ users who represent those enjoying digital music content via mobile phones. The survey clarified their styles in listening to digital music content, so as to obtain an insight into the future direction of music-listening styles.

Future of the Digital Music Content Market in Japan: Changes in Music Content Consumption

The *Survey on the usage of iPod and Chaku-uta®* was conducted in the period between December 2004 and February 2005. In-depth interviews were held with three male and female iPod users in their 20s and 30s, and with three male and female Chaku-uta® Mobile users in their 10s and 20s.[2]

Comments From iPod Users

What follows are typical comments made by iPod users on their style of enjoying music:

I find the Random Play function to be very refreshing. I can 'rediscover' songs on CDs that I did not pay much attention previously. [...] I can store a lot of songs without having to worry about how much space is left. Now, I am storing whatever songs I have, even ones that I would skip if I am playing it on CD. [A 37-year-old man who has used iPod for 1.5 years, SOHO, 6,000 songs are held]

I now realize how much I have restricted myself with frameworks of genres and artists when listening to music. The Shuffle function highlights the raw power of individual songs. [...] Occasions like that have broadened the range of music genres I listen to, making me feel like trying out CDs I would never have dreamed of listening to before. [26-year-old woman who has used iPod for 1 year, office worker, 1,500 songs are held]

I never used to carry music around, but now I do not go anywhere without my iPod. This has widened the variety of occasions I listen to music, for example, while on a train or on the way home after a drink. [...] There are times when a song I frequently listened to on CD sounds very different on a portable player, because of various situations you are in at the time. That gives me fun. [39-year-old man who has used iPod for 6 months, office worker, 700 songs are held]

As suggested in the results of the quantitative survey, they typically—to some extent—have a self-contained approach in music entertainment. Their remarks illustrate new ways of enjoying music (consumption styles) they have attained through hard-disk music players like iPod. For them, a hard-disk music player is a device that allows them to randomly enjoy music out of a greater selection of songs than previously possible in conventional devices (cassette player, MD player), loaded from their CD collection. A hard-disk music player is a true portable music player strictly for personal use. In order for the device to be self-contained, it must be able to carry a massive number of songs, which in turn, facilitates random playing. This random playing then releases listeners from the boundaries of existing music context (by genre, by artist, etc.) and invites the creation of new contexts, thereby enhancing the self-contained nature even further. They are enjoying music in this cycle.

For them, consumption of music content is not about listening to each individual song, but about enjoying a stream of music. It must always be a fresh string or stream of music different from what they have already experienced previously. Their consumption of digital music content is characterized as *self-contained context consumption*. This is an emergence of a new style of music consumption, only possible for hard-disk music players like iPod. The style is facilitated with the concept of *play list* in iPod and other devices. The ability to compile a new string or stream of music, has diluted the concept of *album*, presented conventionally from package providers and artists as producers, and encouraged individual users to compile their own music streams. Consequently, music is increasingly evaluated on the merit of each song. One example is the way iTunes Music Store presented its proliferation scale in the unit of individual songs downloaded, rather than albums. This kind of presentation appears to depict a transition of mentality, with listeners focusing more on individual songs, rather than embracing the supplier-defined unit of *album*.

The following comments are derived from Chaku-uta® Mobile users on their style of enjoying music:

During a break time at work, I just leave my mobile phone to play songs to provide some background music. [...] They are all songs that everyone knows, and will not trigger any music talk. However, it is better than having no music, and stimulates conversation. [...] I don't mind if each song may be just 30 seconds long. It is actually better to have short tunes to enjoy them with my colleagues and build up a lively atmosphere. [25-year-old man who has used Chaku-uta® Mobile for 6 months, office worker, 10 songs are held]

I like upbeat Techno music. I use these types of songs as Chaku-uta, and play them during break time when my friends are around, so that I can show them how to dance to the tunes. [...] The other day, I had my mobile hanging around my neck, and playing Chaku-uta, as I danced across a Shinjuku intersection with my friend. [21-year-old woman who has used Chaku-uta® Mobile for 6 months, university student, three songs are held]

I might listen to and check out music with my friends, but I am more likely to use it as the Sleep Timer when I go to bed. [...] I can operate it by hand, and put it on charge at the same time. It is very convenient. [...] I don't care about (each song being the ring tone length of 30 seconds and) not having the complete song. I fall asleep as I listen to the same songs repeatedly. [19-year-old woman who has used Chaku-uta® Mobile for 1 year, vocational school student, five songs are held]

The analysis of the quantitative survey results also indicated that persons entering the digital-music-content market from now use *both computer-based music players and mobile phones*, and *use music to enhance their relationship or communication with their friends and acquaintances* instead of merely enjoying music by themselves. Comments from Chaku-uta® Mobile users substantiate the tendency, that is, using music as a tool for sharing various occasions with friends.

As part of the quantitative survey described earlier, people were asked how they use ring tones and Chaku-uta® on mobile phones. The top three answers were as "ring tones (87.3%)," "alarm clock (60.4%)," and "other alarm sounds (46.3%)," The fourth highest ranked answer, however, was to "enjoy them alone as music" (44.0%), and 41.7% said they "enjoy them together with friends or use them to entertain others"—as such indicating that people are beginning to enjoy mobile-downloaded tunes as stand alone songs with friends.

What can be noted in these comments is that songs are enjoyed in the ring tone length of 30 seconds, rather than in their entirety, which is quite different to that of hard-disk music player users, who consume a massive amount of randomly replayed music in various contexts. Their consumption style is summarized as "sharing the occasion of playing popular songs, rather than personal favorites with others to magnify enjoyment." What counts is how good each NETA (=song as conversation topic) is, rather than how many songs you have in store. Their consumption of digital music content is characterized as "NETA consumption to be shared among friends." For them, Chaku-uta® Mobile is perceived as a "music player that plays 30-seconds of everyone's favorite songs for a shared experience." The emergence of a new service called Chaku-uta® has brought about this new style in music consumption, while now, the style seems to transform formats of music content.

Conclusion

As we have examined, Japan's digital-music-content market—which started off with the distribution of ring tones as one mobile phone service—has embraced the arrival of fully fledged digital music players and online stores, both designed to be used via computers, such as iPod and iTunes Music Store. From the viewpoint of hardware competition, the market has now entered a stage of combined development of mobile-phone-based devices and computer-based devices. It has brought about two contrasting consumption styles with distinctive characteristics (computer-based and mobile-phone-based consumption of digital music content), and diversified people's styles in enjoying music at the same time.

People who use a computer-based means to enjoy digital music content, have a self-contained style of consuming music in a specific context, loading a hard-disk music player with a greater amount of music from their personal CD collection than previously possible and enjoying songs in random order. In contrast, people who use mobile-phone-based devices, employ a mobile phone as a communal music player for playing 30-second tunes of high popularity and consume music as topics (information) for sharing various occasions with friends or enhancing the atmosphere.

At present, these styles are separate tendencies and can be observed among users of hard-disk music players and users of mobile phones as music players as two extremes. However, a steady proliferation of hard-disk or USB flash-memory music players may cause these styles to merge on the side of individual users. Competition between two types of devices has created two distinctive styles of listening to music. Now, each user may start using both of these devices at the same time, hence adopting both styles alongside each other. Such a user may eventually begin to seek both of the styles in one of the two types of devices, which may amount to hardware integration, brought about by the symbiosis of the two different music-listening styles. Closely paying attention to consumer behavior and practices in the future will then give way to rich empirical data to be used to develop and elaborate the stream of thought outlined in this study further.

Further Reading

Institute for Information and Communications Policy. (Eds.). (2005). *Henbou suru contents business. (Contents business.)* Tokyo: Toyo keizai shinpo sha.

Masuda, S. (2005). *Sono ongaku no sakusha toha dare ka.* Tokyo: Misuzu shobo.

Masuda, S., & Taniguchi, F. (2005). *Ongaku mirai kei.* Tokyo: Yosen sha.

Ministry of Internal Affairs and Communications. (Eds.). (2005). *Information and communications in Japan 2005.* Tokyo: Gyousei.

Tsuda, D. (2004). *Dare ga ongaku wo korosu no ka.* Tokyo: Shoei sha.

Yoshimi, S. (2004). *Media bunka ron. (Invitation to media cultural studies.)* Tokyo: Yuhikaku.

Endnotes

[1]   The survey was conducted by Macromill Inc. in Japan and Zoomerang, Inc. in the U.S. And, it was organized by Hakuhodo Institute of Life and Living and Hakuhodo DY Media Partners' Media Environment Laboratory.

2   The survey was conducted by Oval Communication and was organized by Hakuhodo Institute of Life and Living and Hakuhodo DY Media partners' Media Environment Laboratory.

Section II:
Commerce, Community, and Consumer-Generated Content

Chapter V

"You're In Our World Now."™
Ownership and Access in the Proprietary Community of an MMOG[1]

Sal Humphreys, Queensland University of Technology, Australia

Abstract

This chapter considers how the interactive and social nature of massively multiplayer online games (MMOGs) presents challenges to systems of organisation, control, and regulation used for more conventional media products. It examines how the interactive structures of games cast players as producers of content, not merely consumers. This productive role creates a distributed production network that challenges the ideas of authorship which underpin copyright and intellectual property. The role of the publishers is shown to encompass community as well as intellectual property management. The communities generated within these games are a key source of economic benefit to the publishers. The contract that determines the conditions of access and the forms of governance inside proprietary worlds is considered in light of this newly intensified relationship between commerce and community. Questions are raised about the accountability of publishers, the role of the market, and the state in determining conditions of access.

Introduction

MMOGs are a form of new media that challenge, and will reshape, many of the conventional practices associated with media. These intensely social games, in which hundreds of thousands of players create communities and content with each other, exceed many boundaries associated with the organisation, regulation, and control of media. In particular players help constitute these games through their production of game play, derivative works, secondary economies, and strong social networks. This disrupts some of the key foundations underlying other media. For instance, productive players challenge both the institutions of intellectual property and discourses of consumer rights. The creation of ongoing communities inside proprietary worlds raises issues about the terms of access and the recourse to justice such communities have. The role that contract law takes in determining the rights of players has implications for a much broader set of online applications which can be defined as *social softwares*.

In this chapter I will explore the structure of MMOGs, looking at how the emergent quality of these games necessarily means that authorship resides in part with the players. The ceding of some control to the players leads to contention and disagreement. Dialogue between developers, publishers, and player communities indicates an ongoing struggle for power in some areas. I will explore how the rise of active fan and *mod* communities (players who modify games in various ways or create new artwork and other content for games) has led to the development of new business models, where publishers seek to harness the innovative and creative capacities of players. Who should own the results of players' labours, who can exploit the intellectual property in fan-created items is very much dependent on the type of business model being employed by the publisher. These distributed production networks present some major challenges for all stakeholders in the process.

However, fan-based creation of new game objects is not the key focus of this chapter. The even more interesting feature of MMOGs, and the one that presents an even greater challenge to current practices, is the value of the social networks. MMOGs rely on subscription-based models for revenue, and as such, the ongoing and long-term involvement of players is key to their success. The ways in which social networks are facilitated through the structures of the games are explored, and it becomes clear that the commercial success of these games is very much bound up in the affective investments of players. The stronger the social ties within the game, the longer the player will subscribe. This intensified relationship between commerce and culture raises interesting and contentious issues.

If players conduct large parts of their social lives inside the proprietary spaces of game worlds, the terms of access to those spaces become very important.

Access is not only to the content created by the developer, but to the other players and to their own electronic identities. The end user licence agreements (EULA) and terms of service (TOS) to many games are one-sided contracts that work to the benefit of the publishers. As managers of intellectual property, publishers are used to dictating terms which work to the benefit of themselves and the authors of the works they are managing. With social applications such as MMOGs however, they have become managers not only of intellectual property but of communities as well. The level of accountability publishers have with regard to their player communities is shown to be very low. Decisions to ban players and deny them access to their communities and their own electronic identities are made without any requirement of a neutral point of view or fairness. With no appeal mechanisms in place, the contracts institute an unseemly high level of power for the publisher over players' affective connections and identities.

I argue in this chapter that commonly used neo-liberal discourses of the empowered consumer, which hold that players, as consumers, have the power to exit from the product if they find the management of the service unfair, ignore players' role as producers, as well as the high cost of exit. I also argue that understanding MMOGs in terms of more conventional media properties, and thus in terms of intellectual property, ignores the role of affect in the production of value in MMOGs.

Finally, I look at the ways in which the unruly player populations challenge and circumvent the various formal and legal restrictions imposed by publishers. Player productivity and agency may well lead to individual experiences of empowerment through these games. However the terms of access ultimately rest with the publisher and as such represent the power to terminate such experiences of connection and empowerment. Thus the contracts which determine the terms of access are set to become major areas of contention and dispute.

MMOGs

Computer games are an immensely successful form of media, rivalling Hollywood box office in industry annual turnover (Newman, 2004, p. 3; Prensky, 2001) and achieving a high level of penetration into the entertainment market in many countries. In the U.S., sales figures of video and computer games in 2003 were $7 billion (Entertainment Software Association, 2004). Comparably high figures apply in the UK, Europe, South Korea (where broadband accessibility has enabled network play); and increasingly, China and other Asian markets. Unlike other, more narrative based media, computer games exploit the cybernetic feedback loops available through the technology to deliver a form of content that allows the user to *do* things with the text. Computer games of all types establish a relationship between the player and the game that is different from the conventional narrative text's construction of the relationship between reader and text. Because of the goal-driven nature of games, the emotional engagement with the text comes, not from the engagement with characters and events such as occurs in conventional narratives, but because the player is an actor themselves. The engagement comes because the player is the performer, and the game evaluates the performance (Juul, 2001). Crucially the game can assess a player's performance and *adapt* according to that performance. This means the game can present greater challenges to the player as their skill improves (typically implemented through a levels-based structure). This adaptability is often key to a game's success. It represents responsiveness to the player's actions or performance. How games *work* as texts is very different from conventional narrative texts.

What is implicated in these observations is the issue of control. In a conventional narrative, although the author is not in control of the many interpretations of the text that will occur, he or she is in control of the crafting; the structure; the order of events; the building of tension; the withholding and revelation of information; and so on (Cameron, 1995; Ryan, 2001). In a game some of this control is ceded to the players, who determine to a greater or lesser extent what will happen next. Control for the developer is asserted through the structures of rules, the coding of object behaviours, and the parameters of the game world they create. Players will construct their own trajectories and game play with more or less freedom depending on the tightness of the control imposed by the developer. But the power dynamic in the dialogue between player and developer is quite different from the negotiations between author and readers of a more conventional narrative text.

MMOGs, as a subgenre of the computer games field, represent a particularly interesting case of the negotiation for control of the text. MMOGs can be cast as emergent texts. Unlike some often single-player games which dictate narrow pathways through a game along a particular trajectory, MMOGs are emergent—the rules and parameters of the games are set, and to some extent shape the possible game play—but the direction of play and the events that unfold are largely determined by the players themselves.

The more this quality of emergence is incorporated into media environments, the more the issues of control and authorship will arise. What is implied in the practice of interactivity, in the construction of emergent environments, is that the users will be creators in a distributed production network. As Leadbeater (2000) has pointed out:

The more knowledge-intensive products become, the more consumers will have to be involved in completing their production, to tailor the product to their needs ... In a knowledge driven economy, consuming will become more a relationship than an act ... with the consumer as the last worker on the production line ... (pp. 32-33)

The importance of this consumer creativity cannot be underestimated. A production shared between developers and players redefines the concept of authorship and this becomes problematic when dealing with conventional copyright and intellectual property laws which mobilise idealist notions of Romantic authorship. How can such a system cope with distributed production spread across not only paid workers in a development house, but also what have traditionally been thought of as consumers—the players. The more productive the players become, the more stretched these systems of understanding and regulating media will be (Humphreys, 2005b).

MMOGs are persistent worlds which allow players to meet and play inside shared environments online. Although console games are increasingly incorporating network play into their capacities, initial MMOGS have been PC-based Internet games. In South Korea, where broadband penetration is high, and where PC Baangs (Internet gaming cafés) are very popular, MMOGs have attracted large populations of players. *Lineage* was the most successful of the initial raft of MMOGs, with over 3 million subscribers in South Korea and a further 1 million in Taiwan (Herz, 2002a). In the Western world, *EverQuest* was for many years the most successful, at one time holding a subscriber base of 450,000. Other notable early Western MMOGs were *Ultima Online* (which was the first MMOG to really develop a large and persistent player base) and *Star Wars Galaxies*. More recently the publisher Blizzard's *World of Warcraft* achieved figures of over 1 million subscribers in July 2005 (Blizzard Entertainment, 2005).

Players tend to be dedicated, and given the complexity of game play in most MMOGs, casual play is difficult. Surveys carried out by Kline and Arlidge (2002) and Yee (2001) put the average playing time of *EverQuest* players between 20-24 hours per week, with "hardcore" players spending up to 40 hours or more a week inside the game. It is the role of these players in producing value for the games that I want to examine now.

Redefining Content in
an Interactive Environment

Many computer games have generated very active communities of fans who create their own artwork and objects to import into their game and to share with other players. These *mod* (after modification) communities of fans bear some resemblance to the fan fiction writer communities that have sprung up around films and television series (Hills, 2002; Jenkins, 1992). They create new *skins* (artwork including customised clothing) for their characters or avatars, new levels (environments) to play in and sometimes new AI (artificial intelligence characters to play against) for importing into their games. Occasionally players create entirely new games using the game engine from a favourite game. The very successful game *Counter-Strike* is the product of a team of hardcore players who collaborated to make a new game using the *Half-Life* game engine. *Counter-Strike* has won numerous player and industry awards. Some developers and publishers have been quick to harness this creative and often innovative activity, releasing tools for players to use to create extra content for games and facilitating the uploading and swapping of such content between players (Banks, 2002; Herz, 2002b).

Indeed some companies have moved to a business model where they release a platform and rely on players to create most of the artwork/content. The role of the developer and publisher becomes one of service provider and community facilitator (Humphreys, Fitzgerald, Banks, & Suzor, 2005). Auran for instance, the developer and publisher of a train simulation game, *Trainz*, relies on fan groups of dedicated train enthusiasts around the world who create trains and tracks modelled on their local railway systems. Thus there are content developer groups for *Trainz* in the UK, the U.S., Sweden, Australia, and numerous other countries, all keen to create detailed representations of their favourite local trains and tracks. These fans swap their content and their knowledge on how to build them—sometimes for free and sometimes for money, depending on the motivations of the player-creator. Whether player-creators are allowed to own the intellectual property in their own creations depends on the business model and attitude of the publisher. Auran allows players to own their IP and to trade their content commercially. Other publishers claim all IP in the player-created content and disallow commercialisation of it by the players. *The Sims* is another example of a game heavily reliant on player-created content (up to 90% of content is created by players according to Herz [2002b]), but Electronic Arts, the publisher, does not allow commercial trading of content created for the game by players.

Many of the MMOGs do not have the facility that allows players to upload their own objects and artwork into the game. There are some straightforward practical reasons for this. In a persistent dynamic world, which may host up to 10,000 players on a single server, and run 50 servers or more, ensuring the smooth technical running of a server becomes much more difficult if new, player-created objects need to be constantly integrated into the world, not only for that player but for every other player on that server as well. *Second Life*, which is a persistent world (but not a game—it is an environment but lacks the goals and built-in rewards and rules of a game), allows users to create their own objects in the world. This is the exception rather than the rule for persistent virtual worlds. *Second Life* TOS are such that the players own the intellectual property in their creations. Linden Labs, the publishers, have implemented Creative Commons licencing for their users in an effort to enable smooth interchange of objects between players. Linden Labs are very clear that they see the main source of innovation and creativity in their world as emanating from the users (Ondrejka, 2004).

Whether players and users are given the right to own the in-game objects, and whether the objects are created by the players or the developers, a secondary market has sprung up on the Internet in which these items are traded for real money (Castronova, 2001; Dibbel, 2004). Their status as property is not really under dispute any longer. Hunter and Lastowka (2004) assert in relation to games and game items that "…no obvious reason exists prohibiting the recognition of legal interests in intangible virtual properties" (p. 294). The issue then becomes what kind of access or exclusions are agreed to in relation to those objects by users/players and developers/publishers through TOS or EULAs. One option is for the publishers to claim all rights of ownership in the objects, and the rights to exploit the value in those objects. Implementing Creative Commons licencing is another. Or, as Benkler (2004) suggests, a further option is to implement the GNU Free Documentation licencing (the form of open source licencing adopted by wikipedia) that effectively creates no exclusions at all.

What I want to address now is the idea that content is more than the coded objects and artwork in these environments. The idea that Benkler (2004) raises, which I want to explore further here, is that it is not the digital objects that we should be focusing on. Referring to these online virtual worlds Benkler says: "… it is a form of social software, mediating a social relation among individuals…" (2004, p. 1). Benkler's attempt to shift the debate away from who should own the virtual spoon or sword offers an opportunity to begin to understand online interactive environments as more than intellectual property.

When a player logs into an MMOG such as *EverQuest* what he or she engages with is much more than what the developer has created. The world and the objects in it have indeed been coded by the developers. But game play is made not purely through engagement with these things. Game play happens through engaging with both the world and its objects and *with other players*. Solo play is not much fun in these games, although it is possible. However MMOGs tend to be structured to actively reward social play and discourage solo play. *EverQuest* for instance is not a game where you can fight other players (apart from on a dedicated player-versus-player server). The idea is to team up with other people and fight computer generated opponents. Most computer generated opponents after the early levels of the game are impossible to kill through solo play. The game rules and the game engine code both work to structure social play as the norm. The establishment of in-game communities is an integral part of a games' success.

Thus, while some of the engagement for a player may come from mastering skills inside the game, to a greater or lesser extent, the other source of engagement comes from interacting with other players. What constitutes content in the game is only partially created by the developer. Even in games where players cannot make their own objects for the game, they are still creating game play and content that other players engage with. There are a number of implications that arise from thinking about content in this way.

Firstly, it requires rethinking the model of production from the more conventional linear structure: a chain of events that begins with an author (or team of authors), who create and finish a text, which is published and distributed by a publisher to an audience under particular conditions of copyright. The MMOG product is not finished by the *author*. It continues to develop after publication. Furthermore, after publication the content is created by both the paid developers and the unpaid labour of the players. Rather than linear, the production model is recursive and networked. Rather than a single author (or developer team known as author) there are multiple authors.

Thus, secondly, a networked or distributed production model brings into question the idealist conception of the romantic author upon which much copyright is based. How does intellectual property law articulate with collaborative social production? Is it an appropriate form of law to be applied in this context? The complexity of intersecting interests and rights in an environment that embodies social as well as property elements, and production as well as distribution issues, raises serious challenges to the paradigm of intellectual property. In a proprietary environment the implication is that in-game communities are owned and controlled by publishers. Rather than accepting the key terms of the debate, which tend towards arguments about who should own the intellectual property in particular works, it may be more pertinent to ask: Should some things be owned at all?

These are issues that have been explored in relation to indigenous, oral, and folklore cultures which have had to interface with economies based on individual property rights. Solutions for protecting the collectively held rights of those cultures in such contexts have tended to entail the introduction of new mechanisms (and displacement of old ones) for understanding them as property. But when social relations and processes become subject to a property regime they are reified—what was fluid becomes fixed, what was process becomes a *thing*, a commodity.

Coombe points to the ways in which copyright or IP law freezes:

... into categories what Native peoples find flowing in relationships that do not separate texts from ongoing creativity production, or ongoing creativity from social relationships ... (Coombe, quoted in Smiers, 2002, p.128)

Engagements with property law produce particular effects and kinds of truths about the medium in question. Invoking property law can preclude other understandings and shape practices in particular ways.

In current contexts, it seems almost inevitable that intellectual property should be the lens through which this multi-user online medium is viewed. Intellectual property shapes the institutional practices surrounding it. But as Frow (2000) points out, the teleological assumptions that accompany arguments of inevitability need not be accepted. Institutional practices (for instance those of the publishing industries) are the result of a historic series of strategic moves made by the stakeholders and represent the enactment of particular power relations. These can be countered in equally specific and strategic ways. The framing of all issues pertaining to this area as property issues closes down other debates that might be had. As Coombe (2003; glossing an argument put forward by Vaidhyanathan) suggests:

... once all questions of authorship, originality, use, and access to ideas and expressions become framed in terms of property rights, discussion simply seems to end and maximum protection seems ordained; how can one argue in favour of theft? (p. 3)

If one looks at what constitutes content in an MMOG environment and understands it as being social interactions as well as bits and bytes of code, then it seems that questions about authorship and property may not be the right questions to be asking. Thus I want to turn now to the role of affect in producing value, and the issues raised by these new forms of interconnections between commerce and culture.

The Value of Social Networks

Most MMOGs run as subscription-based games. As such, they rely on players having a sustained interest in the game. Single player games more often involve a point-of-sale interaction between the publisher and the player. The player engages with the game until they have "cracked" it—mastered it—and then moves on to the next game. MMOGs do not have an end. Players may engage with an MMOG for upwards of 5 years. While the content supplied by the developer and publisher may be one of the reasons for this extended engagement, the key reason will be the strength of the social ties a player develops within the game. The stronger the ties, the longer the engagement, and the longer the monthly subscription rolls in for the publisher. The commercial value of the game is thus very much linked to the social networks generated within the game. This intensified relationship between commerce and culture is one which brings up interesting challenges and issues for both businesses and players.

Developers design their games to reward social play and discourage solo play. While the quality of emergence ensures they cannot predict with total certainty how a game community will unfold, they can structure into the rules and parameters of the game environment affordances which encourage social engagement. For instance, rewards may be greater when slaying a computer generated opponent (mob) in a full group than when slaying it solo. Some higher level mobs may be impossible to kill without a group. In games such as *EverQuest* slaying a higher level mob can require a raid of several hours and up to 70 players. The ability to organise a group of 70 players to be in one place and fight cooperatively against a joint opponent demands a strong, established network of social contacts as much as it implies strategic and fighting skills.

Most MMOGs offer some kind of infrastructure that allows people to form guilds, or clans—ongoing social groups—that can create the basis for networks that persist over time. Such structures might include: chat channels that allow easy communication between group members, even when not colocated in the game; tags that identify players publicly as belonging to a particular group; locations within the game that "belong" to the group and where they can meet; tools for creating distinctive group emblems; and so on. These structures do not necessarily mandate the kind of social relations which are built, they more facilitate the building of ties.

My own research in *EverQuest* showed that guilds ranged in type from the ultra competitive, efficient, and dedicated *über* guilds that expected their members to raid five or six nights a week for four or five hours a night, to more "family" oriented guilds which focussed less on ultra high achievement and more on friendly, helpful social interaction. I interviewed one player who patiently worked his way through an 8 month admission process, attending five or six raids a week, to get into what he considered to be the most elite guild on his server. On the other hand, one guild I joined and stayed with for several years seemed to run more like a soap opera. Friendships and romantic liaisons were formed and broken; in-guild marriages celebrated; alliances with other guilds made and broken; bouts of group petulance and mass sulking were followed by an exodus of half the guild; recruitment drives were mounted; and various other ebbs and flows of goodwill and rancour kept the members engaged and active. The sometimes repetitive game play, which some of the players had mastered years ago, was made fun again by the social engagements required to pursue it. Raids could be completely absorbing; requiring concentration; coordination of players and groups; and skills on the part of individuals. They could result in triumphant teamwork or abysmal failure and "total mass wipeouts," but as one player told me, you could bond with your group better if you had experienced adversity and obliteration together.

Given the amount of time many of the players spend inside MMOGs it seems clear that at least some are conducting their social lives within the game worlds. They are forming enduring relationships of one kind or another with other players. Sometimes there is a crossover between online and off-line relationships, with players who know each other off-line playing together inside the game. Sometimes players meet off-line having initially met online. As such, the communities within the game can be seen to exceed the boundaries of the game. But on the whole, the communities conduct their main activities within the proprietary spaces of the publisher.

Terms of Access

6.   *We may terminate this Agreement* (including your Software license and your Account) and/or suspend your Account immediately and without notice if you breach this Agreement or repeatedly infringe any third party intellectual property rights, or if we are unable to verify or authenticate any information you provide to us, or *upon gameplay, chat or any player activity whatsoever which we, in our sole discretion, determine is inappropriate and/or in violation of the spirit of the Game a*s set forth in the Game player rules of conduct, which are posted at a hotlink at www.everquestlive.com. (extract from the EverQuest EULA, emphasis added. Sony Online Entertainment, 2005)

The previous paragraph is taken from the *EverQuest* EULA that all players click through each time they log on. The agreement is some seven pages long, and if the player wants to understand some of the terms they must consult the

EverQuest Web site (for instance the Rules of Conduct they agree to in the EULA are only found on the Web site, and consist of a further eight pages of text). It seems doubtful that many players read through the entire document. The contract is not negotiable. It is a manifestly one-sided contract which works in favour of the publisher and to the detriment of the players. Its terms may be changed without notice or negotiation at any time, it lays claim to all player created content, and it allows the publisher to disclose information about players to government agencies and other private entities at its own discretion.

The EULA represents the point where contract law intersects with a number of other areas of law and renegotiates the boundaries. The right to determine what conditions of governance will exist in a particular game world are premised on ownership of that world by the publisher or developer. Taylor (2002) has noted:

... we increasingly live in a world in which opting out of technological systems is becoming more and more difficult ... and yet participation within them pushes us to accept structures we might oppose. (p. 233)

With the advent of online virtual worlds, we see an increase in the number of people conducting their community life and social relationships within proprietary spaces. The publishers wield power over players through both intellectual property and contract law. The power they exert has the capacity to limit the access people have to their own electronic identities and their communities. This power is based on, as Hardt and Negri (2000) point out, an increasingly abstracted concept of private property, coupled with contract law which is able to reset the terms of engagement between the parties. Contracts are often able to get individuals to waive their rights, and courts are increasingly allowing this to occur.

It is worthwhile highlighting here how contract law can individualise an arrangement, and thus override the collective rights that may be protected by law focused on a more "universal" public good. However, as parts of our lives are increasingly conducted in proprietary spaces, those spaces take on the characteristics of a public commons, and the role of the publisher begins to resemble that of a state. If the publisher is to usurp the state and its powers by redefining law through private contracts, perhaps it is time for the "real" state to intervene and regulate what the terms of those contracts might be. Leaving this regulation to the marketplace is not an adequate solution, given the lack of real interest the marketplace has in citizen rights, justice, or equality.

The value of affect, of social and emotional investment and its relationship to economics is not easily articulated. Developers and publishers know that the social relationships and the emotional investments of players are the key to a successful MMOG. Businesses know about and utilise affect and cultural production as part of their economic strategies (Jarrett, 2003). Communities and social networks can create "site stickiness" on the Internet. Brand loyalty is a result of an affective process of creating and harnessing desire in consumers. The economic value of affect in the networked, knowledge economy is huge. The intangible nature of affect makes its commodification hard to measure. In a discussion of intellectual property in this context, affect is often ignored or erased—it has no place in a discourse of property. However, rather than ignore it, it may be time to broaden the range of discussion that occurs around interactive media products to encompass the role of affect. Does utilising affect for commercial gain come with any obligations or systems of accountability?

The creation of subscription-based virtual game worlds has generated the creation of communities. How are these communities to be managed? Do game participants hold all the rights of an ordinary off-line citizen—the right to the same protections and freedoms? Is a publisher under any obligation to treat the game world community fairly? For instance, in the EULA for *EverQuest*, cited previously, Sony Online Entertainment (SOE) reserves the right to ban players' accounts (and therefore access to the game) on a number of grounds, including if the player plays "against the spirit of the game" (SOE, 2005). Such a catchall term in effect gives SOE the right to terminate the service for pretty much any reason it wants. There is no system for appealing such a decision. This is the case with many other games and online environments, including various AOL, EA, and MSN services.

[I]t is disturbing to learn that online intermediaries (the companies who create online spaces—currently, games, but in the future, private internets) now have "ownership" of online identities. These providers may not be very accountable or transparent, and their rules may be effectively unreviewable by any terrestrial court or legislature. This means online intermediaries will be handing out "law", whether we like it or not. Online intermediaries are a different source of law than those we are used to (such as courts and legislatures). (Crawford, 2004, p. 219)

Although it is clear that publishers need to be able to ban players from their games if they are "griefing" other players (cheating or being outrageously disruptive and antisocial)—there is no guarantee that all players operate with the same understanding of griefing (Foo, 2004) or that publisher decisions on this will be fair or right.

A private online intermediary has no particular legal requirement to be neutral as to viewpoints or actions of users. Courts will defer to extraordinarily broad (and ever-changing) terms of service for these online worlds. So the law of identity online is private, contractual law. The use of force online—the removal of identity—has been handed over to private parties. (Crawford, 2004, p. 221)

In current neo-liberal discourses of the empowered consumer in the market-place, the consumer is seen as endowed with agency and the ability to make choices between products. If a player does not like the style of governance in a game they should change games. To a certain extent this is possible. However the role of affect comes into play here in significant ways. As discussed, players create communities within MMOGs. This entails often significant investments of time and affect. And once embedded into a community, once many of a players' friends are to be found within a game, then the cost of leaving the game is very high. Building friendships is a time-consuming process. Accruing social status, constructing networks, building reputations, are all activities that players invest time and affect in. The high switching costs for the player mean they are not *free agents*, able to move through the market at will. Changing games is not like changing your brand of jeans. Their agency and mobility is constrained by the affective elements of their investment in the game. And let us be completely clear about the fact that the investment of the players in this way is directly, economically beneficial to the publishers. It is the networks and communities that keep players' subscriptions coming in year after year.

There are two key things of interest here. The first is that the affective and time investments of players create part of the content of the game—they are co-creators of the game with the paid developers. As such, it is limiting to conceptualise players as consumers. They not only consume, they also produce. As what they produce gives them a sense of ownership in the game (and at the very least a sense that they own their own identities online), and constrains to some extent their ability to leave, a discourse of consumerism which locates their power as residing in their *exit power*, fails to adequately encompass what is at stake. In fact it offers a very diminished position of power to the players. Thus the discourse of the players as consumers erases their role as producers. And we should not fail to notice that their productivity is very profitable to the publishers.

Second, because affect and social networks and communities are intangible, and not properly thought of as property, they are erased from discourses which frame these media products as intellectual property like any other media property. Interactivity and networking—the two key aspects that differentiate *new media* from more conventional media thus raise serious challenges to such discourses.

These characteristics highlight that in a new media environment, with actively productive users, what is produced bears little resemblance to the other products dealt with by intellectual property law. Not only is the process of production no longer linear, the authorship multiple, and the product never "fixed" like a conventional text, but the nature of networked, collaborative environments is such that communities and social relations are central to the product. The legal rights of people participating in proprietary worlds accessed through contracts need to be considered. The terms of the contracts currently are manifestly one-sided and seem to diminish participants' access to administrative justice at the very least.

The Chaotic Unruliness of Players

The previous discussion deals with the formal and legal structures associated with MMOGs. But as with any emergent and social environment, the actual practices of the players and the publishers differs somewhat from such formal mechanisms of control. As with any community, online or off-line, proprietary, public or private, behavioural norms are established and policed by the participants as much as by an outside body or institution.

Communities can be to a greater or lesser extent self-governing. Publishers cannot wholly determine every norm within the game through code and customer service policing. Any social group will have ways of establishing and policing community norms. Regulation of conduct can be enforced through a variety of social mechanisms. The public shaming of cheats—shouting the name of "loot stealers" through the zone for instance—can be a means of enforcing certain norms. Group norms vary across the different communities found within the same game. Some guilds are very hierarchical, others more like a drunken party of equals. Some work towards cohesive team actions, some run like a primetime soap opera. Some groups may establish role-playing norms and others ridicule them. Clashes between groups with differing norms may cause more widespread discontent within the game.

Publishers have a great deal of latitude in how they choose to intervene in the communities. Decision making with regard to community governance can rest to a great extent with the players if that is how the game is designed. The MMOG *A Tale in the Desert* was an example of a game where players were able to suggest and vote on in-game rules and government, up to a point. The balance of power can shift according to the game, but to some extent will be reliant on the nature of the game itself and whether, for instance, having player populations vote on rule making in the game actually fits with the themes of the game.

In a series of interviews conducted in 2003, I encountered a variety of attitudes towards the role and conduct of customer service among players. Some were adamant they would rather seek their own solutions to in-game disputes—be they at the personal or the broader- and inter-guild level. They did not want any external, customer-service-based intervention in disputes. Others said they were quick to report to customer service what they perceived to be bad behaviour or violations of codes of conduct. Most had dealings with customer service over bugs and technical glitches that left them stranded in places they were unable to shift from themselves. I encountered a number of players who had stories about the perceived inconsistencies in the decisions meted out by customer service. Several told stories of being very confused as to what actually constituted an "exploit." Trouble seemed to arise around the finer points of when play is actually cheating and when it is just clever, expert play from someone who knows the game inside out. I heard stories of players who had warnings placed on their accounts or who had been banned for acts they considered to be perfectly reasonable or to have been misinterpreted by the customer service team (Humphreys, 2005a).

The key issue here is not whether the player was right and the customer service team wrong, but that there is no dispute resolution system in place that can hold the customer service team accountable for its decisions. If a player feels their account has been banned unfairly, where do they go to appeal the decision? If there is misunderstanding about the rules, or differing interpretations of the rules, where can this be argued?

It is at this point, where there is uncertainty or ambiguity about the governance of the community, that the role of the publisher as community manager most obviously becomes problematic. Given the level of investment some players have in the game, and given the value that their investments add to the game for the publisher, is it enough to say "well, there are other games in the market, they can just move on to one of them instead"? Should a player be expected to wear the high cost of a poor decision made by a possibly overworked customer service team, or should they have access to a system of appeal? Should publishers be able to insist on such contracts without these mechanisms in place?

Many players circumvent the customer service team's efforts at policing—buying new accounts (against the terms of the EULA) at online auction sites. However this can be a costly process—high level characters cost many hundreds of U.S. dollars at the online player auction houses. The secondary economy surrounding MMOGs (in which players buy and sell in-game money, objects, and characters), is an indication of the ways players exceed the boundaries laid down in contracts. The trade being done in in-game items through auction houses—the secondary markets—was estimated to be worth $880 million at the 2004 *State of Play Conference* at the New York University Law

School (Salyer, 2004). Almost all MMOGs explicitly ban this kind of trade, although some publishers are beginning to work out ways in which they can become the brokers in this market and make money from it themselves, but this model is currently still in its infancy. Whatever the arguments for and against such secondary economic activities, the practice of banned players going online and buying new high level characters still represents a cost to the player for an action on the part of the publisher that could be construed as unfair. The rebuilding of social status and identity is also implied in this process.

Players may be significantly empowered on a personal level through their playing of MMOGs. I conducted one interview in the course of my research with a woman whom I had encountered inside *EverQuest*. She was a guild leader in a guild with several hundred members. She played about 40 hours a week. She knew just about everything there was to know about *EverQuest*. Other guild members turned to her for advice and sought her expertise on many aspects of the game. She organised raids and led them a number of times a week. She had a range of characters, all of whom had "partners" online—some were married, others were strategic alliances, and others she characterised as mere flirtations. She held considerable status amongst her peers and was seen as competent and capable. When I travelled to meet this woman and interview her, she turned out to be disabled, limited in her mobility, and unable to get work outside the home. She lived in a basement flat with her husband and two children. She did not really like her husband, but felt unable to leave the relationship because of her financial and physical dependence upon him (she could not, for instance, tie her own shoelaces due to her disability).

For her, *EverQuest* was a place where she could access social status, recognition for her leadership abilities, romance, and friendships that were unavailable to her in her off-line life. That *EverQuest* was a source of empowerment for her could not be in doubt. There is, however, a difference between this kind of personal empowerment and the structural power relationship that exists between her and the publisher. In this relationship, the publisher holds the power to deny her access to *EverQuest*. All the positive empowering aspects of creating and engaging with online social activities and social networks mean nothing if you cannot actually access them. Thus, I want to make clear the distinction between the kinds of power players that may develop within the game, and the kinds of power involved structurally between players and publishers around the issue of access.

Players have held protests inside games—for instance, in *Star Wars Galaxies* where a swathe of players were banned by customer service after a "duping" scam was implemented by one player. Rather than tracking down the source of illegally duped (duplicated through exploiting a bug in the code) items, any player who had bought one was banned by the customer service staff. These players were unaware of the duped status of the item they bought, but were banned nonetheless. A protest of several hundred players was held in a particular zone of the game. Players were transferred out of the zone by the customer service team and had their accounts warned (a flag that precedes banning).[2] It was an interesting event for the ways in which it became obvious that the customer service team were the holders of structural power—able to deny access with no accountability. The players held exit power—they could leave in protest and take their business elsewhere—but for many this represented too great a loss to contemplate. While many of the banned accounts were eventually reinstated, the customer service team were actually under no obligation to do so.

Thus while players can be seen to exercise a certain amount of agency within MMOGs, creating their own communities and game play and experiencing various forms of personal empowerment through their activities, there are ultimately structural limits on that agency. While it is in the interests of the publisher not to alienate the communities it is managing inside a game, this constraint on their behaviour is not enough to ensure players are treated fairly and that access to their online identities and communities is maintained in an accountable manner.

Conclusion

MMOGs represent one of the most interesting turns that interactive media have taken—subscription based, interactive, emergent, social, networked—they exploit many of the features of "new media" that are new. They are much more than repurposed "old" media. They are an exemplary knowledge economy product. MMOGs embrace the productivity of their users and turn it to the advantage of publishers very successfully. But this new form also brings with it challenges to conventional publishing and legal practices. The regulation of such media is a complicated proposition, particularly in relation to the fair treatment of individuals and communities conducting their social lives within the game worlds. While it is probably *simplest* to argue for a free market solution to the questions of governance, I have argued that this latest interface between consumer/citizens and media corporations may require more complex treatment. If online identities and online communities are owned by a third party, the conditions of access to them become crucial. As we come to live more and more of our lives inside proprietary spaces, what role are governments to take in ensuring our fair treatment? Can we afford to let our commonly held public rights devolve into a series of one-sided contractual arrangements with corporations that work in the interests of profit above all else?

While MMOGs may seem like a fringe example in terms of the numbers of people they attract, the issues raised by their structure and the business models used to maintain them, will become important ones across a broad spectrum of applications which also utilise Internet-based social software. Their reliance on distributed production and the value of social networking, with all the inherent contradictions with copyright and intellectual property laws, and their need for social governance, flag what will become major and complex issues for businesses, law makers, and users. The central role of affect and its intersection with commercial imperatives requires further consideration from all parties.

The users of such applications (be they games or other online environments) take a very active role in constituting the content and may in the future be less willing to accept the very uneven TOS currently on offer. But in a world of constrained choices, where the market does not in fact offer the kinds of terms users might wish for, the role for policy making and regulation will become clearer.

References

Banks, J. (2002). Gamers as co-creators: Enlisting the virtual audience—A report from the net face. In M. Balnaves, T. O'Regan, & J. Sternberg (Eds.), *Mobilising the audience* (pp. 188-212). Brisbane: UQ Press.

Benkler, Y. (2004, November). *There is no spoon.* Paper presented at the State of Play 2, Law and Virtual Worlds Conference, New York Law School.

Blizzard Entertainment. (2005, August 29). *World of Warcraft® surpasses 1 million customer milestone in North America.* Press release. Retrieved August 30, 2005, from http://www.blizzard.com/press/050829-wow.shtml

Cameron, A. (1995). Dissumulations. Illusions of interactivity. *Millennium Film Journal, 28,* 33-47.

Castronova, E. (2001). *Virtual worlds: A first-hand account of market and society on the cyberian frontier.* (CESifo working paper series no. 618.) Fullerton: California State University, Center for Economic Studies and Ifo Institute for Economic Research (CESifo).

Coombe, R. J. (2003). Commodity culture, private censorship, branded environments, and global trade politics: Intellectual property as a topic of law and society research. In A. Sarat (Ed.), *Companion guide to law and society* (pp. 349-384). Oxford: Basil Blackwell.

Crawford, S. P. (2004). Who's in charge of who I am?: Identity and law online. *New York Law School Law Review, 49*(1), 211-229.

Dibbel, J. (2004). *Playmoney*. Retrieved December, 14, 2004, from http://www.juliandibbell.com/playmoney/2004_04_01_playmoney_archive.html#108209506356337766

Entertainment Software Association. (2004). *Top ten industry facts*. Retrieved November, 9, 2004, from http://www.theesa.com/pressroom.html

Foo, C. Y. (2004, December, 6-8). *Redefining grief play*. Paper presented at the Other Players Conference, IT University of Copenhagen, Denmark.

Frow, J. (2000). Public domain and the new world order in knowledge. *Social Semiotics, 10*(2), 173-185.

Hardt, M., & Negri, A. (2000). *Empire*. Cambridge, MA: Harvard University Press.

Herz, J. C. (2002a, October 8). The bandwidth capital of the world. *Wired*. Retrieved May 6, 2003, from http://www.wired.com/wired/archive/10.08/korea_pr.html

Herz, J. C. (2002b). Harnessing the hive: How online games drive networked innovation. *Release1.0, 20*(9), 1-22.

Hills, M. (2002). *Fan cultures*. London: Routledge.

Humphreys, S. (2005a). *Massively multiplayer online games. Productive players and their disruptions to conventional media practices*. Unpublished doctoral dissertation, Queensland University of Technology, Brisbane.

Humphreys, S. (2005b). Productive players: Online computer games challenge to conventional media forms. *Communication and Critical/Cultural Studies, 2*(1), 36-50.

Humphreys, S., Fitzgerald, B., Banks, J., & Suzor, N. (2005). Fan based production for computer games: User led innovation, the drift of value and the negotiation of intellectual property rights. *Media International Australia, 114*, 16-29.

Hunter, D., & Lastowka, G. (2004). Virtual crimes. *New York Law School Law Review, 49*(1), 211-229.

Jarrett, K. (2003). Labour of love. *Journal of Sociology, 39*(4), 335-351.

Jenkins, H. (1992). *Textual poachers: Television fans and participatory culture*. New York: Routledge.

Juul, J. (2001). Games telling stories? A brief note on games and narratives. *International Journal of Computer Game Research, 1*(1).

Kline, S., & Arlidge, A. (2002). *Online gaming as emergent social media: A survey*. Vancouver, British Columbia, Canada: Media Analysis Laboratory, Simon Fraser University.

Leadbeater, C. (2000). *Living on thin air*. London: Penguin.

Newman, J. (2004). *Videogames*. London: Routledge.

Ondrejka, C. (2004). Escaping the gilded cage: User created content and building the metaverse. *New York Law School Law Review, 49*, 81-101.

Prensky, M. (2001). *Digital game-based learning*. New York: McGraw-Hill.

Ryan, M.-L. (2001). Beyond myth and metaphor—The case of narrative in digital media. *International Journal of Computer Game Research, 1*(1).

Salyer, S. (2004). Recorded conference session, State of Play II, NYU Law School. Retrieved December 10, 2004, from http://web.stream57.com/nylaw/102904_virtualproperty0004.htm

Smiers, J. (2002). The abolition of copyrights: Better for artists, third world countries and the public domain. In R. Towse (Ed.), *Copyright in the cultural industries*. Cheltenham, UK: Edward Elgar Publishers.

Sony Online Entertainment (SOE). (2005). End user licence agreement. Retrieved November 3, 2005, from http://eqlive.station.sony.com/support/customer_service/cs_EULA.jsp

Taylor, T. L. (2002, June 6-8). *Whose game is this anyway?": Negotiating corporate ownership in a virtual world*. Paper presented at the Computer Games and Digital Cultures Conference, Tampere, Finland.

Yee, N. (2001). *The norrathian scrolls*. Version 2.5. [Electronic version]. Retrieved October, 17, 2002, from http://www.nickyee.com/eqt/report.html

Endnotes

[1] "You're in our world now" ™ is a registered trademark of Sony Computer Entertainment America Inc. and was used as a slogan for the game EverQuest for a number of years.

[2] For player commentary on this event see: http://intrepid.galaxyforums.com/index.php?showtopic=7190&st=0http://www.warbucket.com/ibforums/index.php?act=ST&f=23&t=17655 (accessed 2/9/2004)

Chapter VI

Games and Advertisement:
Beyond Banners and Billboards

David B. Nieborg, University of Amsterdam, The Netherlands

Abstract

The use of digital games for the promotion of goods and services is becoming more popular with the maturing and penetration of the medium. This chapter analyzes the use of advertisement in games and seeks to answer in which way brands are integrated in interactive play. The branding of virtual worlds offers a completely new range of opportunities for advertisers to create a web of brands, and it is the usage of marketing through games that differs considerably. This chapter offers a categorization of advertgames and will address the use of advergames from a developmental perspective, differing between commercial games with in-game advertisement and dedicated advergames. Where TV commercials, print ads, and the World Wide Web rely on representation for the conveying of their message, advergames are able to add the extra dimension of simulation as a mode of representation, resulting in various interesting game designs.

Introduction

The increasing sociocultural and economic importance of digital games not only caught the attention of politicians, academics, and journalists but advertisers as well. Modern day gamers complement their use of the television screen with playing games, and use their PCs for Web browsing and buying books online as well as gaming. Marketers may have found their way around in the cinema and the television set; but the virtual world has yet to be fully explored. Slowly but steadily, the adaptive character of advertisement is spilling over to digital games. Besides money earned from the original purchase and subscriptions another revenue stream may become equally important for game publishers and developers. Why have digital games become such an interesting medium for advertisers? And in which way are brands integrated in interactive play? This chapter seeks an answer to both questions.

Digital play on its part can no longer be seen as child's play. The question is, if games ever have been child's play. Due to the graphic nature, but also the complexity and sophistication of many contemporary PC games, children are not by default the primary target group of game publishers. As stated elsewhere in this volume, the average age of a gamer is not 13, not even 20, but 29, while 59% percent of the players are male. A significant number (43%) of all of all U.S. *gamers* play online and the gender breakdown of online players is similar to the overall demographics (ESA, 2004). And when gamers do play, they take their time. They have to, as contemporary console games for the big three—Xbox, PlayStation 2, and GameCube—as well as the majority of PC games, allow gamers to invest dozens of hours of their free time.

Single-player, narrative-driven role playing games such as the *Final Fantasy* series can take hours to complete, more open ended simulation games such as *The Sims* series or the *Rollercoaster Tycoon* series can grip the short attention span of Generation Y even longer, and online multi-player games can in theory be played indefinitely, for those considering playing games as an essential part of their lives. For the "hardcore" gamers, gaming is part of their lifestyle. The complex social worlds online multi-player games have become, makes playing such games even more rewarding from a sociocultural perspective, as discussed by Sal Humphreys elsewhere in this volume (Chapter IV). Spending 5 hours a day—on average—playing *Counter-Strike* with friends or clan mates, or playing 6 hours a day—role playing as a level 60 Night Elf Rogue in *World of Warcraft* with guild mates—is not an uncommon activity at all.

The *Online Games White Paper 2003* by the International Game Developers Association (2003) estimates the U.S. market size of PC CD-based online games at less than 5 million gamers, and the PC Web-based category at 50 million (or more) gamers. The growing broadband penetration in the United States, Europe, and parts of Asia proves to be invaluable for the distribution of all sorts of digital content, and games are no exception to these advancements. As game technology gets cheaper and more pervasive, the group of online PC gamers is projected to steadily grow over the coming years. The introduction of massive multiplayer online role playing game (MMORPG) such as *World of Warcraft,* showed the remarkable smooth distribution of a subscription-based game among millions. Only a month after the games' introduction on the Chinese market, the Warcraft population increased with 1 million new gamers, surpassing the 4 million player limit worldwide (Schiesel, 2005). *Counter-Strike* and *Counter-Strike: Source,* the most played, online *first-person-shooter games*, facilitate online game play for 2.4 million players every month.[1]

As such, digital games are arguably the most influential product of contemporary computer technology. Many aspects of the omnipresent and growing cyber culture are surfacing in this new form of digital amusement and profound questions regarding the complex interplay of marketing, technology, and culture are yet to be addressed. Kline, Dyer-Witheford, and de Peuter (2003) gave their take on the interaction among game technology, game culture, and marketing and argue that game culture has become part of "a web of synergistic advertising, branding and licensing practices spreading through contemporary popular culture" (p. 21). The commodification of digital play is commonplace and games as "the ideal commodity in the post-Fordist society" are natural inhabitants of this new high-technology capitalistic society. The post-Fordist society, also dubbed "post-industrial capitalism" and "information capitalism," signals "changes in the workplace, in patterns of consumption, in media of communication and in the role of government" (Kline et al., p. 64). It is a move towards perpetual innovation, from material to experiential commodities and towards the development of media, information, and digitization. This society seems to welcome the synergy of advertisement and games with arms wide open.

The "eyeball" time of gamers is worth billions of dollars. Game technology enables developers to develop true-to-life simulations and as a result games steadily move outside their role of entertainment technology. Games are increasingly used for education, testing of (military) technology, and propaganda. Games have become more than just mere entertainment (Nieborg, 2004, 2005). And because of the interactive and configurative nature of game technology, advertisement in games can go far beyond static in-game banners, posters, and billboards.

Consider the horrifying First Person Shooter game *Doom 3*. The in-game personal digital assistant (PDA) of the player provides vital clues as how to navigate through the Mars base where the main character is trapped. During the game, dozens of e-mail messages become available on the PDA, some of which praise the fictive company Martian Buddy—"the latest interstellar marketing venture" (Martian B uddy, n.d.). As it turns out, investigative players, such as the author of this chapter, find out that surfing to martianbuddy.com provides a code to unlock a weapons locker. With an unforeseen wink to the subject matter at hand, the Web site explains its purpose: "Martian Buddy represents the best in direct marketing advertisements" (Martian B uddy, n.d.). The game developers are not far from the truth—the semi-annoying spam e-mails evidently did their work as the Martian Buddy Web site had more than 470,000 unique visits within 3 weeks after the release of the game. Naturally, the imaginary Martian Buddy brand is easily replaced by a global brand of choice.

The example of the fake Martian Buddy brand helps to pinpoint several essential elements in discussing games and advertising. The starting point of any analysis on games should always be the emphasis on its ludological nature, as games are systems "in which players engage in an artificial conflict, defined by rules, that results in a quantifiable outcome" (Salen & Zimmerman, 2004, p. 80). Static in-game advertising may seem like a viable way to market a product or service, and in many ways it is, but games as rule-bound, interactive texts favor more than just an interpretive reading practice. Gaming is at the same time a configurative practice, combining "ends, means, rules, equipment and manipulative actions" (Eskelinen, 2001). The PDA in *Doom 3* is not merely encountered during a play session, it is operated by the player and a player cannot progress without using the device. Playing games involves engaging with the game's simulation model in a creative fashion. In this way, the process of "reconfiguration," creatively repurposing the rules of a game, could complement configurative gaming practices (Raessens, 2005, p. 380). It is my belief that the forward leaning (inter)active nature of game play, whether or not they enable a reconfigurative mode of participatory media culture, should always be considered by those including marketing messages in digital play.

Today, the implementation of branded game designs takes various forms and shapes. In the following section the distinction between different sorts of advergames will be fleshed out after which a detailed case study of the PC game *America's Army*, will focus on the most elaborate form of advergaming, as it is wholly designed as a branded game experience.

Understanding Advergames

The number as well as the sophistication and implementation of game-based advertisement (or advergames) are becoming more popular with the maturing and penetration of the medium. An advergame could be defined as the integration of advertising messages in an online game and is increasingly used as an integral part of Internet marketing and advertising strategies to promote goods and services to potential consumers (Buckner, Fang, & Qiao, 2002). Chen and Ringel (2001) distinguish three ways in which messages can be incorporated in games. The first is associative advergaming, that is, driving brand awareness "by associating the product with the lifestyle or activity featured in the game" (p. 3), the second illustrative advergaming, in this way the product is heavily featured in the game, and a third way is demonstrative advergaming, featuring "the product or brand name in incidental ways" (p. 4). In addition, advergames can also serve as online tracking tools. By both active and passive data gathering, advertisers can learn from customers and collect all sorts of demographic data, e-mail addresses, and data on online behavior. The topology of Chen and Ringel offers a starting point to discuss the use of games for marketing purposes. But as they ignore the interactive nature of games, a different categorization will be proposed to deepen the understanding of both games and advertisement.

As the various examples in this chapter will make clear, game technology enables developers to incorporate the modes discussed by Chen and Ringel (2001) in more than one way in a single game. This chapter offers a different categorization of advergames and will address the use of advergames from a developmental perspective. There are considerable differences between simple tennis games featuring a company's logo and slogan, a high-profile commercial release developed for profit showing in-game ads, and state-of-the-art simulations offering immersive marketing experiences. In this chapter two main categories of advergames are proposed based on the rationale of a game, that is, advertisement in commercial games, hereafter *in-game advertisement*, versus *dedicated advergames*. The former category consists of commercially developed games, aimed to sell as many units as possible to profit both the developers and publisher. The latter category games are solely made to advertise. Both categories are inhabited by subcategories. These subcategories focus on the formal aspects of games, distinguishing between non-game-play integrated advertisement (logo's, slogans, banners, and billboards) versus game-play integrated advertisement. This second subcategory consists of advertisement integrated into the game's ruleset.

Advertisement in Commercial Games

The first category of games featuring in-game ads holds games containing some sort of brand placement. Similar to movies and television series, advertisers can insert praise for their goods in a commercial game in two ways. On the one hand, developers can choose to insert static advertisement, similar to a banner on a Web site or a billboard on the background in a movie or television series. The exploratory research of Chaney, Lin, and Chaney (2004) found that first-person-shooter players, regardless of their experience with the genre, did recall encountering static advertisement in the form of billboards during game play, but did not recall a brand's name 15 minutes after. In this particular study, gamers were focused on playing the game, rather than paying attention to the (branded) environment.

On the other hand, developers can harness the interactive nature of games and blend an advertisement message into the game play. The moving picture equivalent of game-play integrated advertisement would be the cars of James Bond—for example, the BMW Z8 or the Aston Martin V12 Vanquish. Bond's use of his specially prepared and luxurious cars, bear direct relevance to the movie's plot. After all, a master spy needs a fast and powerful car to impress his opponents or in order to escape after a successful mission. It should be noted that the distinction between game play and non-game-play integrated ads is to a certain extent a theoretical one, many games have incorporated both mechanisms.

Let us now take a closer look as to how the two forms of in-game advertisement function in today's for-profit games. The popular and much debated game *Grand Theft Auto: San Andreas* is an interesting example in this respect. Albeit the game has no real world in-game advertisement, it could be regarded as a proof of concept as to how to use interactive play for marketing purposes. As it happens, the game does show a great range of fake advertisement—ranging from promiscuous sex jokes to nods at previous games in the franchise. *Grand Theft Auto: San Andreas* is available for the PlayStation 2, Xbox, and the PC and is best described as an urban simulation game. The player navigates the Afro-American avatar Carl "CJ" Johnson through the state of San Andreas, modeled after the state of California. At the beginning of the game CJ arrives at his mother's home in the city of Los Santos, where he meets his old "homies" and the games' mission structure sets off. The player can freely explore the enormous virtual world of San Andreas by foot or by using various vehicles, for example, trains, planes, automobiles, golf carts, and forklifts.

The game space is modeled after three real world cities—Los Angeles, Las Vegas, and San Francisco with similar architecture and atmosphere. Because of its plentiful real world references, there are numerous opportunities to advertise various goods or services. It is likely that the controversial character of the game made many advertisers hesitant to put up a signpost in San Andreas. The inclusion of a brand without prior consent can lead to difficulties as shown in the PlayStation 2 game *The Getaway*. This game contains 50 square kilometers of virtual London where gamers have to fulfill all sorts of driving missions. The game pictured a scene where a criminal was dressed up as a British Telecom technician, after which British Telecom protested, resulting in the subsequent removal of the "advertisement" in future versions.

The easiest way to advertise goods in *San Andreas* is through the use of billboards alongside the road—a clear form of non-game-play integrated advertisement. To achieve missions in the game, players have to cover great amounts of terrain and road signs, and billboards are already a natural part of the game space. However, gamers do not have to interact with the billboards in any way. For instance, the billboards do not offer any secret codes to unlock doors. An opportunity to add game-play integrated advertising would be branding clothing of the main character. It is possible to completely customize the appearance of CJ, ranging from various outfits (e.g., police uniforms, country or medic clothes), to watches and sun glasses. As new clothes make CJ look "cool" and improve his "appearance," it also positively influences his "respect" and thus clothes become integrated into the overall game play. Designers could go as far as to let the computer-controlled characters make positive remarks about certain brands—encouraging a certain outfit.

Similarly, the game features various unbranded cars which will take the player to the gym to build muscles or to one of the fast food restaurants, such as Cluckin' Bell Happy Chicken (a Taco Bell/KFC parody) where the player can eat a Cluckin' Big Meal and have a glass of Sprunk (a parody of the soft drink Sprite). Nelson (2002) found that when brands are integrated into the game play: "for example, the car selection in a racing game—short term recall is enhanced" (p. 89). And while driving their randomly picked cars, the players of *San Andreas* can visit Well Stacked Pizza Co. or Burger Shot. Similar to the fake ads of Martian Buddy in *Doom 3*, Cluckin' Bell has a Web site at cluckinbellhappychicken.com, including the Cluckin' Bell Happy Chicken theme song and a list of the menus. Despite these various marketing opportunities, all these brands still are self-referential and they are part of the appeal of the game series—that is, the fake brands consist of typical *Grand Theft Auto* humor.

The games' soundtrack is one of the few in-game real world references in *Grand Theft Auto*. The moment the player gets into a (stolen) car, he can opt for one of the nine radio stations, ranging from a modern rock station to a country channel. A month after the release of the PlayStation 2 version of the game, an 8-CD, stand-alone version of the soundtrack box set hit the market, featuring all in-game radio stations. The box is clearly primarily meant as a collector's item rather than a marketing opportunity. Games do however prove to be a valuable medium to market (new) music or bands. Rapper Snoop Dog for example, let his single *Riders on the Storm* debut in the race game *Need For Speed Underground 2*. The *Need For Speed Underground 2* soundtrack is part of the EA TRAX initiative. The game industry's biggest publisher Electronic Arts (EA) teamed up with several record companies and started TRAX to promote new music in their sports games:

Record labels partner with EA because they understand videogames are a powerful channel for exposing new music to a large core of young opinion leaders. Record companies also realize the valuable demographics of gaming; its "cool" factor; the buzz and the size of the interactive entertainment industry have put videogames at the center of mainstream entertainment.[2]

In this way gamers might find their way to the latest hits via their games, rather than via their peers, p2p software, or the radio. In the same way that publishers put out press releases for movies and games, they put out independent press releases for a games' soundtrack.

For a long time, games have been part of the complex intertextual web of popular culture (cf. Marshall, 2002). Initial research points to the direction that gamers do not object to the use of in-game advertisement, arguing that (fake) advertisement makes the game space more "real" (Hernandez, Chapa, Minor, Maldonado, & Barranzuela, 2004; Molesworth, 2003; Nelson, 2002; Nelson, Keum, & Yaros, 2004;), whether this (perceived) additional realism is effective has yet to be seen (cf. Chaney et al., 2004). An expressive example of the "need" for advertisement and the idea it increases a virtual world's authenticity, is a free downloadable user-made modification (*mod*) redecorating the virtual landscape of *Grand Theft Auto III*. The mod, ironically dubbed *RealGTA3* (or *RGTA*), is assembled and partly developed by a Czech modder, and contains a collection of many *Grand Theft Auto 3* modifications "trying to make GTA3 more realistic by adding real cars, buildings or advertisements all over Liberty City."[3] The mod could as well be named the best of international brands mod with in-game advertisement for McDonalds, Pepsi, Coca-Cola, IKEA, Media Market, Pizza Hut, and the inevitable Czech beer brand Pilsner Urquell. The long list of mod developers from all over the world who contributed to *RGTA* suggests the willingness of amateur software developers to take part in the voluntarily act of branding virtual worlds.

From Banners to Power-Ups

The willingness to consume, to experience, or even to co-develop advertisement is shown in a number of today's persistent MMOGs, such as *There* and *Second Life*. These worlds as well show a mixture of both game-play and non-game-play integrated in-game advertising. In the virtual playgrounds, such the one of *There*, users are able to produce their own (noncorporate) brands and use the same branding techniques as clothing companies to market their goods. With the use of time, money, and technical skill, users are able to rival with corporate branded goods in regards of reputation within the virtual world (Book, 2004). Advertisement in MMOGs shows the active appropriation of brands used in the social and economic interests of gamers.

Some players actively choose to incorporate brands into their game experience to construct their online personae. In this way, the game world becomes an index of consumers rather than products, signifying consumers as cultural entities (Pennington, 2001). By a carefully constructed web of brands, consumers can market themselves within chaotic online worlds deprived of the necessary signifiers to construct one's identity. That a personality can be defined by naming a number of brands shows the former Web site Branddating.nl. Here visitors associated themselves with several brands to distinguish themselves from other daters, in addition with their gender, age, and place of residence. Research into MMOGs suggests that younger age groups have a more positive attitude towards advertisement and branding in virtual worlds than adolescents and adults (Book, 2004). This fits with the demographics from the Branddating.nl Web site where a majority of the daters were fairly young as well.

As said, the technological and innovative character of game technology can open up a window of opportunity for innovative and daring marketers. The tactical first-person-shooter game *SWAT 4* introduced customized in-game ads in their first (mandatory) patch. The marketing firm Massive Incorporated specializes in technology-linking ads with specific game audiences and already has some major game publishers among their clientele. When gamers play *SWAT 4* they will randomly encounter in-game ads such as Coca-Cola or Gamefly.com posters and data is sent back to the Massive Incorporated ad servers detailing which ads are looked at by gamers and for how long. In this way the advertisers can specifically target online gamers with ads of their taste, thereby changing static, hard coded, in-game product placement into truly interactive dynamic advertisement, although still not game-play integrated. It is even possible, as is done in the MMOG *Anarchy Online*, to include full-motion video and audio ads.

Soft drink company Red Bull has integrated its product in the platform game *Worms 3D* where it serves as a power-up. A clever integration, oddly shaped power-ups with ever weirder results are part of all games in the Worms series. In the game a can of Red Bull serves as a powerful simulation of the Red Bull slogan "Red Bull gives you wings." In a similar way game publisher Ubisoft and Sony Ericsson Mobile Communications made a deal to include the Sony Ericsson P900 and the T637 camera phone in the stealth game *Tom Clancy's Splinter Cell Pandora Tomorrow*. The phones are integrated in the game play, similar to *Doom 3*'s PDA, as gamers have to use the mobile phone to receive messages from headquarters and to locate their position. And during hour-long single player game sessions, gamers are continually exposed to Sony Ericsson's technology up to a point where they have to make a photo of an opponent with the T637 camera phone.

Big corporations, such as McDonalds, already invest in branding online worlds. In *The Sims Online* users can purchase a McDonald's food kiosk, an element deliberately integrated into the game play. Book (2004, p. 13) demonstrates that the McDonald's food kiosks "function more as billboards than anything, they do not live up to their interactive potential." Pointing out that game-play integrated advertisement is not necessarily more successful than the non-game-play integrated subcategory. While both modes of in-game advertisement may become more ubiquitous, the sociocultural, political-economic, and technological characteristics of digital play facilitate yet another form of commodified game play, games focused on one product or service; the dedicated advergame.

Dedicated Advergames

The category of dedicated advergames inhabits a wide array of games, ranging from simple Internet advergames, mostly using Macromedia Flash technology, to sophisticated online worlds. A distinction can be made between three subcategories of dedicated advergames. First, there consists a wide range of singular dedicated advergames. Secondly, there are transferal dedicated advergames, and thirdly there is the subcategory of experiential dedicated advergames.

The first subcategory of simple nonpersistent advergames are probably the widest employed subcategory of dedicated advergames, for its low costs and simple development cycle. The notion of singularity derives from the games' focus on single-style game play. A singular advergame only has one core game-play element, such as games focusing on motor skills or (e.g., a race game), problem solving (e.g., a puzzle game). Many of these games are modeled on the classic games of yesteryear, such as *Pacman* or *Tetris*. A puzzle game with *Tetris*-style game play could be turned into a dedicated advergame by making it appear on a specific Web site in a pop-up window. Gamers who are interested can play the game on the spot or sometimes download it to play on a moment of choice. Other advergames offer a new but familiar design. Car manufacturer Jaguar promoted their new S-type R model with a Flash game offering an online Urban Golf course.[4] The car in the back of the game had nothing to do with the actual game play. A player has to finish a Golf course in central London and the hole is replaced by a red postbox. Players who supply their e-mail address can win golf lessons from a pro.

These simple advergames arguably lack the game play to engender immersive play and are primarily used to raise brand awareness and direct visitors to the various Web sites for more information. The games have their own Web sites or may pop up when visiting a random Web site and cannot be saved to one's computer, thus the game becomes a random encounter and in many cases the nonpersistent achievements—that is, points—do not encourage gamers to play the game again. Making the game available off-line, on the other hand, can aid the viral distribution of a game and thus its marketing message. In the Jaguar advergame example, players may send the Web site's URL to their "mates" via the Web site and can compete to beat the top scores. The International Game Developers Association (IGDA) in their *Online Games Whitepaper* promote these kinds of advergames as "a powerful and effective tool for delivering branding and advertising messages" as these games tend to be "sticky," nonintrusive and able to generate various demographic data of consumers (2003, p. 35). As said, small PC Web-based advergames can tap into a large group of 50 million U.S. gamers, whereas PC CD-based games, such as *The Sims* or *Rollercoaster Tycoon 3*, have a much smaller potential market of less than 5 million U.S. consumers.

A more sophisticated form of dedicated advergaming are games offering a transferring experience, or what Chen and Ringel (2001, p. 3) would call "associative advergaming." Here brand awareness is raised through lifestyle association. The subcategory of transferal advergames may also feature the advertised product and thus can be seen as an illustrative advergame—offering as much in-game product exposure as possible. The sole intent of these kinds of advergames is to put users into contact with its brand and harness a positive game experience within a controlled and branded (persistent) online world. The games in this subcategory may or may not contain any links to external Web sites of the advertised service or product and does not enable gamers to actually experience a particular product or service.

A successful example, in terms of the amount of visitors and time spent on the Web site is the online world of *Coke Music*, developed by order of Coca-Cola.[5] *Coke Music* has all the elements of an MMOG and contains all kinds of simple social activities, which can be very time consuming, ranging from chat to the production of simple music compositions. The technology is completely Web based and gamers can only play online. Established in 2002, this Web site counted "over a million views a day, the number of new visitors increases monthly with 200,000, and people spend about 25 minutes on the site" (Van der Graaf, 2004). Additional gain for Coca-Cola is added through putting out surveys to collect various gamer data. The Coca-Cola brand is omnipresent and many ad campaigns in other media slip into *Coke Music*—and vice versa.

The example of the branded world of *Coke Music* shows how existing game genres can be repurposed to fit the advertisers need. Built upon the template of the commercial game/chat environment of *Habbo Hotel*, Coca-Cola successfully appropriated the game mechanics of a proven game concept and offers a free branded alternative. *Habbo Hotel*, developed by the Finnish company Sulake Labs, is a moderated, Web-based chat environment with many franchises all over the world. It is a huge success among young children and has 3 million unique users visiting virtual hotels within 16 countries on four continents. As both *Habbo Hotel* and *Coke Music* are free games, the choice between both games may be somewhat arbitrary and has a social dimension. In a way Coca-Cola's virtual world is more than a game; it is a social structure:

(...) based on the constant negotiation of cliques, inner circles, in-crowds and social drama that is enacted throughout a variety of settings. The corporate sponsor is just as likely to be completely ignored in the pursuit of these activities, especially when more powerful metaphors can be found. (Book, 2004, p. 21)

This observation shows that the complexity or sophistication of an advergame does not equal (instant) success for the advertised product or service. There is always such a thing as good game design. A brand may be cleverly integrated into the game play or to put in the words of Hernandez et al. (2004) a brand may be congruent and thus less intrusive, creating meaningful play is an art in itself (cf. Salen & Zimmerman, 2004). Young gamers may freely wander through the branded world of *Coke Music*, whether or not they will associate their own lifestyle with the soft drink's brand is a question certainly worth further analysis. Next, the third subcategory of dedicated advergames will be discussed— experiential advergames.

Experimental Marketing

Games add the representational mode of simulation to the marketing mix. In games, brands can be shown repeatedly and through carefully branded simulations, games enable consumers to "transfer meaning to themselves, defining themselves as cultural entities" (Pennington, 2001, p. 50). But the gift of interactivity adds a significant "bonus level," through game-play products or services can be experienced. The intangible and arbitrary associations evoked by brands as symbols, become tangible, allowing gamers to experience what it is like to drive a car or being a soldier by immersing themselves into carefully constructed virtual simulations. Economists Pine and Gilmore (1999) offer a useful concept to understand this new marketing paradigm: "Cyberspace is a great place for escapist experiences" (p. 34) and the game can stage such memorable experiences, situating itself within existing community structures and design conventions in order to offer a "show." This shift is in line with the notion of "the experience economy," where the former offerings of the commodity economy are replaced by an economy relying on staging memorable and personal experiences.

The branding of virtual worlds offers a complete new range of opportunities for advertisers to create a web of brands. Brands get their meaning partly through opposition (Pennington, 2001) and the previous example of *RealGTA* shows the low technical, social, and virtual barriers of the branding of virtual worlds. Major global brands such as Microsoft, IBM, General Electric, and Intel do not have the advantage of being able to create experiential branded simulations. Computer software and hardware and consumer appliances seem to miss a central point to create meaningful play. Coca-Cola bypassed this problem by facilitating social interaction in a branded virtual world where teenagers can chat and come together within a branded community. Car manufacturers are arguably one of the other few major brand holders being able to tap into existing game genres and develop engaging experiential simulations, that is, a racing game rather than a branded simulation, for example, a puzzle game sponsored by a car brand.

An interesting example of a successful experiential dedicated advergame, from an economic perspective, is the PC game *America's Army*.[6] This game goes beyond a transferal experience as it is a game that relies mainly on the simulation of combat. The state-of-the-art game facilitates rich and immersive virtual experiences, showing consumers virtual insights in an interactive world previously not accessible to the general public. "By creating leads and traffic through America's Army's design and characteristics, the Army's brand is not about 'just a logo. It is much more, namely, it is the experience that occurs when a gamer comes into contact with the Army's game" (Van der Graaf & Nieborg 2003, p. 329).

For most players *America's Army* is first and foremost an online multi-player-tactical, first-person-shooter PC game. Developed by the U.S. Army, the game is freely available on various Web sites and the games' design is inspired by other popular first-person-shooter games such as *Counter-Strike* and *Tom Clancy's Rainbow Six*. In *America's Army* the player takes the role of a U.S. Army soldier and engages in man-to-man combat against human opponents in authentic environments by using a range of real-life weaponry in order to complete a mission or objective. *America's Army* is primarily a multi-player game. The single player part entails several training missions, which need to be completed in order to unlock certain roles, such as a medic or a sniper.

America's Army could be seen as a simulation of the U.S. Army, many unrealistic elements from the first-person-shooter genre are changed. For realism's sake, the game play is much more structured and bound by the rules of physics and warfare. Players become soldiers with a persistent record. Shooting team members is ruled out and maps, weapons, and roles cannot be changed. In *America's Army* you will always be put in the boots of a U.S. Army soldier. Through the use of a software trick every gamer sees himself and his team as U.S. soldiers and the other team as the Opposing Forces (OpFor) and vice versa.

America's Army is not the only advergame issued by the U.S. military to promote its services. There is the free downloadable real-time strategy game *Guard Force* to aid recruitment for the U.S. Army National Guard. While the U.S. Marine Corps was heavily involved in the development of the first-person-shooter, training tool spin-off *Close Combat: First to Fight*, this game is a commercial game with game-play integrated advertisement. Gamers have to buy the game and its primary goal is to sell as many copies as possible. The U.S. Navy issued the action game *Navy Training Exercise (NTE): Strike & Retrieve*. This game however is a transferal-dedicated advergame as the game play does not directly simulate the activities of Navy recruits. *America's Army* then is marketed as a combat experience, and by simulating U.S. Army values through a true-to-life infantry combat experience, the Army educates gamers about soldiering. How *America's Army* works as a dedicated advergame and an experiential marketing tool, will be explored more in depth in the following analysis.

Military Advertisement

With the end in 1973 of the mandatory military service, better known as the draft, the U.S. military had to rely on its recruiting efforts to enlist personnel for its new All-Volunteer-Force. Over three decades later, the U.S. military has to persuade more than 200,000 recruits annually to fill its ranks, but one of the biggest problems facing contemporary recruiting efforts still is its effectiveness. Today, the U.S. armed forces rely on three pillars for their recruiting efforts. First, there is a 15,000 strong force of recruiters. Second, various (financial) incentives are available upon joining and in order to raise awareness, and third, to help recruiters reach their target groups, the military invests heavily in advertisement. From 1998-2003, the total advertising budget for military recruiting almost doubled from $299-$592 million while the total recruiting budget approached $4 billion

(General Accounting Office, 2003). In order to keep up with contemporary marketing, the U.S. Army created the "U.S. Army: An Army of One" brand.

As any other brand, the U.S. Army brand needs constant expansion—a process taking up enormous amounts of financial recourses. To expand the Army brand, the U.S. Army sponsors a NASCAR (National Association for Stock Car Auto Racing) racing team, a NHRA (National Hot Rod Association) Top Fuel team, and a NHRA Pro Stock Bike team. And in line with the ubiquitous transgressive character of brands (Pennington, 2001), there are three (official) Web stores offering licensed material with the "U.S. Army of One" logo and slogan on it, ranging from clothing to mugs, playing cards to key rings, and other knick-knacks.[7] With half of the military advertising funding going to the Army and the constant need to reinvent and explore new advertisement platforms, there is room to experiment and try new initiatives to reach the core group of 18- to 24-year-olds. Probably the most high profile advertising experiment of all, could well be *America's Army*.

It was the advergame dimension, the Army's goal of attracting more recruits, that became at the conception of the project, the guiding design rationale. The U.S. Army does not label *America's Army* as a recruiting tool or an advergame, but as a strategic communication tool (e.g., Davis, 2004). The goal of the game is to inform popular culture rather than to persuade and to raise awareness rather than directly recruit, which is done by U.S. Army recruiters. Raising both the awareness of the U.S. Army brand and the U.S. Army as a possible career are central to the design of the game and its community. With less influencers, people with a positive attitude towards the Army and a willingness to communicate this attitude present in the U.S. society (e.g., former soldiers), the Army has to rely on other mechanisms to enter the "consideration set" of America's youth. "So when a young person turns 18—17, 18—and they start to think about what their options are for the future, what does that list look like? Go to college? Get a job? Hang out with my friends? We want 'join the Army' to be one of those lists of options" (Department of Defense, 2001). With this statement, the former Secretary of the Army, Louis Caldera, articulated one of the main goals of the "Army of One" campaign.

What makes *America's Army* fairly unique is that it could be considered one of the first multidimensional games (Nieborg, 2004, 2005). Analysis shows that the game has more than an advergame dimension. It is used to train U.S. Army soldiers as well as to educate gamers about the U.S. Army—the *edugame* dimension. Through off-line PowerPoint lectures followed by multiple choice tests and through online game play, gamers may learn what it takes to be part of the "Army of One." The games' third dimension is its use as a test tool. New military technologies are carefully modeled in the game, allowing military experts and soldiers to test these future weapon systems in the virtual world, after which they can be easily incorporated into the edugame dimension. Gamers can be tested as well. Similar to off-line test tools, such as the Armed Services Vocational Aptitude Battery (ASVAB) freely available at U.S. high schools, the U.S. Army is able to virtually test the aptitude of potential Army recruits. The fourth and last dimension of *America's Army* is its propaganda dimension. The game is both an example of a public affairs instrument, as an instrument of public diplomacy, as it shares many of the same goals and characteristic of both strategic communication tools. However, it is the role of *America's Army* as a tool of public diplomacy that signals a shift away from the advergame dimension towards the *propagame* dimension. Both dimensions still interact and reinforce rather than replace each other. The initial goal of a recruitment aid and raising the brand awareness of the U.S. Army is partly bypassed when looked at the global use of the game, thereby giving way to the propagame dimension.

Encapsulated in the first-person-shooter genre are several key features ready to be appropriated for (successful) digital marketing. The U.S. Army as a brand transformed into the *America's Army* brand and appears able to tap seamlessly into existing game community frameworks. Kierzkowski, McQuade, Waitman, and Zeisser (1996) provide five distinct recommendations for success in digital marketing, all of which are present in the production, distribution, and consumption of the official U.S. Army game. First, there is the advertisement on and alliances with gaming Web sites such as GameSpy.com and Gigex.com. Second, providing participants with a stimulating and motivating game is evident in *America's Army's* much acclaimed realism. Third, participants are instantly rewarded and have the prospect of beating top scores. This is constructed by the extensive and persistent honor system which gives a gamer certain credits and acknowledgement among peers as well as goals to aim at (e.g., getting more honor points than a peer). Fourth is the identification of user preferences by providing choices within the game. In *America's Army* players can play in theatres of operation all over the (virtual) world, playing different rolls and familiarizing themselves with a plethora of weapons. And the fifth and final aspect is retaining users which is partly taken care of by the community, which consists of the official homepage with its message boards, several (semiprofessional) affiliates and fan sites and several IRC channels. Game communities are known for their collaborative and peer-supporting character (Jenkins, 2002; Newman, 2004) and *America's Army* is no exception to this rule.

One of the questions asked by every journalist and academic unfamiliar with *America's Army* is: "is the game effective and do you have figures showing how many people joined?" Such figures are nonexistent and the design of both the game and the community are not set up in a way that such data can easily be obtained. One thing about *America's Army* as an advergame is clear; the game is extremely cost effective. The game cost $4 million a year from 2000-2003.

With a breakdown of $2 million in wages, $300,000 for game engine costs, and $1.5 million in operational costs (Zyda, Mayberry, McCree, & Davis, 2004). In the upcoming years, staffing costs and licensing fees are likely to grow. The $20 million spent on the game pales into insignificance considering the following remark: "The Army estimates *America's Army* has the potential to save some $700M-$4B per year" (Zyda, 2002, p. 9).

Conclusion

In a society where even sand can be branded, the competition for attention is enormous (cf. Klein, 1999). Advertisement in our post-modern, media-saturated world is omnipresent but at the same time extremely fragmentary. The eyeball time of young people has become a commodity in itself, with every medium fighting for attention trying to sell audiences to a growing pool of companies and brand owners. Over the years and with the maturing of the medium, childn's play has become heavily commodified (Kline et al., 2003). Product placement in digital games is ubiquitous and gamers seem to praise the efforts of game designers to include their favorite brands in a game to make the game space more "real." The console hardware developers have become established brands themselves, up to a point where gamers identify themselves with the hardware. Gamers even have names for such aficionados: "fanboys." As a result "The industry has come full circle: conditions for its spectacular growth were set in existing youth-oriented media niches; now for gaming is itself poised to create marketing opportunities for other corporations that are seeking to target the youth audience" (Kline et al., 2003, p. 236). The multiple identities of gamers as both fans and consumers are not without consequences, the voluntary activity of play becomes intertwined with the discourses of a commodified game culture.

Where TV commercials, print ads, and the World Wide Web rely on representation for the conveying of their message, dedicated advergames add the extra dimension of simulation. The ever-rising processing power of computer chips, doubling every 18 months according to Moore's law, enables rich and immersive virtual experiences, showing consumers virtual insights in interactive worlds previously not accessible for the general public. It is the usage of marketing through games that differs considerably. Commercial games increasingly include some sort of marketing message. Increasingly, dedicated advergames are used to advertise, varying from singular advergames which may be freely distributed via popular Web sites or on a company's homepage, to the more sophisticated experiential advergames, which encompass elaborate, persistent, virtual worlds.

As the early abstract games of *Pong*, *Spacewar,* and *Tetris* turned into lifelike and realistic simulations, developers are now able to turn their intertextual references into commercial representations and simulations. Games as one of the new intertextual commodities have to:

... posses the elasticity to incorporate the imaginary reconfigurations of its images, stories and products by users. Although corporations protect their trademarks and images, they have also developed sophisticated structures and architectures that allow certain images of their film or game to float freely across the Internet as promotional sirens of their cultural commodity. (Marshall, 2002, p. 76)

America's Army is a successful example of such a cultural commodity, marketed as a simulation of the U.S. Army. Game-play-integrated advertisement seems to be favored by gamers over non-game-play integrated forms—a cleverly integrated branded car of PDA adds flavor to a game and aids brand recall. Advergames can move beyond in-game banners and billboards. However, while the goal of brand placement is raising brand awareness (Nelson, 2002), interactive entertainment is able to move beyond this marketing model as well. *America's Army* shows that gamers are able to learn (U.S. Army) values, basic skills, and a considerable amount of knowledge and information, just by playing the game. Gamers willfully subject themselves to minute long PowerPoint lectures to advance in the game. A career in the U.S. Army is literally played out. In *America's Army*, the U.S. Army brand is ubiquitous and encompasses all modes of advergaming.

The game constantly supports brand awareness, for the brand and its simulation are interchangeable. By using various new media technologies, the U.S. Army is able to directly reach their target group in an active and engaging manner that corresponds with the media use of today's youth. Being able to simulate conflict by using existing game design conventions, the U.S. Army both redefines elements within the first-person-shooter genre and taps directly into the very fabric of popular culture. In a similar way *Coke Music* is based on the popular format of *Habbo Hotel.* The question would then be if the designers and publishers of future advergames are willing to leave existing game genres behind and if, through innovative game design, they not only will profit from game technology and culture, but contribute to it as well.

References

Book, B. (2004). *These bodies are FREE, so get one NOW!: Advertising and branding in social virtual worlds.* Social Science Research Network. Retrieved August 25, 2004, from http://papers.ssrn.com/sol3/papers.cfm ?abstract_id=536422

Buckner, K., Fang, H., Qiao, S. (2002). Advergaming: A new genre in Internet advertising. *SoCbytes Journal, 2*(1).

Chaney, I., Lin, K., & Chaney, J. (2004). The effect of billboards within the gaming environment. *Journal of Interactive Advertising, 5*(1), 54-69.

Chen, J., & Ringel, M. (2001). *Can advergaming be the future of interactive advertising?* Retrieved September 1, 2005, from http://www.locz.com.br/ loczgames/advergames.pdf

Davis, M. (Ed.). (2004). *America's army pc game vision and realization.* San Francisco: U.S. Army and the Moves Institute.

Department of Defense. (2001). *Army announces new advertising campaign.* Retrieved August 22, 2004, from http://www.defenselink.mil/transcripts/ 2001/t01102001_t110army.html

Entertainment Software Association (ESA). (2004). Top ten industry facts. Retrieved December 10, 2004, from http://www.theesa.com/pressroom.html

Eskelinen, M. (2001). The gaming situation. *Game Studies, 1*(1). Retrieved from http://www.gamestudies.org/0101/eskelinen/

General Accounting Office. (2003). *Military recruiting: DOD needs to establish objectives and measures to better evaluate advertising's effectiveness.* Washington, DC: United States General Accounting Office.

Hernandez, M. D., Chapa, S., Minor, M. S., Maldonado, C., & Barranzuela, F. (2004). Hispanic attitudes toward advergames: A proposed model of their antecedents. *Journal of Interactive Advertising, 5*(1), 116-131.

International Game Developers Association (IGDA) Online Games Committee. (2003). *IGDA Online Games White Paper.* San Francisco: IGDA.

Jenkins, H. (2002). Interactive audiences? The collective intelligence of media fans. In D. Harries (Ed.), *The new media book.* London: BFI.

Kierzkowski, A., McQuade, S., Waitman, R., & Zeisser, M. (1996). Marketing to the digital comsumer. *The McKinsey Quarterly, 32*(3), 5-21.

Klein, N. (1999). *No logo.* New York: Picador.

Kline, S., Dyer-Witheford, N., & de Peuter, G. (2003). *Digital play—The interaction of technology, culture, and marketing.* Montreal, Canada: McGill-Queen's University Press.

Marshall, D. P. (2002). The new intertextual commodity. In D. Harries (Ed.), *The new media book*. London: BFI.

Martian Buddy. (n.d.) Homepage. Retrieved May 16, 2006, from http://www.martianbuddy.com

Molesworth, M. (2003, November, 4-6). *Encounters with consumption during computer-mediated play: The development of digital games as marketing communication media*. Paper presented at the Level Up: Digital Games Research Conference, Utrecht, Holland.

Nelson, M. R. (2002). Recall of brand placement in computer/video games. *Journal of Advertising Research, 42*(2), 80-92.

Nelson, M. R., Keum, H., & Yaros, R. A. (2004). Advertainment or adcreep? Game players' attitudes toward advertising and product placements in computer games. *Journal of Interactive Advertising, 5*(1), 3-30.

Newman, J. (2004). *Videogames*. London: Routledge.

Nieborg, D. B. (2004). *America's army: More than a game*. Paper presented at the Transforming Knowledge into Action through Gaming and Simulation, München, Germany.

Nieborg, D. B. (2005). *Changing the rules of engagement—Tapping into the popular culture of America's army, the official U.S. army computer game*. Unpublished masters thesis, Utrecht University. Retrieved September 1, 2005, from http://gamespace.nl/thesis

Pennington, R. (2001). Signs of marketing in virtual reality. *Journal of Interactive Advertising, 2*(1), 43-55.

Pine II, B. J., & Gilmore, J. H. (1999). *The experience economy: Work is theatre & every business a stage*. Boston: Harvard Business School Press.

Raessens, J. (2005). Computer games as participatory media culture. In J. Raessens & J. Goldstein (Eds.), *Handbook of computer game studies* (pp. 373-388.). Cambridge, MA: MIT Press.

Salen, K., & Zimmerman, E. (2004). *Rules of play: Game design fundamentals*. Cambridge, MA: MIT Press.

Schiesel, S. (2005, September 6). Conqueror in a war of virtual worlds. *The New York Times*, E1, column 4.

Van der Graaf, S. (2004). Viral experiences: Do you trust your friends? In S. Krishnamurthy (Ed.), *Contemporary research in e-marketing* (Vol. 1, pp. 166-185). Hershey, PA: Idea Group Publishing.

Van der Graaf, S., & Nieborg, D. B. (2003, November, 4-6). *Together we brand: America's army*. Paper presented at the Level Up: Digital Games Research Conference, Utrecht, Holland.

Zyda, M. (2002). 2002 In the MOVES Institute. MOVES Institute. Retrieved August 14, 2004, from http://www.movesinstitute.org/MOVESactivity2002.pdf

Zyda, M., Mayberry, A., McCree, J., & Davis, M. (2004). *From Viz-Sim to VR to games: How we built a hit game-based simulation*. Monterey, CA: The MOVES Institute.

Endnotes

[1]   Retrieved September 4, 2005 from http://steampowered.com/status/status.html

[2]   Retrieved September 1, 2005 from http://www.info.ea.com/downloads/eatrax.doc

[3]   From the RGTA Web site General Info section located RealGTA.net. Retrieved August 23, 2004, from http://www.doupal.cz/realgta/info.htm.

[4]   Retrieved September 1, 2005 from http://www.jaguarurbangolf.co.uk

[5]   See: http://www.cokemusic.com

[6]   America's Army is continually updated and there is no finished version of the game. The first version, released July 4, 2002, was dubbed America's Army: Recon, followed by America's Army: Operations and America's Army: Special Forces. Each Special Forces update has its own label, for example, America's Army: Special Forces (Direct Action) v2.5, released October 13, 2005. During each update, content is added and the game's design differs constantly.

[7]   See for example: http://www.armyproducts.com/default.aspx, http://shop.ipledge.com and http://armyofone.usptgear.com. Retrieved August 22, 2004.

Chapter VII

Digital Petri Dishes:
LiveJournal User Icons as a Space and Medium of Popular Cultural Production

Alek Tarkowski, Polish Academy of Sciences, Poland

Abstract

Internet applications such as Web-based blogging and instant messaging tools or social networking sites often provide their users with the possibility of displaying small graphic elements. Such "pictures" or "icons" allow users to represent and mutually identify themselves. This text is an analysis of user icons displayed on the LiveJournal blogging site. I treat such a user icon as a medium with particular characteristics and patterns of usage. LiveJournal users use such icons to participate in what John Fiske (1992) calls popular culture. A case study of user icons discloses the life cycle of the media form, during which a medium with initial characteristics coded by its creators begins over time to support a wide variety of uses, innovation in usage, and active participation in culture. In this chapter, I consider user pictures and practices that are tied to them as an example of the manner in which popular culture functions in the digital age.

Introduction

LiveJournal is one of the more popular blogging tools, a Web-based application that allows users to run an online diary or journal. LiveJournal at its nascence was itself a result of user innovation. It was written by a 19-year-old programmer named Brad Fitzpatrick as a tool that would allow him to stay in touch with high school friends after leaving for college. LiveJournal's user base has been constantly growing and in early September 2005 there were almost 8.2 million registered journals and 1.4 million users who have updated their journal in the preceding month. Although the exact historical data on LiveJournal growth is not readily available, such data is for the purpose of this chapter insignificant, despite the general hype surrounding the growth of blogging. Neither are these numbers quoted to prove the importance of the site, as cultural significance cannot be easily quantified into statistical figures. It is the scale of the phenomenon, which involves hundreds of thousands of Web pages, users, and communities formed by them, that is important. It is the scale of a fair sized city, a size at which any phenomenon must be internally varied and heterogeneous.

As an online publishing system, LiveJournal is a tool that can be used for production, exchange, and reception of cultural content. Furthermore, this content and the interface with which it is produced forms an axis for communication and formation of social associations. LiveJournal's architecture is designed to support interaction, in particular by enabling the creation of "communities." These collectively written journals are spaces for discussion, similar to online forums. Each community, treated as a media form, is an anchor for a collective of users that expresses itself in the community's online space and is commonly thought of as a community as well. Posts and comments are both instances of personal expression and traces of interactions between users. They are shared and public because they have been archived by the system, while other aspects of these interactions remain invisible, as they took place in private spaces and channels or even beyond the Internet. Although LiveJournal is constantly being accessed in the present, its public space has a historical, archival character as it consists of content stored in LiveJournal servers. A community of users communicating through LiveJournal constructs in parallel a community as a media form, a record of own interactions stored as the system's content.

Defining LiveJournal as a blogging site has its consequences. Blogging is a phenomenon that is a prime example of what Woolgar (2002) calls the cyberbolic social studies of the Internet, based on "...synoptic, top-down (and often unexplicated) depictions of technical capacity and effect" (p. 4). We can instead think of LiveJournal as simply an online infrastructure for publishing content. It is a digital medium primarily designed to support textual communication and to remain open—it has few restrictions or even guidelines regarding the produced content. There are almost no preferred themes, style guidelines, or editorial policies, except for the general standards of decency, to which users must adhere. The only significant limitation is the difficulty of publishing multimedia content, as LiveJournal does not provide users without paid accounts with server space for content other than text.

A distinction should be made between LiveJournal as either an application designed by its administrators or a material, technical artifact—and LiveJournal as it is perceived by its users. The relative simplicity of the application means that it is the content and not the medium itself that defines user's experience. While sharing the label "LiveJournal journal," individual sites can greatly vary and the system itself can have different meanings for different users. The heterogeneity of uses, themes and interests, or communities means that there is no "typical," model use of LiveJournal, no synoptic description it will fit into (Woolgar, 2002).

LiveJournal as a system has a border that is porous and only roughly relates to the symbolic limits of the livejournal.com domain, making it even more difficult to consider LiveJournal as a single medium and a homogeneous environment. At the level of code and content, users outsource the storage of visual content to other servers and service providers. Links from the site constantly direct the viewer beyond LiveJournal. At the social level, LiveJournal is but one tool and space in a wider digital environment. Users use this tool to varying degrees and ascribe to it varying degrees of importance. Activity at the LiveJournal site is for a vast majority of users only a part of their online activities, which in turn are only one aspect of their media-saturated lives. The porous character of LiveJournal means that its users and components "pertain to them by one side only, but through the other sides, ... escape from the world they constitute" (Tarde, 1999, p. 80).

User Icons in the Context
of The LiveJournal Site

A *user picture* or *user icon* is a graphic selected by the user and displayed on his/her journal. To some extent, it is designed as a visual counterpart to the username. According to the intentions of LiveJournal designers, these pictures serve to represent the user, disclose elements of his/her identity. The LiveJournal FAQ states that "[u]ser pictures are icons or avatars used to represent yourself, your moods or feelings, your interests, etc. They are displayed in numerous locations on LiveJournal ..." (asciident 2005). An icon appears on a user's journal page, a *user info* page containing selected information about the user appears alongside posts and comments authored by the user.

When it comes to choosing an icon, system administrators provide only a limited set of guidelines that pertain solely to the technical and code levels of an icon. Each picture has to be a .GIF, .JPG, or .PNG file, not larger than 100x100 pixels and with a file size not greater than 40kb. While the definition of the user icon does suggest that the image should be iconic in nature, it is not explicitly stated that a user picture must be a picture of the user. The only limitations concern use of explicit content. LiveJournal FAQ informs users that their pictures, especially the default one, are freely accessible and therefore potentially available to any user. Thus the default picture cannot contain explicit content, while other user pictures can be of a more graphic nature.

A user with a free account is entitled to an *icon pool* of three different pictures, while with a paid account the number increases to 15 different icons. With an additional purchase, a user with a paid account can raise their total number to 100. Additional user icons are one of only a few extensions of the paid suite that a user can purchase. LiveJournal allows users to upload pictures, select the default one, and assign keywords, which later are used to select a picture accompanying particular posts and comments.

LiveJournal FAQ provides little advice about creating an icon and formatting it so that the technical limitations are met. In order to do so, access to and at least basic competency with graphics or photography software is required. The FAQ states only that: "[y]ou have the option to create a userpic yourself. In order to do this, you will need an image-editing program. If you do not have an image-editing program, you may wish to use your favorite search engine to find one. You can also find a userpic from a website or from a LiveJournal community" (asciident 2005).

Therefore a user does not have to follow any rules or guidelines regarding the creation and usage of icons, and neither is much guidance given. Due to this lack of prescribed uses, and to minimal technical limitations (the size of the image being the only significant one), a user icon is an open tool. An analysis of user icons on LiveJournal shows that with time the way they were used went beyond the simple representation imagined by system's designers. The ability to freely create icons is coupled with the possibility of selecting, from one's icon pool, an icon appropriate for the given situation. This allows users to control both a user pool, which can be considered a way of visualizing their personality or identity, as well as the default icon displayed on a user's journal and icons shown alongside posts and comments. In this manner a seemingly simple feature becomes a potentially versatile medium for not only representing, but also expressing oneself and communicating with others. As we will later see, the usage of icons commonly goes beyond displaying one's photograph.

The user icon as a medium and a body of specific user icons are the subject of this chapter. An icon is a *media species*, as well as a population of individual icons. The species itself has its own life cycle, as uses develop and evolve over time and initially prescribed uses become but a starting point for cultural innovation. It is through contact with users that an icon becomes a hybrid of initial assumptions or specifications and ever new practices, expectations, and imaginations. We can compare the difference that exists between prescribed and actual uses to the distinction between *langue* and *parole* made by De Saussure (1991). User icons can be understood as serving several purposes at once: (1) a tool designed by LiveJournal programmers to fulfill a certain function both within a single journal and in a system of hyperlinked journals; (2) a tool and medium made available to the users, who adapt it to their own uses and needs, transforming its function and potential; or (3) a body of cultural content stored by users on LiveJournal servers and displayed as user icons.

The user icon is a layered phenomenon. A tripartite layer model has been initially proposed by Benkler (2000), who distinguished the physical, code and content layers of the Internet. In the case of user icons, the influence of the physical layer is of secondary importance, as it does not directly affect the icon that exists in an environment formed by several sublayers of the code and content layers, such as the World Wide Web and the LiveJournal application. I therefore distinguish instead between the layers of code, content, and interaction. At the level of code, an icon is a field in an individual database entry, which can store a bit of content data that meets a set of requirements. At the content level, an icon is an image visible in the user's browser. At the interaction level, icons are material artifacts to which cultural practice and social behavior are tied.

The life cycle of an icon as a medium begins when the icon is a potential form with a prescribed usage defined in its code layer. At a later stage, the user icon turns into millions of existing images and displays a complexity and variety typical of the everyday life of LiveJournal users, in which these icons, as tools and objects of popular culture, are involved.

The use made of an icon by a user is influenced by several factors present at different layers of an icon. It is partially defined by the architecture of the icon's code, partially by a prescribed usage, which is a norm defined by LiveJournal's creators (and enforced not only through system's code), and partially by individual experience: by observing other's icons and uses made of them—a collective history of icon usage.

LiveJournal icons are an interesting cultural phenomenon for several reasons. Firstly, they constitute an opportunity to analyze the relation between an initially prescribed use and the actual use patterns developed by users. Or put in other words, to analyze the differences between the imaginations of the creators and users. Media designed as open and interactive have a potential to support cultural innovation. The end-to-end argument (Saltzer, Reed, & Clark, 1984) describes a telecommunication network like the Internet, which by remaining open and simple, effectively hands over control of the service to end users and thus fosters innovation of usage (Lessig, 2000). Alongside improved innovation, an end-to-end network has normative benefits: greater diversity of participating groups and weaker third party control or censorship (Sandvig, 2002). Uses that icons are put to become varied with time and grow beyond the frames set by LiveJournal's creators. Like the Internet, both the LiveJournal system and its user icons form a medium that does not discriminate against transmitted content. In each case, an open code layer supports a varied and vibrant culture at the content level. The Internet thus has a recursive structure and its parts display similar characteristics to the Internet itself. Embedded in the online media environment are media forms that serve as both containers for content and content-generating structures. Multiplicity and variation of forms that grow from a relatively simple and limited medium proves the hypertrophic nature of modern culture. The user icon is but one simple feature of a single online application, yet it involves a wide number of users and supports varied and lively cultural production.

It is difficult to find direct parallels to user icon usage in off-line or predigital culture. The production of user icons depends on the ability to cheaply and easily find, copy, and transform content, offered by digital tools. When searching for similarities we can compare LiveJournal icons and their uses to:

1.   fashion elements, such as pins, t-shirt designs, or patches;
2.   scrapbooks with clippings from color magazines;
3.   teenage bedrooms, filled with posters and photos;
4.   graffiti, stencils, stickers, and other forms of individual expression in public space; and
5.   ID documents or membership cards.

My analysis focuses upon icons as symbolic tools and the varied uses made of them. I am less interested in their content and avoid interpreting their meaning or significance. An accurate interpretation is difficult if not impossible and we should heed the warning of Barthes, who describes the "terror of uncertain signs" (Barthes, 1977, p. 39). The meaning of visual content is almost limitless and thus uncertain when they are placed out of context and not fixed by text information, as is often the case in digital media, characterized by an ease of recombining content.

First of all, it is often difficult not only to establish the origin and authorship of a given icon, but also to ascertain whether the given content is a product of the media industry or a popular cultural production. This is due to the fact that homemade, visual Web content can today be of similar quality as commercial content, especially in the case of objects that are relatively small and of low resolution. High levels of cultural competence are required to identify content and to understand the web of allusions, parallels, and citations weaved by LiveJournal users. Secondly, a single icon is displayed in the multiple contexts of different Web pages, text, and other images. It has a different meaning when displayed alongside all of the user's icons in the icon pool, different when present—like a digital crest—in a prominent place at the user's journal and yet another when displayed alongside individual posts and comments. A researcher can also easily extract icons from the system and attempt to analyze them on their own. Following Barthes (1977), we should interpret the meaning of icons as only one layer in a wider web of meanings. However, this would quickly force us to deal with the complexity of analyzed environment, which I tried to avoid by focusing on the user icon as a single, simple feature. LiveJournal content in general, as experienced by the researcher, is separated from the everyday lives of its users and creators, it is but one aspect of a whole largely invisible to a student of online culture.

I believe though that we can also think of icons as a medium with which the researcher can visualize a given cultural phenomenon. While researchers of new media still lack tools for analysis and interpretation of online materials, the visualization of cultural phenomena through a focus on their visual aspect can be a valid method for dealing with encountered complexity. Bendyk (2002), in his analysis of the Bovine Spongiform Encephalopathy (BSE) epidemic, shows how public perception of the threat—an infectious particle known as prion—was changed by visualization techniques: "3D visualization software made the prion, until then an abstract concept for most people, come alive" (Bendyk, 2002, p. 154). Bendyk observes that visualization can provide insight that is imprecise or even false, but the same can occur when we try to grasp complex phenomena with concepts. The term translation (*traduction*) is used in Actor Network Theory to describe a process of reality construction, in which a single actor speaks on behalf of others and imposes upon them his/her own description, and therefore construction, of reality. In the process, "identity of actors, the possibility of interaction and the margins of manoeuvre are negotiated and delimited" (Callon, 1999, p. 203). Translation involves opening and closing of phenomena, so they can either be disclosed as complex or made to look like simple "black boxes." Cyberbolic analysis of new media is criticized by Woolgar (2002) as an example of translation that takes a complex phenomenon and translates it into a homogeneous system with uniform uses and effects.

User icons exist in a space where mass media content and popular cultural content, arising out of everyday life, meet. They therefore allow the researcher both to trace the boundary line and study interactions between the two spheres. We can see how the online lives of LiveJournal users, represented in digital traces such as user icons, are no longer part of the everyday, but are rather elements of the process of popular culture. LiveJournal icons are one of many tools through which people negotiate their relations with dominant cultural content and construct their mediated lives.

User icons are many things at once. They form interface spaces between a dominant culture produced by media industries and the everyday realities of users. They are also tools used by users to build identities with the help of dominant media products and they inject these identities into the shared cultural sphere. They are hybrids formed from cultural, media and technical elements.

Popular Culture in the Predigital Era

LiveJournal user pics are a manifestation of popular culture. Fiske (1992) defines popular culture as the process, in which resources provided by a dominant cultural system are excorporated by subordinate users, who make their own culture out of it. By focusing upon excorporation, rather than incorporation of people in the system, Fiske provides an alternative to a pessimistic approach to modern culture that has its roots in the works of the Frankfurt School. Fiske assumes that "[t]he people are not a passive, helpless mass incapable of discrimination and thus at the economic, cultural and political mercy of the barons of the industry" (Fiske 1987b). Attempts at incorporating them made by the dominant cultural system are a sign of popular vitality and creativity.

Popular culture is not pop culture and the adjective *popular* does not describe a popularity measured by top hits lists. Popular culture is an autonomous cultural sphere created by and for people at the interface between the dominant cultural industries and everyday life. According to Fiske (1992), cultural commodities circulate not in one, but two different and partially autonomous economies. They are produced in the financial economy of the dominant cultural industry, but later transfer to the cultural economy, in which consumers are also producers. In this second economy production is not for profit, and it is not the products of the dominant cultural industry but meanings and pleasures that are the most important circulating commodities (Fiske 1992). The dominant culture provides the popular culture with resources, but it only to some extent controls their later transformations. Popular culture is a sphere of active reception, interpretation, and transformation of content produced by dominant cultural industries, mainly the mass media. While in itself it is active and vital, popular culture is described by Fiske as always a reaction to the dominant culture. Some cultural commodities have the potential to trigger popular cultural activity. They have an open character and invite new uses or interpretations. Such cultural innovation can be based not only upon the acceptation, but also evasion or opposition to encountered meanings.

There are therefore different terms in which the relationship between dominant cultural industries and popular culture can be described. The majority of metaphors used are based on the concept of conflict or combat. Eco describes activities that "restore a critical dimension to passive reception" or "urge the audience to control the message and its multiple possibilities of interpretation," as semiological guerrilla warfare (Eco, 1987, p. 144). Michel de Certeau speaks of poachers, who encroach and steal cultural goods without being caught or even subject to the laws of the territory (De Certeau, 1998). Fiske (1992) writes that popular culture has to do with treachery, robbery, sleight-of-hand games played with the cultural industry: "To attract consumers is to attract tricksters; encouraging consumption encourages trickery, robbery, *la perruque*" (p. 41).

Jenkins (1998) suggests that metaphors of conflict account for only one stream of popular cultural activity, one which he calls "culture jamming". He distinguishes it from "cultural poaching". Cultural jamming is more radical and closer, as an intellectual position, to the pessimism of the Frankfurt School. Culture jammers define themselves as outsiders who attempt to liberate their own lives and the lives of others from the mass media that encroach and invade their lives. Cultural poaching in turn is rather a form of cultural symbiosis or parasitism that works not beyond the cultural system, but within its bounds. Poachers participate in the dominant culture, but see themselves as creators and reject the possibility of being marginalized to the position of passive receivers. Both strains of popular cultural activity thus attempt to fulfill the postulate of semiotic democracy, according to which in a good society each one should participate in the creation of meanings that circulate in a culture (Fisher, 2001; Fiske, 1987a). While both are forms of collective cultural action, jamming attempts to achieve what Melucci (1996) calls a breach of the limits of compatibility of the cultural system, while cultural poaching exists largely within the system's limits. It is the latter of these two strains that the most popular cultural activities present at LiveJournal fit into.

Protest activities are traditionally understood as antagonistic, system-breaching, collective actions. Cultural poaching does not fit this definition, as it does not attempt to breach the system's limits. Galloway (2004) believes that we need to redefine protest because of the changing nature of power, against which it is directed. Galloway describes a form of distributed, decentralized control, which has been gaining importance in the modern world. It is a procedural form of power exhibited for instance by protocols running at the code layer of the Internet. Resistance to distributed control cannot be based upon the traditional notion of protest, but the concept of hypertrophy: "The goal is not to destroy technology in some neoluddite delusion, but to push technology into a hypertrophic state, further than it is meant to go ... Then, during the passage of technology into this injured, engorged, and unguarded condition, it will be sculpted anew into something better, something in closer agreement with the real wants and desires of its users" (Galloway & Thacker, 2004). Popular cultural activity at LiveJournal is an example of such hypertrophic cultural activity.

Digital Media and the Transformation of Popular Culture

Fiske wrote *Understanding Popular Culture* in 1989, 2 years before the invention of the World Wide Web by Tim Berners-Lee and several years before rapid growth of Internet use began. Popular culture, according to Fiske, circulates in the context of three types of content: primary texts or original cultural commodities; secondary texts that directly refer to them, such as reviews, criticism, or advertisements; and tertiary texts that are the process of everyday life: conversations, patterns of dressing, acting, or dwelling.

In the dominant mode of popular cultural activity, people take ready-made products and replace ready-made meanings with ones they themselves produce. Commodities that are reused later in the process of popular culture are according to Fiske (1992) poor in meaning, insufficient, "resources to be used disrespect-fully, not objects to be admired and venerated" (p. 123). Popular culture takes these incomplete cultural objects and fills them with meanings that make them relevant in everyday life. In this manner, a contradictory culture is formed. It relies upon simple, even unimaginative resources provided by the dominant cultural industry and produces content characterized by "subtle complexity, dense texture of human sentiment and of social existence" (Fiske, 1992, p. 120). Popular culture uses all three types of content, but by itself produces only tertiary texts. Among these most numerous are conversations, through which viewers, readers, and listeners redefine the meaning of cultural commodities. It is also produced through dress styles, patterns of behavior, and lifestyle choices. Ephemeral manifestations of popular culture coexist with cultural commodities without displacing them. "With very few and very marginal exceptions, people cannot and do not produce their own commodities, material or cultural, as they may have done in tribal or folk societies. In capitalist societies there is no so-called authentic folk culture ..." wrote Fiske (1992, p. 27). Predigital times were a period of the Dark Ages for popular creativity (Lessig, 2001). The production of autonomous content, that is, content not derived from commodities produced by cultural industries, was marginal and its distribution was limited and local.

The relation between two segments of contemporary culture, as described by Fiske (1992) or De Certeau (1998), are based upon several key dichotomies: large and small; constant and in flux; and cumbersome and nimble. John Fiske explained the distinction between dominant and popular culture by describing the former as "places" built by the powerful and the latter as "spaces" temporarily set up in these places by the weak (Fiske, 1992). De Certeau (1998) describes the powerful as cumbersome, unimaginative, and over organized. These traits allow "the weak," or producers of popular culture, to dwell in dominant content, appropriate it, and to "speak [their own] meanings with their language" (Fiske, 1992, p. 36).

The difference between dominant and popular culture is related to the type of media at the disposal of the two cultures. The cumbersome and slow character of dominant culture is in part an effect of the relative stability and durability of media and objects, to which it is tied. Dominant cultural commodities often take the shape of relatively durable material artifacts like newspapers, books, DVDs, or toys. Otherwise they gain significance and importance as content is broadcast into—so as to almost saturate—the majority, if not the whole, of a society. Actor Network Theory uses the term *immutable mobiles* to describe objects that retain their shape and characteristics while moving through space and time (Law, 2000). With such objects, and thanks to their durability, power can be enforced and sustained at a distance. An analysis of popular cultural activities shows that such objects are not necessarily immobile. Cultural commodities enforce certain meanings, but at the same time are open to appropriation and reworking of carried meanings. "To be popular, the commodities of the cultural industries must not only be polysemic—that is, capable of producing multiple meanings and pleasures—they must be distributed by media whose modes of consumption are equally open and flexible" (Fiske, 1992, p. 158). In other words, with time and at a certain distance, they become mutable.

In contrast, the creators of popular culture are quick and nimble, unencumbered by products that need to be distributed or property that needs to be protected. Popular culture is not a cultural industry and does not need legal, distribution, or marketing apparatuses. Material artifacts of popular culture, if any, were distributed in circuits that were either local or marginal and in both cases informal and based upon a nonfinancial economy. Lacking the capability to produce immutable mobiles, popular culture is unable to widely propagate its own meanings.

Digital media have transformed popular culture as much as they are changing the shape of the media market and cultural industries. Today, popular culture still exists at the borderline between dominant cultural content and everyday life, yet the growing popularity and diffusion of digital media in the society means that this interface space is, to a growing extent, digital and online. Mizuko Ito (in press) describes how contemporary popular culture is characterized by a coupling of collective imagination with digital technologies. These have revolutionized the popular production and distribution of symbolic goods by lowering the costs, time, and effort necessary to produce and distribute cultural products. Through these technologies, meanings that were until now ephemeral became anchored in relatively stable digital content.

Since the last decade of the 20th century, the growing influence and popularity of the Internet and other digital media transformed the conditions in which popular culture is both produced and distributed. Digital media gave popular culture the ability to distribute—at least potentially—content at a speed and range comparable to the capabilities of broadcast media. Most of these changes have by now been well documented, and the Internet is commonly described as capable of lowering all sorts of costs that hinder cultural production. Increased ease with which people can actively participate in their culture significantly affects the process of popular culture.

Yet the character of popular culture is most profoundly changed by the fact that digital media give people the potential to produce symbolic goods that are no longer ephemeral, scarce, and only locally available. Digital popular culture is capable of producing not only what Fiske defined as tertiary, but also secondary texts (Fiske, 1992). Potentially digital media enable people even to create their own primary texts, a body of autonomous cultural content that is closest to what Fiske calls "authentic folk culture" (Fiske, 1992, p. 27). Digital popular culture is thus able to acquire its own immutable mobiles, objects that can propagate in digital environments, allowing popular culture to grow in size and significance.

Predigital popular culture existed on a small scale, partially invisible to the dominant culture with its cultural industries, which it easily tricked, thus remaining beyond the latter culture's scope of control (Bey, 1985; Fiske, 1992). This changed with the digital means of symbolic production and communication, when every operation involved making a copy (Lessig, 2004). Once ephemeral activities now produce relatively durable, immutable objects, and cultural poachers are now leaving traces of their own actions. Digital environments allow institutions that form dominant cultural industries to easily and efficiently monitor, track, and mine for data. In this manner, the circulation of materials can be controlled or measured, for instance to protect their own intellectual property or to provide data needed to adjust future production and marketing. They also facilitate reciprocal appropriation of popular cultural practices and aesthetics by cultural industries (Jenkins, 1998).

Cultural poaching has been explained as *bricolage* (Jenkins, 1998), the art of "making do with whatever is at hand." Popular cultural production was the domain of the bricoleur: "someone who works with his hands and uses devious means compared to those of a craftsman" (Levi-Strauss, 1966, p. 16). A bricoleur works with a set of parts that is neither planned nor invented—but found, assembled, and appropriated in the conditions of relative scarcity.

Introduction of the digital media into the society has also improved the availability of "raw materials" needed for popular cultural production. In predigital times, before the Internet, cultural commodities could be received as push media broadcasts or had to be bought. The growing World Wide Web places, at the disposal of its users, a rapidly growing body of digital content. Most of this content can be easily accessed and duplicated, albeit cultural industries attempt to an ever greater extent to curb uncontrolled usage through legal and technical means (Lessig, 2004). Content that is accessible on the World Wide Web is much greater than that available through push media, and access to it is often freed from financial constraints. In such conditions, time or attention span and not money become a crucial investment. In a condition of cultural plenitude, when a great range of materials is always at hand, popular cultural production resembles grazing more than poaching. Due to the vastness of contemporary culture, rational selection is not often possible. Due to limited attention spans we are more than ever choosing from but a thin slice of a culture as a whole. Popular cultural production still makes do with what is at hand, but in a digital era this is a strategy for coping with excess and not scarcity. Bricolage is a mode of experiencing and appropriating a culture characterized by complexity, in which no order is visible and whose elements cannot be "drawn together and properly assembled" (Law & Mol, 2002, pp. 14-15).

As a result of a partial transfer online of both dominant and popular culture, the two spheres began resembling each other to a greater extent. The changing conditions of popular cultural production and distribution weakened the distinction between cumbersome dominant culture and nimble popular culture. Online, all cultural phenomena begin coexisting in a single symbolic space, which furthermore is collectively imagined as a space in which the digital aspect of the process of everyday life is situated. Primary, secondary, and tertiary cultural texts coexist and interact in a relatively homogeneous space of the Internet and the World Wide Web, under protocological control of basic Internet protocols at the code layer of the medium (Galloway, 2004). Equally important are the decreased distance and difference between dominant and popular culture, as well as a mutual contamination occurring between these two cultures and everyday life. This according to Lash and Urry (1994) is characteristic of what they call the post-modern condition, in which cultural forms increasingly form a part of social reality that is not distinguished as different or specific. In post-modernity, "an audience is sensitized to the reception of such cultural objects because of 'semiotics of everyday life' in which the boundary between the cultural and life, between the image and the real, is more than ever transgressed" (Lash & Urry, 1994, p. 135).

Popular Culture at Code and Content Layers of LiveJournal

Predigital popular culture could have been imagined as existing in spaces temporarily established at the border or interface, with the dominant culture. In the digital era, the Internet and World Wide Web have provided an environment in which places—symbolic, but nevertheless real—of popular culture can be created. LiveJournal users are not poaching its online cultural resources, but rather producing popular culture in a place that in their imaginations can be inhabited, settled upon. It is a place where humans often dwell only temporarily, as proved by the majority of blogs left fallow by its creators. Still content dwells forever or at least until the death of the server. While our everyday lives remain in constant flux, their record on the Internet, or the objects of online popular culture, remain and are largely static. This is the "dark matter that gets left behind to molder in data vaults and arcane archives as we progress into a great digital future" (Nolan & Levesque, 2005, p. 35). LiveJournal is a place, not a space of popular culture. In this place, popular meanings are not injected into preexisting content by rogue actors, but constitute primary content produced there. Raw digital materials, that is, cultural commodities, are not produced on-site, but brought into the LiveJournal environment. However, to fully understand the process of popular culture at LiveJournal, we should once again distinguish between the code and content layers. At the code level, users took an informational infrastructure crafted by LiveJournal's creators and adapted the relatively open tools to their own needs. The LiveJournal system itself is to an extent sluggish and unimaginative, dependent upon a certain path coded into its interface and database, a certain historic condition in which Brad Fitzpatrick decided to write the system, and a simple view of future uses imagined by the system's creators. These coded tools have been taken by users and appropriated for new uses. While the code remained the same, LiveJournal as a digital tool grew beyond its initial boundaries.

Furthermore, some of the new and innovative uses of LiveJournal have repurposed it as a tool for the digital production of popular cultural content. LiveJournal is also what Fiske (1992) calls a producerly cultural form. Although accessible and open, it has "gaps ... wide enough for whole new texts to be produced in them" (p. 104). With time, LiveJournal became a space in which popular culture could be performed. Elements of its coded infrastructure could be treated as tools for popular cultural production. LiveJournal user icon is one such tool, originally imagined as a method of personal representation that at some point started being used for popular reuse of dominant content.

The LiveJournal User Icon as
a Site of Popular Culture

User icon usage does not follow a single pattern, but is rather a family of uses that begins with a limited set of uses envisioned by system's creators and then evolves into a dynamic system of both conformist and innovative uses. The user icon was initially designed as an iconic sign that signifies its user based on the principle of similarity. It has been later redefined into a primarily symbolic sign. The relation between the sign and the user became based upon an arbitrary, agreed convention. User icons contain faces and cropped facial details; celebrities, fictional characters, animated characters, and other people; animals and cartoon creatures; slogans and drawings; landscapes and objects; actors, musicians, and models; users, friends, and strangers. To some extent they retain their prescribed function, so that every image displayed can be interpreted as signifying a given user. Yet we must assume that in the case of many icons the representation of the user is neither the sole or primary goal. The sum of all LiveJournal user icons is a quite faithful visualization of culture as a whole, albeit divided into fragments the size of 100 pixels to a side.

While the interpretation of user icon content goes beyond the scope of this chapter, it is worth making several remarks in this regard. Such an interpretation is a daunting task and does not provide direct insight into the lives and identities of users, hidden behind "photo shopped" layers of images. Nolan and Levesque propose that it is never a real identity, but only an "identity map" (2005, p. 35) that can be recreated from online content—an approximation of the real person. It is worth adding that such identity maps are created not just by researchers and human hackers described by Nolan and Levesque, but by all users. An online persona does not have to take the form of a three-dimensional virtual visualization. More commonly, it is an imaginary actor constructed by others on the basis of available content relating to the given person.

If we treat the user icon as a tool for visualization of contemporary culture and society, then the icon suggests that we live in a reality in which the lines between mediated content and real lives became blurred. The space of user icons is an environment, in which representations of users coexist mostly with cultural commodities. The ecosystem of LiveJournal user icons is monotonous and depleted, inhabited by users, celebrity images, and other mass mediated content, texts, and slogans and abstract or digital backgrounds. Given the possibility to freely represent and express oneself, users opt to rework cultural commodities and insert themselves into their mix. Other than photographs of oneself, there are few signs of primary cultural texts produced by users who do not choose to represent or express themselves with images of loved ones, favorite objects, or places that are part of their everyday, off-line existence.

As is the case with every medium, LiveJournal users are to a varying extent innovative in their use of icons. Of all users, two partially overlapping communities, *fandom* and *icon makers*, are most involved in innovative cultural production with the use of icons. Fans participate in a culture in a manner that is extravertous and hypersocial (Ito, 2005), active enthusiastic and partisan (Fiske, 1992). Fandom prefers cultural poaching to jamming, a mode of appropriation that is dialogic with the dominant culture and respectful of mainstream consumption of the media (Jenkins, 1998). Cultural poachers mainly care about the right to self-expression and reworking of cultural material for their own interests and pleasures. "Fans respond to this situation of an increasingly privatized culture by applying the traditional practices of a folk culture to mass culture, treating film or television as if it offered them raw materials for telling their own stories and resources for forging their own communities" (Jenkins, 1998). Icon making is a hobby, a form of digital craftsmanship and artistic production. For icon makers, a user icon is not just a medium, but also a popular art form. Both types of groups perform popular culture with the use of a user icon, a medium provided by LiveJournal's creators; dominant mass mediated content and a repertoire of techniques of icon creation. For fandom communities, style and techniques developed by icon makers are of secondary importance to playful appropriation of meanings and expression of attachment to their favored cultural commodities. Icon makers place greater emphasis upon cultural production of icons as an artistic activity. In both cases, icon *pics* become a symbolic currency that circulates within these communities, used to express oneself, but also to sustain social relations and establish an individual reputation.

While practically every LiveJournal user is an icon maker, I reserve the term for those users that pay particular attention to this medium and furthermore self-define themselves as such. Icon making is hypersocial. It reflects "forms of sociality augmented by dense sets of technologies, signifiers, and systems of exchange" (Ito, 2005, p. 6), which according to Ito are characteristic of the popular culture of youth and children today. Online hypersocial relations are based in textual conversations taking place in makers' and communal journals, but are first of all sustained through the circulation of icons.

Icon makers have developed a specific aesthetic and style. User icons made by them are usually a collage of three elements: a human face or figure, a short text or slogan, and an abstract pattern or design serving as the background. Icons seem to have evolved into a form that most fully utilizes the limited resources at hand (in particular screen and server space) to perform digital popular culture— that is, to signify user's attachment, involvement, and interaction with cultural commodities.

Icon makers communicate through specialized journals and communities that can play several different functions. They can be: (1) virtual "shops," in which makers accept requests from others; (2) showcases of works; or (3) competition spaces with contests that establish the value of works and artists. Icon making is a social activity and icon makers usually compare their works, accept commissions, or allow others to copy and reuse their icons. It is a community based upon an economy of reputation and the circulation of user icons. A maker's reputation depends upon the quality of his/her works: aesthetic merit, ability to perform popular cultural appropriation, and technical skill.

The last factor seems especially interesting, as makers pay much attention to icon-making techniques. Icon making requires skills with two-dimensional graphics software; an understanding of disc space usage by graphic files and factors that affect their size; and know-how of appropriate digital brushes, fonts, and techniques. Many icon makers are distinguished by an understanding of the relation between displayed content and the code layer of an icon. Icon making is similar to the *demoscene*, a hacker subculture whose members competed to create short but intense digital graphics called demos. It also has parallels with the "5k contest," a Web-design competition organized since 1999, in which designers create Web sites of no more than 5kb in size.

While icon makers naturally have varying skills and talent, some of them fit the description of what Leadbetter and Miller (2004) call Pro-Amateurs: "committed and networked amateurs working to professional standards" (p. 9).

Of all LiveJournal users, fans and icon makers are communities that have developed most unorthodox uses for the user icon. To give a final example, a text field set up in the system as a space for a short description of an icon has been used in icon-making communities to attribute the authorship of the author—a function that is crucial in a nonfinancial economy based upon reputation. In such a case, the original function of the icon—the representation of a user—is pushed beyond the icon's boundaries. System's administrators later introduced the possibility of commenting icons, possibly in reaction to this practice.

Ito (2004, 2005) describes popular culture of Japanese youth as a coupling of two "sociotechnical innovations": the hypersociality mentioned previously, supported by digital communication and file-sharing networks, with what she calls "media mixes." A media mix "integrates different media forms through licensed character content" (Ito, 2004, p. 31), a "heterogeneous but integrated web of reference" (Ito, 2004, p. 31) anchored in cultural commodities and technologies. Media mixes, argues Ito, create relatively open and porous intertextual networks with which popular culture can interact.

The content reused at LiveJournal is part of wider media mixes, in which images of celebrities or fictional characters are present as well as videoclips, posters, movies, newspaper and magazine articles, t-shirts, DVDs, and so on. Yet LiveJournal seems detached from such mixes. Ito (2005) describes a process of constant negotiation that occurs between dominant and popular interests inside Japanese media mixes. Cultural industries are absent at LiveJournal and do not attempt to commodify or profit from popular cultural activities occurring on the site. LiveJournal is indeed, paradoxically, invisible to the powerful. We can only assume that the site itself retains its autonomous character only because the everyday lives of its users have already been colonized. Yet LiveJournal is not a site of a popular cultural rebellion directed at the dominant culture, but a space in which consumers decide to perform acts of cultural poaching and grazing.

Conclusion: Petri Dishes and Digital Folk Culture

A user icon is an empty "container": a field in the database, a bit of space on a server, a space on a journal's Web page. Such a container is itself a simple form that expresses minimal preferences regarding the content that it can store. We can compare it to a petri dish filled with a selective medium, upon which a bacterial culture can flourish. This metaphor accounts both for the robustness of activities rooted in a simple media form and for the organic manner in which patterns of usage develop over time. We can draw a conclusion from the case of user icons that popular cultural activities flourish when anchored in already existing content and structure. As long as the architecture is not too restrictive, users are drawn by the presence of some (not necessarily optimal) interface and architecture, the presence of social and cultural conventions, and the presence of others. LiveJournal is like a city, whose "dwellers are not necessarily smarter than other human beings—but the density of space occupation results in a concentration of needs. And so questions are asked in the city that have not been asked elsewhere ..." (Bauman, 2003, p. 104).

I used the example of LiveJournal user icons to present the life cycle of a digital medium, characterized by a relation between a medium that is open at the layer of code and culture that flourishes at the level of content. As such, it is a case study of the robustness and capacity to innovate that is inherent in popular culture. I argue that the Internet is both filled with digital petri dishes of varying size and itself shares structural characteristics with the LiveJournal user icon.

References

asciident. (2005). FAQ—Userpics. Retrieved September 10, 2005, from http://www.livejournal.com/support/faq

Barthes, R. (1997). *Image-Music-Text.* New York: Hill and Wang.

Bauman, Z. (2003). *Liquid love. On the frailty of human bonds.* Cambridge, UK: Polity Press.

Bendyk, E. (2002). *Zatruta studnia. Rzecz o wBadzy i wolnosci. [Poisoned Well. On Power and Freedom}.* Warszawa, Poland: Wydawnictwo W.A.B.

Benkler, Y. (2000). From consumers to users: Shifting the deeper structures of regulation toward sustainable commons and user access. *Federal Communications Law Journal, 52*(3), 561-579.

Bey, H. (1985). *The temporary autonomous zone, ontological anarchy, poetic terrorism.* Retrieved September 10, 2005, from http://www.hermetic.com/bey/taz_cont.html

Callon, M. (1999). Some elements of a sociology of translation: Domestication of the scallops and the fishermen of Saint Brieuc Bay. In M. Biagioli (Ed.), *The science studies reader* (pp. 67-83). London: Routledge.

De Certeau, M. (1998). *The practice of everyday life.* Minneapolis: University of Minnesota Press.

De Saussure, F. (1959). *Course in general linguistics.* New York: Philosophical Library.

Dery, M. (1993). *Culture jamming: Hacking, slashing and sniping in the empire of signs.* Retrieved June 15, 2004, from http://www.levity.com/markdery/culturjam.html

Eco, U. (1987). *Travels in hyperreality.* London: Picador.

Fisher, W. W. (2001). Theories of intellectual property. In S. Munzer (Ed.), *New essays in the legal and political theory of property.* Cambridge University Press.

Fiske, J. (1987a). *Television culture.* London: Routledge.

Fiske, J. (1987b). TV: Re-situating the popular in the people. *Continuum: The Australian Journal of Media & Culture, 1*(2), 56-66. Retrieved September 10, 2005, from http://www.mcc.murdoch.edu.au/ReadingRoom/1.2/Fiske.html

Fiske, J. (1992). *Understanding popular culture.* London: Routledge.

Galloway, A. (2004). *Protocol.* Cambridge, MA: The MIT Press.

Galloway, A., & Thacker, E. (2004, March 24). The limits of networking. *Nettime*. Retrieved September 10, 2005, from http://amsterdam.nettime.org/ Lists-Archives/nettime-l-0403/msg00090.html

Ito, M. (2004, Winter). Technologies of the childhood imagination. *Items and Issues, 4*(4). Retrieved September 10, 2005, from http://www.ssrc.org/ programs/publications_editors/publications/items/online4-4/ito-childhood.pdf

Ito, M. (in press). Technologies of the childhood imagination: Yugioh, media mixes, and everyday cultural production. In J. Karaganis & N. Jeremijenko (Eds.), *Structures of participation in digital culture*. Durham, NC: Duke University Press.

Jenkins, H. (1998). *The poachers and the stormtroopers: Popular culture in the digital age*. Retrieved September 10, 2005, from http://web.mit.edu/ cms/People/henry3/pub/stormtroopers.htm

Lash, S., & Urry, J. (1994). Postmodernist sensibility. In A. Giddens, D. Held, S. Loyal, D. Seymour, & J. Thompson (Eds.), *The polity reader in cultural theory* (pp. 134-140). Cambridge, UK: Polity Press.

Law, J. (2000). *Objects, spaces, others*. Retrieved September 10, 2005, from http://www.lancs.ac.uk/fss/sociology/papers/law-objects-spaces-others.pdf

Law, J., & Mol, A. (2002). *Complexities: Social studies of knowledge practices*. Durham, NC: Duke University Press.

Leadbetter, C., & Miller, P. (2004). *The pro-am revolution. How enthusiasts are changing our economy and society*. London: Demos.

Lessig, L. (2000, March 27). Innovation, regulation and the Internet. *The American Prospect, 11*(10). Retrieved September 10, 2005, from http:// www.prospect.org/print/V11/10/lessig-l.html

Lessig, L. (2001). *The future of ideas: The fate of the commons in a connected world*. New York: Random House.

Lessig, L. (2004). *Free culture. How big media uses technology and the law to lock down culture and control creativity*. New York: The Penguin Press.

Levi-Strauss, C. (1966). *The savage mind*. Chicago: University of Chicago Press.

Melucci, A. (1996). *Challenging codes. Collective action in the information age*. Cambridge: Polity Press.

Nolan, J., & Levesque, M. (2005, February). Hacking human: Data-archaeology and surveillance in social networks. *ACM SIGGROUP Bulletin, 25*(2), 33-37.

Reed, D., Saltzer, J., & Clark, J. (1984). End-to-End arguments in system design. *ACM Transactions on Computer Systems, 2*(4), 195-206.

Sandvig, C. (2002, November 22-23). *Communication infrastructure and innovation: The Internet as end-to-end network that isn't.* Paper prepared for the AAAS/Columbia/Rutgers Joint Research Symposium with the Next Generation of Leaders in Science and Technology Policy, Washington, DC.

Tarde, G. (1999). *Monadologie et socialogie.* Paris: Les Empêcheurs de penser en rond.

Woolgar, S. (Ed.). (2002). *Virtual society? Technology, cyberbole, reality.* Oxford University Press.

Section III:
Creative Industries

Chapter VIII

Creative London?
Investigating New Modalities of Work in the Cultural Industries

David Lee, Goldsmiths College, University of London, UK

Abstract

This chapter considers the emergence of the discourse of creativity in contemporary economic, political, and social life, and the characteristics of emerging labour markets in the cultural industries. In particular it is concerned with analysing the working experiences of a number of individuals working in the cultural industries in London. Using a critical theoretical framework of understanding, it examines the importance of cultural capital, subjectivisation, governmentality, network sociality, and individualization as key concepts for understanding the experience of labour in the creative economy. This chapter considers how creative individuals negotiate the precarious, largely freelance, deregulated and de-unionised terrain of contemporary work. As the economic becomes increasingly inflected by the cultural in contemporary social life, the terrain of experience of individuals working in these expanding sectors has been neglected in cultural studies. This chapter seeks to critically intervene in this area, arguing that the "creative" turn in contemporary discourse can be seen to mask emergent inequalities and exploitative practices in the post-industrial employment landscape.

Introduction

Everywhere we turn in contemporary society, we are being encouraged to be creative. In today's "knowledge economy," where we are told we are "living on thin air" (Leadbeater, 1999) the imperative to be creative has taken on the ideological force of a moral edict: something that we should all aspire to. Influential political literature tells us that we are living in the "Creative Age" (Bentley & Seltzer, 1999), commentators speak of the rise of the "creative class" (Florida, 2002) and businesses are told to display "creative leadership" (Guntern, 1998). Indeed creativity is no longer presented as a choice in such discourse; it becomes compulsory if one is to survive the vicissitudes of global capitalism. A vast plethora of books from self-help literature to popular psychological literature as well as an extensive range of discursive political activity seeks to assure us that creativity is something that we can all achieve, if only we try. As Osborne (2003) argues, "in psychological vocabularies, in economic life, in education and beyond, the values of creativity have taken on the force of a moral agenda" (p. 507).

Creativity, as a key structural necessity of cultural production, has come to be seen as a constitutive element of the contemporary economy. One of the defining features of our times is the ever-increasing fusion of the cultural with the economic within society (see Jameson, 1991; Lash & Urry, 1994). Ours is an economy of "signs and spaces," increasingly dominated by the media, by brands, by advertising, in short by signifying practices. As Lash and Urry (1994) argue "[e]conomic and symbolic processes are more than ever interlaced and interarticulated; that is…the economy is increasingly culturally inflected and … culture is more and more economically inflected" (p. 64). The structural needs of late capitalism demand creative workers in a wide range of areas. The huge growth in the creative industries is concomitant with the emergence of the notion of the *creative economy*. As such, Wang (2004) claims that "'[c]reativity' is redefined as an enterprise sector, intrinsic, not external, to the contemporary technologically-accented knowledge economy" (p. 11). In contemporary society creativity becomes a central element of the discursive regime of the new economy, in which the demands on the individual to demonstrate flexibility, entrepreneurship, and innovation have taken on the hegemonic power of ideology.

In the United Kingdom, the ethos of creativity has become an integral part of the New Labour government. The overt fusion of culture with politics can be seen both as a rebranding exercise as evident in the Cool Britannia project and as a vital component of the bid to transform Britain into a leading global knowledge economy.[1] Yet the creativity explosion is not one that emanates purely from the heavy hand of the state, it also becomes a matter of governmentality, in the Foucauldian sense,[2] one that encourages the development of techniques of the self,[3] and is a discursive process that has become embedded within our very subjectivity. Subsequently, we live in a society where everyone not only wants to be creative but is told and believes that they can be.

This chapter considers the working experiences of a small group of cultural producers working in London's creative economy as a way of exploring the sociological significance of the cultural economy within the context of late modernity. It investigates why creativity has become such a central component of the discourse of everyday life, and how it has become entwined with the social, the political, and the economic. Exploring the importance of identity, reflexivity, and individualization for these "cultural intermediaries,"[4] I argue that the precarious routes that they are obliged to take through the spheres of employment within the creative economy are indicative of a radically transformed world of work. As the relationship between the cultural and the economic becomes ever more entwined in modern society, the question of how these cultural producers negotiate the terrain of the new economy is vital. The new modalities of work in the cultural industries, which are largely freelance, flexible, and entrepreneurial, can be seen as templates for how we are all increasingly having to negotiate our working lives in a state that is "permanently transitional" (McRobbie, 2004).

As today's cultural producers make highly individualized pathways through their working lives, and as the notion of the "portfolio career" becomes more common place, we can see how the traditional notion of a career is radically altering; no longer a "job for life," work becomes transitional and insecure. The increased individualization of late modern social life means that these knowledge workers must "seek personal solutions to systemic contradictions" (Beck & Beck-Gernsheim, 2002, p. 22): they must live with the ever-present possibility of "the breakdown biography" (p. 3). It is clear from my research that the working lives of cultural producers are increasingly precarious. At the same time culture has been appropriated by the state and by transnational corporations for neo-liberal, free-market purposes. With this in mind, the fundamental and underlying questions driving my research for this chapter are: what purposes does the "creative turn" serve within contemporary society, and what are the subjective experiences of those individuals who are working inside the creative economy?

Structurally, the argument that follows is split into two key sections. The first section is a theoretical discussion that seeks to contextualize the cultural economy within the larger historical and social framework of late modernity. This will examine the key literature both in terms of theorizing the cultural economy and also more specifically the research that is available into the study of cultural production and the sociology of work. Through an examination of recent academic and political literature I will attempt to define the scope of the creative economy, and its political significance. Then I will explore the increasingly cultural nature of economic life, followed by an analysis of the inherent reflexivity and individualization in contemporary society and the significance of this for my research. This will be followed by a review of the literature within both media and cultural studies and sociology that helps us to understand the working lives of cultural producers, assessing the importance of subjectivity, discourse, and governmentality.

The second section is an analysis of interviews carried out between July and August 2004 with four individuals working within the creative industries in London. I will attempt to ground the theoretical discussion of the essay in the actual lived and situated experiences of these individuals. The subjects of this analysis come from a variety of backgrounds and ages. All are working within the creative industries as defined by the Department of Culture Media and Sport (DCMS).[5] They have a personal investment with the notion of being "creative" in terms of what they do. As such they fit the criteria of subjects for whom being creative is a deeply important aspect of their lives, and for whom, as Rose (1990) would suggest, "[w]ork is a essential element in the path to self-fulfilment" (p. 118).

Theorizing the Cultural Economy

Worldwide, the creative industries sector has been among the fastest growing sectors of the global economy. (Cunningham, 2004, p. 110)

First let us turn to a consideration of what the creative industries actually are, and how we can assess their social, economic, and political significance. The cultural workers inside the creative economy are employed in a huge variety of different roles, within a rapidly transforming area. In recent years, creative industries have become the subject of intense promotion within political and economic discourse. In 1998 the British government defined the creative industries as being comprised of music, performing arts, publishing, software, TV and radio, film, designer fashion, advertising, arts and antiques, crafts, design, architecture, and interactive leisure software (DCMS, 1998). They are defined as "those industries which have their origin in individual creativity, skill and talent and which have a potential for wealth and job creation through the generation and exploitation of intellectual property" (DCMS, 2001, p. 5).

Concomitantly, in recent years creativity has been put at the top of the political and economic agenda on a global basis. Leadbeater (1999) has declared that "the real assets of the modern economy come out of our heads not out of the ground: ideas, knowledge, skills, talent and creativity" (p. 18). In the U.S., Florida (2002) has announced that there is a dominant new social group in society that he calls the "Creative Class":

[i]f you are a scientist or engineer, an architect or designer, a writer, artist or musician, or if you use your creativity as a key factor in your work of business, education, health care, law or some other profession, you are a member. With 38 million members, more than 30 per cent of the nation's workforce, the Creative Class has shaped and will continue to shape deep and profound shifts in the ways we work, in our values and desires, and in the very fabric of our everyday lives. (p. 9)

On the more local level that I am describing in London, creative industries have become central to regional policy to promote economic growth. A recent report on London's creative industries, *Creative London*, shows the scale of growth of this sector in recent years (London Development Agency, 2004). According to this research, the creative industries contribute £21 billion to London's gross domestic product; one in every five new jobs created in London is in the creative industries, and the sector as a whole now accounts for more than 500,000 jobs in the capital (London Development Agency, 2004). This makes the creative economy second only to financial services in terms of its economic significance in the capital.

Cultural Capitalism

The structural demands of late capitalism mean that increasing numbers of people are now making a living within the creative industries. Jameson (1984) detected the centrality of cultural production to the workings of advanced capitalist economies, asserting that post-modernism, both as a historical condition and as a new cultural aesthetic marked by pastiche, irony, depthlessness, and heterogeneity, needs to be understood from a material, economic basis. Post-modernism occurs in a society where culture has become inextricably connected with the economy and where: "aesthetic production ... has become integrated into commodity production generally: the frantic economic urgency of producing fresh waves of ever more novel-seeming goods at ever greater rates of turnover, now assigns an increasingly essential structural function and position to aesthetic innovation and experimentation" (Jameson, 1991, pp. 4-5). This shift is also one away from an industrial society into a so-called post-industrial society, where services rather than manufacturing and industry have become the economic dominant (Bell, 1973). This supposedly "weightless" economy creates an increased need for cultural producers. In our consumer society, goods have a built in obsolescence and advertising and marketing become crucial. As such, culture becomes not only a major aesthetic consideration, but is also the major driving economic force within society.

More recently Lash and Urry (1994) have argued that we live in an economy of "signs and spaces." By this they mean that business processes have become increasingly acculturated in modern social life, so that the value of a commodity, for example, is indissociable from the power and symbolic capital attached to its "brand." As they note, "[w]hat is increasingly being produced are not material objects, but signs." In this process, "goods often take on the properties of sign-value through the process of 'branding,' in which marketers and advertisers attach images to goods" (Lash & Urry, 1994, p. 15). Structurally, this means there are ever-greater numbers of people working to produce symbolic content. As Lash and Urry (1994) assert: "[w]e thus live in increasingly individuated and symbol-saturated societies in which the advanced-services middle class plays an increasing role in the accumulation process. This class assumes a critical mass in the present restructuration: as symbol-processing producers *and* as consumers of processed symbols working and living in certain towns and cities" (p. 222).

Reflexive Modernization

As the cultural has become fused with the economic, the ongoing processes of individualization and reflexive modernization provide a theoretical framework for understanding the new modalities of work for cultural producers. A number of commentators have examined the processes of detraditionalization that have occurred through modernization, and the impact of this on the individual where subjects become increasingly "reflexive" and are compelled to seek structure and meaning to their lives through a plethora of personal lifestyle choices (see Beck, Giddens, & Lash, 1994). Individualization has become a key trend in contemporary social life, occurring as people are disembedded from traditional social ties of kinship, class, and geography and become more fluid and mobile in their social relationships. As Lash (2002) writes, "individualism is a result of the retreat of the classic institutions: state, class, nuclear family, ethnic group" (pp. 9-10).

This process has profound consequences for the individual. Subjects in individualized societies must take responsibility for themselves. If things go wrong, the answer lies not with society, but with their own personal failings. Indeed, "'individualization' consists in transforming human 'identity' from a 'given' into a 'task'—and charging the actors with the responsibility for performing that task and for the consequences (also the side-effects) of their performance" (Bauman, 2002, p. 15).

Explaining this dynamic, Giddens (1992) argues: "[t]he self today is for everyone a reflexive project—a more or less continuous interrogation of past, present and future. It is a project carried on amid a profusion of reflexive resources: therapy and self-help manuals of all kinds, television programmes and magazine articles" (p. 30). This is certainly evident for my interviewees, who are self-monitoring and order their identities through personal narratives which present themselves as life choices. The "creative" turn which I have described can be seen as a key element of the ongoing process of individualization within late modernity, something for the self to aspire to, that which will bring self-fulfillment. As such it becomes part of the "lifestyle" culture of contemporary society, an individual route to potentially transform one's domestic life, relationship—even one's identity.

Researching Contemporary Cultural Production: The Missing Link

Why has the study into the working lives of cultural producers been so neglected in recent years by academics? Firstly, such work is "production heavy," and "requires intense periods of immersion in the field of study" (Schudson, 2000, p. 257). Access is also a central issue. Although academics have some contact with media professionals and cultural intermediaries, in order to do valid research in this field one needs to have very strong contacts, as gaining access to busy media and creative professionals is a painstaking and time-consuming process. Furthermore, production research has been seen by some as overly celebratory of the industries it studies, in that it "succumbs to the superficial glamour" of the world it attempts to study (Garnham, 1990, p. 11). Critics have also questioned the validity of the methodology of ethnographic research in media and cultural studies, claiming that the interview technique misses the larger questions of power, decision making, and economics within media organizations (Garnham, 1990).

Theorizing Work in the New Cultural Economy

In recent years, however, a number of writers have attempted to make sense of the transformed working landscape of contemporary cultural producers. For example, McRobbie's (2000) engagement with recent social theories of reflexivity, network cultures, governmentality, and individualization has produced some crucial insights into modalities of work within the cultural economy. Addressing Garnham's (1990) point, she acknowledges that there is always the fear that "this kind of work can often convey the field of study as being more autonomous and more cut off from the network of powerful institutions that are its conditions of existence" (McRobbie, 2000, p. 258). However, drawing on the insights of theorists such as Rose (1990, 1999), she argues that the self-promotional strategies used by creative workers that emphasize the glamour of what they do are in fact critical factors in the study of this field: "I would propose that it is precisely the creative dimension, the dynamics of self-promotion and also the sociological nature of 'the glamour' that now ought to be the focus of attention in studies of cultural workers" (McRobbie, 2000, p. 258). Of course, such rewards are only available to a tiny elite of cultural workers, and following this path comes at the expense of job security, decent pay, and a whole array of worker's rights, which are sacrificed on the altar of creativity.

Discourse analysis also provides a convincing means of understanding the role of creativity as a loaded signifier involved in the formation of work-based identities. For example, Du Gay's research (1996, 1997) investigates how workers come to identity with beliefs that closely echo the needs and normative demands imposed on them by capitalism and by the companies that they work for. Du Gay's research exposes the centrality of culture within the contemporary workplace. His insights are essential for understanding the discursive power of creativity for those employed within the cultural industries, as a way of creating "better" contemporary workers. Du Gay suggests that there is a clear reason for this turn to culture in the workplace—profit—in which, "'[c]ulture' is accorded a privileged position ... because it is seen to structure the way people think, feel and act in organizations. The aim is to produce the sort of meanings that will enable people to make the right and necessary contribution to the success of the organization for which they work" (1996, p. 41). Equally, Miller and Rose (1990) argue that economic governance operates through subjects, and so needs to connect with an individual's subjectivity in order to be effective. As they explain, there is an economic rationale for this process: "[g]overnment ... is a 'personal' matter, and many programmes have sought the key to their effectiveness in enrolling individuals as allies in the pursuit of political, economic and social objectives" (Miller & Rose, 1990, pp. 327-328). The promotion of creativity can be interpreted as a fundamental part of economic discourse and governmentality, one in which the creative lifestyle as an individual choice has a wider economic and political purpose. As they suggest: "[o]rganizations are to get the most out of their employees ... by releasing the psychological strivings of individuals for autonomy and creativity and channelling them into the search of the firm for excellence and success" (Miller & Rose, 1990, p. 330). These processes play a vital role in the formation of identity for cultural producers, as we shall now see.

The Cultural Producers

I have chosen to separate the analysis of my interviews into three central themes. Firstly, I will examine the economic realities of making a living in the cultural industries. Secondly, I will explore the importance of creativity to my interviewees. Finally, I will analyse the emergence of *cultural individualization* within the creative economy, through my participants' experiences. Work for these individuals has become a site of intense flux, compelling them to be entrepreneurial and to sell themselves on the labour market on a constant basis. This has had a negative impact on their personal lives in some cases. Yet for all this, these cultural producers loved their work, and the "freedom" that their creative labour gave them. As such, work for them has become a terrain of great risk but also of opportunity and great satisfaction. In the pages that follow I will try to make sense of the complex and often contradictory evidence that I have amassed from my research.

A Risky Business: Making a Living in the Cultural Economy

The working lives that I describe illustrate a shift in which the traditional notion of a career or job for life is disappearing; instead people are more likely to be in a state of semi-employment or multi-activity work. As Beck (2000) argues: "[t]he normal work situation ... has begun to break down, and a political economy of insecurity and differentiation has developed in place of an economy of state-guaranteed social security" (p. 53). For growing numbers of people the "portfolio career" is emerging, filling the vacuum left by the permanent job. This is certainly the pattern of work as experienced by my interviewees. For example, Mark (personal communication, August 2004), the co-founder of a small advertising firm, described the lack of security that he experiences in work:

It's not particularly secure. I mean we constantly have conversations about it, will we be able to continue, have we got enough money? It's hard to say, I've only ever got about 30 days where I'm certain [of work].

Similarly, Catherine (personal communication, August 2004), a television producer/director working in the independent television sector, finds her working life highly precarious at times. When asked about the average length of a contract, Catherine replied:

I've got a long one at the moment, 8 months. But I've had a weekly contract before ... that's about as bad as it gets! Three months is very common for a documentary. I've never had anything longer than 8 months.

Catherine described the tension between managing a creative career in a self-entrepreneurial way and the impact that it can have on your emotional life:

At times I feel incredibly insecure ... The positive way of trying to look at the career is always looking for new skills and new challenges and just keeping moving, taking the work that comes my way. But the actual feeling, what it's actually like to work really, really hard and be off to Africa one week talking your way into a jail cell and then fly back and the project is over and you're unemployed again and all your contacts say that there is no work about, can be very harsh really. Hard on yourself.

Daniela is an established freelance journalist, who has worked for a large number of national newspapers and magazines over the course of her career. Because of this, she has very good contacts in the business, and finds work more easily than most in her field. But she is still prone to the fluctuations of fashion and of the market, and has experienced the insecurity of creative work the hard way. When working for a national newspaper she told me how suddenly they terminated her contract when it became financially necessary:

When they had a budget overspend they had to get rid of me and bring the job in-house because that's how they were going to save £11,000 a year ... they just phoned up and said 'Could you file your copy? Oh and by the way we don't need you any more.' (personal communication, August 2004)

"Ducking and Diving": The Portfolio Career

A significant trend that my analysis shows is the emerging "portfolio career" pattern for those employed in cultural production. As the "job-for-life" disappears, and the insecurity of project-based work increases, subjects in the cultural economy are compelled to find a number of ways to make a living. It quickly became clear that in addition to the attendant insecurity of creative work, my participants have to juggle any number of different projects at a given time. They are forced to become highly entrepreneurial, commodifying themselves on the labour market, always on the lookout for the next project. According to Catharine:

As a researcher or assistant producer most people spend the last few weeks of their contract looking around for work, because when people want to hire you they want you the next Monday.

Daniela provided particularly telling evidence of the portfolio career pattern.

When the Internet came up British Airways head-hunted me, At this point I was working at The Times *two days a week, I was doing my television critic stuff for the* Daily Mail *and I was doing other freelance stuff—so I had like an office job a steady contract and other bits and pieces, and then British Airways wanted me to set up their internet site ... so I've got a little portfolio. Then I've got this rock festival that I'm setting up in Nebraska which is something completely different.*

Daniela is performing a juggling act to ensure a steady flow of capital. She was an exemplary case study of a creative worker for whom "[t]he norm now is a kind of middle class 'ducking and diving'" (McRobbie, 2002a, p. 525).

Ellie also finds it necessary to combine a number of jobs to make a living as an artist. Insecurity and transition form a staple feature of her working life. She makes very little money from her artistic practice and sees it as an investment in her future career. In order to survive she teaches sculpture part-time on an art foundation course and does occasional telesales work to supplement her income. She has little security in her teaching work and no formal contract in her telesales work.

Networking: A Club Culture

To survive in such a precarious, flexible situation, where one goes from project to project at a dizzying pace, the ability to network becomes crucial. Daniela states:

I think you do have to network and I think a lot of people do it and I think there's a lot of brown-nosing going on. You have to rely on contacts, you have your favourite commissioning editors who you actually socialize with ... you become friends with the people who commission you and you almost expect them to hand you pieces like you're their favourite pet.

How can we understand the emergence of the network as the dominant paradigm of contemporary social and economic life? Castells (1996) argues that fundamental changes in communications technology, most importantly the development of the Internet and instantaneous global communications systems, mean that we have entered the age of the "network society." In this emergent society, labour markets have undergone intense changes. As Castells (1996) suggests: "[c]apitalism itself has undergone a process of profound restructuring, characterized by greater flexibility in management; decentralization and net-working of firms both internally and in their relationships to other firms; considerable empowering of capital vis-à-vis labour, with the concomitant decline of influence of the labor movement; increasing individualization and diversification of working relationships" (p. 1). As creative workers are increasingly freelance, mobile, and have no fixed stable workplace, the network becomes increasingly important in terms of finding work, socializing, sharing information, and learning new skills.

Taking this into account, interestingly my analysis shows that most of my participants had an ambivalent relationship to the networking culture that they operated in. While admitting its centrality to success, it was also seen as something potentially vulgar, not something that they overtly associated themselves with doing. It seemed that there was a code to "correct" networking.

The Centrality of "Cultural Capital"

If networking is the new paradigm for finding work and maintaining a career in the new cultural economy, then a critical question arises: who has the skills to get on in this "club culture" and who does not? Clearly, successful networking in London's creative economy can be seen to take place in a rigid hierarchy of taste, with definite social codes and norms. Navigating this terrain successfully requires high levels of "cultural capital" in order to facilitate access to the network and to provide an individual with the communicative and cognitive skills to succeed in this environment (Bourdieu, 1984).

All of my interviewees can be said to possess high levels of cultural capital. Middle-class, university-educated, they epitomize Bourdieu's definition of "cultural intermediary," a group that: "comes into its own in all the occupations involving presentation and representation (sales, marketing, advertising, public relations, fashion, decoration and so forth) and in all the institutions providing symbolic goods and services. These include the various jobs ... in cultural production and organization which have expanded considerably in recent years" (Bourdieu, 1984, p. 359). My interviewees instinctively knew how to behave in the closed worlds of their professions and how to work the cultural economy to their advantage, where networking is so vital. Evidence of their skills can be seen in these comments:

Mark: *You've got to have the interpersonal skills—they are the most important things. (personal communication, August 2004)*

Catherine: *How do I network? Just pop an e-mail, make a call, be charming. (personal communication, August 2004)*

The networked economy becomes increasingly discriminatory in terms of who has access and who does not while hard-fought battles over workers' rights and antidiscrimination laws are sidelined. As McRobbie (2002) argues, networked labour markets in the creative industries are far more open to subtle forms of discrimination and exclusion: "[w]hat we see ... is the emergence of working practices which reproduce older patterns of marginalization (of women and people from different ethnic backgrounds), while also disallowing any space or time for such issues to reach articulation. In this case the club culture question of 'are you on the guest list?' is extended to recruitment and personnel, so that getting an interview for contract creative work depends on informal knowledge and contacts, often friendships" (p. 533).

Cultural Individualization

The working lives of this group of cultural producers are acted out against the backdrop of an accelerated individualization within contemporary society. My analysis suggests that the creative economy is peopled by atomized workers, who connect through networks but have lost a wider sense of workplace politics and labor solidarity. Because they have no fixed communal workplace, their experience of work is innately individual, as they move with such speed from project to project and place to place. For Daniela, modern technology exacerbates the atomizing process:

When you're freelance you've got the Internet and everything, you can do your shopping on the Internet there becomes very little reason for you to walk out of your front door. I could be here for a whole week and never go out.

Finding "Pleasure In Work"

Despite the pains that they feel at such precarious working lives, my participants were all at pains to stress how much they love their jobs, and the sense of freedom and fulfillment it gives them. They expressed a deep ambivalence towards their working lives. As seen previously, they were open about their concerns at the insecurities and the stresses of individualization, of living and working in a culture requiring constant risk taking. Yet at the same time they emphasized their great personal satisfaction in being creative, and in the pleasure they derive from their work. In central ways, "creativity" acted as a panacea for the structural pains of making a living under such pressures:

Daniela: *I love the fact that I can come up with an idea, and have the freedom to turn it into a story that lots of people then enjoy reading. I'm lucky to have that, so many jobs are really boring.*

Mark: *It's a way of expressing yourself, of doing work that doesn't necessarily feel like work, you know?*

In particular, my participants all stressed the satisfaction they derived from "doing their own thing," and of escaping the dull confines of a nine-to-five office job, which they associated with tradition and a lack of autonomy and fulfillment.

Ellie: *I think it's about freedom maybe, having freedom about choices I make, in terms of what I do and what I think about.*

Daniela: *I know for a fact that I really need to believe in what I'm doing. I can't just do it for the money.*

As Ursell (2000) suggests, for creative workers "pleasure derives from the scope they are finding for aesthetic self-expression" (p. 819). This helps to explain why contemporary cultural producers actively choose their occupations and sometimes work for very little money or even for nothing, even though they experience insecurity and exploitation. The pleasure and satisfaction that these workers derive from their jobs, even in the face of deeply (self) exploitative working practices, serves a structural function that legitimizes the workings of late capitalism. The individualized pleasure in work that my participants feel can be understood in terms of how the discourse of creativity has a disciplinary effect on workers. In a culture where creativity is prized as an "inner quality" that will bring self-fulfillment, it becomes a discursive regime: "regimes of power all the more effective since they are connected with freedom and self-realization" (McRobbie, 2002b, p. 104). As Ursell (2000) suggests, in the creative economy, "one constructs one's self with a view to marketability and value-adding propensities" (p. 810). Thus commercial consumption regimes and lifestyle politics so evident in contemporary society act as potent technologies of the self, creating individuals who are "seeking identity in work, whose subjective desires for self-actualization are to be harnessed to the firm's aspiration for productivity" (Rose, 1990, p. 244).

Conclusion

My research into the rapidly evolving and amorphous creative industries signals a number of trends, each of which would provide fertile ground for further research. In examining the personal implications of the creative economy focusing on the experiences of my respondents, I have only been able to sketch out some preliminary and tentative shifts. However, the results are striking, and if they can be said to be indicative of wider developments in this field, and indeed in the economy at large, they signal a significant transition in contemporary labour markets.

My analysis suggests that creative workers are compelled to find new ways of managing their careers in increasingly individualized ways; in the absence of a job-for-life, and with the need to juggle a variety of projects in their attempts to work the cultural economy, these knowledge workers are having to find complex pathways through their working lives, routes which insist that they become reflexive, adaptive, and in the absence of workplace politics that they become their own support structures. They are truly "entrepreneurs of the self" (Du Gay, 1997, pp. 301-303).

Creative workers are at the vanguard of the new economy model of work in terms of how they experience flexible capitalism, freelance economies, networking, and work that is defined by mobility, atomisation, rapid deskilling, self-exploitation, multiple sites, insecurity, entrepreneurialism, and flux. In their biographies we can begin to understand the logical progression of neo-liberal values, the fusion of the cultural with the economic and the impact of the network society on work in the age of "soft capitalism." Cast adrift in the flows of the creative economy, my interviewees all exist in a constant state of risk at work, yet the rewards are deeply uncertain for as Sennett (1998) argues, "new market conditions oblige large numbers of people to take quite demanding risks even though the gamblers know the possibilities of reward are slight" (p. 88).

A future world of work characterized by semi-employment, risk, and insecurity is the logical conclusion of the neo-liberal winner-take-all market. Such a breakdown of certainty and meaning can be glimpsed in my participants' working lives. As Sennett (1998) asks, "How can long-term purposes be pursued in a short-term society? How can durable social relationships be sustained? How can a human being develop a narrative of identity and life history in a society composed of episodes and fragments?" (pp. 26-27). This is the dilemma for my participants working in the creative economy of London. And as Beck (2000) suggests, it may be one that will face us all: "[t]he high-wire balancing act is becoming the paradigm for individual biography and social normality. Become a life-artist or go under: such is the alternative that is posed everywhere" (p. 118).

References

Bauman, Z. (2002). Individually together. In U. Beck & E. Beck-Gernsheim (Eds.), *Individualization*. London: Sage Publications.

Beck, U. (2000*). The brave new world of work*. Cambridge, UK: Polity Press.

Beck, U., & Beck-Gernsheim, E. (2002). *Individualization*. London: Sage Publications.

Beck, U., Giddens, A., & Lash, S. (1994). *Reflexive modernization: Politics, tradition and aesthetics in the modern social order*. Cambridge, UK: Polity Press.

Bell, D. (1973). *The coming of post-industrial society: A venture in social forecasting*. New York: Basic Books.

Bentley, T., & Seltzer, K. (1999). *The creative age: Knowledge and skills for the new economy*. London: Design Council/Demos.

Bourdieu, P. (1984). *Distinction: A social critique of the judgement of taste*. London: Routledge.

Burchell, G., Gordon, C., & Miller, P. (Eds.). (1991). *The foucault effect: Studies in governmentality*. London: Harvester Wheatsheaf.

Castells, M. (1996). The information age: Economy, society and culture (Vol. 1). *The rise of the network society*. Oxford, UK: Blackwell.

Cunningham, S. (2004). The creative industries after cultural policy. A genealogy and some possible preferred futures. *International Journal of Cultural Studies, 7*(1), 105-115.

Department of Culture Media and Sport (DCMS). (1998). *Creative industries mapping document*. London: DCMS.

Department of Culture Media and Sport (DCMS). (2001). *Creative industries mapping document*. London: DCMS.

Donzelot, J. (1991). Pleasure in work. In Burchell et al. (Eds.), *The foucault effect: Studies in governmentality*. Hemel Hempstead, UK: Harvester Wheatsheaf.

Du Gay, P. (1996). *Consumption and identity at work*. London: Sage Publications.

Du Gay, P. (Ed.). (1997). *Production of culture/cultures of production*. London: Sage Publications.

Florida, R. (2002). *The rise of the creative class, and how it's transforming work, leisure, community and everyday life*. New York: Basic Books.

Foucault, M. (1988). Technologies of the self. In H. Luther et al. (Eds.), *Technologies of the self: A seminar with Michel Foucault* (pp. 16-49). Cambridge: University of Massachusetts Press.

Garnham, N. (1990). *Capitalism and communication: Global culture and the economics of information*. London: Sage Publications.

Giddens, A. (1992). *The transformation of intimacy: Sexuality, love and eroticism in modern societies*. Cambridge, UK: Polity Press.

Guntern, G. (Ed.). (1998). *Risk-taking and creative leadership*. London: Shepheard-Walwyn.

Jameson, F. (1991). *Postmodernism, or, the cultural logic of late capitalism*. London: Verso.

Lash, S. (2002). Individualization in a non-linear mode. In U. Beck & E. Beck-Gernsheim (Eds.), *Individualization*. London: Sage Publications.

Lash, S., & Urry, J. (1994). *Economies of signs and spaces*. London: Sage Publications.

Leadbeater, C. (1999). *Living on thin air: The new economy*. London: Viking.

London Development Agency (LDA). (2004). *Creative London*. London: LDA.

McRobbie, A. (1999). *In the culture society: Art, fashion and popular music*. London: Routledge.

McRobbie, A. (2000). The return to cultural production case study: Fashion journalism. In J. Curran & M. Gurevitch (Eds.), *Mass media and society* (pp. 255-267). London: Arnold.

McRobbie, A. (2002a). Clubs to companies: Notes on the decline of political culture in speeded up creative worlds. *Cultural Studies, 16*(4), 516-531.

McRobbie, A. (2002b). From Holloway to Hollywood: Happiness at work in the new cultural economy? In P. Du Gay & M. Pryke (Eds.), *Cultural economy* (pp. 97-114). London: Sage Publications.

McRobbie, A. (2004). Everyone is creative? Artists as pioneers of the new economy. In E. B. Silva & T. Bennett (Eds.), *Contemporary culture and everyday life* (pp. 184-210). Durham, UK: Sociology Press.

Miller, P., & Rose, N. (1990). Governing economic life. *Economy and society, 19*(1). In P. Du Gay (Ed.), *Production of culture/cultures of production*. London: Sage Publications.

Osborne, T. (2003). Against 'creativity': A philistine rant. *Economy and Society, 32*(4), 507-525.

Rose, N. (1990). *Governing the soul: The shaping of the private self.* London: Routledge.

Rose, N. (1999). *Powers of freedom: Reframing political thought.* Cambridge University Press.

Schudson, M. (2000). The sociology of news production revisited (again). In J. Curran & M. Gurevitch (Eds.), *Mass media and society* (pp. 175-200). London: Arnold.

Sennett, R (1998). *The corrosion of character: The personal consequences of work in the new capitalism.* New York: Norton.

Ursell, G. (2000). Television production: Issues of exploitation, commodification and subjectivity in UK television labour markets. *Media, Culture and Society, 22*(6), 805-827.

Wang, J. (2004). The global reach of a new discourse: How far can 'creative industries' travel? *International Journal of Cultural Studies, 7*(1), 9-19.

Endnotes

[1]   "Cool Britannia" was New Labour's strategy on coming to power in 1997 to promote the UK as a cultural powerhouse and as a world leader in the creative industries.

[2]   "Governmentality" relates to Michel Foucault's theory of power. The term refers to the techniques that exist to encourage individuals to act upon themselves in ways that serve particular ends (see Burchell, Gordon, & Miller, 1991).

[3]   Techniques of the self are those practices which "permit individuals to effect by their own means or with the help of others, a certain number of operations on their own bodies and souls, thoughts, conduct and ways of being, so as to transform themselves in order to attain a certain state of happiness, purity, wisdom, perfection or immortality" (Foucault, 1988, p. 18).

[4]   The notion of the "cultural intermediary" derives from the work of French sociologist Pierre Bourdieu. Bourdieu (1984) argues that the cultural intermediaries are a new economic class, who work in the culture industries, serving the needs of an economy characterized by a massive expansion of the cultural sphere.

[5]   The DCMS definition of the creative industries includes music, performing arts, publishing, software, TV and radio, film, designer fashion, advertising, arts and antiques, crafts, design, architecture (DCMS, 2001).

Chapter IX

Digital Cinema as Disruptive Technology:
Exploring New Business Models in the Age of Digital Distribution

Nigel Culkin, University of Hertfordshire, UK

Norbert Morawetz, University of Hertfordshire, UK

Keith Randle, University of Hertfordshire, UK

Abstract

The distribution and exhibition of motion pictures are at a crossroads. Ever since the medium was invented in the 1890s the "picture" has been brought to the spectator in the form of photochemical images stored on strips of celluloid film passed in intermittent motion through a projector. Now, at the beginning of the 21ˢᵗ century, an entirely new method has emerged, using digitally stored data in place of film and barely needing any physical support other than a computerised file. This opens an intriguing portfolio of revenue-generating opportunities for the movie exhibitor. This chapter will give an overview of current developments in digital cinema (d-cinema). It will examine potential new business models in an industry wedded to the analogue process. The authors will consider the strategies of companies at the forefront of the technology; implications associated with the change; and how different territories might adapt in order to accommodate this transition.

Introduction

In this chapter we will consider how the transition from film to digital product is likely to affect an industry that has been wedded to an analogue process for more than 100 years. Rather than contributing further to the debate about the qualities of competing technologies or the creative merits or demerits of digital product, this chapter will focus on the development of potentially new business models in the global film industry. The authors will examine the strategies of the companies at the forefront of the technology; the financial implications associated with change; and how different territories are adapting in order to accommodate this transition.

D-Cinema: An Idle Revolution?

Ever since 1999, when George Lucas launched *Star Wars: Phantom Menance* on four digital screens in America, prophets of d-cinema (that is using digitally stored data in place of film) have proclaimed that it will change the film industry forever. Six years later d-cinema is still far away from wide implementation.

Belton (2002) has even declared d-cinema to be a "false revolution" because it does not transform the nature of the motion picture experience for the audience, stating that "One obvious problem with digital cinema is that it has no novelty value, at least not for film audiences." He argues that in a marketplace in which the word "digital" sells consumer products, "it is digital sound (and not digital projection) that marks for consumers the entry of motion pictures into the digital era."

His arguments cannot be easily dismissed especially when considering the explicit goal of digital projector manufacturers to produce an image quality that *equals* that of traditional film prints. Slater (2002) has compared the cinema exhibition chain of traditional film and electronic/d-cinema. When looking for an answer to the question what problem electronic/d-cinema is trying to solve, he could not find "one single good technical or operational reason why the whole system should be replaced" (p. 43), with film being high quality, flexible, and most important future proof.

Still key players in the industry seem to be determined to make d-cinema happen, such as John Filthian, president of the National Association of Theater Owners (NATO) in America, who has said that "digital cinema will be the biggest transition technology in the history of the movie industry" (Baird, 2004).

The Dilemma

However, with just over 120,000 screens worldwide, the cinema market has been deemed too small to support any major technological innovation by itself (*Screen Digest*, 2003). This means that no manufacturer is currently in the position to produce a digital projector at such a competitive price, that exhibitors could afford to pay for the switching costs themselves. Consequently, the matter of financing the conversion to d-cinema has been passed on to distributors, who are claimed to benefit the most from d-cinema by saving on print costs.

The problem is further intensified, when more than one company for d-cinema equipment tries to serve the market, and more than one standard exists. For distributors however, it does only make sense to fund d-cinema conversion, if a single standard exists (similar to the 35mm standard), otherwise the cost savings of digital are offset by producing several masters for different standards.

Thus the need arises for a clearly specified standard—an issue that took the participating players more than 6 years to resolve.

These players can be categorized into three basic groups: equipment manufacturers, institutional players, and distributors. In the following section the major players and their stakes in d-cinema will be introduced briefly while reflecting on their role in the search for a single standard.

Setting a Standard, Shaping the Market

The earliest attempts to gain a dominant market position and to set standards have been made by the main competitors in digital projector manufacturing, Texas Instruments (TI) (DLP Cinema), Sony (GLV), and JVC (D-ILA).

While JVC's position in the market has been marginalised, TI has licensed its DLP Cinema technology to projector manufacturers such as Barco, Christie Digital, and DPI/NEC and has by doing so gained an early advantage for its standard over Sony. It soon became evident however, that a working business model for d-cinema has to include not just a projector, but must consist of a bundle with digital distribution and server hardware. The main competitors in this area are companies such as QuVis, GDC, XDC, and AccessIT.

As technology companies are clearly wedded to their own solutions, pointing out flaws in competing technologies while downplaying the shortcomings of their own, institutional players stepped in to help specify a single standard and support the development of d-cinema.

In the U.S. the institution in charge is a special commission (DC-28) of the Society of Motion Picture and Television Engineers (SMPTE), in Europe it is the European Digital Cinema Forum (EDCF), in Japan the Digital Cinema Consortium of Japan (DCCJ NPO), and in China the State Administration of Radio, Film, and Television (SARFT).

The power of these institutions has however been limited, as they tend to avoid taking sides and promote all solutions equally.

In 2002 the Digital Cinema Incentive (DCI) was formed, a joint venture of the seven major Hollywood studios (Disney, Fox, MGM, Paramount, Sony Pictures Entertainment, Universal, and Warner Bros.) that has dwarfed the importance of the other institutions to establish guidelines for d-cinema into insignificance. Although it still is the SMPTE that ratifies technical standards for cinema and television in America, even Peter Symes, vice president engineering at SMPTE has to admit that "the DCI represents a significant party of interest" and it was very unlikely that the SMPTE could reach consensus on something if the DCI was in favour of something else (Crabtree, 2004).

In July 2005 the DCI had published its final overall system requirements and specifications for d-cinema. In their guidelines they have opted for a scalable solution from 2K to 4K and have therefore left the decision which projector technology will be used in theatres to the market.

They have however selected JPG2000 as the image coding system to be used in the delivery of digital motion pictures. This decision is very likely to eliminate competing systems, such as various MPEG standards or newcomer eTreppid from the market and forces all major manufacturers to comply with the standard (Crabtree, 2004).

DCI specifications have consequently been branded to be synonymous with the term *d-cinema*, as Tim Partridge, senior vice president and general manager of the professional division for Dolby Laboratories has explained: "I think we [Dolby Laboratories] use the terms in what has become the standard way. D-cinema to us means DCI standard equipment, E-cinema is everything below that" (DCR, 2005b).

The question arises, why the *d-cinema revolution* still has not fully begun, when the dominating market forces (the Hollywood studios) can so easily safeguard their interests. One might argue that all they have to do, to continue their international market supremacy, is to replicate the existing power structure and apply it to the d-cinema market. What does stop them? Can the hesitancy of the "majors" to move along with d-cinema quickly be interpreted as an indication of concern about the impact the digital transition will have on the industry?

D-Cinema: A Disruptive Technology?

Digital cinema [...] is perhaps the most significant challenge to the cinema industry since the introduction of sound on film. As with any new technology, there are those who want to do it fast, and those who want to do it right. As we move down this path, let's not forget the lesson learned with the introduction of digital audio for film in the '90s. Cinema Digital Sound, a division of Optical Radiation Corporation, was the first to put digital audio on 35mm film. Very, very few remember CDS, who closed their doors long ago. Such are the rewards for being first. (MKPE Consulting LLC, 2005)

As the previous statement shows, there are considerable risks attached with moving into a market too fast. Indeed some of the companies who tried to find an early foothold in d-cinema have already closed their business in this field (most notably Boeing).

However as the literature on *disruptive innovation* and *disruptive technology* has pointed out, one of the biggest risks for incumbents in any market is to move too slowly.

Disruptive innovation and disruptive technology are emerging and increasingly prominent business terms describing a revolutionary change in an industry (Thomond et al., 2003). The term disruptive technology was first marked by Christensen (1997) to describe a technological discontinuity that causes the failure of incumbents in a market. Danneels (2004) defines disruptive technology as a technology that changes the bases of competition by changing the performance metrics along which firms compete. Customers seeking certain benefits determine which attributes they value in a product, with different customer groups valuing different attributes. New products based on a disruptive technology have different attribute sets than existing products. They tend to have initially a lower level of performance on dimensions relevant to mainstream market segments but have higher performance on dimensions valued by remote or emerging market segments. Christensen (2000) has characterized disruptive technologies as typically "simpler, cheaper, and more reliable and convenient than established technologies" (p. 192).

When the disruption has established itself in an underserved customer segment, major players may be displaced as disrupter's develop new wealth opportunities. The consequences of not securing disruptive innovations can be "far more devastating than simply lost opportunities or lost market share" (Thomond et al., 2003, p. 6). Following these definitions d-cinema can easily be identified as a disruptive technology.

In the following sections we will map out current important issues stopping incumbents from embracing the technology and exploiting its full potential. We will show how d-cinema changes the basis of competition in the industry and helps new markets to emerge. We will also show how incumbents can slow down the development to their advantage, and in doing so deliberately risk losing niche markets.

Single Standard vs. Consumer Market

One of the prerequisites for a wide roll out of d-cinema has been the readiness of tested equipment. There is a broad consent among industry experts that the problems of digital projectors with image quality have now been solved. However the availability of technology that meets the requirements has not propelled the number of installed d-cinema projectors tremendously. Walt Ordway, chief technology officer for the DCI, does not see a wide implementation of d-cinema for at least 4-6 years, although an initial roll out could take place "in the next year or so." Ordway notes that one problem with the systems that are currently fielded is their lack of security constraints and a common standard (DCR, 2005a).

On an exhibitor's wish list for regulators of d-cinema, a common global standard would rank among the top objectives.[1] There are two rivalling technologies in the projector market, namely TIs 2K (DLP) standard, and Sony's 4K (GLV) standard.[2] TI has invested an "unspeakably large amount of money" (Screen Digest, 2003, p. 30) into its DLP technology, revealing the exact amount not even to its shareholders, and currently controls the market. Sony on the other hand keeps announcing its 4K projector and plays on the preference of studios for a 4K solution. Despite Sony's de facto, zero-market share, the DCI (in which Sony is a member) has endorsed both 2K and 4K standards when choosing the JPEG 2000 codec for studio d-cinema release masters.

Although the revenues from the high-end d-cinema market can be substantial, the real market to be won is the home cinema market. For both companies the market for d-cinema is therefore a kind of branding exercise for reaping rewards in the consumer electronics (CE) market. The underlying logic (e.g., for TI) is the following:

Cinema audiences will see the DLP logo before the start of every film in a d-cinema and come to associate it with the highest quality of picture

*viewing. They will then seek it out or of opt for it in their local CE market.
(Screen Digest, 2003)*

The situation is similar to the introduction of digital sound into cinemas, which was also seen as a preliminary battle "for the potentially much more lucrative market for digital sound in the home" (Belton, 2002, p. 101). During the 1990s three different companies tried to establish their proprietary technology as a cinema standard, namely DTS (Universal/MCA), SDDS (Sony), and Dolby digital (Dolby Laboratories). Since each standard was able to capture a sufficient market share, multi-standards in cinema sound continue to exist.

Multi-standards in d-cinema are certainly not a desired outcome for film distributors as well as exhibitors. Still, as long as d-cinema is only considered as a prefacing market for the companies who actually develop the technologies in use, standards will be an issue.

A Market with Network Effects

One of the reasons why a common standard is so desirable is that the market for d-cinema exhibits positive consumption and production externalities. Positive consumption (network) externalities exist, when the value of a unit of the good increases with the expected number of units sold (Economides, 1996).

If both TI (2K) and Sony (4K) establish their incompatible projectors in the market, the market is split into two different networks, one for 2K projectors and one for 4K projectors. Each of these networks consists of sellers (the Hollywood studios plus independent content producers) and buyers (exhibitors). If an exhibitor installs a 2K projector he joins the 2K network, and the utility of this projector increases with every exhibitor who joins this network because the increasing size of the (2K) market increases the expected utility of all partici-pants as they have more partners to trade with. This is especially true for the Hollywood studios, as for them the utility of the market is at a maximum, when there is only one standard (either 2K or 4K) and they can trade with all the exhibitors without incurring any additional costs.

Charles Swartz, CEO of the USC Entertainment Technology Center, has stressed the importance of a single, global, interoperable standard for d-cinema by referring to 35mm which had all these characteristics; the single standard ultimately enabled film to become a "medium of tremendous power" (Crabtree, 2003). A situation with a double standard would therefore not be progress but a step backward for the industry.

Waiting for Sony

As a vertical integrated corporation Sony faces competition on each stage of the value chain, with contradicting objectives adding to the complexity.

Being a member of the DCI, Sony, the studio, has been able to secure that the DCI agreed on scalable format standards from 2K to 4K, and has thereby strengthened the position of Sony, the projector manufacturer. On the other side however, it has also agreed to accept rival technology as a standard.

There is a strong and compelling argument that says that since the studios are the real beneficiaries of d-cinema (through print savings) they should also fund the projector installation (Baird, 2004).

One possible way to realize this funding sees the majors setting up an independent financing entity that allows cinema owners to decide on their own on how to use the funds to upgrade their cinemas along DCI standards (Kilday, 2004).

If this happens, Sony will find itself in the contradictory situation, where as a member of the DCI it will have to (directly or indirectly) subsidize its competitors in equipment manufacturing.

As an equipment manufacturer Sony competes against TI and its licensees Christie Digital, Barco, and NEC. It has to do so because it wants to protect its market prospects in consumer electronics, where it again competes against TI licensees, for example, Samsung, Sanyo, or Marantz.

On each stage of the value chain Sony has more to lose than its competitors (the subsequent market) but it is also the only player that can exacerbate power at a higher level by participating in the DCI. Although Sony has not even proved yet that its 4K projector is more than a functioning prototype, it is therefore still a market force one has to take into account.

Sony's strategy clearly is to play on time, and by cleverly doing so, it has managed to stay in a race that otherwise would have been long over. Through repeatedly announcing its 4K projector it has raised industry uncertainty and stopped investments. As Travis Reid, president of the cinema chain Loews Cineplex said:

... the fact that (a 4K projector) exists is making everyone stop to think, and admitted that if there was no deployment (of 4K), then 2K would have been the initial rollout. (Sperling, 2004)

An exhibitor quoted in *Hollywood Reporter* said that:

They [Sony] are clearly trying to slow down the forward momentum of 2K being adopted and rolled out. It will be interesting to see how they've come along to being a real live projector; there are a lot of studios saying, "If this is close, then let's wait." TI [Texas Instruments] can't be happy about it. (Sperling, 2004)

Doug Darrow, Project Manager for d-cinema at TI challenges Sony with the strong argument that it has not demonstrated that 4K projectors will actually work in theatres for a few years, in contrast to TI. However, this argument could backfire. If there is no pressing economic need (and there is none) to switch to digital projection immediately, then exhibitors and studios might well postpone their investment decisions and wait to see if Sony's 4K projector can deliver.

TI has expressed little interest in the race to 4K and focuses on the commercialisation of 2K, with "the biggest challenge not lying in resolution but in costs" (Kaufman, 2004).

A Complex Transition

John Fithian, president of the National Association of Theatre Owners (NATO), states "it is fairly clear that studios will fund the transition," since "they will save a tremendous amount of money from the conversion" (Baird, 2004).

The modus operandi of this transition is far away from being "fairly clear," though. The rollout plan that determines which cinemas will get converted first must be consensually negotiated with all interest parties. Should the transition start only in North America or internationally, by state, by exhibitor, by market, or where low technology and penetration allow for fast entry? (Fuchs, 2004b).

The Board of directors of the NATO (2004) has formulated a resolution of requirements that need to be fulfilled for the transition to be a success. A key point for them is that interoperable, reliable equipment is in place (both NATO and DCI have pledged for a beta testing phase) that at least equals the image quality of 35mm. The equipment must further be easy to upgrade at reasonable cost, as technology advances; must be built around clearly defined standards; and has to be produced by competing multiple vendors.

For exhibitors a desirable financing plan for the transition has to ensure that all movie complexes and auditoriums, regardless of size or geographic location can participate within reasonable time, studios are committed to provide digital content, and exhibitors can independently select the equipment, and own it at the end of the financing period. Furthermore they ask for a "no dark screen" policy, meaning that films play in a nonrepudiate manner unless the exhibitor attempts to play the film in a completely different venue and that they can decide on their own about schedules, advertisements, trailers, and other content (NATO, 2004, p. 3).

From a studio point of view, subsidising the full cost of the equipment without any obligations to exhibitors does not seem to be a very healthy economic proposition. A solution that does not contain any obligations to exhibitors to show content is a de facto cross-subsidisation for independent filmmakers, as they will benefit from the installation without contributing to the costs.

In the question of ownership therefore rests a crucial point in the transition to d-cinema. The immense undertaking to convert thousands of screens in America and internationally is not an "everyday" logistic and organisational challenge. To resolve the major issues it will take time. For the moment this will delay the d-cinema revolution further, as exhibitors have little incentive to enter the market on their own before the studios have come to a decision.

The New Digital Deal

The paralysis that results from the funding problem has left the market for the moment to third-party players.

A first wave of third-party players proposed to pay the upfront costs for digital projectors in return for a fee (per-print, per-screening, per-ticket, or an annual contract) and promised to ensure that there is no shift in the balance of power between distributors and exhibitors (*Screen Digest*, 2003). The success of these companies (with some exemptions such as Kodak) has been very modest so far. In 2003 Boeing Digital Cinema closed its d-cinema business that was once projected to bring $1 billion a year in revenue (Gates, 2003). At the same time, Technicolor has scaled down its ambitions and based on latest reports, Elsacom is still in the testing phase.

A new wave of investment into d-cinema comes from state initiatives and independent film distributors. By targeting niche markets these players fragment the market and can then gradually expand their business into the mainstream.

These dynamics are reflected in Christensen's (1997) disruptive technology framework. He argues that incumbents are resource dependent (Pfeffer & Salancik, 1978) on their most demanding customers and focus their investment towards innovations that are valued by their mainstream customers. In contrast to this, new entrants are not constraint by and can not rely on an existing customer base, thus they are "forced to identify consumers who value the new features offered by the new technology and support its further development" (Adner, 2002).

In this regard, it seems as if the first wave of new entrants into d-cinema failed to correctly identify these "new customers." Most of these ventures were aimed right from the beginning at the mainstream market, ignoring the importance to segment the market that has been strongly underlined by Moore (1991). This is in stark contrast to the new wave of entrants, who are very focused on niche markets, namely the distribution of independent content.

It is remarkable in this context that major new initiatives (e.g., the UK Film Councils Screen Network) are state driven. So far government support for the film industry was mainly aimed at subsidising film production, often resulting in the so-produced films not finding exhibition and reaching only a very limited audience. The idea to provide distribution and exhibition for this content through installing digital screens is a strong shift away from the traditional production-oriented subsidy logic to a more market oriented one. It directly addresses a market failure in exhibition that provides only very limited "screen space" to "art-house" films.

While d-cinema might potentially help independent filmmakers to overcome the market barriers to distribution, this does not necessarily mean that the even bigger barriers of consumer habits and tastes can be overcome as well. The American film industry has shaped audience tastes for generations resulting in a market share of up to over 90% in Western countries. Although this domination might be a portrait of distorted consumer preferences, resulting from restricted consumer choice offered in local cinemas, the majority of mainstream audience taste is unlikely to change overnight. It will take more than access to the market to re-win significant audience shares for independent (European) cinema. Nevertheless higher exposure to content is an essential first step to alter cinema goer's habits in the long run.

Implications for the Current Structure of the Film Industry

As the aforementioned examples clearly show, d-cinema not only allows smaller competitors to carve out viable market niches but can bring completely new markets into existence. Remote areas whose access to audiovisual content that has been limited so far will now be as easily reached as regions with developed infrastructures. Both developments will increase competition: Firstly through players who fragment the market and then try to expand their strongholds into the mainstream market, and secondly through companies who operate from new strong domestic markets.

Without additional costs in supplying additional "prints" for screens, economies of scale that have shielded Hollywood studios from low-budget competitors for nearly a century are eradicated. Consequently, the release of a film will become "less of a financial decision and more of a marketing decision" (TI, 2003). If this will truly give independents leverage remains to seen.

The majors themselves have hardly ever regarded printing costs as an obstacle to distribution. With "ultrawide releases" (3000+ prints) on the rise (*Screen Digest*, 2003), d-cinema opens the door to an ever higher pervasiveness of Hollywood product.

The studios have recently shortened the time lags between release dates in international markets and global, simultaneous, film starts have become a trend (e.g., The Matrix II, III, Star Wars, Harry Potter, Lord of The Rings). One reason for this might be that the Internet has facilitated the development of a global film audience with increasingly convergent tastes. This audience readily turns to pirated copies of films if time lags between national releases are too long. The combination of d-cinema and global simultaneous film starts is likely to propel this trend further with studios staging and marketing their productions as global events for a global box office.

Another advantage studios will take along into the era of d-cinema will be their business model of a portfolio approach to film production and distribution. The strategy to spread risk onto a slate of films is even more effective with d-cinema: If a film is a success, studios can immediately supply additional screens at virtually no cost, if a film is a failure, it can be withdrawn without bearing the sunk costs of film prints.

In this context d-cinema appears to be less a disruptive but rather a sustaining technology for the majors. Sustaining technologies are consistent with a firm's business model (Christensen & Raynor, 2003) and improve the performance of established products through the "current technology product paradigm" (Kostoff, Boylan, & Simons, 2004). D-cinema bears both the characteristics of a sustaining and a disruptive technology, making it difficult to recognize the distinction. It is exactly this failure to address technological innovations appropriately that according to Christensen causes successful incumbents to stumble or even disappear from the market.

Historically, the film industry has already mastered a number of disruptive technologies (e.g., television, video recorder), despite its traditional reluctance to embrace new technologies. Its nostrum on how to deal with new technologies seems to be a combined strategy of vertical disintegration and diversification, which has led to an oligopolistic industry structure.

During the 1990s the major studios diversified themselves into the independent market by setting up or buying independent distributors (New Line Cinema, Miramax, Fox Searchlight, etc.), a trend that is likely to be intensified by d-cinema. Thus, if entrepreneurial firms take advantage of the disruptive technology d-cinema and "redefine current markets" (Kostoff et al., 2004) the majors might simply counter them through acquisition and integration into their corporate structure.

As local independent distributors develop an expertise on how to successfully handle "difficult" films in their markets, the majors might also begin to disintegrate further and try to outsource some of their distribution to these companies in the same way that they have outsourced production through flexible specialization (see Christopherson & Storper, 1986, 1989).

As the importance of a physical distribution structure diminishes their means to keep control over the industry would then be through controlling intellectual property rights as well as keeping a strong stake in development, packaging, and financing and providing expertise in film production, marketing and distribution to contractors.

The Hold Up Problem

Figure 1 shows a simplified model of money flows in the traditional film industry value chain and in a system of d-cinema (a comprehensive discussion on profit calculation and accounting practices in the Hollywood studio system can be found in Daniels, Leedy, & Sills, 1998).

In the current system, box office receipts are first split between exhibitors and distributors. Exhibitors are the first to deduct their expenses, the value they appropriate is E. Distributors then deduct their *distribution fee*, which is intended to cover their overhead costs (offices, corporate expenses, distribution efforts) and the *distribution expenses* (prints and advertising). The distribution fee varies according to geographic area and market between 25% and up to 50% of the revenue. The value the distributors appropriate is D. The remainder, P, is allocated to the producers of the film.

After the transition to a system of d-cinema, cost savings arise: distribution expenses are reduced through cutting print costs, distribution fees are lowered through reduced studio overhead. It will be interesting to see if studios can appropriate the added value they have created through cost savings for themselves or if they will have to share it with the other parties. If studios pay for the transition costs, they are likely to demand the added value on the ground that they have paid for it (scenario 1 in Figure 1). However, if a new distributor enters the game at this stage ("Maverick distributor"), he/she would be able to offer both exhibitors and producers a better deal than the existing studios (scenario 2, Figure 1), since the distributor can pass on the cost savings to them without having paid for them. In this scenario, studios will eventually have to pass on cost savings to producers as well, if they do not want to continuously lose potential box

Figure 1. Money flows in the film industry / the hold up problem of d-cinema

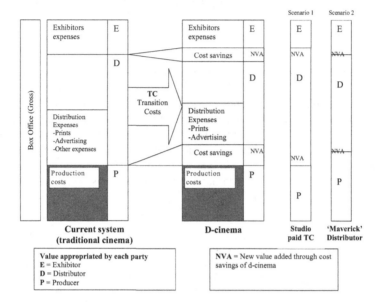

office hits to maverick distributors. The prospect of being held up by other parties in the value chain in the long run is therefore another factor that severely decreases the studios financial incentive to pay the transition costs for d-cinema.

Companies like Hollywood Software already offer independent film distributors and producers to outsource the distribution of entire release slates or individual films to their company. Hollywood Software is a major player that provides information systems to the industry (including the majors) that automatically create sales charts, track film bookings, print shipment orders, and credit payments (Hollywood Software, 2005). The company is a subsidiary of one of the largest server and d-cinema platform manufacturers in the market, Access Integrated Technologies (Access IT). AccessIT has bought and recommissioned all 28 installed d-cinema systems from Boeing Digital Cinema in 2004, placing itself in the "centre of the digital revolution" (Fuchs, 2004a). Their most recent development is the Theatre Command Console which supports multiple brands and models of d-cinema projectors and is operated through an easy-to-use graphic interface. The president and COO of the company, Dave Gajda has said:

The idea is to have fingertip access to and control of all critical d-cinema operations, including print-movements and pre-show content such as advertising and trailers. Whether on-site by the manager or directed remotely from the central home office, ..., operators can easily employ a single user interface to simplify training and flexibly integrate multiple technology solutions into a unified system. (Fuchs, 2004a)

This gives rise to a tangible set of questions about training needs of staff and the transition to d-cinema. Slater (2002) has predicted that the new projection equipment will use built-in diagnostic software and straightforward test routines. As a consequence d-cinema projectors will be far easier to remotely control when connected via a cinema management system that both controls their inputs and outputs. AccessIT's Theatre Command Console is therefore a predecessor to an era where it will be possible to look after hundreds of screens in the country from a single control room (a situation that already has come true for UK broadcasting [Slater, 2004]).

The simplicity of a graphical interface and remote control dismisses concerns from exhibitors that new digital projectors will require advanced technical knowledge (McQuire, 2004) but could mean bleak prospects for some projector staff.

Conclusion

In this chapter we have tried to situate current developments in d-cinema within Christensen's framework of disruptive technologies. We have focused the attention on what we see as the major players in d-cinema, namely the major Hollywood studios and have tried to map the implications of d-cinema on the relationships within the film industry value chain. It was shown that the market for d-cinema exhibits network externalities and that therefore a common standard is desirable. The discussion on standards also revealed the conflicting interests a diversified and vertical integrated corporation such as Sony faces, as the competition in d-cinema becomes a "preliminary battle" for the CE market. As a major incumbent, Sony is able to delay the progress of the whole transition to d-cinema for its own benefit, a strategy worth examining more closely.

We have also briefly outlined some of the complexities linked to organising a satisfying transition to d-cinema for all parties.

The emergence of new markets and new entrants into the d-cinema market was examined in respect to the implications for major players in the industry. Although d-cinema was found to benefit independent players that can carve out market niches, it was also shown that the majors have a strong leverage to exploit the technology to their advantage. However, the combination of a change in the terms of competition and a potential hold up problem, are likely to lead to a further diversification and possibly a further disintegration of major distributors.

In addition we have discussed important issues associated with d-cinema, such as alternative content, training, and digital rights management.

Further research is needed to explore strategies of new entrants and incumbents in this market, survey successful and unsuccessful business models, and discuss how the research on d-cinema can contribute to and be enriched by literature on strategic management and disruptive technologies. Interesting research questions are related to the performance of third party initiatives such as the UK Film Council's Screen Network (2005); the complexity of organising a transition to d-cinema for the mainstream market; and the role of diversified, vertically integrated corporations in the process of setting standards for d-cinema, branding for subsequent markets, and market fragmentation.

In conclusion it shall be mentioned that d-cinema has not solved the problem of long-term digital storage yet. As Phil Feiner, CEO of the renowned optical service company Pacific Title Digital, has remarked: "It's not archival" (Parisi, 2004). Digital intermediates are stored on magnetic tapes that have an archival life of 30 years at best. In contrast, a three-strip black-and-white masters, the current archival standard, lasts as long as 1,500 years. This means that even if a film is shot, edited, distributed, and projected digitally, in the end it has to be transferred to film.

Therefore, in the uncertain future of d-cinema, at least one thing is for sure: Even if the "d-cinema fairy" converts all the screens in the world overnight to digital, traditional film is still going to stay with us for a very, very, very long time.

References

Adner, R. (2002). When are technologies disruptive? A demand-based view of the emergence of competition. *Strategic Management Journal, 23,* 667-688.

Baird, K. (2004, April 22). *The age of digital movies is coming (or so it seems).* Las Vegas: Sun Herald.

BBC News. (2005, March 20). *Irish cinema 'set to go digital'.* Retrieved March 23, 2005, from http://news.bbc.co.uk/go/pr/fr/-/2/hi/uk_news/northern_ireland/4365875.stm

Belton, J. (2002). Digital cinema: A false revolution. *October, 100*(1), 98-114.

Christensen, C. M. (1997). *The innovator's dilemma.* Harvard Business School Press.

Christensen, C. M., & Raynor, M. E. (2003). *The innovator's solution. Creating and sustaining successful growth.* Boston: Harvard Business School Press.

Christopherson, S., & Storper, M. (1986). The city as studio – The world as backlot: The impact of vertical disintegration on the location of the motion picture industry. *Environment and Planning. D: Society and Space, 4,* 305-320.

Christopherson, S., & Storper, M. (1989). The effects of flexible specialization on industrial politics and the labor market: The motion picture industry. *Industrial and Labor Relations Review, 42*(3), 331-347.

Crabtree, S. (2003, August 27). Single, global standard eyed for digital cinema. *The Hollywood Reporter.*

Crabtree, S. (2004, June 21). Studios pick digital system. *The Hollywood Reporter.*

Culkin, N., & Randle, K. R. (2003, Winter). Digital cinema: Opportunities and challenges. *Convergence: The Journal of Research into New Media Technologies, 9*(4).

Culkin, N., & Randle, K. R. (2003, August 25). Stelios v America, the latest big screen bout. *The Guardian,* p. 19.

Daneels, E. (2004). Disruptive technology reconsidered: A critique and research agenda. *Product Development & Management Association, 21,* 246-258.

Daniels, B., Leedy, D., & Sills, S. (1998). *Movie money: Understanding Hollywood's (creative) accounting practices.* Los Angeles: Silman-James Press.

Department for Culture, Media and Sport (DCMS). (2002). *The implications of digital technology for the film industry.* London: TSO.

Digital Cinema Report (DCR). (2005a). *The big picture.* Retrieved March 14, 2005, from www.digitalcinemareport.com/thebigpicture_53.html

Digital Cinema Report (DCR). (2005b). *A conversation with Tim Partridge.* Retrieved March 14, 2005, from www.digitalcinemareport.com/qatimpartridge.html

Economides, N. (1996, October). The economics of networks. *International Journal of Industrial Organization, 14*(6), 673-699.

Fuchs, A. (2004a, September). Gaining access: Former Boeing digital sites re-lit & linked by satellite. *Film Journal International.* Retrieved March 25, 2005, from http://www.filmjournal.com/filmjournal/search/article_display.jsp?vnu_content_id=1000692659

Fuchs, A. (2004b). The Hollywood Titanic. ETA Conference Asks: Is D-Cinema the Iceberg. *Film Journal International.* Retrieved March 25, 2005, from http://www.filmjournal.com/filmjournal/search/article_display.jsp?vnu_content_id=1000729613

Gates, D. (2003, December 2). Condit steered Boeing to be No. 2. *Seattle Times.* Retrieved March 23, 2005, from http://seattletimes.nwsource.com

Giardina, C. (2004). Independent thinking. *The Hollywood Reporter* (Ed.). White Paper: Digital Intermediates, p. 14.

Hollywood Software. (2005). *Indiedirect.* Retrieved March 14, 2005, from http://www.ukfilmcouncil.org.uk/news/?p=D4A15778059152EF9EkRn 2455D6C&skip

Hubbard, P. (2002). Screen shifting: Consumption, 'riskless risks' and the changing geographies of cinema. *Environment and Planning A, 34,* 1239-1258.

Huettig, M. D. (1944). *Economic control of the motion picture industry.* MPhil dissertation, University of Pennsylvania, Philadelphia.

Husak, W. (2004) Economic and other considerations for digital cinema. *Image Communication, 19,* 921-936.

Kaufman, D. (2004). DI facilities adopt 2K Projectors. *The Hollywood Reporter* (Ed.). White Paper: Digital Intermediates, pp 10-11. Retrieved March 14, 2005, from http://www.hollywoodreporter.com/threast/pdfs/di_ whitepaper.pdf

Kilday, G. (2004, March 25). Studios shifting d-cinema stance: Hint at subsidizing transition. *The Hollywood Reporter.*

Kostoff, R.N., Boylan R., Simons, G.R. (2004). Disruptive technology roadmaps. *Technological Forecasting & Social Change, 71,* 141-159.

Litman, B. R. (1998). *The motion picture mega industry.* Needham Heights, MA: Allyn and Bacon.

McQuire, S. (2004, February). Slow train coming? The Transition to digital distribution and exhibition in cinema. *Media International Australia incorporating Culture and Policy,* p. 110.

MKPE Consulting. (2005). *Humble thoughts.* Retrieved March 14, 2005, from http://mkpe.com/digital_cinema/index.php

Moore, G. (1991). *Crossing the chasm.* New York: Harper Business Press.

(NATO) National Association of theatre owners (2004, November 18). *Digital Resolution.* Retrieved March 14, 2005, from http://www.natoonline.org/ DigitalResolution%2011-18-04.pdf

Parisi, P. (2004). Aged to perfection. *The Hollywood Reporter* (Ed.). White Paper: Digital Intermediates, p. 15. Retrieved March 14, 2005, from http://www.hollywoodreporter.com/threast/pdfs/di_whitepaper.pdf

Pfeffer, J., & Salancik, G. R. (1978). *The external control of organizations: A resource dependence perspective.* New York: Harper & Row.

Schilling, M. et al. (2005, January 21). Conquering Alexander. *Screen Int.*, p. 4, 6.

Scott, A. J. (2002). A new map of Hollywood: The production and distribution of American motion pictures. *Regional Studies, 36*(9), 957-975.

Scott, J. (2005). *On Hollywood. The place, the industry.* Princeton University Press.

Screen Digest. (2003*). Report on the implications of digital technology for the film industry.* London: Screen Digest.

Slater, J. (2002, August). *Electronic cinema—A business as much as a technology. Ingenia, 13,* 41-46.

Sony. (2005, March 15). *Digital cinema gets to billing with Sony, Landmark Theatres Alliance.* Retrieved March 23, 2005, from http://news.sel.sony.com/pressrelease/5701

Sperling, N. (2004, October 22). Double standards. *The Hollywood Reporter.* Retrieved March 25, 2005, from http://www.hollywoodreporter.com/thr/film/feature_display.jsp?vnu_content_id=1000682865

Texas Instruments (TI). (2003, June 9). Interview with Director Bryan Singer. Retrieved March 21, 2005, from http://www.dlp.com/dlp_cinema/dlp_cinema_feature_article_brian_singer_interview.asp

Texas Instruments (TI). (2005, March 15). *George Lucas and James Cameron to highlight digital cinema and 3D movies at ShoWest 2005.* Retrieved March 23, 2005, from http://www.dlp.com/about_dlp/about_dlp_press_release.asp?id=1232

Thomond, P., & Lettice, F. (2002). *Understanding and enabling disruptive innovation.* Doctoral paper. International Ecotechnology Research Centre.

UK Film Council. (2005, February 26). UK film council selects arts alliance digital cinema to manage world's first large scale digital screen network. Press Release. London

Von Sychowski, P. (2003). *Digital cinema business models: The global outlook.* London: Screen Digest.

Endnotes

[1]   In fact it is one of the primary objectives of a resolution by the board of directors of the National Association of Theatre Owners in America (NATO, 2004).

[2]   JVC does not seem to actively participate in the competition at the moment.

Chapter X

Access to the Living Room:
Triple Play and Interactive Television Reshaping the Producer/ Consumer Relation

Eggo Müller, Utrecht University, The Netherlands

Abstract

Whereas the advent of interactive TV has been discussed as one of the key added values of digitization and convergence of "old" and "new media" for years, current marketing strategies of the big players in the Dutch telecommunications market avoid the term interactivity. *Providers promise users "more fun" and increased ease of media consumption when connected digitally to the media world by offering broadband Internet, cable television, and telephone services in one package. They aim at another added quality of interactive media consumption: gaining access to the living room means gaining access to consumption patterns that can be traced back to the individual consumer. This article discusses media convergence and the current development of interactive television in the context of the reconfiguration of the relation between producers and consumers in the new online economy.*

Concepts of Interactivity

For almost three decades, one magic word has dominated professional and public debates on the future of television: *interactivity*. The story goes that when finally provided with a return channel, our "good old television" would become a true means of real two-way-communication. Viewers would not only compose their own program schedules, watch any program at any time, get more background information, and do their shopping at home, they would also contribute to and participate in programs and would even become directors themselves. Although the first field tests of interactive television services in the U.S. in the 1970s, then still based on analogous technologies, failed (Richeri, 2004), and although audience research in the early 1990s still showed that the average public was not ready for interactive television programming (Berghaus, 1995), the industry's expectations remained optimistic, especially since the introduction of the Internet in the early 1990s; progress in digitization and compression of audiovisual information; and household's fast growing computer and broadband penetration. The convergence of television and computer-based communication technologies would help to finally disseminate the envisioned interactive television or multimedia system (Owen, 1999; Van Vliet, 2002).

This vision of the industry was echoed by a new brand of media theory that in the name of technological potentials of new media uncritically promoted a fundamental transformation of traditional power relations that were inherent to "old-fashioned" broadcast media and their traditional forms of mass communication. For example, Pearce (1997) praised this "interactive revolution" in a McLuhanian style:

The interactive revolution is [...] about creating machines that extend our mental and creative faculties, that enable us to store, manage, and most important, share massive amounts of knowledge on a global level. It is about using powerful tools to create our own educational and entertainment experiences rather than passively accepting that which is fed to us by so-called experts. It is about the dissolution of boundaries and the translation of all thought into a common vocabulary. Binary code is the digital Esperanto that is leading concurrently to individual empowerment and worldwide unity. (p. xvii)

According to this view, the New Media technologies would fundamentally transform the relation between producers and consumers. Through interactive media, consumers would increasingly gain control of the means of production and distribution, contribute to public opinion, and participate in cultural production processes. Interactive media would help to empower the, by then passive, media consumers and transform them, as the argument goes, into active "prosumers" (Toffler, 1981).

Pearce's (1997) view can be characterized as a quite extreme example of what Boddy (2003) has called the "polemical ontology" (p. 191): the ideological self-promotion of a new medium that highlights the technological features and social advantages of the new medium and, at the same time, disparages those of the old media. In the past few years, this utopian view has been challenged by more critical if not dystopian accounts of New Media (Andrejevic, 2003) and especially by the development and introduction of interactive television. As Kim (2001) and Kim and Sawhney (2002) argue, the concepts of interactive television as envisioned by firms rooted in the traditional television business do not sufficiently take advantage of the new possibilities interactive technologies provide to extend the user's control of mediated communication. On the contrary, according to Kim and Sawhney, interactive services such as enhanced television, video-on-demand, or Web TV as developed by the TV industry cannot be regarded as "interactive" at all. These services fail to realize the "inherently" participatory, empowering, and democratic potential of the new computer-based communication technologies:

[...] interactive TV requires television to change its historically and culturally built-in centralized character. Due to this built-in bias, the TV communication model limits interactivity to mechanical transactions, while the center retains in control. In interactive TV, 'interactivity' is artificially grafted onto TV without taking into consideration the contradiction between interactivity and TV. (Kim & Sawhney, 2002, p. 224)

This view obviously implies a normative definition of the concept of interactivity and subsumes that there are inherent qualities of a technology as such. Like many other scholars, Kim and Sawhney (2002) define interactivity in qualitative terms as the radical sharing of power and control between producers and consumers in mediated communication (Jensen, 1999; Pearce, 1997; Rafaeli, 1988)—a quality that has to be unfolded when interactive television is developed. But as numerous studies of technological innovation have shown, technology is constructed in a social environment and thus shaped by the economic, political, and cultural contexts in which a technology is developed, realized, and introduced (Bijker & Law, 1992; Williams, 1974; Winston, 1998). In an international survey of producers' and developers' concepts of interactivity concerning the new interactive technologies, Van Dijk and De Vos (2001) have shown that the concepts of experts working in television-based industry differs significantly from those experts affiliated with the world of the Internet. Television defines interactivity "as an extension of current TV with a number of additional facilities" (p. 457), while interactive applications on the Internet are associated with the transformation of the television viewers "into users and producers of audiovisual programs, or into more active participants in e-commerce by making continuous price comparisons and by offering products themselves" (p. 457). Depending on different business models, different concepts of interactive TV are developed. Considering the economic, political, and cultural power of the established transnational media firms that invest massively in the growing online economy, and engage in the development and exploitation of interactive services and applications, their concept of interactivity will increasingly shape interactive media technologies and, as a consequence, reconfigure the relationship between producer and consumer in the media and communication market. In the following paragraphs, the launch of the Windows Media Center and the competition of the distributors of digital television on the Dutch market will be discussed as two indicators of this reconfiguration.

Targeting at the Living Room

When Microsoft launched the Windows XP Media Center Edition 2005 in the beginning of 2005, the magic word that for decades propagated the key-added-value of new digital media in public and scholarly discourses did not show up even once in Microsoft's Dutch marketing campaign. Instead of promoting "interactivity," the company chose a more accessible value in simply promising: "It's more fun." On Microsoft's Web site, the advantages of the new system software are explained in the following tempting words:

Microsoft Windows XP Media Center Edition 2005 lets you do everything other Windows XP PCs do—and a whole lot more. Browse the Web, play your favorite PC games, e-mail and instant message your friends, and install and use programs designed for Windows XP. Media Center also delivers a powerful yet familiar way to enjoy all of your digital entertainment—photos, music, TV, movies, home videos, radio, and a world of applications and services whether you're sitting in front of your Windows desktop or across the room with a remote control. Media Center is your all-in-one PC and home entertainment center. (http://www.microsoft.com/windowsxp/mediacenter/evaluation/features.mspx)

The same is true for Hewlett Packard's (HP) marketing campaign of its new Media Center PC that was released at the same time, dovetailing with Microsoft's new version of the system software. The Dutch folder for HP's Media Center PC shows four young people sitting on a huge designer couch in front of a big flat screen television enjoying the new possibilities of the Media Center. One of the male participants points to the significant start menu on the big TV screen with its standard options that suggest a personalizing character of the applications: Online Spotlight, My Videos, My Pictures, My TV, My Music, More Programs, and so forth. The text praises the following advantages of the Media Center PC:

HP introduces the HP Media Center for the living room. TV and stereo, your pictures and films, Internet and many other technological triumphs all in one set. Operated by only one remote control and a very easy accessible menu on your television screen. The whole family will enjoy anything that home entertainment offers to you. That's what we call Digital Entertainment. (Hewlett Packard, 2005, p. 1)

The marketing campaign of a Dutch computer brand adapted this model of addressing the consumer in terms of the accessibility, ease of technical handling, and the promise of personal entertainment. As the flyer for the Paradigit Enjoy TV 2005 promises:

The Enjoy TV 2005 transforms your living room into the ultimate media center. In one top designed system you'll combine the best of a computer and home entertainment! Beyond that, the Enjoy TV2005 is noiseless. All your photographs, videos and music documents will be accessible from your couch. You'll be able to pause and rewind all your TV programs 'live.' Programs to be recorded, you'll chose in the online program guide by pressing just one button. (Paradigit, 2005, p. 1)

By deliberately avoiding the term *interactivity* and replacing it with concepts like "fun," "entertainment," or "easy handling," these marketing campaigns obviously aim at a more and more crucial target: the living room as the headquarter of a family's media consumption. The Media Center PC is designed to replace different analogous hardware systems such as the stereo and VCR, by *one* computer. This central computer is not only used to digitally store and manage a family's music, photos, videos, and computer games. Logged on to the Internet, it also allows e-mailing, surfing on the Internet, e-banking, online shopping, and so forth. It can be used for Internet information retrieval as well as for downloading any information, service, or entertainment product required. Although in technological terms it is not necessary to login when starting up the computer, using a Media Center PC would practically imply that the user will be connected to the Internet at any moment that they are engaged with media. The Media Center software is designed in such a way that listening to music, watching "regular" television programs, or archiving photographs would mean that the user *is* connected, unless he or she actively changes the default options of the software. For the industry this is not only a prerequisite in terms of exploiting online services and e-commerce, but according to experts the interesting fact arises that whenever the consumer is connected to the Internet, any act of consuming a media product or an online service can be monitored, registered, and related to the individual's profile. As Bertelsmann Group media consultant Carel Mackenbach explained bluntly in a Dutch TV documentary on the future of the media market, this data is the target of the media and communication industry:

If you look at the big international media concerns, be it Bertelsmann, AOL/ Time Warner, or Vivendi: these are global players that engaged in television, radio, and print at the same time, and right at the moment there is a battle for the consumer going on in The Netherlands and in Europe. All these concerns are investing in pan-European databases of consumer profiles on a large scale. The following generation of consumer databases does not just register names, addresses and more or less accidental subscription of a daily newspaper, it registers behavior like what you think about certain topics, when you buy goods or when your require a financial service of a certain type or when you plan to change your telephone provider and what the reasons are to do so. (Rottenberg, 2005)

Compared to data utilized by traditional audience research such as the Nielson Media Research, the "new generation" of data Mackenbach (Rottenberg, 2005) refers to is of special value for providers and advertisers. These data not only register patterns of media and consumption behavior, they can be related to profiles of individuals. An individual user's phone numbers would be accessible to the provider when the user has subscribed for all three services, Internet, television, and telephone, the so-called triple play or "multi play."

Although regulations and privacy legislation do prohibit the industry from registering such personal data, the example of Californian-based provider and distributor of personal or hard disk recorders TiVo clearly shows that there is no technological problem in doing so. In the U.S., TiVo is a widespread brand of digital video recorder that not only allows users to capture television programming on internal hard disk storage for later viewing, it also registers viewing habits and program preferences of the individual viewer in order to help him to "personalize" the overall television programming: a TiVo preselects and records a user's preferred programming and alerts the viewer when a preferred shows is on. Therefore, these digital video recorders are also known as "personal video recorders." The crucial difference between this and average hard disk recorders that have been marketed in the last few years all over the world, is that a TiVo must be connected via a telephone line to the provider that not only sends the program schedule to the hard disk of the user, but also registers his or her viewing habits. As Martin (2001) has convincingly shown by analyzing the log files automatically transmitted from the individual TiVo box at home to the TiVo headquarters, these files not only tell down to the second what has been watched, which commercials have been skipped, and what moments have been rewound and played again. According to Martin's (2001) findings, TiVo:

gathers enough information to track back individual user's home viewing habits while apparently promising not to do so; could identity the personal viewing habits of subscribers at will; has a much more explicit privacy policy disclosure on its Web site than in the printed material that accompanies the purchase of the product. (p. 2)

Though TiVo spokespeople admit that TiVo could investigate an individual's viewing habits, they recurrently deny that TiVo would do so (Charny, 2004). However, taking Carel Mackenbach's statement into account, the long term strategy of cable distributors, telephone companies, and Internet providers is obvious: gaining digital access to the living room means access to an enormous capital in the online economy, by providing information about individual user's consumption habits (Rottenberg, 2005).

Only against this background can one understand the enormous competition in the Dutch telecommunication market that arose in 2004 when the former national postal and telephone company, KPN (Royal Dutch Post) launched the first set top box in the Dutch market for terrestrial digital television broadcasting. As the former national telephone provider, the KPN has traditionally held a strong position in the market of (mobile) telephony and broadband Internet. Yet since about 96% of television broadcasting is distributed regionally by commercial cable companies, only a few public channels are broadcasted terrestrially and there is no significant satellite penetration (Koetje, 2003), KPN would miss television programming as an indispensable part of a future triple-play strategy. Media experts expected—then and right now—that by means of new media technologies replacing the good old "telly" in the living room, one could get the economically crucial access to the average family's living room, since television was and still is the most frequently used domestic medium.

The competing cable distributors took their chance and denied KPN access to cable distribution, while getting the coaxial cable system ready for broadband Internet, analogous and digital telephony and for digital television distribution for themselves. In neighboring countries such as Flanders, the government forced entrepreneurs to agree on one common standard accessible for digital encoding for any provider (Baaren, 2006). In Germany, public and commercial broadcasters defined one standard for terrestrial digital broadcasting (DBV-t). However, in The Netherlands, the Dutch authorities defined neither a common standard for digital broadcasting, nor one for terrestrial, cable, or satellite distribution. The result of this neo-liberal policy is that besides the KPN there are other competitors on the market offering television via the cable—each using its own exclusive standard to encode the digital signal: cable television companies that formerly operated only regionally such as Casema and Essent, but also UPC and Versatel, two competitors that operate nationally (Gorter, 2005, pp. 28-29). Some of these and some new competitors prepare digital television distribution via the next generation of broadband Internet (ADSL-2); each company making use of its own standard and thus set top box, respectively smart card, offering its own, exclusive package of TV channels via Internet Protocol Television.

According to market research held in June 2005, a total of 30% of the Dutch consumers said that they were interested (19%) or might be interested (11 %) in subscribing for a triple-play package to get digital television, broadband Internet, and telephony for a relatively cheap price (Heliview Nieuws, 2005). However, the competing companies use different standards to gain exclusive access to the living room. Their strategy is based on the expectation that in the long run exclusive access will be the gold mine of the online economy. As the former owner of one of Europe's biggest independent television production companies, John de Mol, revealed in a television interview in August 2005, providers would invest 1,500 euros for any consumer subscribing to digital television. John de Mol had just launched a new television channel called TALPA on the highly competitive—and according to experts saturated—Dutch television market. TALPA is De Mol's second attempt to conquer Dutch television. His first attempt to market a commercial sports channel failed within only a few months, when too few viewers subscribed (Maarsen, 1999, pp. 108-123). As opposed to this short-term strategy targeting a niche market, John de Mol's new TALPA enterprise is designed as a family channel. As a business plan it only makes sense when seen as a strategy that anticipates the crucial transformation of the television market in the context of a developing online economy.

At the moment, De Mol's TALPA is broadcasted as free-TV and accessible via all television providers within the Dutch market. It is part of the various analogous or digital cable TV packages and can be received digitally via satellite (CanalDigitaal) or terrestrial (KPN Digitenne). But there is one significant exception: UPC's digital television package does not contain John de Mol's TALPA that owns the exclusive rights for live broadcast and other coverage of the national football competitions. As everywhere in Europe, coverage of national football has been the most attractive programming for decades. De Mol, who up until 2005 held a total of 42% of the Versatel stocks, cooperates closely with Versatel, whereas UPC is next to the regional cable distributors, Versatel's fiercest competitor on the market of digital TV and triple-play packages. In the long run, TALPA will only be accessible for subscribers of exclusive digital TV packages or as pay per view, as De Mol honestly announced in a TV interview on the occasion of TALPA's release. According to his strategy, TALPA's exclusive national football coverage would help TALPA and thus Versatel too, to achieve a dominant position in the Dutch television market. De Mol's enormous investment in his new television network is not just the realization of the multi-millionaire's old dream of owning a television channel, but follows a well-calculated economic strategy aimed at the business model of future interactive television. Television functions as a portal that not only provides exclusively access to the living room, but also one that cashes in on and registers any form of (media) consumption.

Corporate Industry's Redefinition of Interactivity

Although the Dutch television market has nationally specific characteristics, the business strategies of the Dutch television industry can be seen as an example of international developments. Television is no longer developed and marketed as a distinct medium, but is part of a media center in the living room that gives users access to many different types of media and other forms of consumption. At the same time, it makes the living room accessible to the industry in terms of consumption patterns and consumption behavior. Both an individual's actual consumption and the data registering these acts of consumption as a personal profile are cashable, and thus form the economic sources for media concerns in the online economy. Whereas the promise of interactive TV and the new interactive media was that the user would gain control of media communication, these developments point to a reconfiguration of the relationship between the industry and the audience that can not be correctly described in terms of "participation" or "empowerment" of the user as active citizen. In his fundamental critique of the new online economy Andrejevic (2003) describes this redefinition of the relationship between industry and users in terms of an increasing exploitation of the users' consumption:

Interactive media are rapidly being assimilated into an economic framework in which participation has nothing at all to do with power sharing. [...] Instead of power sharing, the contemporary deployment of interactivity exploits participation as a form of labor. Consumers generate marketable commodities by submitting to comprehensive monitoring. They are not so much participating, *in the progressive sense of collective self-determination, as they are* working *by submitting to interactive monitoring. The advent of digital interactivity does not challenge the social relations associated with capitalist rationalization, it reinforces them and expands the scale on which they operate (pp. 196-197, emphasis in original).*

Here Andrejevic (2003) describes the result of a well-known process in media history. Following a phase of invention and appropriation by amateurs and activists, economically promising new media technologies will subsequently be incorporated by the established concerns on the market. That which in a first utopian phase of the invention is discussed and appropriated as a means of communication, is turned into a medium of distribution tailored to industry interests (Zielinski, 1999). Regarding the Internet, this process has been referred to as the "normalization of cyberspace" (Resnick, 1998, p. 48).

Looking at the recent and current development of the so-called interactive television that uses the return channel to register user profiles and behavior, the advent of the "prosumer" era should no longer be embraced with enthusiasm. In this media order a user who is logged on and connected whenever he or she consumes media or other services, cannot *choose not to* interact. The media center in the living room, be it a Media Center PC or a set top box, interacts behind the user's back all the time thanks to the return channel. Instead of being the "active prosumer" one should think of the future fettered consumer as the "conducer." The conducer has no option but to collaborate, intentionally or unintentionally, at any given time, being seduced by the ever increasing entertaining value of contents, applications, and services of the converged media center in the living room. The interactive revolution is not just about people—as Pearce (1997) has put it—it's about a reconfiguration of power relations between the industry and the consumer.

References

Andrejevic, M. (2003). *Reality TV: The work of being watched.* Lanham, MD: Rowman & Littlefield.

Baaren, E. (2006). *Achter de schermen van iTV: De institutionele ontwikkeling van digitale interactieve televisie in Nederland en Vlaanderen. (Behind the screens of iTV: The institutional development of interactive television in The Netherlands and Flanders.)* Unpublished masters thesis, Utrecht University, Utrecht, The Netherlands.

Berghaus, M. (1995). Zuschauer für interaktives Fernsehen. Ergebnisse einer qualitativen Befragung. (Interactive television and its audience. Results of an empirical study.) *Rundfunk und Fernsehen, 43*(4), 506-517.

Bijker, W. E., & Law, J., (Eds.). (1992). *Shaping technology/building society: Studies in sociotechnological change.* Cambridge, MA: MIT Press.

Boddy, W. (2003). Redefining the home screen: Technological convergence as trauma and business plan. In D. Thornborn & H. Jenkins (Eds.), *Rethinking media change. The aesthetics of transition* (pp. 92-100). Cambridge, MA: MIT Press.

Charny, B. (2004, February 5). TiVo watchers uneasy after post-Super Bowl report. *CNet News.Com.* Retrieved September 12, 2005, from http://news.com.com/2100-1041_3-5154219.html

Gorter, E. (2005). *Televisie: Van Nipkowschijf tot harde schijf. Apparatus en discours rond digitale televisie in Nederland. (Television: From Nipkow disc to hard disc. Apparatus and the discourse on digital television in The Netherlands.)* Unpublished masters thesis, Utrecht University, Utrecht, The Netherlands.

Heliview Nieuws. (2005, June 6). Interesse in multi play aanbod is aanzienlijk… (Notable interest in multi play supply) *Heliview Nieuws.* Retrieved September 12, 2005, from http://www.heliview.com/Applications/Helivieu.nsf/Nieuws/ID=160

Hewlett Packard. (2005). *HP media center edition 2005.* [Folder]. Amstelveen.

Jensen, J. F. (1999). Interactivity: Tracking a new concept in media and communication studies. In P. Mayer (Ed.), *Computer media and communication* (pp. 160-188). Oxford University Press.

Kim, P. (2001). New media, old ideas: The organizing ideology of interactive TV. *Journal of Communicaiton Inquiry, 25*(1), 72-88.

Kim, P., & Sawhney, H. (2002). A machine-like new medium: Theoretical examination of interactive TV. *Media Culture and Society, 24,* 217-233.

Koetje, H. (2003). *Advis commissie switch-off: Afschakelen om digitaal door te starten. (Advisory board switch-off: Switch off and take off digitally.)* The Hague, The Netherlands: Ministry of Enonomics.

Maarsen, M. (1999). *Betaalde liefde. Voetbal, van volkssport tot entertainment-industrie. (Soccer: From the people's sport to entertainment industry.)* Nijmegen, The Netherlands: Sun.

Martin, D. (2001, March 26). *TiVo's data collection and privacy practices.* Retrieved September 12, 2005, from http://www.cs.uml.edu/~dm/pubs/TiVo%20report.htm

McChesney, R. W. (1996). The Internet and U.S. communication policy-making in historical and critical perspective. *Journal of Communication, 46,* 98-124.

Owen, B. M. (1999). *The Internet challenge to television.* Cambridge, MA: Harvard University Press.

Paradigit. (2005). *Paradigit enjoy TV 2005.* [Folder]. Eindhoven.

Pearce, C. (1997). *The interactive book. A guide to the interactive revolution.* Indianapolis, IN: Macmillan.

Rafaeli, S. (1988). Interactivity: From new media to communication. In R. P. Hawkins, J. M. Wiemann, & S. Pingree (Eds.), *Advancing communication science: Merging mass and interpersonal processes* (pp. 110-134). Newbury Park: Sage Publications.

Resnick, D. (1998). Politics on the Internet: The normalization of cyberspace. In C. Toulousee & T. W. Luke (Eds.), *The politics of cyberspace* (pp. 48-68). New York; London: Routledge.

Richeri, G. (2004). The history of interactive TV. In F. Colombo (Ed.), *TV and interactivity in Europe* (pp. 57-68). Milano: Vita e Pensiero.

Rottenberg, F. (2005). *De Media en de market, de kijker en de macht. (The media and the market, the audience and the power.)* VPRO, NL 2005. Retrieved October 15, 2005, from http://www.vpro.nl/tegenlicht/afleveringen/23/901551/

Toffler, A. (1981). *The third wave.* London: Pan Books.

Van Dijk, J. A. M. G., & De Vos, L. (2001). Searching for the Holy Grail. Images of interactive television. *New Media & Society, 3*(4), 443-465.

Van Vliet, H. (2002). Where television and Internet meet. *E-View,* 02-1. Retrieved September 12, 2005, from http://comcom.uvt.nl/e-view/02-1/vliet.htm

Williams, R. (1974). *Television: Technology and cultural form.* New York: Schocken.

Winston, B. (1998). *Media technology and society: A history.* London: Routledge.

Zielinski, S. (1999). *Audiovisions: Cinema and television as entr'actes in history.* Amsterdam, The Netherlands: Amsterdam University Press.

Chapter XI

Screening in High Standard:
Innovating Film and Television in a Digital Age through High Definition

Bas Agterberg, Utrecht University, The Netherlands

Abstract

This chapter introduces the innovation of television by looking at the development of high definition television (HDTV). It argues that the way that the interaction of technological, industrial, and political actors has been crucial in several stages of the development of this innovation. Central question is how industry, broadcasters, and consumers have debated and defined a medium and consequently redefine a medium through innovations. The complexity and the way actors have played a part within the changing media environment is analyzed by looking at the necessity for technological change of the television standard, by relating the media film and television in transition from analogue to digital and by studying case studies of political debates and policy in Europe and the United States.

Introduction

As a domestic medium, television has basically not changed since the 1950's. The programming, the way of viewing and the technological quality of the image all suggest that the medium's history is a stable one. The major changes have been the introduction of colour in the 60's and cable and satellite in the 80's, offering more channels. The VCR influenced the viewers' possibilities for time shifting. Despite these changes William Uricchio (2002) argues that the applications, cultural status and our assumptions regarding the medium have hardly changed over the past half-century. Digitalisation has offered new possibilities for the medium, but so far consumers have hardly adopted digital television. One of the developments associated with Digital Television (DTV) has been the innovation of the television screen in High Definition Television. This chapter explores aspects that have affected the so far unsuccessful implementation of HDTV.

The way in which innovation of a medium is promoted often resembles the discourse that was used with the introduction of a previous medium; in the case of Digital TV it's for instance radio and television. William Boddy (2004) argues that the digital moving image has been celebrated within "compelling imaginary scenarios of work and leisure, identity and community" (p. 1). Obviously the cultural and economic stakes in the transition from analogue to digital should be considered by looking at the way the media have been anticipated, debated and taken up by the industry, politics, and audiences.

Technology has to be considered as a cultural construct, so it is essential to look at the way that medium has developed. In terms of television this means how industry, broadcasters and consumers have debated and defined a medium and consequently redefine a medium through innovations.

Within this context the introduction of High Definition Television offers a compelling case study for the pattern in such a technological innovation. The changing media environment is studied by looking at the necessity for technological change of the television standard, by relating the media film and television in transition from analogue to digital and by studying case studies of political debates and policy in Europe and the United States.

Developing the High Standard

The process of defining a standard for the television image at the beginning of the medium shows the complex interaction of different actors involved in television technology.

The standard for the black and white television image has been set in the 40's and 50's and for colour in the 50's and in the 60's. Andreas Fickers (2004) argues that in the process of standardisation three actors or terrains were active, the technological, the industrial and the political. The standardisation of the television image has an important political dimension. The difference in the development of colour television in the US and Europe is exemplary for this process. In the U.S. the Federal Communications Commission (FCC) already forced the television industry in 1948 to develop colour TV by freezing the granting of frequencies for television. In 1950 the National Television Committee (NTSC) was founded to create a colour television standard compatible with black and white. In cooperative research of the American radio and television industry an electronic and compatible system was developed within three years. The FCC made the NTSC, with 525 lines, the U.S. standard of colour TV in 1953. In Europe however the black and white television standard was still debated in the beginning of the 50's. Colour would not be introduced until the 60's. The different European countries—Britain, Germany and France—had different standards, PAL (625 lines) and SECAM (819 lines). National interests were more important than the European interests at that moment. The international authorities and organisations such as the International Telecommunication Union (ITU), founded in 1865, and the International Consultive Committee for Radio Transmission (CCRT) did not have the authority to prevent the different standards. As Andreas Fickers (2004) concludes, the decision remained a national one. The choice for a television standard could not be made on the basis of quality of the picture and thus became a political and industrial decision. For the industry the prospect of a reasonable share was better than ending up as the "losing" system. The introduction of two standards of colour television in Europe in 1967 was the result.

The world standards of television are still NTSC (525 lines), PAL (625) and SECAM (625). The digitalisation of media technology makes the improvement of the quality of the screen only a matter of time. However, the development of so called High Definition Television started decades ago and what seems to be a matter innovation of the quality of television has become an interesting case to show the effects of the transition from analogue to digital, in terms of the changing roles of industry, global politics, of broadcasters and the convergence of different media like television, film and computer.

Defining a New Standard

The Japanese public broadcaster NHK worked on a new television standard since 1968. The idea was to design a system of 1125 lines and a wide screen ratio of 16:9. The necessity for research seemed a bargaining strategy of NHK, according to Winston (1998) it was tradition to use technological advances such as colour or teletext for the renegotiating of the domestic television licence fee level with the Japanese government.

When NHK presented the new HDTV system at international meetings, the quality of its images was admired, but the innovation was observed with suspicion.

During the meetings of the CCRT in 1983 in Algiers a worldwide standard for HDTV was mandated. Three years later, in 1986 at a meeting in Dubrovnik HDTV was put on hold. Technically it was the incompatibility with the existing television standard that was considered a problem by many countries. Yet more important was a socio-economical fear for a Japanese take over that led to a hold.

By putting the world standard for HDTV on a hold in 1986, Winston (1996) slows down the process of innovation, because of fear of losing a market share. Int was not the technology, but the economic stakes that suppressed the potential of HDTV (p. 94). This period can be considered the first phase in the development of HDTV.

Technologically the HDTV of the 80's was far from perfect. Although most of the technical problems could be solved within the near future, it was an analogue system in a digitalizing world. The signals of High definition require a lot of bandwidth, which means that consumers would only get one fifth of the number of television channels. It was however the digital High Definition could use compression techniques to solve this problem.

Most important was that in the 80's the infrastructure was not equipped to deliver HDTV. Therefore in the early stage HDTV was no competitor for film or television in production, distribution or exhibition. It was however promoted as a challenge to the existing concepts of film and television. It was believed that HDTV would change both media fundamentally.

The introduction of HDTV in the 80's has to be considered within a broader range of changes. William Boddy (2004) argues that the new TV delivery systems of cable and direct broadcast satellites, the ongoing consolidation of the telecommunications and computer industries, the international trend toward broadcast deregulation, and the growth of significant new transnational entrepeneurs all point to the late 1980s as the beginning of a period of the greatest change in global television since the decisive growth of international television in the second half of the 1950s. HDTV can thus only be understood in an international context in which the infrastructure and political deregulation play a crucial part in the development (Berghaus, 1994).

Innovating Audiovisual Media

The objective for improving the quality of the image was to achieve an electronic equivalent 35mm film. If the television screen equals the cinema, how does it affect the film industry in terms of production, distribution and exhibition?

Francis Ford Coppola claimed he would never make movies on 35mm again after shooting *One from the Heart* in 1981 with Sony's HDTV equipment (Winston, 1996). Coppola's film failed, costing him his Zoetrope studio and he continued making films on 35mm.

Film industry has in general responded conservatively to digitalisation. Brian Winston (1996) shows in *Technologies of Seeing* that Hollywood responds conservatively to innovation by analysing the way in which Hollywood responded to colour film, 16mm film and HDTV.

In film production nowadays, digital techniques such as video assist for instant reviews of what is shot on film during production on the set, editing and creating visual effects in postproduction are in general use. The shooting and exhibition have remained analogue in a 35mm standard. Some films used the video camera as an aesthetic choice, such as *The Blair Witch Project* (1999) or the Danish DOGMA 95 films. In the case of *The Blair Witch Project* the documentary look, the suggestion that the depicted events actually took place, was also used for a new way of promoting the film through the Internet. Despite specific use of new technologies, these examples do not differ much from traditional ways of producing and releasing a film.

High Definition however offers the possibility to change cinema fundamentally. In shooting a digital file would replace the vulnerable celluloid. Exhibition would even be possible through satellite, involving no material at all. Costs would especially be reduced in distribution and exhibition. How have different actors play a significant part in a possible change to digital cinema so far?

Both film and television are considered "old" media. In this case you might say that in terms of organisation of industry and content the traditions have led to a resistance to innovations.

Thomas Elsaesser (1998) argues that "For this remarkably stable product, digitalisation is a contradictory factor, at once an ingenious technical process of translation, generation and storage, and the totem-notion around a notoriously conservative industry is in the process of reorganizing—and this eventually means reinventing—itself in order to do much the same as it has always done" (p. 203). The Hollywood industry has already changed a lot after 1950, the blockbuster films and cinema are only one part of a marketing of products such as related video games, theme parks and the video/DVD market, the pay tv and cable tv.

Within the film infrastructure the exhibitors have no gain in investing in new digital equipment. The distributors would benefit, but are unable to invest in theatres. For Hollywood the change for delivering digital films would only work if it could deliver digitally worldwide. The complex interaction in distribution and exhibition means that little has changed so far.

The transformation of film and television cannot be restricted by looking at the technological innovation, but has to be considered as a fundamental transformation of the concept of the media. Siegried Zielinski (1999) argues that 'the particular constellations that arise in this way under the hegemony of the culture industry, structure the process historically' (p. 19) He distinguishes four dispositif arrangements, the production of illusions of motion in space and time with the aid of picture machines, the cinema, television and advanced audiovision, The transformation is a process in which the periods overlap, interlock, attract and repel each other. In this sense we do not only look at the way the innovation has been developed and implemented, but how it redefines the existing media in a changed system of advanced audiovision that differs fundamentally from the traditional constellations that we knew as cinema and television.

The International Politics in Technological Innovation

In the development of HD it has been the electronics industry that has played a major part Although HDTV became a public debate in the 80's, different countries already researched new standards. The American Society of Motion Picture and Television Engineers (SMPTE) set up an HDTV Study Group in 1977. Initially they felt that home HDTV would depend on audiences becoming used to the standard first in the theatres. But without the interest of the film industry, the researchers introduced it as a new television standard.

In Japan, Europe and the US the electronics industry used the technology debate for lobbying in politics to make governments invest in research.

After 1986 the innovation of HD became a national interest. As Republican congressman Norman Lent put it in 1989 "our future competitiveness in high tech electronics could be at stake here", or even more fundamental as another republican said "[HDTV] *is* one of the most important inventions of the 20th century. This is a crown-jewel product" (Winston, 1996, p. 95).

In comparison to the 60's the European Community had in the 80's gained power as a political force. The European Commission launched its strategy on HDTV in 1985. The five year program was called Eureka and was aimed at cornering a lucrative multi-billion dollar market for European electronics companies. It was to help producers, broadcasters and studios to make HDTV format programs.

The Dutch electronics giant Philips and French company Thomson worked together to develop a European HDTV standard. At first it was the analogue MAC device that was subsidized by the EC. In Japan the government supported the electronic industry to develop the MUSE system. Both examples indicate the high expectations for the national electronic industries in the development of HDTV. Despite a political lobby, the US government was reluctant to subsidize the industry. In 1989 Jeffrey Hart argued that the U.S. policy should adapt a national standard to add to U.S. competitiveness in consumer electronics and second that the formation of R&D consortia to develop HDTV technologies should be encouraged and assisted. In short term the development of HDTV was interesting for producers of semi conductors because the digital TV needs much more chips than the Standard Television.

During the 90's the electronic industries tend to cooperate intensively in research and development of new television sets. Philips and Thomson worked in Europe, but also participated in an American research program with Sarnoff Research Laboratory, thus creating a win-win situation (Anonymous, *Economist*, 1992).

Implementing the New Screens

During the early 90's the first steps in implementing HDTV were taken. In Europe the industry and several (public) broadcasters worked together to produce and screen a growing number of programs in 16:9 with 1250 lines as standard. It was meant to boost the sales of 'wide screen' televisions.

The European countries also created national platforms to promote the changes. In the Netherlands the HDTV Platform was established in December 1989 as a national mechanism to prepare for the introduction of HDTV (Van der Louw, 1990). Basically, coordination, research, information and international cooperation were the key issues for this platform. The foundation was formed by the National Broadcasting Corporation (NOS), the Broadcasting Service Corporation (NOB), the Dutch Telecom service (PTT Telecom), the association of Cable Antenna Operators and Authorities (VECAI) and Philips. Three governmental departments were involved.

The platform had three taskforces, one to stimulate the number of HDTV productions, one to coordinate transmission and one to investigate other electronic services of HDTV (van der Louw, 1990).

Subsidizing HD productions, demonstrating programmes at festivals and re-search, made promotion for HD. A channel, TVplus, was created in 1991. It broadcasted four hours HD weekly.

Transmission of the HDTV signal became one of the crucial problems to be solved. Therefore cable operators were essential. In the Netherlands 90% of the country is supplied through cable. Although the network was not able to transmit the HD data in the early 90's, solutions were foreseen in the near future (van der Louw, 1990).

The proposed non-broadcast services were for instance HDTV pictures of collections of various museums, or an HDTV theatre showing public events. Most of these services in fact reflect the way in which television was promoted in the 30's and at trade shows throughout Europe and the U.S. in the 40's and 50's.

The platforms were the cooperation between the local governments, cable and telecom organisations and local industries. In the Netherlands the platform played an important part to promote the use of HDTV, but the long term development was decided by European politics.

In the U.S., the FCC played a central part in developments. In 1987 the FCC began to define the technical and juridical aspects of HDTV. In 1990 it held an open entry for the new HDTV standard. The compatibility with the existing NTSC was to be ensured and the enhancement signals were to be sent through a second channel. This solution was possible because in parts of the U.S. there were still channels available. None of the three main consortia, that were in the game for the frequencies, offered the solution. For the FCC it was clear that the digital TV would be the solution and therefore the three consortia were asked to cooperate. In 1993 a so-called Grand Alliance was founded with the companies Zenith, AT&T, General Instruments, that also had MIT and several small companies. To prevent Anti-trust lawsuits, European Philips and Thomson were included as well as the promise to release the patented technology (Kleinsteuber, 1994).

In the meantime the EC debated the subsidy, the standards and implementation. The idea was to renew the EUREKA project. But the UK vetoed the program, because it argued that the analogue-based system would be overruled by the digital development in the U.S. Other arguments were the advantages such as interactivity and suitability for all forms of distribution, terrestrial, cable and satellite. Some European members feared that the fact that British view on European subsidies was motivated by the fact that British electronics industry was foreign owned.

The EC launched the Advanced Digital Television Technologies, Eureka 1187 in 1994. The Dutch Platform wrote that one and a half year were lost due to the debate and that it meant the end of the European HDMAC system. According to the platform it was a pity because HDMAC was semi digital and it did not share the American optimism on the digital HD. Despite an initial European initiative in developing HD, once again a division within the EC resulted in a slowdown of the process.

By the mid 90's HDTV was a technology that mostly interested the electronic industries, hardly anyone was interested in the content. " The only people talking about HDTV are those who are developing it" according to management consultant John Rose (*Economist*, 1994)

In 1993 Philips announced it was halting its production of HDTV sets and would review its entire strategy if the EC would not come up with the promised subsidy (Barnard, 1993).

For the success of HDTV, not only a subsidy for developing the technology and the infrastructure was required, but also the introduction to the market needed state intervention. However the growing tendency towards liberal market policy made governments careful in subsidizing implementing an innovation like HD.

It turned out that neither the broadcasters, nor the consumers were interested. Was there no audience because there was no content? Or were broadcasters right that the audience did not want to buy expensive HDTV sets?

When television was introduced in the late 40's it was the medium itself that was being sold From manufacturer Allan B. Dumont, "…. Sell television on what it can do for the customer. You are selling more than just a gadget—you are selling television itself" (Boddy, 2004, pp. 53-54). With HDTV the customer knows what television as a medium offers. As van Vliet (2002) observes, "HDTV does not work, because better picture and sound quality do not change Sesame Street."

During the 90's there is a growing market for wide screen televisions, although they only partly offer the quality of the high definition. Advertisements appeal to quality of the screen in relation to lifestyle, offering status, financially as well as a sign of taste. The flat screens of the late 90's are an example of this. However a massive breakthrough has not been achieved.

By the end of the 90's there were two HD world standards, of 1080 and 720 lines. Most technical problems in HD equipment and delivery were solved, so there was no reason why broadcasters and audiences would not adopt the new standard. But in fact especially in Europe at that moment HDTV was unimportant for the broadcasting industries.

The End of HDTV?

During the 90's the attention for HDTV faded. The Dutch Platform wrote in September 1994 that all goals had been achieved within four years. It suggests that it created the infrastructure, but denied responsibility for the implementation of HD (Van Eupen, 1994). The way in which HDTV was studied and promoted showed a technological interest, but failed to take into account the social status of film and television at the period. The audience was not attracted to HD by initiatives such as activities by the platform, in 1996 the platform was resolved (Vos, 2000).

None of the initiatives in Europe and the U.S. in the early 90's led to a regular production and screening of HDTV. In 2000, a Dutch professional production magazine Call Sheet wrote:

if you wonder when the HDTV format will be there? It will not. Some years ago the NOB (facility service television) has thrown all standards and equipment over board, and thus all broadcasting in HD are history. All well known manufacturers have developed HD techniques, but aim at the US, where special TV-stations broadcast in this standard. In the Netherlands HDTV is restricted to some experiments. (Een overzicht, p. 12)

The failure of HDTV is international. The innovation was promoted within the context of television, but did not add anything to the existing concept of television. Brian Winston (1998) offers a model for development of technologies in which this interaction of competence of science is related to social necessity and processes of diffusion. If we consider the case of HDTV in this model, the lack of social necessity and the way of diffusion have been crucial in the innovation's slow acceptation.

Even in several studies at the end of the 1980s noted some of the problems. *Is HDTV a new medium?* was the question at a conference organised by German broadcaster ZDF in 1990. (Lüscher, Paech, & Ziemer, 1991). It was an attempt to discuss the innovation in an interdisciplinary approach, looking at technical aspects, the aesthetics of HDTV and the social consequences of the changes of television.

According to participants a change of content for HDTV was required due to the quality of the screen. As long as there would be compromises with the existing forms of television, HDTV would fail. One of the conclusions was that the innovation could only be successful after 2000 (Lüscher et al., 1991).

Why have governments and electronic industry tried to start the medium a decade earlier? There is a similarity in the development of television standards in Europe in the 50's. Fear of a monopoly made it more attractive to get a part of the cake instead of risking getting none at all.

Consequences of the transformation of this new medium were issues that put the relation of viewer and medium into question. It was the VCR, cable and satellite that played a significant part in debates on changing media environments. Only few academics discussed issues such as telepresence and a development in aesthetics that would change the concept of television in terms of its social status. At the start of the 90's none of these changes were related to digitalisation, for instance in interactive services in television and other media. It was only five years later that the debate on media shifted to concepts of interactivity and connectivity. HDTV, however, has hardly been part in this debate. Of the few studies, the most compelling one is Brian Winston's case (1996), set as an example for his model technological development and views on how we tend to forget the process of media changes.

Reviving HDTV in a Digital Context

A third phase of HDTV started when it was linked to digital television in the U.S.

Digital television is most of all the change in accessibility of large quantities of digital content on a huge scale. It was no longer cinema that was related to television, but television partly merging with the Internet. The consumer's needs individualize and therefore new services are directed to the individual demands, for instance in electronic program guides (EPG) and video-on-demand (VoD). Harry van Vliet (2002) argues DTV will affect the content, economics and politics of the television business. In short term digital television has not been a commercial success. William Boddy's (2004) examination of digital television's distinct fortunes in the U.S. and GB offers revealing insights into some of the most persistent and difficult issues in media historiography, including roles of national culture, market structures, and ideological valence in setting the course of technological innovation.

In 1997 the FCC granted the free duplicate UHF channels to each U.S. broadcaster. The strategy was due to the political lobby by the broadcasters, in cooperation with the consumer electronics industry, who were hoping to revive the domestic market. The FCC planned to shut down and auction off all analogue television channels by 2006. Even in a continuing internationalization of media ownership and programme flows, the nationalist sentiment remained a crucial element within political debates.

Immediately after the allocation, broadcast executives expressed reservations about the costs involving HDTV for networks and consumers. The HD broadcast made only one channel available, whereas multicasting in standard definition and interactive services were more attractive for broadcasters.

Only CBS started to produce HDTV programs. But with the approaching 2006 deadline, other broadcasters started to do the same. By 2003 both ABC and CBS delivered their entire prime-time slate of about 15 hours a week in high definition (Snider, 2003).

Despite the slow start in the new millennium more HD content is produced in the U.S. By the end of 2004, 10% of U.S. households had a television capable of displaying HDTV. The question is whether this is the critical mass of 12.8 million sets to make a turning point in the technology's adoption (Harrison, 2005).

In the UK the development of digital television has not been related to HD. The difference between the U.S. and the UK in infrastructure is significant. Britain had a low penetration of cable, only five terrestrial channels and a satellite service by Rupert Murdoch delivering to 3.6 million households. In this context two digital services were launched in Britain in 1998. The first one was Murdoch's new digital satellite service of BskyB, offering 140 channels, and the second one OnDigital by a consortium of ITV broadcasters, offering 30 channels. BskyB offered limited interactivity, OnDigital none at all. The number of channels, all in standard definition, was the main selling point. Despite 1.2 million subscribers, OnDigital failed due to a variety of problems, technological as well as in marketing and management.

Yet digital television in the UK is successful, 44% of British household had digital television in 2003, more than anywhere in the world (Boddy, 2004). Especially BskyB was successful. To attract the audience Murdoch had given away set top boxes to subscribers in 1999.

Digital television in Britain offered nothing new, but due to the infrastructure its selling point was the number of channels. Within Europe differences in infrastructure have probably determined the adoption of digital television. In the Netherlands the liberalisation of media politics resulted in seven new commercial channels within 15 years, apart from three existing public ones and some regional channels. With a cable penetration of 90%, Dutch viewers receive about 20 foreign channels and some pay TV channels. In 2004 Dutch Telecom company KPN was the first to offer a digital service. Several cable companies, also offering telephone, Internet and television services, soon followed KPN. In 2005 Internet provider Versatel started offering all football matches live. About 10% of Dutch consumers switched to digital television by 2005. In a European context the development is similar to a country like Germany (Döbler, Mühlenfeld, & Stark, 2003).

Although the innovations have not been successful yet, it shows the instability of the media constellations. First of all cable companies and telephone companies offer services in delivering a variety of services in Internet, television and telephony. Another thread for existing models of broadcasting are technological devices such as the digital video recorder—especially its possibility of recording and watching with a small delay changes television's sense of liveness or simultaneity. The fear of advertisers and commercial networks is a decrease of revenues. Therefore ways of advertising and participating in programmes or offering onscreen services will change content of television.

These changes will affect the social position of television in terms its relation to the audience. As Boddy (2004) quotes a newspaper statement by BBC chairman John Birt, "the end may be in sight for broadcasting as a communal experience" (p. 86). Of course the traditional models of broadcasting will exist in future, but not be as dominant as it used to be in the second half of the 20th century. Changes in the relation to the audience and the way cultural products are consumed have and will change in digitalisation if television and Internet tend to merge.

With the development of digital services, HD has become a small part in the discourse on changing media. Yet in recent years it seems to become more important. The U.S. strategy definitely plays a part. The necessity to produce HDTV has resulted in an increase in HD productions. The improvement of the equipment is another reason. Within the context of digitalisation changes within cinema create possibilities as well.

To promote digital cinema, the European Media program has subsidized a project offering equipment to arthouse cinemas at low costs. The condition is to screen national and European films digitally. Especially documentaries have found a possibility for theatrical release.

It seems that it's not the Hollywood industry that initiates a change to digital high standard, but the marginalized media industry. Most European films are low budget and the production costs are hardly affected by producing digitally. But because public broadcasters and national film funds finance most European films, by stimulating digital cinema they also play a part in distribution and screening.

Although Peter Greenaway already used HD in his feature film *Prospero's Books* (1989), in 2003 the first Dutch feature was to be shot in HD completely. In postproduction the film *Pipo and the PPParelriders* was transferred to 35mm released in theatres. Since then more films have been shot digitally and some of them also released digitally. The film *0605* (2005), a conspiracy thriller about the murder of politician Pim Fortuyn in 2002, was even first released on the Internet by co-producer and provider Tiscali. It caused a media hype, but eventually only a few people did download, pay and watch the film.

Now that broadcasters, independent producers and related industries seem to adopt the HD technology, the consumers will have to follow. Although so far consumers have not adopted HDTV, for several reasons HD will become standard for consumers. Even computer monitors have a higher resolution than standard television, thus if Internet and Television merge, it might use a higher standard to do so.

Van Vliet (2002) argues that media developments can be considered in the context of what Pine and Gilmore call the new economy, meaning that people do not want 'just' a product, but want an experience. HD as an innovation has been promoted as a new experience. In this sense HD also recalls film historian Tom Gunning's concept of early cinema as a cinema of attraction, because it was the sensation of imagery that was the attraction for the cinema audiences before 1905.

This sense of attraction is reflected in the European broadcaster Euro1080, set up as an HDTV channel. Gabriel Fehervari, a Belgian Hungarian launched the channel in 2004. It aims at producing sports and concerts, making 1200 productions each year. In an interview with Belgium newspaper *De Standaard* Fehervari argues that other initiatives by broadcasters like French TF1 or BskyB make clear that HDTV is becoming more important to European broadcasters (Petitjean, 2005). In the Netherlands regional broadcasters, public channels that deliver to a small market of several million viewers, announced to experiment with HDTV in April 2005 by opening its channel for programmes of Euro1080. But the promotion of a sensation has been the sole attraction of the innovation of HDTV up until 2005.

Conclusion

The case of HD shows that within 25 years the media landscape has changed. The initial innovation of HDTV was the quality and ratio of the electronic picture. The idea was that it would change television and film into a new medium. More important, the development of HDTV was a necessity for the consumers electronics industry; it would boost sales of chips and sales of new sets. The dichotomy between possibilities and necessity has determined the developments of HDTV.

In response to Japanese prototypes, the American and European industry made sure that a new standard would not lead to a Japanese monopoly. National interests made the innovation of television a political issue.

The electronics industry convinced regulators since the 1980's that HDTV is necessary for consumers electronics industry and for the economy. The U.S. and Japanese authorities as well as the European Union have in different ways contributed to the eventual success of HDTV.

Despite political back up, especially in Europe, the implementation of HDTV did not succeed. HD did not only concern the technology of television, but also of infrastructure through cable and satellite. The infrastructure did improve, but broadcasters and film industry were only interested in HDTV in controlling their position within the media. Consumers seemed to be ignored, there was, and perhaps still is, no demand for improvement of the pictorial quality by the audience. By the middle of the 1990s the HDTV hype was over. The European authorities cut subsidies for HD developments. The U.S. authorities granted UHF channels for digital broadcasting in HD to the American broadcasting companies.

After 2000, the digital HD revived. The FCC grant of free spectrum to the broadcasters to produce digital HDTV television may have been crucial for HD, but changes within cinema and the change of interaction between media such as telephony and the Internet has changed the actors involved. New digital services of interactivity change the traditional concept of television as a domestic broadcast medium. The opportunities for theatrical release at low costs, combined with other media for releasing films in high definition standard do offer new ways of thinking about traditional media film and television.

Initially the promise of new content, for instance in a change of aesthetics in programmes or in a concept like telepresence, was discussed as consequence of HD. However the electronics industry was depending on companies that used HD in traditional production. Thus the audience could hardly been shown the advantages of the innovation.

The HD technology has improved over the past 15 years. The compatibility, the definition of a world standard and improvement of camera equipment all made it easier for broadcasters or independent producers to adopt the HD technology. In different ways we see changes in production, postproduction and distribution in which HD plays a part. So far, these changes do not change the traditional concept of film or television. Now that both industry and broadcasters finally plan to use HD, the audience will be forced to buy HDTV-sets. The FCC will shut down analogue television in the near future.

Therefore it can be argued that HD will succeed, due to political and manufacturers persistence. For the audience the main attraction in digital television is the number of channels and interactivity. If HD is associated with these services, consumers will be more eager to adopt.

The digital developments will change the use of "old" media like film and television, although the traditional concepts will remain, at least for a while. The question remains in what way the developments will change socio-cultural concepts. How does digital HD affect ways of production, distribution and exhibition? In what way will it change the content of this Audiovision?

The study of innovating a medium like television shows that an unstable constellation of audiovisual media has developed. The consequences for media organisations, content and audience trends involve many different actors. It's my belief that the process of transition of traditional concepts into a new audiovision will only be developed in adoption and applications of an innovation by new generations.

References

Anonymous (1992, October 3). Big Television, Big deal. *Economist, 325*(7779), 89-90.

Anonymous (1994, September 24). Screened Out, *Economist, 332*(7882), 66.

Anonymus (2000, November). *Call sheet 27* (p. 12).

Barnard, B. (1993, October 1). HDTV – High definition debate. *Europe*, (330), 34.

Berghaus, M. (1994). Multimedia-Zukunft – Herausforderung für die Medien- und Kommunikationswissenschaft: Multimedia future, challenges for the media and communication studies. *Rundfunk und Fernsehen 42. Jahrgang nr, 3,* 404-412.

Big television, big deal. (1992, October 3). *Economist, 325*(7779), 89-90.

Boddy, W. (2004), *New Media and popular imagination.* Oxford: Oxford University Press.

Döbler, T., Mühlenfeld, H., & Stark, B. (2003). Acceptance and diffusion of digital television in Germany. In A. Schorr, B. Campbell, & M. Schenk (Eds.), *Communication research and media science in Europe* (pp. 336-379). Berlin: Mouton de Gruyter.

Een overzicht van IBC Amsterdam 2000 - An overview of International Broadcasting Convention, Amsterdam 2000. (2000). *Call sheet 27,* p. 12.

Elsaesser, T. (1998). Digital cinema: Delivery, event, time. In T. Elsaesser (Ed.), *Cinema futures: Cain, Able or cable* (pp. 201-222). Amsterdam: Amsterdam University Press.

Eupen, T. van (1994). *Handbook HDTV Platform1990-1994.* Hilversum: Netherlands Platform HCTV.

Fickers, A. (2004). De coloribus dispantdem est - About colour is disrupted. The failure of standardising colour TV in Europe. In O. de Wit (Ed.), *Tijdschrift voor Mediageschiedenis - Magazine for Media History* (Vol. 7, pp. 90-117). Amsterdam: Boom.

Harrison, C. (2005, April 30). *HDTV sales keep rising, but content is scarce.* Retrieved August 25, 2005, from http://www.northjersey.com

Hart, J. A. (1989, summer). Responding to the challenge of HDTV. *California Management Review, 31*(4), 132-145.

Kleinsteuber, H. J. (1994). HDTV-Politik; Die Entstehung der hochauflösenden Fernsehtechnik im High Tech-Dreieck Japan, Europa, USA - HDTV Politics, the development of high definition television technique in the tech-triangle Japan, Europe, USA. *Rundfunk und Fernsehen 42. Jahrgang nr, 1,* 5-23.

Louw, A. van der (1990). Paper on founding 'Stichting Nederlands Platform HDTV. Hilversum: Dutch Platform HDTV Foundation.

Lüscher, K., Paech, J., & Ziemer, A. (Eds.) (1991). *HDTV—ein neues Medium? - HDTV—A new medium?* Mainz: Zweite Deutsche Rundfunk.

Petitjean, F.c (2005, May 19). Euro1080 laat Europa proeven van HDTV - Euro1080 does Europe taste HDTV. *De Standaard*, Groot-Bijgaarden (B), 19. Retrieved August 25, 2005, from http://www.standaard.be/Thema/Multimedia/index.asp?articleID=G9AEVERS&subsectionid=11

Snider, M. (2003, January 7). A defining moment for TV. *USA Today*, 7B-8B.

Uricchio, W. (2002). Cinema as television. In D. Harris (Ed.), *New media book.* London: BFI Press.

Van Vliet, H. (2002). Where television and Internet meet. Retrieved March 13, 2002, from *E-view 02-1* comcom.kub.nl/e-view/02-1/vliet.htm

Vos, B. (2000, January). HDTV Platform ter ziele. In *Video&Audio Report* (pp. 40-41).

Winston, B. (1996). *Technologies of seeing.* London: BFI Publishing.

Winston, B. (1998). *Media technology and society.* London: Routledege.

Zielinski, S. (1999). *Audiovisions, Cinema and televsion as entr'actes in history.* Amsterdam: Amsterdam University Press.

Section IV:
Emerging Markets and
Organizational Cultures

Chapter XII

Bringing the Next Billion Online:
Cooperative Strategies to Create Internet Demand in Emerging Markets

Karen Coppock, Stanford University, USA

Abstract

This chapter classifies the types of partnerships employed to increase Internet demand in emerging markets. This classification system, or taxonomy, is based on more than 60 in-depth interviews, about 32 partnerships, designed to create Internet demand in Mexico. The taxonomy first classifies the partnerships into three broad categories based on the number of barriers to Internet usage the partnership was designed to overcome: one, two, or three. The partnerships are then classified into six subcategories based on the specific barrier or combination of barriers to Internet usage the partnership sought to overcome. The six subcategories of the taxonomy are: (1) lack of funds; (2) lack of awareness; (3) lack of uses; (4) lack of funds and lack of uses; (5) lack of funds and lack of infrastructure; and (6) lack of funds, lack of uses, and lack of infrastructure. This taxonomy gives empirical meaning and enables further analysis of this unique and increasingly popular type of partnership.

Introduction

*... it may sound altruistic and it may sound philanthropic, but let me tell you,
it is very concrete ... if we do not invest, if we do not take the time ... we will
never close the digital divide ... and we will never grow these markets ... and
we can never do it alone ... not the government alone, not universities alone,
not even businesses alone, we absolutely have to do it together.* (Omar
Villarreal, President, Latin America and the Caribbean, Motorola)[1]

The focal point of the Internet is rapidly shifting toward emerging markets. The
sale of personal computers (PCs) and Internet access is stabilizing in industrialized countries and profit margins are eroding (International Telecommunications Union [ITU], 2001; Smith, 2001). Market research firms predict that the
growth rates of information and communications technologies (ICTs) such as the
Internet will not return to their previous levels in industrialized markets, but that
future revenue opportunities lie in the developing world countries of China, India,
Russia, Brazil, and Mexico (De Marcillac, 2003). The sheer size of the population
of these five economies, coupled with their low Internet usage rates, make them
extremely attractive markets for multinational corporations. The Internet is also
seen as a powerful tool for socioeconomic development and therefore, governments, nongovernmental organizations (NGOs), and universities are also intent
on increasing their usage in these emerging markets.

The opportunity is clear, yet elusive. In 2001, from 33-50% of the population of
industrialized economies had Internet access, whereas a scant 1% or less of
emerging market citizens were online (ITU, 2002). Billions of people, therefore,
have never surfed the Web nor used e-mail. The reasons for the discrepancy in
Internet proliferation have been widely studied. On the demand side, education
and skill levels, Internet access costs, per capital gross domestic product, and a
lack of access facilities (telephone lines) are all statistically significant determi-
nants of Internet usage rates in emerging markets (Cukor & McKnight, 2001;
Kiiski & Pohjola, 2002). On the supply side, the absence of an independent
regulator and credible regulatory frameworks lead to under investment in ICT
infrastructure, which hinders Internet access rates (Gutierrez & Berg, 2000).

A wide range of initiatives sponsored by a diverse set of organizations have been
launched to increase Internet usage in emerging markets. The Digital Dividends
Project Clearinghouse (http://wriws1.digitaldividend.org/wri/app/index.jsp) created by the World Resources Institute lists nearly 1,000 initiatives designed to
increase Internet usage. At least one half of these initiatives are being implemented through the cooperative effort of two or more organizations. These
include both "traditional" partnerships, or those between two or more private

sector firms, and cross sector partnerships, or those between firms (private sector) and organizations from the public (government) and/or nonprofit sectors (including universities).

The purpose of this chapter is to classify the types of partnerships being used to increase Internet demand in emerging markets. A classification system, or taxonomy, will enable further analysis of this unique type of partnership and is the first step in any new line of social science research.

The chapter is organized as follows. First, I define the concept of market creation and outline the discrepancy between the practice and theory of market creation partnerships. Secondly, I present and explain the Internet market creation partnership taxonomy and provide definitions for each of its six categories. In the third, fourth, and fifth sections of this chapter, each of the three main categories of the taxonomy are explained in detail and examples are provided for each of the partnership configurations. The sixth section provides a high level overview of the methodology used to develop the taxonomy. The chapter ends with a brief conclusion.

Market Creation Partnerships

This chapter focuses on partnerships formed to create new markets, not simply access existing markets. A partnership in this chapter is defined as two or more organizations (i.e., firms, government agencies, NGOs, and universities) that agree (implicit or explicit contract) to share risk, responsibility, resources, competencies, and benefits to achieve a specific objective—in this case, to increase Internet usage rates in Mexico (Nelson 2002).[2]

According to Kotler and Armstrong (2001), one way a firm can expand the size of its market is to develop new users: either by extending into new geographic segments (market access) or by converting nonusers of a good or service into users (market creation). Market access, therefore, refers to market-share expansion, or increasing a firm's proportion of the total sales of a particular good or service on a global level. Conversely, market creation, or converting nonusers to users, is defined as increasing the total sales of a particular good or service on a global level. Because the vast majority of emerging-market citizens do not currently use the Internet or Internet-related goods and services, the focus of this chapter is on market creation partnerships or those designed to convert Internet nonusers into users.

There is a discrepancy, however, between the practice and theory of market creation partnerships. In practice, firms are drawing upon a wide range of

entities—firms, universities, government organizations, and nonprofit organizations—for their market creation partnerships. Scholars such as Kanter (1998)
and Prahalad and Hart (2002) all agree that market creation efforts in emerging
markets require partnerships of diverse configurations. In theory, however, the
conceptual foundations for partnership are largely separated into two categories:
traditional (between two or more private sector firms) and cross-sector (between public, private, and nonprofit organizations) partnerships (Gray, 2000;
Huxham & Vangen, 2001). Not only is this scholarship compartmentalized, but
Nelson (2002) also contends that there is a bias toward the study of traditional
interfirm partnerships.

This research project contributes to academic theory by simultaneously analyzing both traditional and cross-sector partnerships. Specifically, the focus is on
partnerships with a market creation objective. As a first step in this new line of
inquiry, this chapter will classify the partnerships to give them empirical meaning.

Internet Market Creation Partnership Taxonomy

*Classification is arguably one of the most central and generic of all of our
conceptual exercises ... Without classification, there could be no advanced
conceptualization, reasoning, language, data analysis or, for that matter,
social science research.* (Bailey, 1994, p. 1)

High-tech firms are partnering with a wide array of organizations to overcome
the barriers to Internet usage in Mexico and stimulate its demand. These
strategies can be categorized according to the barrier(s) to Internet usage they
were designed to overcome. This classification system, or taxonomy, is based on
a total of 32 Internet market creation partnerships in Mexico. The Internet
market creation partnership taxonomy (taxonomy) is shown in Table 1.

The taxonomy classifies the market creation partnerships into three broad
categories and six subcategories. The three broad categories are the number of
barriers to Internet usage, in Mexico, the partnership was designed to overcome.
The majority of partnerships in this study set out to tackle a single barrier to
Internet usage. Slightly less than one third of the partners set out to simultaneously tackle two barriers to Internet usage. Very few partnerships set out to
simultaneously tackle three barriers to Internet usage. None of the partnerships
included in this study simultaneously tackled all four barriers to Internet usage.

Table 1. Internet market creation partnership taxonomy

INTERNET MARKET CREATION PARTNERSHIP TAXONOMY						
Number of Barriers Tackled by the Partners	SINGLE BARRIER			DUAL BARRIER		TRIPLE BARRIER
Type of Barrier(s) to Internet Usage Tackled by the Partners	Lack of Funds	Lack of Awareness	Lack of Uses	Lack of Funds + Lack of Infra-structure	Lack of Funds + Lack of Uses	Lack of Funds + Lack of Uses + Lack of Infra-structure

This is because two of the barriers (lack of awareness and lack of uses) are mutually exclusive.

The six subcategories of the taxonomy are the specific barrier, or combination of barriers, to Internet usage the partnership set out to overcome. These are as follows:

Single Barrier Partnerships

- **Lack of funds:** The potential user does not have the economic resources to afford Internet access or to acquire the technology or services required to facilitate this access.

- **Lack of awareness:** The potential user is unaware of the value of the technology.

- **Lack of uses:** The technology is not "accessible" to the potential user or does not have value for the potential user due to its current form or the user's profile (education rates, etc.) (Gándara, 2003).[3]

Dual Barrier Partnerships

- **Lack of funds + lack of infrastructure:** The potential user does not have the economic resources to afford Internet access or to acquire the technology or services required to facilitate this access; and the potential user does not have a telephone line to use to access the Internet.

- **Lack of funds + Lack of uses:** The potential user does not have the economic resources to afford Internet access or to acquire the technology or services required to facilitate this access; and the technology is not "accessible" to the potential user or does not have value for the potential user due to its current form or the user's profile (education rates, etc.)

Triple Barrier Partnerships

- **Lack of funds + lack of infrastructure + lack of uses:** The potential user does not have the economic resources to afford Internet access or to acquire the technology or services required to facilitate this access; the potential user does not have a telephone line to use to access the Internet; and the technology is not "accessible" to the potential user or does not have value for the potential user due to its current form or the user's profile (education rates, etc.)

The underlying assumption behind the lack of awareness, lack of funds, and lack of infrastructure barriers to Internet usage is that the technology, in its current form, does offer value, but the potential user is simply unaware of this value (lack of awareness) or unable to tap into this value due to economic (lack of funds) or telephone line (lack of infrastructure) constraints. The lack of infrastructure barrier always went hand-in-hand with the lack of funds barrier in the partnerships cited by the high-tech firms in the sample.

Examples of single-, dual-, and triple-barrier partnership strategies are presented in the next three sections of this chapter. This serves to clarify and further describe the taxonomy and categories.

Single Barrier Partnerships

Approximately two thirds of the 32 partnerships analyzed to develop the taxonomy fall within one of the three single barrier categories of the taxonomy: lack of funds, lack of uses, and lack of awareness. More than half of the single barrier partnerships were between two or more firms, often high-tech multinational firms. The other half of the partnerships consisted of a diverse array of partner configurations (i.e., a private sector firm and a government agency; a private sector firm and a university; and a private sector firm and a nonprofit organization). In the balance of this section, each of the single barrier category types is explained and an actual example of a partnership in this subcategory is provided.

Lack of Awareness

After the double-digit growth of the ICT industry in the late 1990s, spending on ICT-related goods and services plummeted after the turn of the century. The dot com bubble burst, coupled with the overall downturn in the global economy, led ICT investment proposals to be scrutinized as never before. This is particularly true of small- and medium-sized enterprises (SMEs), an extremely large and important market segment in Mexico, and late adopter of Internet-related technologies. Most high-tech executives interviewed for this study believe that the Internet has intrinsic value for both SMEs and larger organizations and many have formed partnerships to build the business case or educate the market on the value of this technology. These partnerships tended to be, but were not exclusively, between two high-tech firms.

Example: Making the Business Case

Partnership: Cisco Systems and the Mexican Ministry of Health

Cisco Systems (Cisco), a $19 billion dollar company, is the "worldwide leader in networking for the Internet" (Cisco, n.d.). Until recently Cisco was the darling of the new economy. Within 10 years of its creation, Cisco had experienced growth rates of up to 50% and at one point had one of the highest market capitalizations in the world. After the turn of the century and with the burst of the dot com bubble, however, Cisco's stock plummeted and for the first time ever it announced layoffs.

Cisco's lackluster performance after the turn of the century, coupled with an overall downturn in the global economy, forced the firm to revisit its sales strategies. In this more austere environment, technology investment proposals were being scrutinized as never before and traditional financial measurements, such as return on investment, were now required to justify these purchases. Cisco equipment would no longer sell by itself, the firm now needed to proactively create new markets for its products.

Cisco relied heavily on the Internet to facilitate the exponential growth it experienced in the 1990s and has incorporated this technology into all facets of its business operations. Cisco has been meticulous in documenting the cost and productivity advantages that resulted from its internal use of Internet technology. Cisco created the Internet Business Solutions Group (IBSG) to share these Internet "best practices" with its key customers.

IBSG provides pro bono consulting services to Cisco's most strategic customers. These services revolve around demonstrating the business case for using Internet technology to solve tangible business problems. Cisco's objective is to help potential customers justify Internet-related investments. Each solution generally involves products and services from multiple providers, including Cisco. Partnerships, therefore, are a large part of the equation and Cisco has a stable set of solid technology partners it knows it can depend on for high quality, integrated solutions.

In Mexico, the IBSG group proactively approached the leaders of e-Mexico, the national connectivity program, and offered them its trusted advisor services. E-Mexico is the Mexican government's strategy to exploit the power of the Internet technology for the delivery of health, education, commercial, and government services across the country. Specifically, Cisco has worked with the Ministry of Health on a medical training project. As in most emerging markets, the public sector is a major technology consumer and therefore a key target for Cisco. By forming strong relations with the e-Mexico team, Cisco hoped to improve its overall positioning within Mexico's federal government.

In a tribute to Cisco's Mexican IBSG team, a representative from the e-Mexico Committee of the U.S. Chamber of Commerce commented that the Ministry of Health's e-Mexico plan is one of the most realistic and feasible of all of the e-Mexico projects. The quality of the actual plan, however, is not Cisco's primary objective. By becoming a trusted advisor to, and partner of, the Mexican government and providing them with Internet-based solutions to concrete business problems, Cisco is attempting to expand the overall market for its Internet equipment.

Example: Educating the Market

Partnership: Alestra and Cisco's Public Forum for Technological Diffusion

Alestra, which markets its services under the AT&T brand name, is a telecommunications provider and the fourth largest Internet service provider (ISP) in Mexico.[4] Since competition was introduced into the Mexican marketplace in 1996, prices for Alestra's core offering—long distance telephone service—decreased by over 60% (Alestra, 2002). Alestra believes that the Internet and data services are key to its survival, but fears that the low number of high-usage Internet customers in the country could hinder its success (Alestra, 2002).

Almost 80% of all of Mexican corporations have less than 15 employees (Osterroth, 2004). These firms are leading the growth of the Mexican economy and are expected to contribute to more than half of the new jobs created in 2004 ("SMEs generate 70% of new jobs", 2004). Alestra's Internet business development director noticed that SMEs were not aware of the capabilities or value of Internet technology. In late 2001 he decided to work on educating this market segment on the value of Internet technology in order to generate new demand in this fast growing and underserved market.

Alestra invited Cisco to partner with it on its SME education initiative. Alestra's parent company, AT&T, has a close relationship with Cisco in the United States and Alestra itself uses Cisco equipment exclusively for its Internet network in Mexico. The relationship was mutually beneficial because as Alestra sells more Internet services, it will need additional networking equipment. Success in this initiative, therefore, would translate into increased demand for both firms. Furthermore, by partnering, the two firms would become solutions providers and not stand-alone hardware or communications service vendors.

The solution was the Public Forum for Technological Diffusion for SMEs. Alestra and Cisco sporadically hosted these sessions in the six principal cities in Mexico. The objective was to educate SMEs on the value of Internet technology, not sell products. No price lists or sales-oriented literature was shown. In the forum events, Alestra and Cisco presented economical alternatives for exploiting the Internet for business gain, and SMEs gave testimonials on their successes in implementing this powerful business tool.

Although these forum events are not sales seminars, Alestra measures success based on the number of leads generated at each session and how many of these led to new sales of virtual private networks. Based on these two indicators, the forum has had very good results. The relationship between the two firms is also very solid.

Lack of Funds

According to World Bank (2004) statistics, Mexico's per capita income was $6,230 in 2003. The vast majority of potential Internet users in Mexico, therefore, do not have the economic resources to afford Internet access or to acquire the technology or services required to facilitate this access. High-tech firms have partnered amongst themselves to decrease the costs of Internet access to create new demand for this service. These partners have employed three main tactics: (1) decrease upfront costs (bundle and finance model), (2) decrease recurring costs (prepaid model), and (3) increase operational efficiency (efficiency model). One firm took an alternative approach and focused on increasing income levels rather than decreasing costs.

Example: Decreasing Upfront Costs (Bundle and Finance Model)

Partnership: Teléfonos de México's Prodigy Internet Plus

Teléfonos de México (Telmex) is the leading communications provider in Mexico and a part of the Carso Group, the largest conglomerate in Latin America ("Latin Trade 100", 2002; Telmex, 2002). Carlos Slim, Chairman of the Carso Group, believes because of the commoditization of long distance telecommunications services, Telmex's primary source of revenues, "we have to move into other areas...the key is the Internet" (*BusinessWeek Online*, 2001). Telmex launched Mexico's first commercial Internet access service, Direct Personal Internet (DPI), in 1997 and although the number of DPI subscribers increased 400% in a single year, this still represented less than 2% of Telmex's customer base (Telmex, 2000). Telmex estimated that it should easily have five times that number of subscribers and set out to accelerate Internet usage in Mexico.

Telmex's Vice President, Internet Platform realized that "to sell the Internet and use the Internet you need a device," or PC. This was an obstacle to Internet growth in Mexico as there were less than 4 million PCs in the entire country in 1998 (ITU, 2000). Many of Telmex's customers could not afford the upfront expense of a PC and consumer credit was severely limited due to the significant defaults associated with the 1994 Peso crisis. Telmex decided to "lower the barriers to entry" by bundling a PC with its Internet service and finance this bundle over a several year period. This is a model telecommunications carriers have used with their commercial customers for years: personal branch exchange (PBX) equipment was bundled with telecommunications services and the telecom company charged the corporate customer a fixed monthly fee. Telmex simply extended this model to the consumer mass market and the Internet arena.

In mid-1999, Telmex introduced Prodigy Internet Plus (PIP) in Mexico. Telmex partnered with a wide array of firms to assemble and distribute this package. The

PIP service included a PC loaded with Microsoft's Office suite of products, 2 years of unlimited Internet access, an e-mail account, and an individual Web page. Subscribers were charged a small down payment upon signing up for the service and the balance was paid via fixed monthly fees charged to their Telmex phone bill. At first, Telmex sold PIP services via a call center, but subsequently it extended this offering to the retailers in the Carso Group of companies (e.g., Sears and Sanborns) for wider distribution.

Telmex and its partners have had to adjust its PIP program various times to stimulate demand. When PIP sales began to level off in 2000, Telmex revised the PIP package and replaced Microsoft's Office for Microsoft's less expensive (and functional) Works suite of products. Telmex passed this cost savings on to its customers and decreased the PIP fixed monthly fee. PIP subscriptions surged as a result. In 2002, PIP sales once again stalled. As before, Telmex adjusted the package, this time replacing Intel processors with a less expensive processor and charging a per-minute fee for Internet access during peak hours. This new offering was called PIP-Home and was designed for students, which would likely use the Internet on nonpeak hours. PIP sales again spiked as a result.

Several of Telmex's competitors state that Telmex's PIP offering has been the most successful program in increasing Internet demand in Mexico and credit it with single handedly doubling Internet usage rates in the country. An anonymous senior executive at Telmex, however, acknowledges that the PIP program has limits, "today we finance computers ... in order to facilitate the purchase of PCs ... it is a method of attacking the lack of purchasing power ... but even this has a limit, when you reach a point when even with this people can't use a computer..."

Example: Decrease Recurring Costs (Pre-Paid Model)

Partnership: Todito and Adatel's Pre-Paid Internet Card

Todito is an Internet portal, electronic commerce (e-commerce) site, and ISP in Mexico (Todito, n.d.). Todito is part of Salinas Group, a large Mexican conglomerate led by Ricardo Salinas, which focuses primarily on the mass market in Mexico. During the dot com boom of the late 1990s, the group's companies became interested in exploiting the Internet and e-commerce. Instead of creating a new Internet company, the Salinas Group acquired a 50% stake in Todito, which was owned by Salinas' brother's Dataflux Group.

Todito's chief executive officer (CEO) recognized that his Internet portal and e-commerce services would be worthless if people could not access the Internet. He believed that one significant barrier to Internet usage in Mexico was the lack of affordable ISP access. Adatel, a small high-tech firm, had approached Todito with a pre-paid Internet solution. Todito's CEO thought that this would be a particularly appropriate solution for Mexico. He notes that pre-paid programs proliferate in the country because the economic uncertainty makes the idea of having a long-term obligation unappealing to most Mexicans. Furthermore, he claims that the average Internet user in Mexico connects to the Internet only 8 hours a month, thus he believed the flat-fee Internet services made hourly rates cost prohibitive for the mass market. A pre-paid Internet card would allow consumers to both control their costs and only pay for the time they are actually online.

Todito and Adatel worked together to develop a "Todito card" prepaid Internet product, which was launched in the spring of 2001. At first, Todito marketed and distributed the Todito card and Adatel provided the actual service. Over time, Todito licensed the technology from Adatel and assumed the service delivery responsibilities. The partnership subsequently ended, but Todito continued with the Todito card product on its own.

The Todito card catapulted Todito from relative obscurity to being the third ranking ISP in the Mexican marketplace in less than 2 years. The profit margins on the card are generous and it is now a profitable business for Todito.

Example: Increasing Operational Efficiency (Operational Efficiency Model)

Partnership: IBM and Telecommunications Providers in Mexico

IBM is the "worlds largest" information technology (IT) solutions and services provider (IBM, 2004). When Gerstner joined the firm as CEO in the early 1990s, IBM was a decentralized, technology-centric firm that was losing billions of dollars a year (Gerstner, 1998). In less than a decade, IBM was once again a highly profitable IT powerhouse and Gerstner a widely acclaimed business guru (Teresko, 1999). Gerstner claims that this successful turnaround is due to IBM's singular focus on developing integrated solutions that will provide its customers with a competitive advantage. The Internet is at the core of IBM's solution-centric strategy, and early on IBM focused on the "transformative power" of the Internet and "ways individuals and institutions derive value" from the Net (Gerstner, 1998).

IBM was the sole firm in the sample that took an indirect approach to tackling the lack of funds barrier to Internet usage in Mexico. Specifically, IBM focused on increasing the operational efficiency of telecommunications providers in Mexico. It realizes that the productivity of telecommunications' infrastructure investments greatly decreases once outside of high-density urban areas. IBM believes that its technology can help increase the efficiency of telecommunications providers, enabling them to offer more services at more economical rates in lower density populations and subsequently lead to increased Internet demand in the country. IBM therefore collaborates with its customers—telecom providers—to assist them with systems integration, processes optimization, and creating and provisioning new services to this client base.

Specific information was not made available on the success of this approach, but it is an innovative way of tackling the supply side of the lack-of-funds barrier to Internet usage.

Example: Increase Income Levels

Partnership: Motorola=educ@Mexico

Motorola has a long tradition of supporting education and viewing investments in education as imperative to achieving its long-term, market creation objectives. Motorola's executive team in Mexico believes that improved education levels lead to enhanced employment opportunities and thus, higher earning potential. As disposable incomes increase, so does the overall market for Motorola's products and services. Additionally, they believe that education can be used to overcome people's fear of technology, again leading to increased demand. Education-related activities, therefore, are a core component of Motorola's long-term expansion strategy in emerging markets, such as Mexico.

In 1999, Motorola launched the Motorola=educ@Mexico initiative. Motorola had been actively engaged with educational institutions since its entry into the Mexican market over 40 years ago, and this program simply organized these efforts under a single umbrella initiative. Motorola has partnered with a diverse range of firms, NGOs, universities, and government agencies to improve education under the auspices of the Motorola=educ@Mexico program.

One specific Motorola=educ@Mexico partnership was between Motorola and the Universidad del Valle de Mexico (UVM). UVM is a large, national, private university in Mexico with a predominantly middle-class student body. Motorola provided UVM with $25,000 to assist it with equipping two computer laboratories on its Lomas Verdes campus, and high-ranking Motorola executives participated in educational-related events at UVM (Romano, 1997). UVM believes that its students must have access to state-of-the-art technology for their laboratory experiments and workshops. The Motorola partnership has enabled UVM to achieve this objective, and the laboratory on its Lomas Verdes campus is the most sophisticated of its 16 campuses.

Motorola's university partners interviewed in this study unanimously agreed that Motorola made great strides in enhancing educational activities in their institutions and they believe this is largely due to the firm's pro-education corporate culture and executive team in Mexico. In an industry where the very survival of a firm depends on its ability to effectively compete for a limited pool of highly trained personnel, Motorola's direct link to the source of this talent could also be a significant competitive advantage.

Lack of Uses

Many potential Internet customers in Mexico are unable to use the technology because of language, literacy, training, and cultural barriers. Lack of Uses could be the single most difficult barrier to overcome, as resolving it requires rethinking the value proposition of the technology and partnering with nontraditional players (educational institutions, government agencies, and/or NGOs). The most common approach to tackling this barrier to Internet usage was to develop new applications and uses for the technology.

Example: Developing New Uses for the Technology

Partnership: IBM's Reinventing Education

High-tech firms have a long history of partnering with educational institutions. These partnerships have traditionally revolved around product donations, which are seen as a method of building brand awareness and future consumers. IBM has taken a distinct approach—it has focused on providing educators and educational institutions with compelling reasons to use its technology. IBM's Director of the Public Sector in Mexico, Lorenzo Valle, states, "it isn't a question of simply implementing Internet services, it is a much more complex problem...the most important thing is that people know how to use it and have a *reason* to use it" (personal communication, 2004, emphasis added).

IBM believes that it is capable of developing technological solutions, but it needed experts in education to help identify and develop value-added uses for Internet technology in academic institutions. The result was IBM's Reinventing Education Program. IBM partnered with a small set of schools to identify systemic problems in education and educational institutions. It then worked hand-in-hand with these schools to develop technological solutions for these problems. These solutions were pilot tested in a school, refined and then, ideally, converted into commercial offerings for the educational marketplace.

One specific result of the Reinventing Education Program was the development of Learning Village software. This software connects schools, libraries, professors, students, teachers, and parents to encourage greater collaboration, communication, and learning. The software was initially developed and refined in conjunction with a school in the United States and in 2004 was introduced to Mexico and Brazil. In Mexico, the Learning Village software will be piloted in the Mexican state of Hidalgo. IBM believes that Hidalgo is an ideal test bed for this software as there are just a handful of advanced firms and universities, a moderate–sized, middle-class population, and a large marginalized and poor community in this state. These characteristics—small upper and middle classes and a large lower class—are representative of Mexico as a whole.

It is too early to evaluate the success of IBM's Learning Village pilot project in Mexico. An evaluation conducted by the Center for Children and Technology, however, reports that IBM's overall Reinventing Education Program has had very positive results on education and educational administration in the United States (Spielvogel, 2001). This program has also helped IBM begin to make a profit in the K-12 education market—a market where IBM had traditionally recorded a loss (Kanter, 2001).

Dual Barrier Partnerships

Slightly less than one third of the partnerships analyzed to develop the taxonomy fall within one of the two dual barrier categories of the taxonomy: lack of funds + lack of uses and lack of funds + lack of infrastructure. Approximately half of these partnerships were formed between a high-tech firm and a university, one quarter were between two high-tech firms, and one quarter involved the participation of high-tech firms and NGOs. In the balance of this section, each of the dual barrier category types is explained and an actual example of a partnership in this subcategory is provided.

Lack of Funds and Lack of Infrastructure

The vast majority of Mexico's Internet subscribers rely on the traditional wire-line telephone network for Internet access. According to the ITU (2002), 14 out of 100 Mexicans, or approximately 45% of households, have a phone line. The number of telephone lines is therefore an artificial ceiling for Internet usage rates in Mexico. This is particularly true for potential users in lower economic levels in Mexico, which tend to live in infrastructure-poor areas (no telephone lines). High-tech firms partnered with a diverse set of entities to simultaneously overcome both the financial (lack of funds) and infrastructure (lack of telephone lines) barriers to Internet usage in Mexico. Todito, for example, was particularly active with dual barrier partnerships and employed two main approaches: providing low-cost, shared-access sites (cybercafe model) and developing alternative, less expensive, access and payment technologies (wireless and prepaid model).

Example: Cybercafe Model

Partnership: Todito and Oxxo's Digicentro Todito

Todito's CEO believes that there are three barriers to Internet usage in Mexico: a phone line, a computer, and an affordable ISP. The Todito prepaid Internet card addressed the last issue—the affordable ISP. The remaining two barriers still prevented large segments of the Mexican population from using the Internet. Todito, therefore, decided to simultaneously leverage the success of its Todito card and tackle the income and infrastructure barriers to Internet usage in Mexico via a new initiative: *Digicentro Todito*.

Todito partnered with one of Mexico's largest chain of convenience stores, Oxxo, which was also one of the primary distributors of its Todito card. These two parties created cybercafes or Digicentros Todito. Customers would use their Todito prepaid Internet cards in the Digicentro Todito to access the Internet from one of the half dozen computers located in the Oxxo store. Oxxo provided the physical and communications infrastructure (telephone lines and space in the Oxxo stores) and Todito provided an affordable method of accessing the Internet (Todito prepaid Internet cards and PCs).

It was envisioned that Todito would benefit by having an additional outlet for its Todito cards and by solidifying its relationship with a key distributor. Oxxo would benefit by selling additional units of a high-volume product (Todito card) and by upgrading its stores and image in line with its "Oxxo of the Future" campaign. To bias the likelihood of success, the first Digicentro Todito was launched in late 2003 in Cancun, a hot spot for foreign tourists. If this launch is a success, Digitcentro Todito cybercafes will be rolled out in the major cities in Mexico and ideally, to all 2,000 Oxxo stores across the country.

Example: Wireless and Pre-Paid Model

Partnership: Todito and Biper's Movilaccess

Todito executives believe that e-mail is the number one application on the Internet in Mexico. In the mid-1990s, Grupo Salinas established a company—Biper—to provide paging services in the Mexico market. The cost of acquiring a pager and Biper's monthly fees were relatively expensive for the mass market for which the Grupo Salinas' companies traditionally catered. Todito's executives believed that if they could lower the price of the device and enable customers to send and receive e-mails paid for by Todito prepaid Internet cards, they could enable an entire new segment of the Mexican market access to the most popular application of the Internet and increase aggregate Internet demand. This solution would overcome both the income (low cost device and prepaid

Internet access) and infrastructure (low levels of telephone lines) barriers to Internet usage.

Todito's business plan was based on three elements: a device priced at less than $50, affordable access fees, and wide-scale distribution. The access fees could be made affordable by using Todito's prepaid Internet access card, which would allow Mexicans Internet access without having to sign a long-term contract. Distribution channels had already been secured for the Todito card and could now be used for this new product. The critical factor was decreasing the device cost from approximately $160 to less than $50.

At the time, the usage of two-way paging technology was declining in industrialized countries. Todito hoped to exploit this mature technology for a few years in Mexico until the country was ready for more sophisticated technology. Todito sought a partnership with a two-way paging technology company. These companies, however, were diverting their resources and energies away from this declining technology and toward more cutting-edge solutions. Todito quickly found that as the technology fades in industrialized countries, the number of firms that offer it decreases, as do investments in the technology.

Todito and Biper were still negotiating with paging manufacturers at the end of this study and it was unclear as to if they could reach the targeted $50 price for these devices. This case is interesting, however, as it demonstrates the limitations of firms and countries in repurposing existing technology for the needs of emerging markets. Leapfrogging, or bypassing mature technologies in favor of cutting-edge technologies, may be the only option in some cases.

Lack of Funds and Lack of Uses

Low income levels often go hand-in-hand with low educational attainment rates. If individuals do not learn computers, IT, and English language skills in school, they may not be able or interested in using the Internet. Firms have partnered with educational institutions and NGOs to simultaneously tackle the income and uses barriers to Internet demand in Mexico. These partnerships generally attempted to increase income levels and to develop new uses for this technology (education and content development model).

Example: Education and Content Development Model

Partnership: Sun Microsystems and UNITEC's E-Business Technology Incubator

Sun Microsystems (Sun) is a "leading provider" of hardware, software, and services that power the Internet (Sun, n.d.). Sun strongly believes in ubiquitous connectivity and its mission is to link "every man, woman, and child on the planet" to the Internet (Sun, n.d.). Sun executives in Mexico perceive that there are at least two primary barriers impeding Sun from achieving this mission in their country: lack of funds and lack of uses. Sun's collaborations with universities are designed to overcome these obstacles and in the long run, create Internet demand in this market.

Since the turn of the century, Sun has executed a variety of strategies directed toward expanding its business around the world and in Mexico. Given Sun's long tradition of collaborating with universities, many of these market creation initiatives were implemented in conjunction with the educational sector. Specifically, these strategies focus on creating employment opportunities, improving education, and diffusing Sun's network-centric technology vision. In the long run, higher educational achievement and increased employment opportunities will lead to improved income levels and people's ability to afford the Internet and Sun's goods and services. Furthermore, Sun focuses many of its university collaborations on developing applications designed to make the Internet "simpler" and less expensive. Sun's Java technology can be used to connect less expensive devices—such as cell phones and personal digital assistants (PDAs)—to the network, decreasing the lack of funds and lack of uses barriers to Internet diffusion.

One specific partnership was the Sun—Universidad Tecnológica de México (UNITEC) electronic business technology incubator (Incubator). In September of 2001, Sun invited UNITEC to participate in its elite Campus Incubator Program. UNITEC is the second largest, private university in Mexico and has a predominantly middle-class student body (UNITEC, n.d.). These two organizations jointly established an Incubator on UNITEC's Atizapán campus outside of Mexico City.

The UNITEC Incubator is equipped with an extensive array of Sun products, so that the students can develop their Java-based business concepts on state-of-the-art technology. Students that enter the Incubator are required to take a significant number of courses on Sun's Java technology. In order to facilitate the technical training, Sun taught and certified three UNITEC professors on Java and has authorized UNITEC to impart Java courses to the students in the Incubator free of charge. The students also received business training and individualized assistance on their business plans

In late 2003, UNITEC announced its sixth business plan competition for entry into the Incubator. Over 300 business plans have been submitted thus far and 20 have been selected for development in the Incubator. The first businesses were slated to exit the Incubator in early 2004. The Incubator Director's top priority in late 2004 was to find venture capital for these nascent companies, an extremely difficult task with the significant decreases in capital being invested in IT solutions and in Latin America after the dot com bubble burst.

Triple Barrier Partnerships

Less than 10% of the partnerships analyzed to develop the taxonomy fall under the triple barrier category of the taxonomy: lack of funds + lack of uses + lack of infrastructure. Very few high-tech firms had the financial capacity and reach to initiate these partnerships and the Mexican government took the lead on the primary initiative in this category—e-Mexico, a national connectivity program. The one exception was a multi-sector relationship between a high-tech firm, a university in the United States, local government agencies, and NGOs.

Lack of Funds, Lack of Uses, and Lack of Infrastructure

Many Mexican high-tech firms segment their market according to socioeconomic level (education, housing, and income levels). The scale ranges from A to E, with A being the highest socioeconomic level and E the lowest. A Mexican newspaper, reported that from 2000 through 2002 the number of Internet users in the highest (A and B+) and lowest (D- and E) socioeconomic levels in Mexico remained relatively constant (Reforma, 2004). This suggests that the majority of programs designed to increase Internet usage in Mexico have attracted new customers primarily from middle socioeconomic tiers. These customers may have faced one or two barriers to using the Internet. The lower on the socioeconomic pyramid an individual is, however, the more barriers to Internet usage he/she likely faces. In rural communities and marginalized sections of urban areas, Mexicans may lack the funds, required infrastructure (telephone lines), and ability to use the Internet. In Mexico, the government and private sector are collaborating to simultaneously tackle these three barriers to Internet usage. The programs extend telephone infrastructure (both wireline and wireless—satellite), developing relevant content, and subsidizing usage fees. In the balance of this section, the only triple barrier category type is explained and an actual example of a partnership in this subcategory is provided.

Example: Subsidized Internet Access, Infrastructure Deployment, and Content Development Model

Partnership: e-Mexico

In December of 2000, Mexico's newly elected President, Vicente Fox, announced a national Internet connectivity program, e-Mexico. By the end of Fox's 6-year presidency, the e-Mexico system would consist of 10,000 digital community centers, which provided free (or highly subsidized) access to computers, the

Internet, and newly developed content in the areas of health, education, electronic government (e-government), and e-commerce-related content. These centers would be placed in public facilities (i.e., schools, government offices) and would connect over 95% of Mexico's population to the digital economy.

President Fox made it clear that he was counting on private sector support for this multi-billion dollar initiative because the federal government did not have the budget, nor technical expertise, to complete it on its own. Shortly after e-Mexico was announced executives from Telmex, Hewlett Packard, IBM, Intel, Microsoft, Sun Microsystems, and other firms all expressed an interest in partnering with the federal government on this ambitious program. Some partnerships simply extended existing global programs to Mexico (i.e., Intel committed to training Mexican teachers via its global Teach for the Future initiative). Other partnerships created new initiatives to contribute to the Mexican government's objectives for e-Mexico (Telmex created eTelmex, an initiative designed to connect 2,445 targeted e-Mexico villages to the Internet).

By mid-2003, President Fox announced that he had connected 3,200 digital community centers to the Internet and created the e-Mexico portal with content in the areas of education, health, e-commerce, and e-government (Fox, 2003). What was not reported, and is not being monitored by the Mexican government, is the actual number of new Internet users on the e-Mexico platform. Access to the technology does not necessarily translate into its usage; particularly if training is not included with the newly deployed access. Furthermore, although the Mexican government pronounced an interest in "partnering" with the private sector to achieve the e-Mexico objectives, it has worked in a more traditional vendor-customer fashion and has submitted requests for proposals and selected its "partners" largely based on price.

Methodology

Four main steps were taken to develop the taxonomy. The first step was to select the partnership population: 25 leading high-tech firms in Mexico. The second step was data collection: data were gathered via more than 60 personal interviews with executives and managers of leading high-tech firms, nonprofit leaders, academic, government representatives, and external experts in Mexico. The third step was data analysis: an iterative process of data reduction, categorization, and testing. The fourth, and last step, was testing: the integrity and exhaustiveness of the taxonomy was tested through a second round of data collection and analysis, and external validation.

Step 1: Select the Partnership Population

A relatively broad population was drawn upon to develop the taxonomy. This population consisted of 25 leading high-tech firms in Mexico and was selected based on three dimensions: (1) market characteristics (industry growth potential, income and population levels, and regulatory framework), (2) industry characteristics (high-tech firms in Mexico), and (3) firm characteristics (firm's market position and physical presence in Mexico). Mexico was selected for analysis because it represents upper-middle income, densely populated countries with substantial competition in the Internet arena. The 25 firms included in the taxonomy population are: Alestra, AMD, AOL, Apache, Avantel, Cisco, Dell, EsMas, Hewlett Packard, IBM, Intel, Juniper, Maxcom, Microsoft, MSN, PanAmSat, Prodigy, RedUno/Uninet, Satmex, Sun, T1MSN, Telmex, Terra Lycos, Todito, and Yahoo.

Step 2: Data Collection

After the population was selected, data were gathered. Two pieces of information were required from the firms to construct the taxonomy: (1) high-tech executives' and managers' *perceptions* of the barriers to Internet diffusion in Mexico; and (2) the partnerships these firms have created, or participated in, to overcome these barriers and grow the market. Interviews were also conducted with the firms' partners and external experts to determine the effectiveness and nature of the partnerships included in the taxonomy.

Before interviews were conducted, both primary and secondary archival records were consulted. These were used to construct a preliminary sketch of the high-tech firms market in Mexico and to develop a list of potential interview candidates.

A total of 13 of the targeted 25 firms agreed to be included in this study. Personal interviews were conducted with a total of 63 individuals: 38 representatives of high-tech firms, 14 of the high-tech firms' partners, and 10 external experts in Mexico. Most of these interviews were conducted during four field research trips to Mexico City: February 2003, May 2003, October 2003, and January 2004. The interviews were semi-structured, face-to-face sessions that ranged from 20-240 minutes.

Step 3: Data Analysis

Vast amounts of data were generated from the interviews. Miles and Huberman's (1994) process of data reduction, data display, conclusion drawing, and verification were used to analyze these data. The first step in the data analysis process was to reduce the data, or to identify and select specific portions of data for analysis. The data in this case were the interview transcript sheets. A coding scheme was developed to enable data reduction. Once the data were reduced, they were displayed in Excel spreadsheets. The data in these spreadsheets were reviewed and labels given to the individual barriers to diffusion. Subsequently, these labels were analyzed to see if there was consistency, or a pattern, in the barriers cited. A great deal of consistency was found and 10 major themes emerged. These themes were further examined and grouped into more concise and overarching categories. The final result of this process was the creation of four categories of the perceived barriers to Internet diffusion in Mexico (lack of awareness, lack of funds, lack of infrastructure, and lack of uses).

Once the perceived barriers to Internet diffusion had been identified and classified, they needed to be associated with the partnerships. Specifically, each of the 32 partnerships was categorized by the specific barrier(s) to Internet diffusion it was designed to overcome. The draft taxonomy was then completed.

Step 4: Validity Assessment

Two primary verification mechanisms were used to increase the validity of the taxonomy: external validation and a second round of data collection and analysis. After the first round of interviews and data analysis, an external expert in the field cross validated the coding of the interview transcripts. This individual coded a representative sample of approximately 20% of the senior executive, interview transcript sheets. The coding results were compared against those of the author of this study and any inconsistencies were reviewed and discussed until agreement was reached. The coding definitions were also rewritten to make them more concise and clear.

Secondly, after completing the first draft of taxonomy, an additional 19 interviews were conducted. The data from these interviews were used to further test the validity of the taxonomy. This additional data suggested that these conclusions are valid and the taxonomy was exhaustive.

Conclusion

This chapter shed light on innovative market creation strategies being implemented by leading high-tech firms in Mexico. The objective was to develop a taxonomy of Internet market creation partnerships. This taxonomy classified the types of partnerships high-tech firms were using to create Internet demand in Mexico. The classification was based on the number and type of barrier(s) to Internet usage the partnership was designed to overcome.

As markets become more saturated in industrialized countries and multinational firms seek additional growth opportunities, market creation partnerships will increase in number and importance. This chapter advances scholarship by developing a classification system for market-creation partnerships. Practitioners can use this tool to identify and understand the diverse models being employed to increase Internet usage and emerging markets. Academics can use this tool as the basis for further empirical analysis of partnerships of this nature. Both society and business will benefit from a greater understanding of market creation partnerships as the barriers to Internet usage have both social and commercial underpinnings.

References

Accenden a Internet Nuevos Grupos. (New Groups Join the Internet.) (2004, June 21). *Reforma*. Business Section.

Alestra. (2002). *Form 20-F: Annual Report for the Fiscal Year Ending December 31, 2001*. San Pedro Garza Garcia, Nuevo Leon, Mexico: Alestra.

Alestra. (n.d.). *Quienes somos. (Who we are.)* Mexico City, Mexico: Alestra. Retrieved February 5, 2004, from http://www.alestra.com.mx/empresa/quienes.shtml.

Baez, G. (2003, February 27). *Pyramid research: Communications markets in Mexico: Overview*. Presentation delivered to the Institute of the Americas Telecom/IT Mexico Roundtable. Mexico City.

Bailey, K. D. (1994). *Typologies and taxonomies: An introduction to classification techniques*, Quantitative Publications in the Social Sciences Series, no. 07-102. Thousand Oaks; London; New Dehli: Sage University Papers.

Cisco. (n.d.). Corporate overview. Retrieved February 13, 2004, from http://newsroom.cisco.com/dlls/company_overview.html

Cukor, P., & McKnight, L. (2001, Winter). Knowledge networks, the Internet and development. *The Fletcher Forum of World Affairs, 25*(1), 43-58.

De Marcillac, P. (2003, March). *International markets: A renewed opportunity*. Presentation delivered to the IDC Analyze the Future Conference, Boston.

Fox, V. (2003, June 5). *Lanzamiento e Inauguración de la Primera Red Satelital e-México. (Launch and Inauguration of the First e-Mexico satellite network.)* Speech delivered by Vicente Fox at the Launch and Inauguration of the First Satellite Network of e-Mexico, Gómez Portugal, Aguascalientes.

Gándara, M. (2003, Summer). Lessons from the field: The less-known dimensions of the digital divide. *STS Nexus, 3*(2), 17-22.

Generan Pymes 70% de los Nuevos Empleos. (2004, May 10). *El Financiero*.

Gerstner, L. (1998, April 27). 1999 IBM Annual Meeting of Stockholders. Excerpted remarks as delivered, Miami, FL.

Gray, B. (2000). Assessing inter-organizational collaboration: Multiple conceptions and multiple methods. In D. Faulkner & M. de Rond (Eds.), *Cooperative strategy: Economic, business and operational issues* (pp. 242-261). Oxford University Press.

Gutierrez, L. H., & Berg, S. (2000, November/December). Telecommunications liberalization and regulatory governance: Lessons from Latin America. *Telecommunications Policy, 24*(10-11).

Huxham, C., & Vangen, S. (2001). What makes practitioners tick? Understanding collaboration practice and practising collaboration understanding. In J. Genefke & F. McDonald (Eds.), *Effective collaboration: Managing the obstacles to success* (pp. 1-16). New York: Palgrave.

IBM. (2004, February 19). *IBM offers solution for regulatory compliance*. Retrieved February 25, 2004, from http://www-1.ibm.com/press/PressSer vletForm.wss?MenuChoice=pressreleases&TemplateName= ShowPressReleaseTemplate&SelectString-t1.docunid=6708&Table Name=DataheadApplicationClass&SESSIONKEY=any&WindowTitle=Press+ Release&STATUS=publish>

International Telecommunications Union (ITU). (2000). *World telecommunications development report*. Geneva, Switzerland: ITU.

International Telecommunications Union (ITU). (2001, January/February/March). *Numbering cyberspace: Recent trends in the Internet world*. International telecommunications indicator update.

International Telecommunications Union (ITU). (2002). *World telecommunications development report*. Geneva, Switzerland: ITU.

Kanter, R. M. (1998, January/February). Six strategic challenges. *World Link*.

Kanter, R. M. (2001, September 10). *IBM's reinventing education* (A). (Case Study 9-399-008). Cambridge, MA: Harvard Business School.

Kiiski, S., & Pohjola, M. (2002, June). Cross-country diffusion of the Internet. *Information Economics and Policy, 14*(2), 297-310.

Kotler, P., & Armstrong, G. (2001). *Principles of marketing* (9th ed.). Upper Saddle River, NJ: Prentice Hall.

Latin Trade 100. (2002, July). *Latin Trade*.

Malkin, E. (2001, June 18). Telmex: Mexico's 800-pound gorilla. *Businessweek Online*. Retrieved December 5, 2003, from http://www.businessweek.com/magazine/content/01_25/b3737725.htm

Miles, M. B., & Huberman, M. (1994). *Qualitative data analysis: An expanded sourcebook*. Thousand Oaks, CA: Sage Publications.

Nelson, J. (2002). *Building partnerships: Cooperation between the United Nations system and the private sector*. New York: The United Nations' Department of Public Information.

Osterroth, M. (2004, May 5). Bajan Telefónicas Tarifas a Pymes. (Telephone companies lower rates for SMEs.) *Reforma*.

Prahalad, C. K., & Hart, S. L. (2002, First Quarter). The fortune at the bottom of the pyramid. *Strategy + Business*, (34).

Romano, L. (1997, April 11). Promueve la Empresa el Desarrollo de Tecnología de Punta en Instituciones como la UVM-Edomex. (Firms are promoting the development of state-of-the-art technology in institutions like UVM-Edomex.) *La Reforma*, Business section.

Smith, J. (2001, July 30). PC: Pretty cheap; Market saturation has made it a computer buyer's paradise. *Rocky Mountain News*, Business (p. 1B). Denver, CO: Rocky Mountain News.

Spielvogel, B. (2001, June). *IBM reinventing education: Research summary and perspective*. New York: Center for Children and Technology.

Sun Microsystems. (2004, January). Company info. Retrieved from http://www.sun.com/company/

Telmex. (2000). *Annual report for the fiscal year ending December 31, 1999*. Mexico City: Telmex.

Telmex. (2002). *Annual report for the fiscal year ending December 31, 2001*. Mexico City: Telmex.

Telmex: Mexico's 800-Pound Gorilla. (June 18, 2001). *BusinessWeek Online*.

Teresko, J. (1999, December 6). Driving success at New Blue. *Industry Week, 56*.

Todito. (2002, October 14). *Todito.com announces the launch of Todito ePAID*. Todito press release. Retrieved January 9, 2003, from http://www.todito.com/paginas/contenido/fc10142002/nt10778.html

UNITEC. (n.d.). *Conócenos*. Retrieved October 10, 2003, from http://www.unitec.edu.mx/Acerca/index.html

World Bank. (2004). *Mexico at a glance*. Retrieved February 13, 2004, from http://www.worldbank.org/data/countrydata/aag/mex_aag.pdf

World Resources Institute. (2003). *Project Clearinghouse*. Washington, DC: WRI. Retrieved December 5, 2003, from http://wriws1.digitaldividend.org/wri/app/navigate

Appendix A: Interviews Used to Develop This Chapter

Personal interviews were conducted with a total of 63 individuals: 38 representatives of high-tech firms, 14 of the high-tech firms' partners, and 10 external experts in Mexico. Most of these interviews were conducted during four field research trips to Mexico City: February 2003, May 2003, October 2003, and January 2004. These interviews were used to develop this chapter and taxonomy. Almost half of those interviewed requested anonymity. Those that agreed to be identified are listed here by name and/or title and organization.

Representatives from High-Tech Firms

- Carlos Baradello, Vice President and General Manager of Latin America and the Caribbean, 1996-2002 (retired), Motorola of Mexico
- Gerardo Barragan, Director of Business Development, Alestra
- Rosendo Canizo, Director of Commercial Sector Services, Sun Microsystems of Mexico
- Eduardo Diaz Corona, VP of Internet Platform, Teléfonos de México (Telmex)
- Jesus Domene, Director of Internal Relations, Motorola of Mexico

- Javier Elguea Solís, Corporate Committee for Human Resources, Grupo Carso (Telmex) and President, Inttelmex
- Adrian Gonzalez, Chief Operating Officer, Todito
- Mauricio Martens, Cluster Unit Executive, Communications Sector, IBM of Mexico
- Mario O'Campo, Director of External Relations, Motorola of Mexico
- Tim Parsa, CEO, Todito
- Henry Peluffo, Director of Marketing, SBCI International, (Telmex)
- Rene Sagastuy, CEO and GM, Maxcom
- Juan Saldivar, CEO, EsMas
- Ricardo Saucedo, CEO, Aranea
- Lorenzo Valle, Director, Public Sector, IBM of Mexico
- Jaime Valles, Sun Microsystems of Mexico
- Omar Villarreal, Corporate Vice President and President, Latin America North, Motorola of Mexico
- Julio Dozal, Researcher and Coordinator of the Center for Digital Culture, Inttelmex
- Manuel Gándara, Researcher and Coordinator of the Center for Digital Culture, Inttelmex
- Maria de Jesús Ugalde, Solutions Manager, Telmex
- Ricardo Medina, Sales Manager, Education Sector, Sun Microsystems of Mexico
- Isidro Quintana, Senior Manager, Internet Business Solutions Group, Cisco of Mexico

High-Tech Firms' Partners

- Walter Bender, Executive Director, MIT Media Lab
- Eduardo Garcia, Director, Technology innovation, University del Valle de Mexico (UVM)
- Bakhtiar Mikhak, Research Scientist, Massachusetts Institute of Technology (MIT) Media Lab
- Edgar Ortiz, Director, Electric Engineering Program, Iberoamerican University (Ibero)

- Alejandro Pisanty, GM, Academic Computing Services, Universidad Nacional Autónoma de México (UNAM)

- Eduardo Rubio, Sub-Director, Internal Information Technology Market, Ministry of the Economy, Mexico

- Patricia Sierra, Director, Cooperation and Exchange Programs, Universidad del Valle de Mexico (UVM)

- Guillermo Vega, Director, Electronic Business Technology Incubator, Universidad Tecnológica de México (UNITEC)

External Experts

- Javier Flores, Commercial Specialist, U.S. Embassy, Mexico

- Investigator, INFOTEC

- Director, Government Relations Group, Mexican Internet Association (AMIPIC)

- Member, eMexico Task Group, American Chamber of Commerce

- Professor, Universidad Autónoma Metropolitana (UAM), Mexico

- Staff member, Universidad Tecnológica de Monterrey, Mexico

Endnotes

[1]   Omar Villarreal, Corporate Vice President, Motorola Inc, and President, Motorola Latin America North, Motorola, interview by author, tape recording, Mexico City, Mexico, February 26, 2003.

[2]   This definition is adapted from the one used in Nelson (2002, p. 46), *Building Partnerships: Cooperation Between the United Nations System and the Private Sector.*

[3]   There are six elements of accessibility: operability (amount of training required to effectively use the technology); intelligibility (degree to which the technology is offered in one's native languages and literacy rate); cultural compatibility (ability of the technology to build upon current communication patterns in a nondisruptive way); relevance (degree to which the technology offers socially useful and relevant content); usability (the simplicity of the technology from a user's perspective); and security (degree to which the technology is secure and respects the privacy of the users). These elements are taken from Gándara (2003).

[4]   For market share information please see, Baez (2003) and for information on Alestra and its relationship with AT&T, please see Alestra (n.d.). in the reference list.

Chapter XIII

Organizing Across Distances:
Managing Successful Virtual Team Meetings

Kris M. Markman, Bridgewater State College, USA

Abstract

This chapter examines the use of computer chat technologies for virtual team meetings. The use of geographically dispersed (i.e., virtual) teams is a growing phenomenon in modern organizations. Although a variety of information and communication technologies (ICTs) have been used to conduct virtual team meetings, one technology, synchronous computer chat, has not been exploited to its fullest potential. This chapter discusses some of research findings related to effective virtual teams and examines some structural features of chat as they relate to virtual meetings. Based on these characteristics, I offer tips for using chat as an effective tool for distant collaboration.

Introduction

Since the Industrial Revolution, technology has played a major role in shaping our work practices. Technologies have brought automation, they have brought standardization, and most of all, technology has brought change. In the 21st century, this change is seen most clearly when we look at the impact that computers have had in organizations. While computers are often employed to help workers, that help is not always wanted or needed (see Sellen & Harper, 2002; Zuboff, 1988). However, wanted or not, computers are inescapable in most modern organizations, and their use has become an important part of how many people communicate at work.

Along with the growth of computer use in organizations, there has been a changing of organizational structures; many organizations now have offices and employees spread across the globe (e.g., Dutton, 1999; Iacono & Kling, 2001; Monge & Fulk, 1999), and they often require those employees to communicate and collaborate with each other. The availability and rapid development of computer technology and the Internet is both part of this challenge and part of the solution. Thus we find that organizations have increasingly turned to the use of virtual teams to meet the challenges of the new global marketplace.

Virtual teams are characterized by having some or all of the team's members located in different geographical locations. This might mean that some of the team members work from home instead of the office, or that members are located in offices in different cities, states, or even countries. Similarly to colocated teams, virtual teams are generally characterized by being project focused, of fixed (and often short) duration, and having revolving membership. Employees may work on more than one team at a time, or may change teams a number of times over the course of 1 year. The challenge to virtual teams is to accomplish the given task with little or no face-to-face contact. And it is this particular characteristic that makes virtual teams an object of research for organization scholars seeking to describe or predict how teams can collaborate effectively at a distance.

Researchers in organizational communication, management, and a variety of other fields have used both experimental and field research to explore the social and technological aspects of virtual team interaction. While there are many points of intersection among these diverse studies of virtual teams, one constant thread observable in the literature is the focus on the end result of teamwork. Although this scholarship has done much to explain the factors that complicate distributed teamwork, these studies—taken apart or together—still do not provide a complete description of exactly how the business of collaboration is achieved within the virtual team.

In this chapter, I will approach virtual collaboration from the perspective of one particular technology: synchronous computer chat.[1] Among the variety of ICTs available for virtual team meetings, chat is one of the most cost-effective, though under-utilized tools. Teleconferencing, a popular choice, offers the familiarity of spoken interaction and immediacy, but can be quite costly, especially if team members are located in different parts of the globe. Video conferencing is a less commonly used alternative (Timmerman & Scott, 2006), one that also provides for real-time, spoken interaction. However, video conferencing can also be an expensive and technically complex tool that can in fact be more distracting than helpful for collaboration (Majchrzak, Malhotra, Stamps, & Lipnack, 2004). Comparatively, communication tools associated with the Internet, including e-mail, instant messaging, and chat, are very low cost and flexible. Although e-mail, instant messaging, and similar asynchronous communication tools are important for successful virtual teamwork, they cannot provide the real-time, multiparty interaction required for team meetings. The fact that chat has been overlooked by virtual teams is a function of the lack of understanding about how the structural features of chat conversation reshape collaboration.

I begin this chapter with a brief review of recent research on virtual teams, focusing specifically on studies of communication and technology use in virtual teams. Based on this review, I will explore how a microanalytic approach to studying virtual team communication can uncover new information about how virtual collaboration works. Next, I will apply this approach by examining the structural features of chat-based conversation and discussing how they differ from spoken interaction. Finally, I will show how an understanding of the structure of chat can translate into specific strategies for using chat to hold virtual team meetings.

What We Know About Virtual Teams

Iacono and Kling (2001) noted that "a major problem identified by organizations is that people must work together (e.g., on cross-functional or global teams) while they are often distributed in time and space" (p. 124). In a meta-analysis of research on communication technology and group communication, Scott (1999) noted a rise in the use of distributed teams by organizations; however, he also found that virtual team research lacked an emphasis "on what it means to be dispersed in this sense" (p. 463). The research that exists does cover a fairly large ground, however, it will be instructive to look first at what we have learned about virtual teams before talking more in depth about what still needs to be learned.

Virtual Teams and Technology Use

The very point of using teams in organizations is to pool the talents of multiple individuals to produce a result that would be better than any one member of the team could produce as an individual. Virtual teams, by their very definition, do not share a common physical space, such as an office building, but they do need to interact in order to work as a team. Thus, technology for communication and collaboration across distance becomes and important facet of managing and studying virtual teams. Following this, scholars have explored the effects of a range of specific technologies, including face-to-face interaction (when available) on virtual team interaction. For example, Robey, Khoo, and Powers (2000) found that when team members used both face-to-face communication (individual travel and meetings) and a variety of remote technologies, the face-to-face interaction was shown to be especially important for socioemotional communication. However, and maybe more to the point, they found that for virtual teams to be successful, they needed the ability to adapt and shape communication technologies to their specific situated purposes. Similarly, in a study of virtual team facilitators, Pauleen and Yoong (2001) concluded that when face-to-face meetings are not an option, familiar technologies such as the telephone can be used for relationship building. They also concluded that the key is channels that allow for "backstage" communication, and that synchronous Internet messaging systems such as ICQ hold promise for those teams without access to face-to-face or telephone interaction.

Rasters, Vissers, and Dankbaar (2002) examined a team whose primary means for communication and formation was e-mail—both individual e-mails between team members and an e-mail discussion list circulated to all members. Although the team also gathered for two face-to-face meetings, they found that the use of different communication media did not result in any significant differences in team members' communication. For example, they noted that *flaming*, a negative communication behavior generally associated with electronic channels, occurred both on the mailing list and in the face-to-face meetings, and that the "face-to-face flames were definitely as intense as their electronic counterparts" (Rasters et al., 2002, p. 748). Although computer chat has not been shown to be widely used in organizational teams, it has been used to conduct experimental research on virtual teams. Aoki (1995) found that the use of quasi-synchronous chat (through Internet relay chat or IRC) by international virtual teams can be problematic, at least for international teams. Time coordination, lack of nonverbal cues, and lack of a shared native language were all factors that made chat both a dispreferred and less effective technology for group performance. Finally, there is also some evidence that more technologies do not always mean higher satisfaction and performance in virtual teams. Carletta, Anderson, and McEwan

(2000) looked at virtual teams who used a multicomponent collaboration system that included audio and video links, a shared whiteboard, and shared computer-aided design capabilities. They found that the teams preferred (and used) the communication features of the system over the collaborative work tools.

Social Aspects of Virtual Teamwork

Research into virtual teams extends beyond examinations of technology use. One common approach has been to compare them to face-to-face teams. For example, Potter and Balthazard (2002) used findings from research on face-to-face teams to study the relationship between interaction style and group performance in virtual teams. Their findings from virtual team interaction on an Internet-based, threaded discussion forum showed that (1) virtual teams exhibit the same range of interaction styles as found in face-to-face groups (constructive, passive, aggressive, or mixed) and (2) that these interaction styles affect group processes in ways that are very similar to those found in conventional groups. Potter and Balthazard concluded that computer-mediated communication (CMC) does not present a de facto obstacle to successful group problem solving, and that groups can and do compensate for any limitations imposed by the medium.

Following a different track, Alge, Wiethoff, and Klein (2003) examined the effects of temporal scope (defined as "the extent to which teams have pasts together and expect to have futures" p. 26) on face-to-face and virtual teams' communicative and decision-making effectiveness. Among their findings were results that indicated that teams with no history (ad hoc and future) shared more information and reported higher openness/trust in face-to-face communication than in the computer-mediated setting. However, for the past teams, their previous knowledge-building experiences erased any differences arising from communications media. Alge et al. (2003) concluded that the important question for research raised by this study is not "does the medium matter?" (p. 35) but rather "how does the medium matter?" (p. 35). In this case, teams without a past history were more effective when communicating face-to-face, while teams with a past history experienced equally effective communication in both conditions. Adding a final wrinkle to the face-to-face versus virtual teams dilemma, Schmidt, Montoya-Weiss, and Massey (2001) found that in their comparisons, the virtual teams made more effective decisions than the face-to-face teams.

Moving beyond comparative research, scholars have attempted to identify the factors important to successful virtual team collaboration. One key area that has surfaced is the importance of communication (Hughes, O'Brien, Randall, Rouncefield, & Tolmie, 2001) and related areas such as trust. Jarvenpaa and

Leidner (1999) examined the relationship between communication behaviors and trust in virtual teams, and found that swift trust can be established by very early communication behaviors. Additionally, task-based communication was important to maintaining trust, and social communication could strengthen trust, once established. Trust was important because teams reporting higher levels of trust were better at managing the complexity of their virtual environments. However, later research by Aubert and Kelsey (2003) found that trust levels among teammates did not have a significant relationship with overall performance effectiveness. They did uncover a more indirect link, finding that teams that did not develop trust had to expend more effort to produce quality work than those teams that had developed trust.

In addition to trust, research has shown other factors play an important role in effective virtual team functioning. The style of interaction that the group as a whole exhibits, as opposed to the personalities of the individual team members, can predict contextual outcomes in virtual teams (Balthazard, Potter, & Warren, 2004). The presence or development of shared understanding among team members has also been shown to be important for positive outcomes (Majchrzak, Rice, King, Malhotra, & Ba, 2000), as has listening and paying attention (Furst, Blackburn, & Rosen, 1999). Additional research has shown that effective virtual teams are able to fit their communication patterns to the task (Maznevski & Chudoba, 2000).

The research reviewed here demonstrates the importance of communication and communication-related factors to the success of virtual teams. Communication is also clearly important to the success of face-to-face teams, and this has lead Timmerman and Scott (2005) to suggest that the important role for research on virtual teams should be to study the differences among these groups, as opposed to the differences between virtual and face-to-face teams. Furthermore, because technology is integral to virtual collaboration, we need to continue to ground our research within specific technological contexts (Lurey & Raisinghani, 2001). One way to accomplish these goals is to use research methods that have not traditionally been applied to the study of virtual teams. In the next section I will explore how one such method, microanalysis of interaction, can add to our understanding of communication by teams using chat.

Examining Virtual Meetings

The Importance of Meeting Talk

In order to understand how to make virtual collaboration more effective, I propose that we focus on the one area where the team qua team exists in its most visible form: the meeting. Meetings are an important part of every organization's success, and they are a frequent occurrence for many employees. Meetings, as organized frames for talk, are where much of the business of organizations gets done (Boden, 1994). When our focus is on teamwork, meetings take on added significance, for it is when the members of the team are interacting together, in formal or informal meetings, that they instantiate themselves as a team. This is especially true of virtual teams, where members may be scattered across a state, a country, or across the globe, and whose interaction outside of the team may be limited.

Studying the talk that occurs in team meetings can provide us with an insider's understanding of how collaborative goals are accomplished (Boden, 1994). Recall that one of the findings of research on virtual teams was the importance of shared understanding for effective teamwork (Majchrzak et al., 2000). Research on conversation has demonstrated that one of the best ways to see how and when intersubjective understanding is achieved is through the study of talk (Schegloff, 1992). Specifically, the use of fine-grained microanalysis applied to naturally occurring interaction has shown that talk is an orderly process with a stable set of practices that interactants skillfully use to make sense of the world and produce social order (Schegloff, 1992). We have also learned that institutional talk (Drew & Heritage, 1992; Maynard, 1992) (i.e., talk in various workplace settings such as doctor's offices, court rooms, and schools) has unique characteristics that separate it from everyday conversation. Overall, this research has demonstrated empirically the importance of micro-level analysis of social interaction as a requirement for contextualizing the macro-level study of human social relations (Psathas, 1995).

Because meetings are important sites for doing the work of organizations and consist, by their very nature, of people talking, we can use the microanalytic approach to develop an understanding of how the structure of talk in meetings affects the work being done. For example, research on face-to-face meetings has shown that the system for turn taking in meetings varies from the system for mundane talk in small, but important ways, and that these variations allow decisions to be made and goals to be accomplished (Boden, 1994). Talk that happens before meetings has been shown to help participants accomplish specific tasks and social functions (Mirivel & Tracy, 2005). Despite some small differences, interaction in meeting contexts such as face-to-face and telephone conferences, where real-time speech is the primary modality, allows the use of the general organizing system for talk, the turn-taking system. However, the introduction of new technologies to meetings, specifically computer-mediated tools, fundamentally changes the structure of interaction. Because the system for organizing talk plays such an important role in developing understanding and therefore also effective collaboration, it is logical to assume that when we move away from the familiar spoken modality and into newer, technologically-mediated communication modalities, we will have to readjust our strategies for organizing our communication. I would like to argue that this is certainly true of chat, and that the structure of chat conversations as applied to virtual team meetings can be uncovered through careful microanalysis of interaction. I will explore this proposition next by comparing the structure of spoken conversation to that of chat.

Collaboration in Chat: Following the Thread

In their ground-breaking work in the 1970s, Sacks, Schegloff, and Jefferson (1974) demonstrated that everyday, mundane talk followed an orderly system of organized rules or principles. The turn-taking system provides participants in a conversation with a scaffold, upon which interaction is built. Sacks et al. described this system, and although the features have been refined and expanded upon over the years, the basic observations have held up through repeated analysis. Several of the features of the turn-taking system for talk are particularly relevant to compare to interaction in chat. One of the basic observations was that in talk, speaker change recurs, that is, we take turns at talking, and generally, one party talks at a time. Microanalysis of talk has also shown that overlap, where one speaker starts talking before the other is finished, is common, but brief. Transitions between speakers with no gap and no overlap are common along with transitions with slight gap or slight overlap. Techniques to allocate turns to new speakers are used; for example, a current speaker may continue speaking, or may select the next speaker to talk. If no next speaker is selected, and the current speaker does not continue, a new speaker may self-select.

By comparison, interaction in computer chat is quite different. Although chat, which allows participants to be logged in to the same "room" at the same time, is generally considered to be a synchronous technology when compared to e-mail or bulletin boards, when compared to speech it is only quasi-synchronous. The turn-taking system for speech works because listeners are able to monitor the ongoing production of turns by speakers. One of the most important characteristics of chat is that this monitoring feature is no longer present. As a result, in computer chat, speakers do not exchange turns at talk as much as they add to

Figure 1. Virtual team meeting chat window

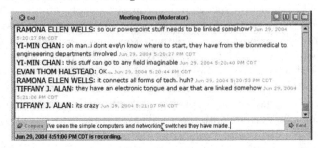

Note: The names of all participants have been changed to protect confidentiality.

the evolving conversation. Participants logged into a chat meeting are presented with a window with two parts; a larger box containing the ongoing conversation, and a smaller box into which they type their posts (see Figure 1). Team members only see each other's turns after they are completed and sent to the chat server; because there is no way to monitor who is currently composing a post,[2] more than one party may talk (i.e., type) at a time. Assemblance of turn taking is presented, because the server lists all posts in sequential order and overlapping posts are not permitted by the server. However, the lack of a truly analogous turn-taking system in chat has given rise to a modified form for organizing conversation.

In the modified chat system, there are no organized transitions between speakers per se, because posts appear in the chat window in the order they were received by the chat server. However, transitions where two posts appear simultaneously (though sequentially) are possible, and gaps (in time) between posts are common. Interestingly, the textual nature of chat conversations means that gaps of time when no one is "speaking" are only noticeable in relation to the last posted turn. When a new post appears in the chat window, it will be located directly beneath the prior post, and unless the server adds a time stamp, there will be no permanent indication of how long the transition between speakers lasted.

Chat systems place no restriction on when participants can begin typing a turn, and because the placement of turns in the chat window is controlled by the server, not by the individual participants, there is little need in chat to explicitly manage the exchange of turns. For this same reason, however, there is a very clear need to organize turns so that their proper sequence can be reconstructed by the participants, because they cannot determine if their posts will be placed adjacent to antecedent remarks. Thus, rather than a system designed to manage speaker exchange, computer chat features an organizing system designed to maintain interactional coherence. The basis for this organization system is not speakership roles per se (i.e., current speaker, next speaker), but rather speaker roles as they pertain to conversational threads.

One feature of many types of CMC that is not present in spoken interaction is *threading*. Threading is a term originally used in computer programming to describe parallel series of code that allowed programs to engage in multiple, simultaneous operations. In CMC, the term *thread* is applied to a conversational topic; individual messages can have one thread or many, and in many CMC systems, such as e-mail, newsgroups, and bulletin boards, messages can be sorted based on their relationships to specific threads. Messages can be read in a strict chronological order, or they can be read chronologically according to thread. Although threading is generally thought of as applying specifically to asynchronous CMC channels, detailed examination of conversation in chat meetings shows that threading is the primary means through which these participants organize their conversations. Threads in chat are not explicitly marked (i.e., through the use of subject lines or the marker "re"), however, in their patterns of turn taking the team members display a very sensitive orientation to the different threads that permeate their conversations. A look at some examples will illustrate how threading works in chat.

In Example 1, two team members, Yi-Min and Tiffany, have been discussing the topics for their project. In line 1, Yi-Min has offered a possible candidate to add to their project, specifically, "ultra wide band." Video recordings made from each team member's computer screen show that Yi-Min pauses after sending line 1, and then resumes typing approximately 12 seconds later. During the same time, however, Tiffany is also typing a post, which she sends (line 2) just 1 second before Yi-Min's post at line 3. Tiffany's post does not directly relate to Yi-Min's post; instead, Tiffany is referring back to an earlier subthread of this conversation. However, the timing of her posts results in it effectively "interrupting" Yi-Min's two related posts at lines 1 and 3. Tiffany is not confused by this interruption, and responds to Yi-Min with agreement in line 4. Yi-Min is also able to keep track of the different threads, and in fact she begins typing a response

Example 1a[3].

1	YI-MIN: ultra wide band is suppose to be a newer technology than the blue tooth
2	TIFFANY: I'm not sure exactly what Dr. Kimbles means by focusing on two technologies, but hopefully wireless as a category works
3	YI-MIN: but nano tech is definately the latest
4	TIFFANY: yeah
5	YI-MIN: i think so...it's going to have a lot of impact on future tech n of course..our future lifestyle
6	TIFFANY: the only thing about the articles Ramona found (and I didn't read them all yet) is that I believe we're supposed to be focusing on what's going on in [city name]

Example 1b. (modified)

Thread 1A

1	YI-MIN: ultra wide band is suppose to be a newer technology than the blue tooth
3	YI-MIN: but nano tech is definately the latest
4	TIFFANY: yeah

Thread 1B

2	TIFFANY: I'm not sure exactly what Dr. Kimbles means by focusing on two technologies, but hopefully wireless as a category works
5	YI-MIN: i think so...it's going to have a lot of impact on future tech n of course..our future lifestyle

Thread 1C

6	TIFFANY: the only thing about the articles Ramona found (and I didn't read them all yet) is that I believe we're supposed to be focusing on what's going on in [city name]

to Tiffany 1 second before Tiffany's post at line 4 arrives in the chat window. At the same time, Tiffany has begun another post that refers to yet another separate thread in the ongoing conversation. To see how skillfully these team members make sense of the altered order of turns in chat, we can rearrange this turn in this example to place related posts adjacent to one another:

In this modified arrangement, what we see is that this excerpt actually contains three separate threads, and that the chat participants must do their own work to mentally rearrange the individual posts to arrive at the correct order. That they do so is evidenced by the lack of any explicit marker of confusion or request for clarification in the chat transcripts. A second, more complex example will further illustrate the skill needed to make sense of threading in chat conversations.

In Example 2, we see more clearly how the thread is the primary structure for organizing chat conversations. This example also highlights the unique abilities

Example 2a.

1	SID: Guess Sid doesn't like us! :-)
2	TIFFANY: let me see if I can look at your trees on blackboard
3	SID: i had to reboot :P
4	EVAN: Haha
5	TIFFANY: oh
6	EVAN: Sorry...!@
7	ICH: if we want some real cool stuff i think we should go interview grad students who are researching this area as well
8	EVAN: At least you were here
9	EVAN: Better then me last week
10	YI-MIN: short cut..hehe

Example 2b. (modified)

Thread 2A

1	SID: Guess Sid doesn't like us! :-)			
4	EVAN: Haha		10	YI-MIN: short cut..hehe
3	SID: i had to reboot :P			
5	TIFFANY: oh		6	EVAN: Sorry...!@
			8	EVAN: At least you were here
			9	EVAN: Better then me last week

Thread 2B

7	ICH: if we want some real cool stuff i think we should go interview grad students who are researching this area as well		2	TIFFANY: let me see if I can look at your trees on blackboard

of CMC over spoken interaction. The first post, line 1, shows how the textual, archived nature of chat can change the conversation. Team member Sid has joined the chat just prior to this segment. Sid had made several attempts earlier in the meeting to join the chat, but because of technical problems, it appeared to the other team members present, Yi-Min and Evan, that he was simply entering and leaving the chat. At that point, Evan sent the following message to the chat, "Guess Sid doesn't like us! :-)." When Sid was finally successful in joining the chat, he exchanged greetings with the rest of the team, and then scrolled up to the beginning of the chat to read what he had missed. It was then that he came across Evan's post, which Sid copied and pasted into his message composition box, and then hit send, thereby recycling Evan's post into his own post in line 1 of Example 2. In effect, what Sid has done is to use an older thread to start a new thread, which he then elaborates on in line 3 with an explanation of his problems from earlier in the meeting.

Sid's thread is not the only one present in this segment, however. At the same time that Sid was copying and pasting Evan's earlier post, Tiffany and Yi-Min were engaged in typing posts that both related to the primary ongoing thread of finding contacts for the team's research project. Again, because more than one participant can type at a time, and because they cannot monitor each other's posts as they are being composed, they also cannot control when messages will "interrupt" other threads. Thus, Tiffany's post in line 2 separates Sid's two related posts in lines 1 and 3. Interestingly, Evan, who had also been typing a message related to a previous thread, stops typing 2 seconds after Tiffany's post, pauses for 4 seconds, and then deletes his turn in progress, and types ""Haha" just as Sid's post in line 3 appears, to which Evan responds immediately with "Sorry...!@." Evan then continues with two more posts designed to follow up on Sid's thread, but they end up getting posted after the message Yi-Min had been engaged in typing. So to see how these posts were threaded by the team members, we can again rearrange them. Posts that relate to the same thread but are not responses will be placed in the same horizontal axis.

What we can see from these examples is how different the experience of following a chat conversation is from following a conversation in spoken interaction. To successfully navigate a chat meeting, participants must, to a certain extent, let go of a temporal understanding of turn taking, and rather analyze messages for their topical relationships. Because placement in the chat window is serendipitous, participants cannot rely on the prior post to help explain the meaning of the most recent post. If participants are not attuned to threads as the primary organization of chat conversation, then they will undoubtedly feel frustrated with this form of communication, especially given how vital shared understanding is for effective teamwork. However, the fact that some teams have been successful using chat leads me to conclude that it does not present an insurmountable obstacle to collaboration, and that, armed with a deeper understanding of why chat conversations can be hard to follow, we can now look to ways to prepare virtual teams for working in this environment.

Tips for Effective Virtual Team Meetings with Chat

We know from the research that use of technology by virtual teams will vary based on the organizational and situational contexts teams find themselves in. We also know that one of the key elements to successful technology implementation in teams is the ability of teams to adapt the technology to their own needs. Therefore, it is important to keep in mind that this set of recommendations is exactly that, helpful tools and suggestions for making chat an effective technology for virtual team meetings. These guidelines should not be thought of as fixed in stone, but should give teams a place to start when undertaking a project of virtual collaboration.

Use of Moderators

Teams of all types with no prior history may experience difficulty getting started, but the remote nature of virtual work can compound this problem. Because of this, discussion moderators can be particularly helpful during virtual team meetings, especially during the beginning phases of the project. The moderator could be a facilitator, someone who is not a part of the team, but who is familiar with the virtual team experience, or the moderator might be a member of the team who is experienced with virtual work. In either case, the moderator should have excellent technical skills and be experienced with the specific chat interface being used. The moderator should serve as a resource for technical support and training and should make sure that all team members have received proper training on the interface before the project starts. The moderator should also be sensitive to the possibility that not all team participants will be able to make sense of the way threading is used in chat conversations, and they may need guidance on how to read each post in its proper order.

Meeting Scheduling and Planning

One of the distinct advantages of chat as a tool for virtual meetings is that they can be scheduled with greater ease and flexibility. However, the nature of chat conversations has the effect of extending the amount of time that it will take to get the work of the team accomplished. Teams using chat need to adjust their expectations and allow more time for pre-meeting talk, both for general socialization, but also to allow for technical issues to be resolved. Because the chat interface allows multiple team members to be typing at the same time, there is the potential to generate more ideas and more talk than might arise in a face-to-face or telephone meeting. This means, however, that it will necessarily take longer for teams to move through each topic. To that end, as with other types of meetings, virtual teams will benefit from the use of agendas. However, agendas for virtual meetings should be relatively short, and the more complex the topics, the fewer items should be included. Virtual teams using chat should find it beneficial to schedule more frequent, shorter meetings as opposed to longer, less frequent meetings.

Interaction Monitoring and Norms

Team moderators and leaders should be aware of the structural features of chat conversation, and should make an effort to foster participation by monitoring the ongoing activity and helping to establish norms for communication. One advantage of the chat interface is that it creates a more egalitarian, collaborative space, because there are fewer ways that individual team members can dominate the conversation. However, the other side to this benefit is that it can be easier for individuals to drop out of the conversation because of the lack of visual reminders of their presence (this is true of any medium that lacks a visual component). Leaders and moderators can help manage this potential problem by making an effort to encourage specific individuals to respond if their participation has lapsed. It is important to note, however, that conversational gaps that appear long by the standards of spoken interaction will be quite common in chat, because posts generally take longer to type than to speak, and because typing speeds vary from person to person. Thus, part of the role of the moderator will be to develop a sense of each team member's chat style, in order to determine when a sufficient amount of response time has elapsed. Moderators should also keep in mind that members can and will multi-task, and may appear silent because they are engaged in a related activity (such as working on a team document) that has removed their attention from the chat environment. The ability to multi-task during the meeting is an advantage of this type of tool and should be encouraged. However, moderators may want to request that team members note prolonged absences in the chat conversation before leaving.

Moderators should also remember that turns will not necessarily be posted adjacent to their antecedent posts, and thus messages that require a response from a specific individual should be specifically addressed to that individual; otherwise the participants may assume that the message is intended for everyone in the team. This is especially important for turns that ask for clarification or explanation. Finally, moderators should encourage the use of shorter, more frequent posts, in order to keep team members attentive to the ongoing flow of ideas and create a sense of progress in the conversation. These practices may emerge spontaneously for some teams; however, moderators may wish to collate these recommendations into a set of explicit conversational norms for the team. Discussing these norms at the start of the team's project can be especially helpful when team members have little or no prior experience interacting in a chat environment.

Conclusion

This chapter has examined how one specific ICT, computer chat, could be used to hold effective virtual team meetings. Chat is a low-cost, flexible alternative to other synchronous technologies such as teleconferencing and video conferencing. Although chat does not provide the same degree of real-time communication as these media, the structure of chat allows for more participation by more team members, thereby increasing the likelihood of positive team outcomes. We have seen that the research on virtual teams covers a wide ground, but that throughout, concerns relating to communication and technology use predominate. To address some of the research gaps, I proposed a new way of looking at virtual meetings by concentrating on the underlying structure of communication in chat. I demonstrated how chat conversations differ from the traditional model for spoken interaction along several dimensions, the most important of which is the concept of threading. We saw that in order to make sense out of the temporally displaced posts in a chat room, participants must be sensitive to the multiple, ongoing topics of conversation. Based on these observations, I offered some tips for making chat an effective tool for conducting virtual team meetings.

Contemporary organizations continue to face the challenges of globalization, and one strategy that will grow in importance is virtual teamwork. As technologies continue to evolve, virtual teams will find that they have a wider range of tools available for use. At the same time, there is no reason to expect that teams will abandon tools that have already proved useful, if only for the reason that learning new tools takes time and energy that could be better spent elsewhere. I have argued that chat, though not widely used, can be a tool that will be both flexible enough for the needs of different teams, and, with some initial guidance, simple enough to use as one way to help virtual teams meet and collaborate. It is likely that there will never be a one-size-fits-all solution to the problem of collaborating across distances, but it is reasonable to expect that particular solutions for particular problems can be developed from continued research on virtual teams.

References

Alge, B. J., Wiethoff, C., & Klein, H. J. (2003). When does the medium matter? Knowledge-building experiences and opportunities in decision-making teams. *Organizational Behavior And Human Decision Processes, 91,* 26-37.

Aoki, K. (1995). Synchronous multi-user textual communication in international tele-collaboration. *Electronic Journal of Communication, 5*(4). Retrieved January 13, 2004, from http://80-www.cios.orgcontent.lib.utexas.edu:2048/getfile%5CAOK_V5N495

Aubert, B. A., & Kelsey, B. L. (2003). Further understanding of trust and performance in virtual teams. *Small Group Research, 34,* 575-618.

Balthazard, P. A., Potter, R. E., & Warren, J. (2004). Expertise, extraversion and group interaction styles as performance indicators in virtual teams. *The DATA BASE for Advances in Information Systems, 35,* 41-64.

Boden, D. (1994). *The business of talk: Organizations in action.* Cambridge, MA: Polity Press.

Carletta, J., Anderson, A. H., & McEwan, R. (2000). The effects of multimedia communication technology on non-collocated teams: A case study. *Ergonomics, 43,* 1237-1251.

Drew, P., & Heritage, J. (1992). Analyzing talk at work: An introduction. In P. Drew & J. Heritage (Eds.), *Talk at work: Interaction in institutional settings* (pp. 3-65). Cambridge University Press.

Dutton, W. (1999). The virtual organization: Tele-access in business and industry. In G. DeSanctis & J. Fulk (Eds.), *Shaping organization form: Communication, connection, and community* (pp. 473-495). Thousand Oaks, CA: Sage Publications.

Furst, S., Blackburn, R., & Rosen, B. (1999). Virtual team effectiveness: A proposed research agenda. *Information Systems Journal, 9,* 249-269.

Hughes, J. A., O'Brien, J., Randall, D., Rouncefield, M., & Tolmie, P. (2001). Some 'real' problems of 'virtual' organisation. *New Technology, Work and Employment, 16,* 49-64.

Iacono, S., & Kling, R. (2001). Computerization movements: The rise of the Internet and distant forms of work. In J. Yates & J. Van Maanen (Eds.), *Information technology and organizational transformation: History, rhetoric, and practice* (pp. 93-135). Thousand Oaks: CA: Sage Publications.

Jarvenpaa, S. L., & Leidner, D. E. (1999). Communication and trust in global virtual teams. *Organization Science, 10,* 791-815.

Lurey, J. S., & Raisinghani, M. S. (2001). An empirical study of best practices in virtual teams. *Information Management, 38,* 523-544.

Majchrzak, A., Malhotra, A., Stamps, J., & Lipnack, J. (2004). Can absence make a team grow stronger? *Harvard Business Review, 82*(5), 131-137.

Majchrzak, A., Rice, R. E., King, N., Malhotra, A., & Ba, S. L. (2000). Computer-mediated inter-organizational knowledge-sharing: Insights from a virtual team innovating using a collaborative tool. *Information Resource Management Journal, 13,* 44-53.

Maynard, D. W. (1992). On clinicians co-implicating recipients' perspective in the delivery of diagnostic news. In P. Drew & J. Heritage (Eds.), *Talk at work: Interaction in institutional settings* (pp. 331-358). Cambridge University Press.

Maznevski, M. L., & Chudoba, K. M. (2000). Bridging space over time: Global virtual team dynamics and effectiveness. *Organization Science, 11,* 473-492.

Mirivel, J. C., & Tracy, K. (2005). Premeeting talk: An organizationally crucial form of talk. *Research on Language & Social Interaction, 38,* 1-34.

Monge, P., & Fulk, J. (1999). Communication technology for global network organizations. In G. DeSanctis & J. Fulk (Eds.), *Shaping organization form: Communication, connection, and community* (pp. 71-100). Thousand Oaks, CA: Sage Publications.

Pauleen, D. J., & Yoong, P. (2001). Facilitating virtual team relationships via the Internet and conventional communication channels. *Internet Research: Electronic Networking Applications and Policy, 11,* 190-202.

Potter, R. E., & Balthazard, P. A. (2002). Virtual team interaction styles: Assessment and effects. *International Journal of Human-Computer Studies, 56,* 423-443.

Psathas, G. (1995). *Conversation analysis: The study of talk-in-interaction.* Thousand Oaks, CA: Sage Publications.

Rasters, G., Vissers, G., & Dankbaar, B. (2002). An inside look: Rich communication through lean media in a virtual research team. *Small Group Research, 33,* 718-754.

Robey, D., Khoo, H. M., & Powers, C. (2000). Situated learning in cross-functional virtual teams. *IEEE Transactions on Professional Communication, 47,* 51-66.

Sacks, H., Schegloff, E. A., & Jefferson, G. (1974). A simplest systematics for the organization of turn-taking for conversation. *Language, 50,* 696-735.

Schegloff, E. A. (1992). Repair after next turn: The last structurally provided defense of intersubjectivity in conversation. *American Journal of Sociology, 104,* 161-216.

Schmidt, J. B., Montoya-Weiss, M. M., & Massey, A. P. (2001). New product development decision-making effectiveness: Comparing individuals, face-to-face teams, and virtual teams. *Decision Sciences, 32,* 575-600.

Scott, C. R. (1999). Communication technology and group communication. In L. R. Frey, D. S. Gouran, & M. S. Poole (Eds.), *Group communication theory and research* (pp. 432-472). Thousand Oaks: CA: Sage Publications.

Sellen, A. J., & Harper, R. H. R. (2002). *The myth of the paperless office.* Cambridge, MA: MIT Press.

Timmerman, C. E., & Scott, C. R. (2006). *Virtually working: Communicative and structural predictors of media use and key outcomes in virtual work teams. Communication Monographs, 73,* 108-136.

Zuboff, S. (1988). *In the age of the smart machine: The future of work and power.* New York: Basic Books.

Endnotes

[1]   For the purposes of this chapter, I define computer chat as any networked computer application that allows three or more parties to converse in the same virtual space in real time. For example, traditional instant messaging would not be considered chat, but the conference function of an instant message program (for example, YAHOO! Messenger™) would meet the criteria.

[2]   This differs from many instant-messaging programs, which include a feature that lets the other party know when his/her interlocutor is typing a message, although parties still do not have access to the content of the message until it is sent.

[3]   Data presented here were taken from chat transcripts collected as part of a larger case study of virtual team interaction. The team was made up of five upper-level undergraduate students at a large university in the south-western U.S. Names and other identifying information have been changed or omitted. Transcripts have not been corrected for spelling, grammar, or punctuation.

Chapter XIV

Working at Home:
Negotiating Space and Place

Tracy L. M. Kennedy, University of Toronto, Canada

Abstract

This chapter explores the work-family interface by investigating home as a potential work space that must still accommodate the social and leisure needs of household members. By examining spatial patterns of household Internet location, this chapter investigates the prevalence of paid work in Canadian homes, illustrates how household spaces are reorganized to accommodate the computer/Internet, and examines how the location of Internet access is situated within sociocultural contexts of the household and how this might affect potential work-from-home scenarios. Data collected from a triangulation of methods—surveys, interviews and in-home observation—also illustrate the relevance of household Internet location from an organizational perspective. The relationship between individuals and business organizations is interactive and integrative, and the home workplace is complex and blurred with other daily social realities, which influence effective work-at-home strategies and potentially shapes productivity and efficiency.

Introduction

The nature of work is changing in today's information society, especially with the prevalence of information and communication technologies (ICTs) in the home. In many instances paid work is relocating to the home, which offers people more flexibility, yet often less clear boundaries between work and household (Sullivan & Lewis, 2001). There has been considerable literature concerning how paid work at home—or telework[1]—is detailed, outlining numerous positive and negative features of working from home, and the impact of paid work at home on the household and organizations (Armstrong, 1997; Dimitrova, 2003; Frissen, 1992; Gurstein, 2001; Haddon & Brynin, 2005; Hardill & Green, 2003; Salaff, 2002; Stanworth, 1997). Despite conflicting analyses and debates about the impact of telework on individuals and organizations, little attention has been paid to the spatial semantics of organizing the location of household ICTs to compliment (or hinder) not only leisure and social use, but also work related tasks and work-at-home scenarios. If indeed businesses and organizations wish to encourage their employees to work at home, then it is important to think about how individuals spatially organize household ICTs and what impact this has not only on work performance and productivity, but also household members.

Most recent statistics in Canada indicate that Canadian Internet use is highest from home, with 62% of households using the Internet at least once a day, on average, from home (Statistics Canada, 2002). Canadian statistics (Statistics Canada, 2001a) also reveal that from 1996-2001, more people chose to work from home then ever before (1,175,760 billion, or 8% of the working population), and that most people who work at home live in urban areas. Having the Internet in the home has changed the way people think about work, how they do their work, and ultimately where they do their work.

This chapter explores the work-family interface by investigating the construction of the home as a potential work space that must still accommodate the social and leisure needs of household members. By examining spatial patterns of household Internet location, this chapter will:

- investigate the prevalence of paid work in Canadian homes,
- provide an overview of household Internet locations,
- illustrate how household spaces are reorganized to accommodate the computer/Internet, and
- examine how the location of Internet access is situated within sociocultural contexts of the household and how this might affect potential work-from-home scenarios.

We also need to consider the relevance of household Internet location from an organizational perspective. While there may be numerous benefits of paid work at home (or telework) to both the individual worker and the organization, there is a need to think about a construction of telework that incorporates individual and business needs and expectations. Examining the practices involved in deciding household Internet location provides sociocultural context to decision-making processes regarding paid work and ICTs in the home: "new organizational, social and personal relationships may accompany these new spatial arrangements, highlighting the entangled interrelations between space, work and organization" (Halford, 2005, p. 20).

The Connected Lives Project

The Connected Lives Project is a Canadian study led by Professor Barry Wellman who heads NetLab at the University of Toronto. The project, funded by the Social Science and Humanities Research Council, consists of six graduate students and numerous research assistants in the greater Toronto area. The goal of the research project is to learn about how Canadians communicate with their friends and family, providing an in-depth investigation of how the Internet is affecting the "everyday life" of Canadians and how the Internet is embedded in daily routines and practices. Where most studies until now have focused on *who* uses the Internet, the Connected Lives Project focuses on *how* different kinds of users (and nonusers) of new communications technologies engage in social relationships and community. The research design employs a methodological triangulation including surveys, interviews, and observations.

Survey: The 32 page survey for the Connected Lives Project was developed between November 2003 and June 2004 by the NetLab research team. English-speaking adult participants over the age of 18 in East York were randomly sampled in June of 2004 and 621 households were sent an information letter regarding the research project and later contacted in person and by telephone to set up interview dates. With a response rate of 56%, 350 surveys were completed between July 2004 and March 2005. Each survey took 1-2 hours to complete. Surveys included questions regarding the use of new communication technologies and the nature of their contact, on and off-line, with friends and relatives that are both near and far.

Interviews: The interview schedule was also developed by the Connected Lives team between September 2004 and January 2005. Participants who completed the initial survey were asked if they were interested in a follow-up interview. The response rate was 85% of those survey respondents who wrote "yes" or "unsure" when asked at the end of the survey if they would be willing to be interviewed. In-home, semi-structured interviews were conducted between February and April 2005 with one fourth of the survey participants (n=87).

The interviews were conducted by Connected Lives doctoral students and took 2-4 hours and provided detailed information about household relations, Internet use, travel behavior, social networks, and information seeking, which provided a better and more comprehensive understanding of initial survey questions. In households with a computer, we asked permission to take a digital picture of where the computer with Internet access was located. This provided NetLab researchers a visual depiction of not only computer and Internet technologies, but also a visual representation of where Canadians are using the Internet in their homes and what is going on around them.

Observations: Once the interview was completed and if the interview participant had a household Internet connection, we asked the participant to demonstrate how they actually use the Internet in their homes. Interviewers observed how participants search for information, particularly information concerning health and culture. Of the 87 interview participants, 43% (n=37) were observed using the Internet. The interviews and observations provide a rich understanding of how Canadians use new communication technologies for interpersonal relations and to obtain information.

Overview of Participants

Race and ethnicity: The Connected Lives Project takes place in East York, a distinct part of the current city of Toronto with a population of 114,240 in 2001 (Statistics Canada, 2001b). Its populace represents a wide range of ethnicities, socioeconomic statuses, and household arrangements, which is reflective of Canadian diversity. For example, 40,620 of the East York population are from visible minorities (Statistics Canada, 2001b). Visible minorities (i.e., nonwhite-Canadians) comprise 27% of the survey sample: primarily East Asians and South Asians, with Chinese-Canadians and Indian-Canadians being the largest groups. This is lower than the 2001 Canadian census report that indicates visible minorities comprise 36% of the East York population. Unfortunately these ethnic groups are somewhat underrepresented in our methodological process because of language and cultural barriers. In most other respects, the data reflect census demographics, including gender, age, income, education, and family composition.

Age, gender and marital status: Fifty-eight percent of the survey respondents are women, with a median age of 45. Fifty-nine percent of the somewhat less representative interview sample are women; with a median age of 49. Nearly two thirds (62%) of the survey respondents are married or stably partnered, as are 68% of the interview participants. Three fifths (61%) of the survey respondents have children; as do a somewhat higher 66% of the interview participants.

Education and income: Forty-three percent of the survey respondents have university degrees, while 27% have a high school education or less. Fifty-one percent of interview participants have a university degree, while only 20% of the interview participants have a high school education or less. The bulk of the population is working class and middle class; median personal income is between $30,000 and $40,000. Sixty-two percent of the survey respondents are doing paid work, thus with a substantially higher median of between $50,000 and $75,000. Thirty-seven percent of all participants are retired, 16% are students, and 13% are full-time homemakers. Others report that they are between jobs, on leave, or have other reasons for not working.

Paid work at home: Twenty-six percent (n=56 and 16% of all participants) of participants reported conducting paid work at home. Of these participants, 91% conduct work related to their main job. Fifty-seven percent of participants who work at home are female. The reasons given for working at home are catching up with work (42%), saves time (37%), saves money (33%), better working conditions (33%). Twenty-six percent note other reasons such as convenience and ease. Participants who work at home report spending an average of 16.5 hours a week on paid work at home.

Discussion

Internet users: The amount of people using the Internet continues to grow. Computer Industry Almanac[2] projects that the worldwide Internet population in 2006 will be 1.21 billion users. On a Canadian scale, most recent statistics (Statistics Canada, 2002) indicate that 62% of Canadians are now online either from home, work, school, or public facilities, with 51% using the Internet from the household. Individuals with higher levels of education, working people with higher income, and those with children still at home are the leading users of the Internet in Canada (Statistics Canada, 2002; U.S. Census Bureau, 2001 states similar findings in the USA). This is also the case for other technology such as telephone, television, and so forth (Dutton, 1999; Dutton, Rogers, & Jun, 1987; also the computer Murdock, Hartmann, & Gray, 1995).

Most of the survey respondents (79%) have at least one computer at home, and 94% of these computerized households are connected to the Internet. Similar to Canadian and American Internet use (Ekos Research Associates, 2004; Rideout & Reddick, 2005), 75% of Connected Lives are connected to the Internet. Comparable to the Canadian mean usage of 12.7 hours per week (Ipsos-Reid, 2005), Connected Lives respondents reported being online a median of 10 hours per week and sending e-mails a median of 21 times per week.

Table 1. Mean number of hours per week spent on Internet activities at home by gender, for those with the Internet (N=235)

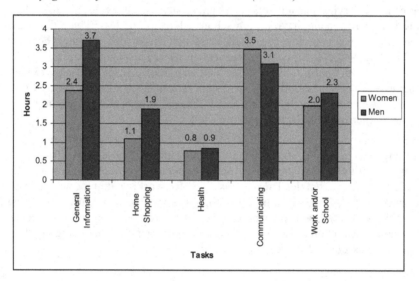

Internet usage patterns: Considerable research has addressed how people use the Internet in general (see Pew Internet and American Life;[3] Howard, Rainie, & Jones, 2001). Overall, there are four general ways of using the Internet—communication, information, recreation, and commerce. Using the Internet for communication—e-mail and instant messaging—to keep in touch with family, friends, coworkers and peers is a popular use for the Internet (Katz & Rice, 2002). Similarly searching for information and Web surfing for leisure interests is also popular, and people are increasingly purchasing products and conducting their banking online.

The use of the Internet by Connected Lives participants reflects similar documented usage patterns. Communicating with others and seeking general information are still the most common uses of the Internet from home, with women spending more hours a week (3.5) communicating with people than men do (3.1 hours). Men spend 3.7 hours per week searching for general information, whereas, women spend 2.4 hours per week (see Table 1). This reflects gendered usage patterns explained in detail in other research (Kennedy, Wellman, & Klement, 2003).

Location of Internet Access

Concerns have been raised about the effects of Internet use on families and households. For example, in 2000 Robert Putnam suggested that computers are partly responsible for the decline of social interaction between family members. However, other researchers indicate this is not the case (see Anderson & Tracey, 2002; Frohlich & Kraut, 2002), as more and more households are spending time on the Internet together in the family hub (if that is where the Internet is located) (Frohlich & Kraut, 2002; Lally, 2002) and incorporating it into their everyday lives. Moreover, it is apparent that family, leisure, school, and work activities are becoming blurred and fuzzy, meshing collectively as schedules and tasks blend together and often overlap.

The presence of the Internet in the household has called for spatial considerations on its placement. New homes being constructed are beginning to reflect the prevalence of computers and the Internet, indicating that the Internet is indeed becoming domesticated (Dutton, 1999), with changes in the design of houses reflecting cultural changes (Frohlich & Kraut, 2002). The experiences and contexts outside the household will also ultimately affect the structure of the home itself (Haddon, 1999).

As well as the choices of technology use—such as telephones, personal computers and televisions—in the home and where they are located is deter-

Table 2. Location of household Internet (N=328)

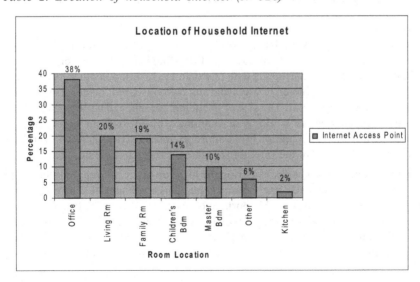

mined by beliefs and attitudes about household organization, which is greatly determined by one's culture, socioeconomic status, and ethnicity (Dutton, 1999). Even the choice of the type of Internet connection—dial-up, high-speed phone or cable, wireless, and so forth—is also dependent on this. The place where household members decide to put the computer/Internet signifies its importance in their lives, from communication hub (Rommes, 2002), to information center (Aro & Peteri, 2003) and from entertainment place to work space.

Deciding Internet Location in the Household

Where to place the computer with Internet access, either in a private office in the home, or in a communal space, greatly affects who uses it, and when they use it (Aro & Peteri, 2003; Frohlich & Kraut, 2002; Haddon & Skinner, 1991). For example, when the computer is placed in a person's private office space, it can deter his/her spouse and children from using it (Haddon & Skinner, 1991). Similarly, if the computer (with Internet access) is placed in a parent or child's bedroom, it can be difficult for other household members to have access to it, for example, when they are sleeping. Household members must make the decision on where to situate the Internet access point. This decision is often contingent on how the computer is perceived; whether the Internet is for work, play, or school will influence where the Internet access point is located. However, there are other factors worthy of consideration as well.

Household Mechanics

East York is located in the greater Toronto area (GTA) with an integration of small wartime bungalows to large-scale homes, and apartment buildings ranging from less than five levels to levels over 25. Fifty-four percent of participants live in houses and 45% in apartments with less than 1% residing in other locations.[4] Internet space is constructed in ways that suit the household; however, external factors are also influential. The size of the home, presence of children, whether a household member is working or running a business from home, and a household member's perception of the appropriateness of the Internet in various rooms will affect where the Internet is located (Frohlich & Kraut, 2002).

One important factor when considering the location of the household Internet is the mechanics of the house itself. Many Canadians are constricted by electrical wiring, telephone jacks, or cable ports in order to connect to the Internet. Few homes currently utilize wireless connections, and Internet Service Providers are generally only offering dial-up, high-speed phone (DSL), or cable Internet access (though this will likely change in the near future). For households using dial-up services, where to put the Internet access point is influenced by the number and location of telephone jacks. The same can be said for DSL, which requires a telephone jack, and cable access which requires a cable port:

Interviewer: *...Your computer is kind of near the front there. Is there any reason you put it over there as opposed to say over here or something?*

Participant #306: *Why over there? Well, because I think—we think—it is the best place, because there is a connection with the telephone. There is connection there, we don't have a connection here. In (another) room we have a connection but we don't have a place to put a computer in there.*

Similarly, this participant notes the age of the home and its constraints:

Interviewer: *Your access point is in the basement, how did you decide to put the computer down there?*

Participant #455: *Well you know, that's interesting because these houses are wired from 1952 so that gives me serious limitations to where I put the computer.*

Granted in houses with multiple computers, this can be remedied by installing a hub or router so that other computers can access the Internet through a single connection. However, the number of households with more than one computer is still low (see Table 3) and purchasing additional computers certainly would be problematic for lower income households. Modems, routers, and wireless cards for personal computers all cost money and may be considered unnecessary luxury items for some people.

Table 3. Number of household computers (N=327)

Number of Home Computers	%
0	21
1	50
2	20
3	7
4	2
5	<1
7	<1

As well, people may not feel they can set up a network connection in their households if they are lacking computer skills and they may not feel comfortable asking someone for help. Importantly, some people are satisfied with using dial-up and do not feel the need for faster access, while others are utilizing DSL or cable access without the need or desire for a wireless network. Regardless, the initial Internet access point is still influenced by where the telephone jacks or cable ports are located.

Another consideration that concerns household mechanics is the layout of the house itself and the number and size of rooms. For example, apartments do not have basements that can be converted into offices or recreation rooms. Often the growth of a household—or having children—converts the initial office space of the childless couple into a child's bedroom, and the computer moves to another spot. In apartments with no children, or single person households that have one bedroom, choices become limited in terms of where to put the computer. For example, one participant notes the restrictions of the layout of the household:

Interviewer: *How did you decide to put the computer in the living room...?*

Participant #561: *That was pretty much decided by the layout of the place. The bedroom would not have had enough space, and there's just not that many locations. It's the layout.*

Interviewer: *Would you rather have it in a different space...?*

Participant #561: *If I had a choice? Yeah.*

Interviewer: *Where would you rather have it?*

Participant #561: *If I had another room, you know?*

Room sizes in apartments also influence decision making, as spaces can become cluttered with the presence of the computer and computer desk in small rooms. One participant reveals how the apartment constrains Internet use from home:

Participant #773: *...The problem is psychological in that being here in this apartment, I feel enclosed like a rat. Sometimes being here one hour, I say I have to go out and do some moving, go downtown...just to breathe some fresh air. Here, being too long and the whole day long, gives a feeling that you are enclosed like a rat in a cage.*

Houses can be a similar challenge in terms of space—the size and number of rooms and the existence of a finished basement will all influence the choice of Internet location. This participant has thought about buying another computer, but is constrained by the number of rooms in the house:

Participant #879: *And if we buy a home with two or three bedrooms, I think we buy another computer.*

Some people are already conscious of office and computer space and potential Internet access points when purchasing new houses, as indicated by this participant (see Figure 1):

Interviewer: *Have you always had (the computers) down there? Have you had (the computers) in other places?*

Participant #439: *Since we've been in this house, no. We've been here about 15 years, and that was one of the reasons why we bought this particular place because of the basement. We thought it was an ideal space for an office. The place we were in before was a smaller semi-detached with an unfinished basement. It was only my husband who was self-employed at that point, but we had his office set up in one of the bedrooms and it was a nightmare. I mean there just wasn't enough room for anything.*

Figure 1. Home office in basement

© 2005 Wellman Associates (Used with permission)

Aesthetics

When East York participants were asked why they placed the Internet access point where they did, aesthetics were important to several respondents. Given the amount of time Canadians are spending accessing the Internet, it seems obvious that the atmosphere or ambience of the computer area should be important:

Interviewer: *What made you decide to put the computer out here? You get the plants and the trees...*

Participant #239: *I sit here, I look out. I see the trees, I see my plants. Ideal. If I had it in the bedroom, which I did some years ago, I'm just looking at the wall, which is terrible. This is ideal.*

Whether for work, play, or education, participants note that the "view" from their computer is important (see Figure 2). Placing the computer near a window to see the garden, the neighborhood, the birds, the greenery, and so forth is motivating, calming, and visually pleasing to Internet users, especially if they are at the desk for many hours. Similarly, placing the computer in an open concept space (such as a living room or family room) provides the user with a less closed-in and isolated feeling than when in a separate room. One participant notes discontent over the initial place of the computer and the changes that were made:

Figure 2. Computer use with a view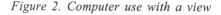

© 2005 Wellman Associates (Used with permission)

Participant #015: *Sitting in the basement with the old computer, I found it too dark and dingy, so we made the office upstairs...what we would consider our computer room upstairs.*

Private Spaces

As Table 2 indicates, the majority of participants indicate that their Internet access point is located in a "private" space; 38% utilize an office space or study, 14% have the Internet in a child's bedroom, and 10% have the Internet in the master bedroom. This gives a total of 62% of participants with Internet access in what might be considered a "private" space. Almost two thirds (59%) of participants who do paid work at home have their computer in an office or master bedroom.

There are some important things to note about these "private" locations. First, we have to remember that often the choice on where to place the Internet access point might be constricted by household mechanics (as discussed previously), therefore, there might not be a *choice* of location, but instead a *default* location of Internet access. In these situations, people make do with what they have and work around notions of public and private spaces within the household.

Second, some of these spaces—office/study or bedrooms—might not be considered "private" spaces for everyone. For example, the office or study may be available and accessible to all household members at any given time, instead of belonging to one particular household member. Privacy becomes something that is negotiated or understood by household members, and may change in different circumstances or contexts. In instances where there is only one Internet access point and more than one user, participants are aware that others in the household need to use the computer. When asked what time of day participants accessed the Internet the most from home, the survey data show that the Internet is used most frequently at home between 5PM and 11PM, when many people have returned home from paid work or school. However, during the interviews, participants report that they access the Internet at times when other household members are not home, or when others are not using it. This indicates that what may generally be considered as a private space in the household—a space that belongs to another household member—may not be so private because everyone in the household feels they can enter at any time.

Privacy means different things to different people. For people doing paid work from home, having the Internet in the household can often be difficult; interruptions by household members can be commonplace, where other household members may not understand the boundaries between work and home when the work is being done at home (Haythornewaite & Kazmer, 2002). Finding a quiet place to work and negotiating household responsibilities becomes tricky for those household members doing paid work or school work and research from home. Participants were also wary of how their working from home might affect others in the household, stating that they do not want to bother others in the household while they are working on the computer.

As well, participants who work from home noted that it was important for them to separate their work life from their home life, and therefore made conscious decisions to have the computer and Internet access in a space where they can go to for work and then leave the room when finished.

Participant #137: *I knew I wanted it (the computer) in my office and not visible, and that I could put it out of the way.*

One participant notes the division of tasks that is separated by the location of the computer:

Interviewer: *Why did you decide to put the computer in that place?*

Participant #848: *...I didn't want it in here. This room is big and I just didn't want it in this room that's all. This is a different kind of room. Right here is where I work mostly, and in that room I read, and you get into a habit, at least I do, of doing things in different places.*

Separating work and home is situated around the designated private work space. An interesting observation that surfaced while researchers were taking pictures of the Internet access point was the comments participants made about the "mess" of the office area. They were very aware that their computer area was laden with papers, folders, and other indicators of use. "Don't mind the mess" comments during the interviews revealed that participants were conscious of this disarray. Participants felt that by having the Internet in a private space that is removed from regular household traffic, they were able to contain the mess and visual disorganization. In these situations, the invisibility of the computer and work space area becomes important:

Participant #421: *I have things all over the desk but I know that nobody's going to touch them. You know what I mean? If I had things sprawled out on the kitchen counter or whatever, I can guarantee that they wouldn't be there when I went back the next night so and we actually had this conversation cause my husband went down there and he was like "when are* *you gonna put the stuff away? Like haven't you finished this project already?" and in my mind I'm saying "Yeah, but there's just that one thing you know I want to put it all together before I put it away" and it's okay if it takes me a couple of weeks to get it because that's out of the way and nobody's going to touch it.*

Communal Places

Some household spaces are more conducive to social interaction. Communal areas such as the dining room; living room or family room; spare room; or basement/recreation room allow household members easy access to the computer and the ability to communicate with others at the same time. Fifty-one percent of respondents indicated the location of the computer with Internet access was in the living room, family room, or kitchen area.

The decision to put the Internet access point in a more communal area that is open to all household members occurs for different reasons in different households. Establishing a multimedia portal is a conscious decision for some participants. Having television, Internet, music, video, or DVD all in one place encourages household members to all be in one place, but perhaps doing different things. This notion of togetherness even though household members might be doing different things is important to many participants. Aside from individual usage of media in the hub of living spaces, participants noted that these more accessible or "public" locations in the home encourage household members to "show and share" what they are doing online. Searching for information online is a common practice in many Canadian households. The kind of information that is being shared is often related to real estate; travel and vacation; home repairs or renovations; or product information. Importantly, participants are not only showing and/or sharing, but they sometimes use the Internet together when planning activities such as movies, concerts, vacations, and so forth. Having the Internet in communal household spaces encourages members to share their online experiences with others. Multi-tasking is also easier when working in communal places, and sharing work time with family time is more permissible, indicating the blurring of work and leisure activities.

Also, while communicating on the Internet is often considered a more personal and private activity, the interviews reveal how households spend communal time communicating together—using Instant Messaging, Audio Chats, and Webcams—with family members outside the household, both locally and globally:

Participant #343: *... when I chat with my family, my wife—she sits with me. She also chats with them. I chat with her family too. So she sits with me, and she chats with her family.*

This is particularly important for immigrants or people with family and friends in other parts of the world, who rely on Internet communication to maintain their ties when people can be very far away. This is not to say that this does not occur in households where the Internet access point is in an office, study, or bedroom. Despite the location of Internet access in the more private spaces of bedrooms and offices, household members are still inclined to use the Internet together or show and share their online experiences. However what is important here is the ease with which this can occur when the Internet access point is located in a communal space and the easy integration of online and off-line that can occur in these collective spaces. Having the Internet in communal spaces can be beneficial for household members because they are spending time together using the Internet. While computers have been blamed for the decline of social interaction between family members (Putnam, 2000), this might not be the case if the Internet is located in living, family, or recreation rooms.

The decision to put the computer and Internet access point in a visible location is opposite to decisions made for the invisibility of the computer. Besides notions of togetherness and communal activities, participants with children stated that they were concerned with being able to see what their children were doing online and being able to track their activities:

Participant #442: *...and then upstairs, we have a master bedroom, two bathrooms, two bedrooms. It's funny, we talked about putting a computer up there, but I don't want the computer out of my sight yet. My husband would like it out of here, just because he aesthetically doesn't like it here. But I told him I don't want it out of our sight. I want it where, when the kids are on it, someone's aware of them being on it, and we can be in tune with it...It's like, if you want to use the computer, you use the computer here, because we're always either in the kitchen or the family room. That's kind of where we live in the house, so it's a great way to monitor the use...*

The sheer presence of an adult in the room may deter children from using the Internet in ways that parents may deem inappropriate. The visibility of the computer also allows parents to monitor how long children stay online, and if they are on too long parents can easily turn off the computer, or end their session:

Interviewer: *Why is your computer out here?*

Participant #810: *We think about the future to buy my son a computer. But not now because I don't want him to stay in his room on the computer. I permit him one hour on computer to play... I don't want him to play [too long], that's why it's here [in the living room]. I can see my son.*

While communal spaces allow for easy monitoring of children's activities, these spaces also allow everyone else in the household to easily view what parents and/ or spouses may be doing. Under the watchful gaze of others, searching for information or communicating with others may be limited or constrained. For household members working from home or doing school work, loud communal spaces may not be as useful or practical as a more private space. Location of the household Internet in spaces that are available to others, or in areas where other household technologies may be (such as the television) affects privacy and concentration (Frohlich & Kraut, 2002).

Contesting Spaces and Places

People are aware of the impact that location has on household Internet access and use. While participants are generally satisfied with where they have their computers, some share discontent with the interviewers. Remodeling rooms, finishing basements, and rearranging layouts reflect the active thought process of where to put the household Internet (see Figure 3).

Interviewer: *So how does that spot work for you? I mean is that somewhere where you think it's going to stay or is there a place that's better?*

Participant #132: *Oh no, hopefully not. Our plan is that—eventually turn— we have a spare bedroom back here that were hoping to turn into a den, so we're gonna hopefully (put the) TV, couch, computer in there...*

Participant's Spouse: *...we just bought a computer hutch with everything centrally there, the laptop and (the) computer as well—everything will be there, fax, scanner...*

Participant #132: *God I hate all that...*

Another participant talks about how an open area was created for computer use:

Participant #232: *...we have an open area on the second floor that we designed on the second story. So, it could have been a 4-bedroom, but I wanted it to be open. So it's like a big landing where the computer is. So when I'm working at home, or doing something at home, I'm available to everybody still. I don't want to be off in a room somewhere.*

Figure 3. Renovating household spaces for the computer

© 2005 Wellman Associates (Used with permission)

What this also reveals is that people have a sense of not only how household members might use the space, but also how it might (or might not) be integrated into the routines and daily tasks of household members.

When remodeling or renovating is not an option, participants who can afford multiple computers use this as a way to challenge constraining household spaces. While purchasing additional computers is often a way to remedy conflicts between household members that occur over Internet use and access, it is also a way to challenge the private and public spaces of the household. In households with more than one computer, often participants will have computers with Internet access in different rooms—locations that are both communal and private so that there is a choice. If one is doing paid work at home, the use of the Internet in the office is a rational choice. If one is online and does not require solitude, Internet access in the living room with others present is an option.

Many participants are aware of the structural limitations that their household presents, whether it is small rooms, lack of phone jacks, or whether the computer is in the office or living room. What is particularly interesting is how some participants are aware of these potential constraints and actively problem solve and negotiate these restrictions. For example, numerous participants have laptops with a wireless connection that allows them to be online whenever they want and in any room they choose. This can take them from the kitchen to search for recipes, to the office for paid work, to the living room for recreation, or leisure pursuits online. Notions of space and place become more fluid if you are able to take the Internet with you wherever you go:

Participant #373: *I'm getting old and stubborn, so now that it's wireless…I want to be where the sun is. I want to be where if it's a cold night, I'll take it down here from upstairs if Chris is not using it and turn on one of the gas fireplaces and be comfortable. So, now that it's wireless, I'm anywhere.*

Other participants are aware of the constraints of desktop computers and stated that rather than buy another desktop computer; they are more interested in transportable Internet usage. This notion of portability indicates not only the diversity of daily Internet usage, but that surroundings matter—and that at different times throughout the day there are different needs and expectations of household Internet use. The context of household Internet use is important here as much as the room arrangements. There is a need to think about how households perceive the Internet in terms of appliance, tool, toy, or perhaps all of these.

Conclusion

The Internet is changing the way household members carry out their daily tasks, whether work, school, or leisure related; it is becoming increasingly integrated into people's everyday lives, and households are utilizing the Internet in different ways from paid work, to communication with family and friends; and general information to more context-specific tasks such as seeking health information for children, looking for recipes for dinner, and planning family vacations.

In this chapter, I have addressed the decision-making process of where to position the household computer and the factors involved in how this decision is made. Household mechanics, aesthetics, private spaces, communal places, and how people contest and challenge existing spatial dynamics in the household are important issues to consider as more people conduct paid work from their homes, more businesses hire teleworkers, and organizations move towards creating new virtual work environments. Space and location of household computers and Internet matters, and these spaces must be perceived and understood in lieu of the household dynamics and processes they are embedded in.

Household Internet location is relevant to an organizational perspective. If we conceptualize the relationship between individuals and business organizations as one that is interactive and integrative, and one that includes not only worker and employee but other household members, then we can say that the home workplace is complex and blurred with other daily social realities—housework, school, children, entertainment, and so forth. ICTs are not used solely for work or employment, and the presence of work-related tasks in the home may complicate this further. Ultimately, these are factors that will influence effective work-at-home strategies and potentially shape productivity and efficiency.

It is difficult to predict whether telework will continue to increase, or whether businesses and organizations will expand further into virtual organizations. However, with the prevalence of the household Internet and the number of people conducting paid work in the home, we might speculate how the construction of households might change. What might the future "smart home" look like? As new housing—apartments, condominiums, and houses—are being built with Internet connections already available[5] (see Hampton, 2001), people may not be faced with issues concerning household mechanics or where to put the computer with Internet access, these decisions might be already made.

In a future where virtual organizations and telework are widespread, we might expect to see new housing complexes with wireless Internet access, larger open concept living rooms, multi-media centers built into living areas, or perhaps even computers with Internet access already present in homes, much like dishwashers, stoves, and refrigerators. Conversely, we might see floor plans for houses reflecting separate "work" environments already loaded with ICTs. It is hard to envision a digital/virtual/smart household that integrates paid employment, education, and family life. I have illustrated in this chapter that individuals and organizations need to unite to ascertain needs, expectations, and outcomes in order to benefit both employer and employee.

As Baines and Gelder (2003) argue, when home is a site of paid work, household members and daily tasks are often incorporated into the telework routine in ways not found in most forms of employment; there are contentions, there is conflict and negotiation—there is everyday life. As a guideline to organizations and business for effective future planning, Shin, Higa, and Sheng (1997) suggest that the implementation of telework can be viewed as a strategic organizational change to improve organizational effectiveness. However, we need to think about the intertwining of "business and pleasure" and "spaces and places" in the context of paid work in the household to overcome barriers and constraints of past teleworker experiences; "spatial hybridity changes the nature of work, organization and management in domestic space, in cyberspace and in organizational space" (Halford, 2005, p. 20).

References

Anderson, B., & Tracey, K. (2002). The impact (or otherwise) of the Internet on everyday British life. In B. Wellman & C. Haythornthwaite (Eds.), *The Internet in everyday life* (pp. 139-163). Oxford: Blackwell Publishers.

Armstrong, N.J. de F. (1997). Negotiating the boundaries between 'home' and 'work': A case study of teleworking in New Zealand. In E. Gunnarsson (Ed.), *Virtually free? Gender, work and spatial choice* (pp. 175-200). Stockholm: NUTEK.

Aro, J., & Peteri, V. (2003). *Constructing computers at home.* Paper presented at the Conference for the Association for Internet Researchers, Toronto, Ontario.

Baines, S., & Gelder, U. (2003). What is family friendly about the workplace in the home? The case of self-employed parents and their children. *New Technology, Work and Employment, 18*(3), 223-234.

Dimitrova, D. (2003). Controlling teleworkers: Supervisions and flexibility revisited. *New Technology, Work and Employment, 18*(3), 181-195.

Dutton, W. (1999). *Society on the line: Information politics in the digital age.* Oxford University Press.

Dutton, W., Rogers, E. M., & Jun, S. (1987, April). Diffusion and social impacts of personal computers. *Communication Research, 14*(2), 219-50.

Ekos Research Associates. (2004). *The dual digital divide IV.* Ottawa, Canada: Ekos Research Associates.

Frissen, V. (1992). Trapped in electronic cages? Gender and new Information technologies in the public and private domain: An overview of research. *Media, Culture and Society, 14,* 31-49.

Frohlich, D., & Kraut, R. (2002). *The social context of home computing.* Retrieved May 23, 2006, from http://www.hpl.hp.com/techreports/2003/HPL-2003-70.pdf

Gurstein, P. (2001). *Wired to the world, chained to the home: Telework in daily life.* Vancouver: University of British Columbia Press.

Haddon, L. (1999). Gender and the domestication of the home computer: A look back. In W. H. Dutton (Ed.), *Society on the line: Information politics in the digital age* (pp. 353-354). New York: Oxford University Press.

Haddon, L., & Brynin, M. (2005). The character of telework and the characteristics of teleworkers. *New Technology, Work and Employment, 20*(1), 34-46.

Haddon, L., & Skinner, D. (1991). The enigma of the micro: Lessons from the British home computer boom. *Social Science Computer Review, 9*(3), 435-449.

Halford, S. (2005). Hybrid workspace: Re-spatialisations of work, organization and management. *New Technology, work and Employment, 20*(1), 19-33.

Hampton, K. N. (2001). *Living the wired life in the wired suburb: Netville, glocalization and civic society.* Unpublished doctoral dissertation, University of Toronto, Canada.

Hardill, I., & Green, A. (2003). Remote working—Altering the spatial contours of work and home in the new economy. *New Technology, Work and Employment, 18*(3), 212-222.

Haythornewaite, C., & Kazmer, M. M. (2002). Bringing the Internet home: Adult distance learners and their Internet, home and work worlds. In B. Wellman & C. Haythornthwaite (Eds.), *The Internet in everyday life* (pp. 431-463). Oxford: Blackwell.

Howard, L., Rainie, L., & Jones, S. (2001). Days and nights on the Internet: The impact of a diffusing technology. *American Behavioral Scientist, 45*(3), 383-404.

Ipsos-Reid. (2005, August 9). *Online news and information seeking: What the future holds.* Report. Retrieved August 12, 2005, from http://www.ipsos-na.com

Katz, J., & Rice, R. (2002). *Social consequences of Internet use: Access, involvement and interaction.* Cambridge, MA: MIT Press

Kennedy, T., Wellman, B., & Klement, K. (2003, Summer). Gendering the digital divide. *IT & Society, 1*(5), 149-172.

Lally, E. (2002). *At home with computers.* Oxford, UK: Berg.

Murdock, G., Hartmann, P., & Gray, P. (1995). Contextualizing home computing: Resources and practices. In N. Heap, R. Thomas, G. Einon, R. Mason, & H. Mackay (Eds.), *Information technology and society* (pp. 269-283). London: Sage Publications.

Putnam, R. (2000). *Bowling alone.* New York: Simon & Schuster.

Rideout, V., & Reddick, A. (2005). Sustaining community access to technology: Who should pay and why. *Journal of Community Informatics, 1*(2). Retrieved May 23, 2006, from http://www.ci-journal.net/viewarticle.php?id=39

Rommes, E. (2002). *Gender scripts and the Internet.* Enshede, The Netherlands: Twente University Press.

Salaff, J. (2002). Where home is the office: The new form of flexible work. In B. Wellman & C. Haythornthwaite (Eds.), *The Internet in everyday life* (pp. 464-495). Oxford, UK: Blackwell

Shin, B., Higa, K., & Liu Sheng, O. (1997). *An adoption model of telework for organizations.* Paper presented at the Hawaii International Conference on System Sciences.

Stanworth, C. (1997). Telework and the information age. *New Technology, Work and Employment, 13*(1), 51-62.

Statistics Canada. (2001a). *Work at home stable while working outside the country increases.* Retrieved May 23, 2006, from http://www12.statcan.ca/english/census01/Products/Analytic/companion/pow/home.cfm

Statistics Canada. (2001b). *East York community profile.* Retrieved May 23, 2006, from http://www12.statcan.ca/english/profil01/Details/details1pop.cfm?SEARCH=BEGINS&PSGC=35&SGC=963520006&A=&LANG=E&Province=35&PlaceName=east%20york&CSDNAME=East%20York&CMA=&SEARCH=BEGINS&DataType=1&TypeNameE=Borough%20%5BDissolved%5D&ID=15196

Statistics Canada. (2002). Retrieved May 23, 2006, from http://www40.statcan.ca/101/cst01/comm10a.htm?sdi=internet

Sullivan, C. (2003). What's in a name? Definitions and conceptualizations of teleworking and homeworking. *New Technology, Work & Employment, 18*(3), 158-165.

Sullivan, C., & Lewis, S. (2001). Home-based telework, gender, and the synchronization of work and family: Perspectives of teleworkers and their coresidents. *Gender, Work and Organization, 8*(2), 123-145.

U.S. Census Bureau. (2001, September). *Home computers and Internet use in the United States.* Retrieved May 23, 2006, from http://www.census.gov/prod/2001pubs/p23-207.pdf

Endnotes

[1]   The meaning of telework itself is often contested within the literature. It can mean working at home or working from home, and often does not include people who are self-employed with their home as the office; or if telework conceptualized better as "homework" (Sullivan, 2003). For the purposes of this chapter, I will refer to telework as any form of paid work in the household that utilizes ICTs.

[2]   http://www.c-i-a.com/pr032102.htm see also http://www.clickz.com/stats/sectors/geographics/article.php/5911_151151

[3]   http://www.pewinternet.org/

[4]   Participants noted basements or condominiums.

[5]   Traveling into Toronto along the Gardiner Expressway, new condominiums now block view of the SkyDome/Roger's Center. All the advertisements for these new homes tout Internet access already available in the units.

Chapter XV

Media Life Cycle and Consumer-Generated Innovation

Yuichi Washida, Hakuhodo Inc. & The University of Tokyo, Japan

Shenja van der Graaf, LSE, UK

Eva Keeris, Utrecht University, The Netherlands

Abstract

This study examines the innovation in communication media, based on empirical survey results from five countries. First, the authors create a general framework of the media life cycle *by exploring the replacement of communication media used in daily life. The shift from voice communications to mobile e-mailing is at the forefront of the media life cycle in the personal communication area. This framework also implies future media replacements in other countries. Second, by comparing two empirical surveys, done in 2002 and 2003, of communication means used among Japanese family relations, the authors discover that certain consumer clusters lead in the innovation of communication media. This framework and discovery can be useful to deal with the vacuum between conventional media studies and the latest information technology.*

Diffusion of New Communication Media

The wide and rapid diffusion of the use of e-mail and mobile phones, called cell phones or currently smart phones in the U.S., has entirely changed the paradigm of human communications. We use e-mail and mobile phones as a part of our everyday life. These two communication means, major products of information and communication technologies (ICTs) during the last two decades, are gradually replacing some conventional communication means, such as physical mailing or talking on fixed phones. These replacements can also change human behavior and may create new social norms and cultures. Obviously, the driving forces behind these replacements are the massive marketing activities of dot com companies and telecom operators.

However, there has been a relatively small number of social science researches on these areas because the technology changes so rapidly. Relentless and endless change of information technology is problematic for academic social science research, when it faces cutting edge technology. That kind of technology always threatens to overturn the conventional social context with rather destructive ways, and then it is difficult for scholars and academic researchers to examine the actual impact of each technology. But, we should not think that a new communication means supported by such a new technology is not a suitable subject for academic research. Looking at it from the viewpoint of social norms and cultural transition, even the newest communication means can be examined scientifically.

The most important point in the examination of the communication means and new technologies is, we believe, the innovation processes that occur while these technologies diffuse among users or consumers. Investigating the changes of interpretation in our society for each communication means and its technology is especially significant from a social scientific viewpoint. According to a common framework of innovation analysis, such as Rogers' (1995), innovation is not merely a technological matter, but the diffusion of a new understanding and behavior toward the technology. Moreover, Von Hippel (1988) examined a lot of examples in which certain user communities can act as sources of innovations. In fact, in some cases suppliers follow the innovations created by users, instead of creating innovations by themselves. By investigating such innovation processes, we can examine the evolution of social norms and emergence of new cultures rather than merely tracing superficial trends of ICTs.

In this chapter, we would like to focus on the role of each user cluster throughout the innovation process that has taken place since new ICTs began affecting human communications. Inevitably, there are many different usage patterns by consumer cluster, such as age, class, family relation, and gender, with new electronic communication means, as well as those within conventional, face-to-face, communication means. Especially, the gender effects on the new communication usage should be considered more. As a matter of fact, many people point out that most ICTs have been developed by males, and thus, principles of these technologies have obviously been "masculine." Rogers also pointed out that especially in the ICT area in the middle 1980s, there was a significant difference of usage and innovation patterns by gender (Rogers, 1986), due to the gap of mathematical performance between male students and female students.

However, in the late 1990s, the situation began to change. Especially when useful graphical user interfaces (GUIs) were introduced into the ordinary consumer market, ICTs became much friendlier to all kinds of people. The wider the penetration of these new communication means has grown, the more supported they have become by ordinary people including women, instead of by masculine techno-fanatics. Based on these intuitive observations, we think that a certain kind of gender study in these areas will have a particular importance.

Central Question and Hypothesis

In this article, we focus mainly on the case of Japanese mobile phone usage. The Japanese mobile phone penetration rate is now approximately 70%, which means the diffusion process has already reached the "majority" stage (Rogers, 1995). In the majority stage, we can see an interesting target-switch phenomenon from male-dominant user clusters to female-dominant ones in Japanese high-tech sectors (Washida, 2005). Moreover, after this target-switch phenomenon, Japanese mobile phone services achieved greater technological innovations. This observation implies that today's prominent innovations of Japanese mobile phone products are driven by the requirements of female users. We would like to call this type of phenomenon *consumer-generated innovation* or *the demand side innovation*, with which we can theoretically define that certain types of technological innovations emerge among users, in other words, the demand side, not the supply side.

In neoclassical economics, however, scholars have thought that all innovations are supplied by producers, and consumers can only choose good products that consist of good technologies and are sold at appropriate prices. This perspective is one of the most basic views in neoclassical economics, in which almost all of the neoclassical economic theories, such as supply and demand curves theory, the economical equilibrium theory, and a series of the marginalism theories, are built. We can say that these theories are some of the fundamental settings of today's capitalism, especially in the 20th century. Moreover, these perspectives and economic theories have deeply influenced the major ideas in conventional media studies. Therefore, in conventional media studies, new technologies that created new media have been considered a "given" element in society. In fact, most innovations in mass media, such as broadcasting technology, writing narratives for various broadcasting programs, creating sounds and visual images, and acting in mass media, were "supplied" by a very limited number of people, compared with the millions of people making up the audience in a society. In other words, in mass media, making innovations has been highly centralized.

However, today's rapid development in the ICTs brings a new stage in media history. The ICT innovations are much more distributed, therefore, not only a small company, but also every ordinary user can make an innovation by adding a new meaning or value to a new technology. Although this characteristic of ICTs is intuitively apparent, few researchers empirically validate the emergence of this new stage of media history. We should say that the distributed character-istic of ICTs and their demand-side innovation effects can be important elements of the innovation in the big picture of media transition history.

The major purpose of this chapter is to examine the innovation process carried by the demand side, and explore the trajectory of near-future media transition. Which medium in which country emerges in the forefront of the media history in taking a global overview of media innovation? How social norms have been compiled in ICT usages? Who actually leads the current ICT innovation in our society? What is the difference between male users and female users? To examine potential answers for these questions, we have conducted two series of empirical surveys. The technical hypothesis for the surveys is addressed in two steps.

First, for Method 1 to identify which medium in which country is at the forefront of the media transition, we have compared frequencies of use of several electronic communication means by country. By examining the result of Method 1, we could learn which electronic communication means is dominant in each country, and which confirmed that mobile phone usage in Japan is in a unique circumstance. Based on the results of Method 1, we concluded that current increase of Japanese e-mailing use via mobile phones should be considered as the forefront of the global media transition. Second, for Method 2 to validate that a certain type of innovation emerges on the demand side, we surveyed, in both 2002 and 2003, the usage patterns of communication means in Japanese families. By comparing these two-year results, we could see changes in usage patterns during the period and distinguish which user cluster has led the change. Moreover, by adding ethnological analyses toward such Japanese usage pat-terns, we concluded that emerging Japanese female usages led major ICT innovations during the period. Details of both methods are explained in the following sections and appendix.

Method 1: Comparative Survey on Communication Media Environment

Method 1 consists of an international comparative survey program, named Media Landscape Survey 2003-2004 (MLS), which includes comparative surveys in the U.S., The Netherlands, Sweden, South Korea, Japan, and China. All six surveys used the same questionnaire translated into each language. The survey targeted people age 15-34. The major purpose of the survey was to examine the communication media environment in each country. The total sample size was 2,578 (details of the surveys are included in the appendix). In each survey we asked respondents about several aspects of communication behavior using fixed phones, mobile phones, e-mailing, instant messaging, and Web logs. Regarding mobile phones, we asked them about both the call usage and the e-mail usage. We also asked respondents whether they used online game sites and music file-sharing sites.

Based on MLS, in Method 1, we compared the usage of several communication means in five countries (the United States, The Netherlands, Sweden, South Korea, and Japan), but not in China. MLS is basically done for those who are interested in using various digital communication means in their daily lives. The five countries are relatively well developed in terms of digital communications, which are common enough to represent "ordinary" life in each country, while China is still developing. For instance, the penetration rate of PCs in China is approximately 5%; therefore, we have to say Chinese results in MLS do not represent "ordinary" Chinese lifestyle to any certain extent. Thus we exclude Chinese data in Method 1.

The purpose of Method 1 is to take an overview of each communication means usage and to map them. By doing so, we try to investigate the meanings of each communication means in the social norms and culture. As we focus on mobile phones in this article, we identify the meaning of mobile phones in the various communication environments. Of course, every country has a unique society and culture that is reflected in each country's usage pattern. However, by comparing five developed countries' results, we can see some general macro tendencies.

Result of Method 1

Tables 1-3 show percentages for each communication means usage per day and by country. In Table 1, we can see the daily usage of calls on fixed phones for personal purposes. In many countries 40-70% of ordinary people make fixed phone calls at least once a day, but not in Japan. Also, Table 1 reflects the same information on mobile phone calls, and we find that the overall tendency is very similar to that of fixed phones. Generally speaking, fixed phones and mobile phones compete with each other, and their usages seem to cannibalize one another. But it is interesting that in our survey, call usage on fixed phones and on mobile phones actually tends to be in direct proportion to one another, rather than in inverse proportion.

As shown previously, people in Japan do not make as many phone calls as do people in other countries. Of course, being a well developed country, Japan does

Table 1. Usage of personal calls on fixed phones and mobile phones per day in each country (in %)

Country	Number of respondents	Frequency of usage
		More than once a day
Personal Calls on Fixed Phones		
Netherlands	177	41.0
Sweden	351	72.9
USA (East Coast)	850	62.1
Japan	400	12.6
South Korea	400	47.0
M	2178	47.1
SD	2178	21.7
Personal Calls on Mobile Phones		
Netherlands	177	63.3
Sweden	351	61.1
USA (East Coast)	850	74.9
Japan	400	31.8
South Korea	400	80.7
M	2178	62.4
SD	2178	18.6

Note. All numbers of data above are verified to have significant differences against the mean with the significance level $p < .05$, in the parametric statistical test - Dunnett test (multiple comparison).

Table 2. Usage of personal e-mailing via PCs or PDAs, and instant messaging per day in each country (in %)

Country	Number of respondents	Frequency of usage More than once a day
Emaining via PCs or PDAs		
Netherlands	177	68.8
Sweden	351	65.7
USA (East Coast)	850	74.8
Japan	400	42.8
South Korea	400	32.8
M	2178	56.9
SD	2178	17.5
Instant Messaging		
Netherlands	177	29.0
Sweden	351	39.8
USA (East Coast)	850	41.4
Japan	400	11.5
South Korea	400	50.8
M	2178	34.5
SD	2178	19.2

Note. All numbers of data above are verified to have significant differences against the mean with the significance level $p < .05$, in the parametric statistical test - Dunnett test (multiple comparison).

not suffer from a weak telecommunication infrastructure. Obviously, the low usage of phones to make phone calls indicates that in Japan voice communications are now being replaced by other communication means.

Therefore, we must determine what other communication means are replacing phone calls in Japan. The most conceivable answer is a variety of text messaging services. Table 2 and Table 3 show the daily usages of e-mailing services via PCs, instant messaging, and e-mailing services via mobile phones, respectively.

Table 2 reflects the usage of regular e-mailing services via PCs and PDAs. E-mailing services have been developed based mainly on PC-based networks. In

Table 3. Usage of personal e-mailing/SMS via mobile phones per day in each country (in %)

	Number of respondents	Frequency of usage More than once a day
Country		
Netherlands	177	28.4
Sweden	351	36.7
USA (East Coast)	850	5.1
Japan	400	51.0
South Korea	400	18.3
M	2178	39.9
SD	2178	22.0

Note. All numbers of data above are verified to have significant differences against the mean with the significance level $p < .05$, in the parametric statistical test - Dunnett test (multiple comparison).

MLS, we classified e-mailing via PDAs as a variation of regular e-mailing services because in many cases of PDA-based e-mailing usage, users are connected by the same type of network as PC-based ones, even though the physical shape of PDA usage is similar to the usage of mobile phones. Interestingly, Table 2 shows a cultural or historical difference of writing behaviors among Western countries and Eastern countries. In Western countries, word processing culture has a long history, reflected in the wider usage of PC-based e-mailing. Conversely, Eastern countries have a long history of handwriting and relatively short history of word processing, and thus e-mail usage in Eastern countries is less popular, although South Korea and Japan have very high penetrations of PCs and Internet usage.

Therefore, according to our data, we cannot say PC-based e-mailing services are effectively replacing Japanese voice communications. Also, Table 2 shows the usage of instant messaging. It is a relatively new, PC-based text messaging service, by which users can see a message automatically as soon as it arrives. Because of its convenience and quickness, instant messaging is becoming popular especially among heavy Net users. Moreover, because instant messaging is usually used among "trusted" relations, it can relatively keep users away from spam mails and virus mails. The five countries in MLS are all well developed regarding Internet connectivity; Table 2 shows that 30-50% of Net users in these countries are using instant messaging, except those in Japan. Only in Japan, the percentage of the instant messaging usage is approximately 10%. Here again, we cannot say that Instant messaging, also a PC-based text messaging service, is replacing Japanese voice communications.

Finally, Table 3 shows the usage of mobile e-mailing services, or short messaging services (SMS). Here we find a popular use of it in European countries and especially in Japan. In the U.S. and South Korea, the usage of mobile e-mailing is not very popular, even though penetrations of mobile phones are not low in these two countries, per se. Interestingly, comparing Table 3 with Table 1, we can see the average shapes of mobile phone usage by country. In the U.S. and South Korea, voice communication is much more superior to mobile e-mail communications, while in Japan mobile e-mail communication is entirely domi-nant. In The Netherlands and Sweden, both voice and e-mail communications are equally popular. Based on this understanding, we can say that in Japan the frequent usage of mobile e-mail communication—in this case more than 60% of total respondents—is replacing voice communication.

The Media Life Cycle

Summing up these survey results, we can envision a framework for the life cycle of a variety of communication media. When a new communication medium appears and becomes popular, an old one becomes obsolete and begins to decline. The important point here is finding a phenomenon of usage decline, rather than merely an emergence or increase of a new medium usage, because a declining phenomenon directly means a replacement of media, and the replacement implies the existence of the media life cycle. In other words, if we observe a declining phenomenon among consumer behaviors, it proves that there emerges a replacement of medium and its technology by other new media and their new technologies. We can define the media life cycle as this alternation of media and their technologies.

In our MLS, the declining phenomenon is seen in the case of Japanese voice communication. We have also found that mobile e-mail communication is becoming the alternative of voice communication. At this point, we cannot see any other declining phenomenon in the other countries. This strongly implies that Japanese society stands at the forefront of the media life cycle due to the wide penetration of mobile e-mail communication.

It is interesting, however, that PC-based text messaging services, such as regular Internet e-mail services and instant messaging, do not seem to replace any other old communication medium, even though many analysts have pointed out that the Internet has started to replace some conventional mass media. For instance, it is true that certain kinds of newspapers, magazines, and music CDs are now in danger of decline due to the massive penetration of the Net media. However, in the personal communication arena that we see in MLS, instead of the mass media arena, the Internet is not a threat for conventional communication media at this point. In other words, there is coexistence between the Internet and conventional communication media.

Comparing mass media and personal communication media, we can also generalize the media life cycle to be a wider map of media transitions, as in Figure 1, which includes a variety of media and technologies we use in our everyday life. The two columns, which follow, represent mass media and personal communication media, respectively, and the four rows represent four generations of media, chronologically. By nature, mass media is based on a one-way communication, from one supplier to many audiences, while personal communication is based on an interactive communication among "one-to-one" relations.

First, Generation A indicates a primitive shape of public communication in each arena, which mainly consists of paper and ink. We can classify various print media, such as newspapers and magazines in mass media and physical mail in the personal communication media. The technology that supports Generation A

Figure 1. The framework of the media life cycle

	Mass Media one-way-based communication: basically one-to-many	**Personal Communication Media** interactive-based communication: basically one-to-one
Generation A: (before the 20th century) The initial shape of public communication system with paper	Mass print media (include newspapers and magazines)	Physical mail
Generation B: (the 1st half of the 20th century) Telecommunication with voice and sound	Radio broadcasting	Calls on telephones (include both fixed and mobile)
Generation C: (the 2nd half of the 20th century) Transferring rich contents with multiple-channels	TV broadcasting (includes cable TV)	Email via PCs (include instant messaging)
Generation D: (beginning of the 21st century) Allowing users to establish communication completely on-demand	Internet portals (include news groups and file sharing)	Email via mobile phones

media was invented several 100 years ago. These media were widely developed as public communication services long before the 20th century. However, because Generation A media are very useful and efficient in many ways, most of them survive as a part of the basic social infrastructure and coexist with new generation media even now.

Second, Generation B indicates the emergence of telecommunications with relatively simple voices and sounds in the early 20th century. We classify radio broadcasting in the Generation B mass media, and calls on telephones in the Generation B personal communication media. The basic technologies that developed the Generation B media were invented at the end of 19th century, but the public communication services for ordinary consumers using these technologies began in the early 20th century. Telecommunications enabled us to communicate, and therefore to overcome any time lag, even when there is a considerable distance between communicators. Inevitably, this was one of the most important developments of the 20th century.

Third, Generation C indicates that we can communicate a great variety of content, such as visual images, movie images, and high quality stereo sounds, through multichannel information distribution systems. TV broadcasting systems and e-mail via the Internet are classified in this category. Thanks to advanced telecommunication techniques and broader bandwidth of transmission networks, we can exchange rich content among ourselves. This revolutionary media environment gave birth to an extremely creative visual culture in the late 20th century. The visual culture is so impressive that it has overshadowed the former generation media. Actually, radio broadcasting began to decline under the influence of TV broadcasting, and physical mail began to decline due to a massive increase in e-mailing. However, as previously mentioned, e-mailing has not begun to replace voice communications at this point.

Finally, Generation D enables us to access rich content whenever and wherever we want. In this sense, Generation D is the second wave in the process of being able to overcome distance and time as Generation B did. However, we need to examine carefully what the difference is between TV broadcasting and Internet portals, or between e-mail via PCs and e-mail via mobile phones.

Let us start with Internet portals and TV broadcasting. When we compare newsgroups in Internet portals with conventional news on TV, what is the actual benefit from it? The answer may be its chronological nonlinearity and ubiquity of news content. From a news list of Internet newsgroups, we can obtain any news in any order we want to see it, while we have to obey the program schedule of broadcasting stations if we want to receive the same content from conventional TV news programs. In general, TV news programs are designed in a chronological order. Consequently, we have to behave synchronously when we depend on TV news. Conversely, if we regularly obtain information from

Internet newsgroups, we are free from such synchronicity, using our limited time resources more efficiently. Moreover, Internet newsgroups are also free from geographic limitations. By nature, conventional TV news programs focus on individual regions and countries, limiting the scope of news content. However, we can watch and read all countries' news simultaneously with Internet portals.

Next, let us examine the actual benefit from using mobile e-mail instead of regular e-mail via PCs. We find the same benefit: a chronological nonlinearity and ubiquity in communicating with others. We can receive and send mobile e-mail immediately, wherever we are. This does not mean that we are only free from geographical limitations of Net accessibility, but also from chronological limitations of communication. As many mobile e-mail users know, constant and seamless connection between friends and family consequently dispels a feeling of time lag between sending and receiving and creates a comfortable feeling of "always being linked." In general, when we send e-mail via PC, we cannot expect the receiver to immediately read it, because the receiver is not necessarily in front of a PC. But in the case of mobile e-mail, especially in Asian and European countries, we can expect the receiver to see the e-mail immediately, even though the receiver may not reply to it instantly. This difference of expectation in the receiver's behavior makes the sender feel more connected. It is curious that the loss of communication time lag leads us to a loss of chronological limitation of e-mailing behavior, even though the actual transaction of e-mail exchange in mobile e-mail is more chronological than regular e-mail via PCs. However, it is unfortunate that in the U.S., due to the low penetration rate of mobile e-mail usage at this point, ordinary U.S. people have not experienced this feeling yet.

One may think these benefits from Generation D are not absolute technological improvements but merely false benefits in the users' minds. However, from the viewpoint of social norms, we believe that the benefit in the user's mind is the most important thing. Users have spontaneously changed the meaning of communication and its technology from *interactive* to *on-demand* in the case of Internet portals, or, from *wireless* to *ubiquitous* in the case of mobile e-mail.

Of course, the framework of the media life cycle shown in Figure 1 may seem to be overly generalized to some extent, and we can be more careful to examine each medium's specific meaning in each period. However, by having a macro viewpoint as in this framework, and especially by observing the replacement of a conventional medium by a new medium, we can understand the meaning of each technology in our society.

Conventional Media Studies
and ICTs Studies

To maintain the theoretical history of media usages, the analysis of the newest media, such as the Internet and mobile phones, is not sufficient at this point. We hope that our framework of the media life cycle can be helpful to fill this vacuum to some extent. One of the most typical of conventional media analysis frameworks is Harold Innis's (1951). He classified various media into two categories, time-binding media and space-binding media, by using the terminology *media bias*. The time-binding media includes manuscripts and oral communications, and are favorable to relatively close communications in a community, while the space-binding media includes all of print media, mass media, and probably current ICTs, and are concerned with today's wide variety of commercialism. Innis and Marshall McLuhan, Innis's colleague at The University of Toronto, thought that media and technologies were "given," and media, per se, could be messages to our society. This approach is so-called *media determinism*, and is a popular approach in media studies, journalism, and critical studies even now. This approach is quite useful to compare the magnitude of influences of various media regardless of the content of each communication. In fact, we can see a variety of examples in which current critical media researchers use a theoretical framework that can be evaluated as a natural evolution of Innis's approach. For instance, Chesbro and Bertelsen (1996) show a media comparison framework using three categories of media classification, oral culture, literal culture, and electric culture, and explore each characteristic of these three types.

The approach of media determinism has been, of course, significant since we have observed the history of media, especially the evolution of mass media and its culture, during the decades in the middle and latter 20th century. But it is also obvious that such types of frameworks are no longer efficient enough to classify the current vast number of emerging media that includes advanced mass media and ICTs. Media determinists think that all kinds of media must be extensions of the human body, in other words, ways of self-expression. In this perspective, technology is always defined as a "given" thing, and thus it is hard to examine the degree of participation of ordinary people within the technological innovation. In the ICT area, innovation and user participation are both indispensable aspects to examine its social impact. Therefore, we have to think that media determinism is not sufficient to become a basis of our media life cycle framework.

On the other hand, Rogers (1986) has also tried to build a new framework of media classifications based on his diffusion theory. He thinks media and technologies should be "variables" in human and organizational communications, instead of a "given" thing (p. 121). This approach is more efficient to include any emerging technology, because we can add a "variable" of communications on the same framework when one new medium emerges. In this article, we basically adopted his approach and tried to widen the map to include the latest situation by adding current ICT analyses. However, Rogers did not sufficiently analyze the dynamics of technological replacements in the media innovations, because in the 1980s and the beginning of the 1990s, no ICT was powerful enough in our society to encompass the conception of the media life cycle. As we showed with a variety of empirical survey results, today we can observe a clear signal of the replacement phenomena between old and new media. Therefore, we can build this media life cycle framework in this article.

By using our framework of the media life cycle, we can foresee the future changes of our communication behavior, both in the sphere of mass media and the sphere of personal communication. In the sphere of personal communication, mobile e-mailing is now replacing voice communications through telephones. In other words, Generation D media can replace Generation B media, while Generation D media can coexist with Generation C media. At this point, this replacement phenomenon appears only in Japan. But in the near future we may observe a similar transition in other countries in proportion to the technological innovation in mobile e-mailing. On the other hand, in the sphere of mass media, we do not observe a similar phenomenon at this point. But according to this theory, Internet portals (Generation D in the sphere of mass media) can replace radio broadcasting (Generation B in the sphere of mass media) in the near future in proportion to the technological innovation. For example, the distribution of new songs from music creators to ordinary listeners, one of the important functions of radio broadcasting, is now being replaced by MP3 music file sharing through a certain kind of Internet portal. In fact, the current MP3 controversy has been caused by a threat against new technology among present media business, not by any theoretical correctness, or any change of the ways of self-expression among music creators. In other words, the anticipation of the media replacement between Generation D and B even in the mass media sphere is already shared widely among many people.

Method 2: A Comparison of 2002 with 2003 in Japan

Our next goal is to distinguish the exact user cluster that leads to innovation in the media life cycle. In this section, we especially focus on Japanese mobile e-mail usage as a good example of the forefront of media innovation. By investigating the forefront of the innovation in detail, we can understand what the innovation of media is.

We conducted a small, preliminary survey in 2002 that had the same questions as the MLS in 2003. Both surveys asked respondents about electronic communications with family members, all of which can represent typical communication patterns in a daily life. By comparing the two-year survey results, we can empirically distinguish one user cluster from another to determine who led the innovation from voice communications to mobile e-mailing. The preliminary survey was taken only by Japanese people aged 18-29. Then we selected a similar respondent bracket in MLS to compare results as precisely as possible.

Table 4 indicates the comparative results of the same question, in the preliminary survey in 2002 and MLS in 2003, regarding the communication rate with six family members using electronic communication means. Here it excludes any face-to-face communication. Due to a slight difference between survey methodologies from 2002-2003, the reactions in 2003 seem to indicate a reluctance to provide information. But, as a whole, we find little difference between the two survey results. The order of the surveyed family members by the communication rate in both survey results is completely the same, and the communication rates

Table 4. Communication rate, using electric communication means in daily life, with family members in Japan (in %)

Person with whom the respondent communicates	Communication rate in each year	
	2002 (n = 89)	2003 (n = 200)
Mother	82.9	81.0
Father	57.3	55.0
Sister	48.0	45.0
Brother	47.3*	31.5*
Spouse	43.7*	29.0*
Cousin	10.9	15.5
M	48.4	42.8
SD	21.2	21.1

Note. All numbers of comparison data between 2002 and 2003 above are tested by the parametric statistical test – T-test. *$p < .05$.

themselves have not changed greatly during 2002 and 2003. It is interesting to note the correlation between the order of family members surveyed and the descending level of their response rate. We can say that, in general, the condition of Japanese communications, using electronic means, among family members has remained unchanged.

On the assumption that the general condition of Japanese communications is unchanged, in Method 2, we wanted to see whether there was any local change in the usage rate among family members during the period. If we could observe that, we would be able to identify the forefront of media replacements along with the media life cycle framework. In other words, who led it, and how did they do this?

Result of Method 2

In this section, in order to make all analyses simple and clear, we examined the survey results based on communications with four major family members, mother, father, brother, and sister, and by four typical electronic communication means; calls on fixed phones, calls on mobile phones, e-mail via PCs and PDAs, and e-mail via mobile phones. Table 5 and Table 6 indicate usage rates for all combinations of family members by communication means. Table 5 shows changes between 2002 and 2003 among male respondents, and Table 6 shows the same result among female respondents.

In Table 5, we notice that calls on mobile phones to brothers significantly decreased during the period of 2002-2003, while there seemed to be no significant change in other respects. On the other hand, in Table 6, we find a couple of significant changes and some interesting tendencies in female usages; calls on mobile phones to both parents tended to decrease, while e-mail via mobile phones with both parents and sisters tended to increase. E-mailing via PCs and PDAs significantly decreased. The means and the standard deviations are indicated in Table 7.

Table 8 focuses on the increase or decrease of each communication means by measuring the average usage rate of each communication means in total amount of usage with four family members. The average usage rate of a communication means x, $AUR(x)$, is defined as:

$$AUR(x) = \frac{1}{n} \sum_{h=1}^{4} u(x,h) \tag{1}$$

Table 5. Comparison of communication media usage between 2002 and 2003 in Japan (in %): Male

Person with whom the respondent communicates	Communication rate		Number of respondents	
	2002	2003	2002	2003
Calls on fixed phones				
Mother	38.7	33.2	31	78
Father	43.5	32.1	23	56
Brother	10.0	10.3	20	29
Sister	6.3	24.4	16	41
Calls on mobile phones				
Mother	45.2	42.3	31	78
Father	47.8	44.6	23	56
Brother	60.0*	24.1*	20	29
Sister	37.5	24.4	16	41
SMS or email via mobile phones				
Mother	12.9	20.5	31	78
Father	4.4	10.7	23	56
Brother	25.0	48.3	20	29
Sister	50.0	39.6	16	41
Email via PCs or PDAs				
Mother	3.2	1.3	31	78
Father	4.4	9.3	23	56
Brother	5.0	10.3	20	29
Sister	6.3	4.9	16	41

Note. All numbers of comparison data between 2002 and 2003 above are tested by the parametric statistical test – T-test. $*p < .05$.

Table 6. Comparison of communication media usage between 2002 and 2003 in Japan (in %): Female

Person with whom the respondent communicates	Communication rate		Number of respondents	
	2002	2003	2002	2003
Calls on fixed phones				
Mother	39.5	42.9	35	84
Father	28.6	29.6	28	54
Brother	0.0	5.9	22	34
Sister	11.1	10.2	25	49
Calls on mobile phones				
Mother	44.2	28.6	35	84
Father	53.6	31.5	28	54
Brother	27.3	26.5	22	34
Sister	14.8	8.2	25	49
SMS or email via mobile phones				
Mother	14.0	25.0	35	84
Father	7.2*	33.3*	28	54
Brother	36.4	52.9	22	34
Sister	59.3	73.5	25	49
Email via PCs or PDAs				
Mother	2.3	1.2	35	84
Father	10.7	3.7	28	54
Brother	36.4*	11.8*	22	34
Sister	14.8*	2.0*	25	49

Note. All numbers of comparison data between 2002 and 2003 above are tested by the parametric statistical test – T-test. *$p < .05$.

Table 7. Means and standard deviations in Tables 5 and 6 (in %)

	Male					
	Means and Stamdard Devioations				Number of respondents	
	2002		2003		2002	2003
Person with whom the respondent communicates	M	SD	M	SD		
Mother	25.0	17.4	25.0	12.0	31	78
Father	25.0	20.7	25.0	15.0	23	56
Brother	25.0	21.5	25.0	15.6	20	29
Sister	25.0	19.2	25.0	12.4	16	41
	Female					
	Means and Stamdard Devioations				Number of respondents	
	2002		2003		2002	2003
Person with whom the respondent communicates	M	SD	M	SD		
Mother	25.0	17.4	25.0	15.0	35	84
Father	25.0	18.4	25.0	12.1	28	54
Brother	25.0	14.9	25.0	18.2	22	34
Sister	25.0	19.9	25.0	29.1	25	49

where $u(x, h)$ is the response number of the communication means x with the family member h ($h \leq 4$), and n is the sum of each number of effective respondents for four questions: communication with mother, father, brother, and sister. The number of $AUR(x)$ indicates the average degrees of presence for the communication means x when a person communicates with all family members. By comparing the $AUR(x)$ in 2002 with that in 2003, we can directly understand the change of presence for the communication means x in ordinary life during the period.

Table 8. Change of communication media usage pattern between 2002 and 2003 in Japan (in point)

Communication means	Communication rate			
	Male		Female	
	2002 (n = 90)	2003 (n = 204)	2002 (n = 110)	2003 (n = 221)
Calls on fixed phones	27.8	27.9	22.7	26.7
Calls on mobile phones	47.8	36.8	36.4*	24.4*
SMS or email via mobile phones	20.0	25.5	27.3*	42.1*
Email via PCs or PDAs	4.4	5.4	14.5**	3.6**
M	25.0	25.0	25.0	25.0
SD	15.6	11.5	7.9	13.7

Note. The numbers of respondents in this table indicate the sum of each number of respondents for four questions (communication with mother, father, brother, and sister). All numbers of comparison data between 2002 and 2003 above are tested by the parametric statistical test – T-test under the total numbers of respondents. $*p < .05$, $**p < .01$.

With regard to calls on fixed phones, there is no significant change. In Method 1, we argued that in Japan, calls on fixed phones are already less popular than those in other countries. However, the result of Method 2 implies that the decline of calls on fixed phones in Japan is not the most current incident. Conversely, it is interesting that, among female respondents, calls on mobile phones significantly decreased, which implies that the forefront of the voice communications decline has started shifting from fixed phones to mobile phones.

On the other hand, we can find very important differences by gender with e-mail communications. With regard to mobile e-mail, we can find a significant increase among female respondents, while e-mail via PCs among female respondents is significantly in decline. Among male respondents, we cannot find significant change of e-mailing behavior via either mobile phones or PCs.

As a whole, this result of Method 2 strongly implies that women in Japan lead the shift of the communication media cycle from voice communications to mobile e-mailing. Among male respondents, we can only observe a tendency of decrease regarding calls on mobile phones, but among female respondents we can observe both a tendency of decrease and a tendency of increase. This fact means that among male respondents the replacement of communication media has just started recently, but among female respondents the replacement is already in progress. Thus, female respondents are in a more advanced stage of the media life cycle.

From an ethnological viewpoint, this tendency has been argued widely in the Japanese mobile phone industry. Since the late 1980s and the beginning of the 1990s, Japanese social ethics regarding female lifestyles have drastically changed and been liberated, as many women are encouraged to have full-time jobs, instead of staying home as housewives. Mobile phones are considered very useful tools to maintain family communications even though women go out frequently. Young girls are ordinarily allowed to stay with their friends until late at night if they make calls or e-mail via mobile phones to their mothers. The sense of "always being linked" caused by a wide penetration of mobile phones is becoming a new social norm in Japan. Many Japanese sociologists say that this new social norm concerning mobile phone usage may generate a new shape of family relations in Japanese society. Japanese women are no longer tied to their family and houses, and owning mobile phones encourages this new ethic. That is why, for women, mobile phones are considered as a symbol of freedom of lifestyle.

Conclusion and Discussion

In this chapter, we started our exploration from the rapid and wide penetration of new communication means such as mobile phones and e-mailing through the Internet. Based on an empirical survey in five countries, (MLS), we examined one of the forefront phenomena of the media life cycle in Japan, in which voice communications are gradually being replaced by mobile e-mailing communications. This discovery of media replacement from an old one to a new one in the Japanese personal communication sphere, and the framework of the media life cycle imply other future media replacements, such as those in different countries or those in different spheres.

Next, we explored deeper details of the media innovation by examining a case of Japanese mobile e-mailing usage. The most significant finding is that, during the period between 2002 and 2003, ordinary female users clearly led media innovations, instead of, for instance, techno-fanatic male users. This implies that certain types of media innovation in Japan have been generated by consumers, in other words, demand side, in which consumers can generate the innovation by choosing appropriate usage of new media in their daily lives, instead of creating new products or developing technologies.

Integrating two conclusions, we can say that the media life cycle is now being processed toward the next stage by the demand side, and during this process, new social norms with the new technology are generated among consumers. In this fashion, we can observe that the media innovation with new technologies is not deterministic, and mobile e-mailing can replace the conventional voice communication by phones, which is an unexpected trajectory of the ICT future for some techno-fanatic analysts.

Acknowledgment

We appreciate the great contributions by Mr. Akira Odani, Mr. Masao Morinaga, Dr. Michael Bjorn, Mr. Erik Kruse, Mr. Kyu-Chol Ban, and Searchina Research Institute, to conduct the MLS 2003. We would also like to thank Dr. Nicholas Jankowski for his giving us important suggestions to our reseach.

References

Chesbro, W., & Bertelsen, D. (1996). *Analyzing media: Communication technologies as symbolic and cognitive system.* New York: The Guilford Press.

Innis, H. (1951). *The bias of communication.* Canada: University of Toronto Press.

Rogers, E. (1986). *Communication technology: The new media in society.* New York: The Free Press.

Rogers, E. (1995). *Diffusion of innovations.* New York: The Free Press.

Von Hippel, E. (1988). *The sources of innovation.* New York: Oxford University Press.

Washida, Y. (2005). Collaborative structure between Japanese high-tech manufacturers and consumers. *Journal of Consumer Marketing, 22*(1), 25-34.

Further Reading

Amor, D. (2002). *Internet future strategies: How pervasive computing services will change the world.* Upper Saddle River, NJ: Prentice Hall.

Angus, I. (2000). *Primal scenes of communication: Communication, consumerism, and social movement.* State University of New York Press.

Brock, G. (2003). *The second information revolution.* Cambridge, MA: Harvard University Press.

Coates, K., & Holroyd, C. (2003). *Japan and the Internet revolution.* Hampshire, UK: Palgrave Macmillan.

Cohen, A. (2003). Real time and recall measures of mobile phone use: Some methodological concerns and empirical applications. *New Media & Society, 5*(2), 167-183.

Dittmar, H., Long, K., & Meek, R. (2004, March). Buying on the Internet: Gender differences in on-line and conventional buying motivations. *Sex Roles: A Journal of Research, 50*(5/6).

Frank, L., & Heikkila, J. (2001). Diffusion model in analyzing emerging technology-based services. In B. Schmid, K. Stanoevska-Slabeva, & V. Tschammer (Eds.), *Towards the e-society, e-commerce, e-business, and e-government* (pp. 657-668). Boston: Kluwer Academic Publishers.

Fransman, M. (2002). *Telecoms in the Internet age: From boom to bust to...?* New York: Oxford University Press.

Fredrick, C. (1999). Feminist rhetoric in cyberspace: The ethos of feminist usenet newsgroups. *The Information Society, 15,* 187-197.

Gill, R. (2002). Cool, creative, and egalitarian? Exploring gender in project-based new media work in Europe. *Information, Communication & Society, 5*(1), 70-89.

Gladwell, M. (2000). *The tipping point: How little things can make a big difference.* Boston: Little Brown & Co.

Harding, S. (1986). *The science question in feminism.* Ithaca, NY: Cornell University Press.

Henwood, F. (1993). Establishing gender perspective on information technology: Problems, issues, and opportunities. In E. Green, J. Owen, & D. Pain (Eds.), *Gendered by design? Information technology and office system.* London: Taylor & Francis.

Katz, J. (2003). *Machines that become us: The social context of personal communication technology.* New Brunswick, NJ: Transaction Publishers.

Martinson, A., Schwartz, N., & Vaughan, M. (2002). Women's experiences of leisure: Implications for design. *New Media & Society, 4*(1), 29-49.

Owen, J., Vega, Y., & Tucker, D. (2003). Investigation of the effects of gender and preparation on quality of communication in Internet support group. *Computer in Human Behavior, 19,* 259-275.

Reponen, T. (2003). *Information technology-enabled global customer services.* Hershey, PA: Idea Group Publishing.

Rommes, E., Oost, E., & Oudshoom, N. (1999). Gender in the design of the digital city of Amsterdam. *Information, Communication & Society, 2*(4), 476-495.

Sekizawa, H., Washida, Y., & Bjorn, M. (2002). *Situation marketing.* Japan; Joong Ang M & B, South Korea: Kanki Publishing.

Shade, L. (1998). A gender perspective on access to the information infrastructure. *The Information Society, 14,* 33-44.

Singh, S. (2001). Gender and the use of the Internet at home. *New Media & Society, 3*(4), 395-416.

Soukup, C. (1999). The gendered interactional pattern of computer-mediated chatrooms: A critical ethnographic study. *The Information Society, 15,* 169-176.

Spilker, H., & Sorensen, K. (2000). A ROM of one's own or a home for sharing?: Designing the inclusion of women in multimedia. *New Media & Society, 2*(3), 268-285.

Tamblyn, C. (1994). She loves it, she loves it not: Women and technology. In *Proceedings of the ISEA '94* (CD-ROM), Inter-Society for the Electronic Arts, Amsterdam, The Netherlands. Retrieved from http://www.isea-web.org/eng/index.html

Turkle, S., (1995). *Life on the screen: Identity in the age of the Internet.* New York: Simon and Schuster.

Turow J., & Kavanaugh, A. L. (2003). *The wired homestead: An MIT press sourcebook on the Internet and family.* Cambridge, MA: MIT Press.

Van Zoonen, L. (2002). Gendering the Internet: Claims, controversies and cultures. *European Journal of Communication, 17*(1), 5-23.

Washida, Y., Bjorn, M., & Kruse, E. (2004). Analysis of diffusion patterns of knowledge and new technology among Japanese early adopters: An ethnological study of product penetrations. *Proceedings of IAMOT 2004* (CD-ROM), International Association for Management of Technology, Coral Gables, FL. Retrieved from http://www.iamot.org

Yoshimi, S. (2000). *Media Jidai no Bunka Shakai Gaku - Cultural and social studies in media era.* Tokyo: Shinyo Sha.

Appendix

The Source of Method 1

Survey name: *Media Landscape Survey 2003-2004* (MLS)

Survey countries, the effective sample populations: 850 samples in the U.S. (east coast), 400 samples in Japan, 177 samples in The Netherlands, 351 samples in Sweden, 400 samples in South Korea, and 400 samples in China (Shanghai area): total 2,578 samples

Respondents: ordinary people who are interested in digital communications, aged 15-34

Sampling procedure: Internet panel survey method, provided by professional survey companies, was used in the U.S., Japanese, Swedish, South Korean, and Chinese surveys. In The Netherlands, a multi-stage recruiting method was used. In the United States, parental permissions had been taken to conduct the survey among respondents aged 15-18.

Response rate: Due to the nature of Internet surveys, it is difficult to fix the precise response rates. However, the average response rate in this Internet survey system is reported as 15-25%. In The Netherlands, the response rate was 25.3%.

Survey date: Oct. 2003 to Mar. 2004

Measurement of reliability: All numbers of data in Method 1 are verified that they have significant differences against each average with the significance level $p<.05$, in the parametric statistical test—Dunnett test (multiple comparison).

The Source of Method 2

Survey in 2002 (preliminary survey):

Respondents: Men and women aged 18-29 living within a 40km radius of the Tokyo metropolitan area

Sample population: 89 respondents (40 males and 49 females)

Setting and sampling procedure: Self-administered questionnaire mailed and left with members of a predetermined panel.

Response rate: 100% (predetermined)

Period: January 2002

Survey in 2003 (in MLS):

Respondents: Men and women aged 20-29 living in Japan

Sample size: 200 respondents (100 males and 100 females)

Setting and sampling procedure: Internet survey

Response rate: Due to the nature of Internet survey, it is difficult to fix the precise response rate. However, the average response rate in this Internet survey system is reported as 15-25%.

Period: November 2003

Measurement of reliability: All numbers of comparison data between 2002 and 2003 in Method 2 are tested by the parametric statistical test—T-test.

About the Authors

Shenja van der Graaf holds degrees in media, business, and performing arts. She has spent time at Utrecht University, Leiden University, and MIT, and is affiliated with the Oxford Internet Institute, Berkman Center for Internet & Society at Harvard Law School, MIT's Convergence Culture Consortium (C3), and the London School of Economics. She was awarded a scholarship from the Dutch Ministry of Education, Culture and Sciences and the Japan-Netherlands Institute in Tokyo. At Hakuhodo's Institute of Life & Living she focused on the Japanese media industry and American and European markets. Starting out with an interest in the Hollywood industry and audience research, she has moved on to the organization of media firms and strategy formation regarding issues of digitization, while employing her experience in an extensive international network of companies including MTV, Sony, BMG, Warner Bros., THQ, Granada, and Endemol.

Yuichi Washida is a research director at Hakuhodo Inc., and a doctoral candidate in the Graduate School of Arts and Sciences at The University of Tokyo, Japan. He is also a research affiliate in the Comparative Media Studies Program at MIT. His research focuses on the social innovation process in the information age. He organized the collaborative research project with Ericsson Consumer & Enterprise Lab and the Utrecht University in 2003, which is one of the basic resources in this book. He is now conducting several interdisciplinary research projects related with the network science, complex systems, innovation studies, and new media studies.

*　　*　　*　　*

Bas Agterberg studied film and television at Utrecht University, The Nether-lands, and Glasgow University in Scotland. He is a professor in film and television at Utrecht University and at the Art Academy of Utrecht. Between 1996 and 2000 he worked as producer for Dutch director Jos Stelling. Agterberg managed the planning and construction of art-house cinema and cultural centre the Louis Hartlooper Complex in Utrecht, where he organised several activities such as lectures and festivals in 2004 and 2005.

Michael Björn is senior expert at Ericsson Consumer & Enterprise Lab (Sweden), where he is currently managing the Consumer Insight and Foresight Program. He earned a PhD in 1997 in database modeling at the Institute for Social Engineering, University of Tsukuba in Japan and received an MSc in 1987 in international business management at the University of Lund, Sweden. His research focuses on consumer trends in mobile media and its relation to social change and social innovation.

Karen Coppock is the director of industry collaboration for the Reuters Digital Vision Program at Stanford University (USA). Prior to Stanford, Coppock spent 4 years with Telcordia, most recently as assistant vice president of strategic accounts, international. Before joining Telcordia, she launched and headed the Latin American regional sales office for Williams Communications. She has also held positions with INTELSAT, SBC, AT&T, Harvard's Center for Interna-tional Development, and the Peace Corps. Coppock received her doctoral and master's degrees in international relations from the Fletcher School, Tufts University. She graduated cum laude in business administration and Spanish from California State University, Chico.

Nigel Culkin is chair and co-founder of the University of Hertfordshire's, Film Industry Research Group (FiRG) (UK), supervisor to a number of research students, and regular contributor to the media. Culkin is co-author of the annual review explaining the effects of digitization on the global film industry titled *Facing the Digital Future: Digital Technology and the Film Industry*. He is also associate dean at the Business School and deputy director of enterprise and knowledge transfer for the university where his main interest is in the area of entrepreneurship education. Most recently Culkin created the Film and Digital Media Exchange (www.fdmx.co.uk), a £2.5 million government funded project designed to create links between the UK's higher education institutions and the UK media entertainment industry. In addition, Culkin is a fellow of the Market Research Society and member of their professional advisory board.

Sal Humphreys currently works as a post-doctoral fellow in media studies at the Queensland University of Technology (Brisbane, Australia) in the Creative Industries Research and Applications Centre, researching digital rights management in creative industries. She completed her doctoral thesis on the role of productive players in MMOGs, using *EverQuest* as a case study. She has published papers in a variety of scholarly journals including *Journal of Communication and Critical/Cultural Studies, Media Arts Law Review, Australian Journal of Communication,* and *Media International Australia.*

Eva Keeris graduated in 2005 from Utrecht University (The Netherlands) in new media and digital culture. She wrote her master''s thesis on game research and play theory. As such, she gave way to the development of several models that provide (game) researchers insight into their academic standpoint on games in specific, and on science in general. At the moment, Keeris is working on a series of children's tales that involve digital play environments.

Tracy L. M. Kennedy is a PhD candidate at the University of Toronto, Canada. Working with Professor Barry Wellman, her dissertation research—"The Digital Home in Canadian Context"—uses quantitative and qualitative methods to examine the prevalence of the Internet in Canadian homes and investigates the implications of the household Internet on social interactions and relationships between family members. Kennedy has attended the summer doctoral program at the Oxford Internet Institute and the University of Maryland's annual WebShop. She is also a lecturer at Brock University and the University of Toronto on the subjects of gender, media, culture, technology, education, and peer cultures.

David Lee is currently undertaking a PhD in the Department of Media and Communications at Goldsmiths College, University of London. His research is concerned with exploring the working lives of freelance production staff in the British television industry, at a time of rapid cultural and technological change. The research involves using ethnographic methods to study cultural production, including interviews and case studies, to give a grounded account of media production within the wider context of reflexive modernization and the "creative economy." Before embarking on this research, Lee worked as a freelance producer in the television industry, within documentary and current affairs production.

Kris M. Markman studies the use of ICTs in the workplace and everyday life. She is specifically interested in using qualitative, microanalytic approaches to explain how different ICTs affect the structure of interaction, and how ICT use influences perceptions of anonymity and identity. Her dissertation research is a case study of collaboration in a computer chat environment. She is currently an instructor in the Department of Communication Studies at Bridgewater State College (USA) and will receive her PhD in communication studies from the University of Texas at Austin in 2006.

Norbert Morawetz received his MA in business and economics from the Karl Franzens University Graz (KFU) of Austria in 2003. His master's thesis on value chains in the American film industry was awarded best thesis 2003 by the Institute of International Management KFU. Since October 2004, he has been studying for his PhD on co-productions and temporary networks in the international film industry at the University of Hertfordshire (UH) (UK). Since June 2005, he has been a research assistant for the Film Industry Research Group at UH, a part-time lecturer in business economics, and an independent filmmaker. His main areas of research are: co-productions, film finance, media, and impact of digital technology on creative industries.

Eggo Müller, Assistant Professor, Institute Media and Re/Presentation, Utrecht University (The Netherlands), received his PhD in cultural studies form Hildesheim University. He has taught in the Media Studies Department at the University of Hildesheim and in the Film and Television Studies Department at the Film Academy Potsdam-Babesblerg. He now teaches media studies at Utrecht University, with a particular emphasis on the social and cultural role of media on contemporary developments of the global television culture and on methodological questions of media analysis. He published a book-length study of love and relationship shows on German television, titled *Paarungsspiele. Die Beziehungsshow in der Wirklichkeit des neuen Fernsehens* (Berlin: Edition Sigma, 1999). His current research focuses on the theory of media entertainment, and he is preparing a research project on the introduction of interactive television; new forms and practices of participation; and the redefinition of public television as social institution.

David B. Nieborg is a PhD candidate at the Amsterdam School for Cultural Analysis (ASCA) and lecturer at the University of Amsterdam, The Netherlands. He holds a MA from Utrecht University. Nieborg's research interests include digital games and contemporary game culture in general and *first person shooter* PC games in particular. His publications explore the implications of the interaction between commercial game culture, technology, marketing, and military communities. He writes on game culture for various Dutch magazines.

Keith Randle, Director, Creative Industries Research and Consultancy Unit (CIRCU) at the University of Hertfordshire (UK), received his PhD from the university in 1999. He has taught organisational behaviour and creativity and innovation management in the Business School and has led or co-led a number of research and consultancy projects with a focus on the film and audio-visual media industries. His recent work has most notably touched upon freelance working in the U.S. film industry and the impact of digital technologies on the film and cinema industries. His current work includes a major EU-funded project on diversity and employment in the UK film and audio visual media industries. He co-founded the Film Industry Research Group (FiRG) with Nigel Culkin.

Alek Tarkowski is a postgraduate candidate at the Graduate School for Social Research at the Institute of Philosophy and Sociology, Polish Academy of Sciences in Warsaw, Poland. His research interests include sociology of media usage, new media theory, and science, technology and society (STS) studies. He is also one of the public leads of Creative Commons Poland, the Polish chapter of an international movement for copyright alternatives.

Imar de Vries began his academic career in 1993 as a student of computational science. In 1997 he switched to theater, film, and television studies; he graduated in 2002 in the field of new media and digital culture. After graduation he continued his work at the Institute of Media & Re/Presentation as junior teacher/researcher, writing his PhD dissertation on the specific characteristics of (usage of) mobile telephony, and on the ways in which these interconnect with culturally idealised ideas of communication. The intermittent results have been presented at the Wireless World Conference in Guildford in 2003, at the Paris-Utrecht Mini Symposium (PUMS) in Utrecht in 2004, and at the Questioning the Dialogue Conference of the International Communication Association in New York in 2005.

Gaby Anne Wildenbos received her BA in theatre, film, and television studies at the Utrecht University, The Netherlands (2004). She specialized in new media. Consequently, she entered the MA program—new media and digital culture—at Utrecht University. Her internship brought her to Hakuhodo Inc. in Tokyo. Here she studied the Japanese utilization of digital products among which mobile phones. In September 2005 she completed her MA degree.

Masataka Yoshikawa is a research director at Hakuhodo Institute of Life and Living. In 1989 he entered Hakuhodo and worked at Marketing Planning Division for 10 years, engaging in planning marketing strategies for telecom companies, information device makers, and entertainment media companies. He established Pocket e-life Lab, a virtual research laboratory that conducted observations on the change of information lifestyle by mobile phones from 2000-2003.

Index

K

Kant 12
Karaoke 61
kawaii 29
Kim 181
knowledge space 3
kogal 23, 44
KPN 185, 202
KPN (Royal Dutch Post) 185

L

Label Mobil 62
Label Mobile 31
lack of awareness 213
lack of funds 213
lack of infrastructure 214
lack of uses 213
LAD 12
Language Acquisition Device (LAD)
     12
layer model 122
LBS 14
level of code 120
life cycle 122
life stages 41
Lineage 80
LiveJournal 119
location based services (LBS) 14

M

MAC 197
market creation 211
MarketReality™ Monitor 37
massively multiplayer online games
     (MMOGs) 76
McLuhanian style 180
media analysis framework 292
media bias 292
Media Center PC 183, 188
media determinism 292
media life cycle 288

media mix 134
meetings 240
men family university 43
MGM 163
MIDI 61
MMOGs 77, 79, 80, 104
mobile communication 2, 22
mobile phones 281
mod communities 81
moderator 250
Motorola 221
MSN 88
multi play 184
multi-standards 166
Murdoch 202
MUSE 197
MUSIC.CO.JP 61

N

National Association of Theater
     Owners (NATO) 161
National Television Committee (NTSC)
     193
NATO 162
network society 155
NGOs 210
NHK 194
NOB 197
NTSC 193
NTT DoCoMo 30, 61

O

OnDigital 202
One from the Heart 195
online diary 119
online economy 182, 185, 186, 187
otaku 23, 44
Oxxo 224

P

Pacman 106
PAL 193